Concept and Form Volume 2

Concept and Form

VOLUME 2, INTERVIEWS AND ESSAYS
ON THE *CAHIERS POUR L'ANALYSE*

Edited by Peter Hallward and Knox Peden

VERSO
London • New York

First published by Verso 2012
In the Collection © Verso 2012

In the interviews © The interviewees 2012
In the Collection © Verso 2012
Introduction © Knox Peden 2012
Chapter 1 translation © Cécile Malaspina, revised by Peter Hallward
Chapters 9 and 15 translation © Cécile Malaspina
Preface and editorial notes © Peter Hallward and Knox Peden
Chapters 10, 11 and 16 translation © Steven Corcoran
Chapters 12, 13 and 14 translation © Tzuchien Tho

1 3 5 7 9 10 8 6 4 2

Verso
UK: 6 Meard Street, London W1F 0EG
US: 20 Jay Street, Suite 1010, Brooklyn, NY 11201
www.versobooks.com

Verso is the imprint of New Left Books

ISBN-13: 978-1-84467-873-0

British Library Cataloguing in Publication Data
A catalogue record for this book is available from the British Library

Library of Congress Cataloging-in-Publication Data
A catalog record for this book is available from the Library of Congress

Typeset in Minion by Hewer UK Ltd, Edinburgh
Printed in the US by Maple Vail

Contents

Preface

Concept and Form is a two-volume work dealing with the 1960s French philosophy journal the *Cahiers pour l'Analyse*. Volume One is made up of English translations of some of the most important texts published in the journal. The introduction to Volume One tries to reconstruct the general context in which the journal was produced, and sketches the main intellectual and political influences that shaped its work. Volume Two collects newly commissioned essays on the journal and interviews with people who were either members of the editorial board or associated with its broader theoretical project. The introduction to Volume Two situates the journal in the context of twentieth-century French rationalism and considers how its commitment to conceptual analysis shaped its distinctive approach to Marxism and psychoanalysis.

These two printed books are complemented by an open-access electronic edition of the *Cahiers*, produced by the Centre for Research in Modern European Philosophy (CRMEP) and hosted by Kingston University London, at cahiers.kingston.ac.uk. The Concept and Form website provides the original French texts in both html and facsimile pdf versions, substantial synopses of each article, discussions of the most significant concepts at issue in the journal, and brief entries on the main people involved with it, as well as full-length French versions of the interviews abbreviated and translated in Volume Two. The materials in these two printed volumes are also included on the website, and posted as pdfs on the Verso website. The website's search box and lists of concepts and names may serve to some extent as a substitute index for the books.

Peter Hallward and Knox Peden

Abbreviations

Where a reference contains two page numbers separated by a forward slash, the first number refers to the original edition and the second to the English translation. When no note accompanies a quotation, the reference is included in the next note.

CF1, CF2 *Concept and Form*, Volume 1 or 2.

CpA *Cahiers pour l'Analyse*. A reference of the form 'CpA 6.2:36' is to page 36 of the second article in the sixth volume of the *Cahiers*, as listed in its table of contents (online at cahiers.kingston.ac.uk, and appended to this volume). Where an English translation for an article is available, inclusion of the English page number follows the French, after a forward slash.

tm translation modified

TN Translator's note

WORKS BY LOUIS ALTHUSSER

ESC *Essays in Self-Criticism*, trans. Grahame Lock. London: New Left Books, 1976.

FM *For Marx,* trans. Ben Brewster. London: New Left Books, 1969.

HC *The Humanist Controversy and Other Writings 1966–67*, trans. G.M. Goshgarian. London: Verso, 2003.

LP *Lenin and Philosophy and Other Essays*, trans. Ben Brewster. London: New Left Books, 1971.

PSPS *Philosophy and the Spontaneous Philosophy of the Scientists*, ed. Gregory Elliott, trans. Warren Montag et al. London: Verso, 1990.

RC [with Etienne Balibar] *Reading Capital* [1968 ed.], trans. Ben Brewster. London: New Left Books, 1970.

WORKS BY ALAIN BADIOU

APE 'L'Autonomie du processus historique'. *Cahiers Marxistes-Léninistes* (Paris: École Normale Supérieure) 12/13 (1966), 77–89.

CM *The Concept of Model* [1969], ed. and trans. Zachary Luke Fraser and Tzuchien Tho. Melbourne: (re)press, 2007.

DI *De l'Idéologie*. Paris: Maspero, 1976.

BE   *L'Etre et l'événement.* Paris: Seuil, 1988. *Being and Event*, trans. Oliver Feltham. London: Continuum, 2005.

LW   *Logiques des mondes.* Paris: Seuil, 2006. *Logics of Worlds*, trans. Alberto Toscano. London: Continuum, 2009.

LS   *Le Siècle.* Paris: Seuil, 2005; *The Century*, trans. Alberto Toscano. London: Polity, 2007.

RMD   'Le (Re)commencement du matérialisme dialectique' [review of Louis Althusser, *Pour Marx* (Paris: Maspero, 1965) and Althusser et al., *Lire le Capital* (Paris: Maspero, 1965)]. *Critique* 240 (May 1967), 438–467.

TC   *Théorie de la contradiction.* Paris: Maspero, 1975.

TS   *Théorie du sujet.* Paris: Seuil, 1982. *Theory of the Subject*, trans. Bruno Bosteels. London: Continuum, 2009.

WORKS BY SIGMUND FREUD

SE   *The Standard Edition of the Complete Psychological Works of Sigmund Freud*, ed. James Strachey et al. London: Hogarth Press, 1953–1974, in 24 volumes. A reference of the form 'SE14:148' is to page 148 of volume 14.

WORKS BY JACQUES LACAN

E   *Écrits.* Paris: Seuil, 1966. *Ecrits*, trans. Bruce Fink, in collaboration with Héloïse Fink and Russell Grigg. New York: W.W. Norton, 2006. References in the form 'E, 803/680' refer to the French/English pagination.

S   *Seminars* (1954–1980), in 27 volumes. A reference in the form 'S11, 278' is to page 278 of volume 11. References are to English translations where available. The published volumes have been edited by Jacques-Alain Miller; Cormac Gallagher has made available some draft English translations.

THE MAIN VOLUMES CITED INCLUDE:

- *Seminar I: Freud's Papers on Technique* [1953–54], trans. John Forrester. New York: W.W. Norton, 1988.
- *Seminar II: The Ego in Freud's Theory and Technique of Psychoanalysis* [1954–55], trans. Sylvana Tomaselli. New York: W.W. Norton, 1991.
- *Seminar III: The Psychoses* [1955–1956], trans. Russell Grigg. New York: W.W. Norton, 1993.
- *Seminar V: The Formations of the Unconscious* [1957–1958], trans. Cormac Gallagher, unpublished manuscript.

- Seminar *VII: The Ethics of Psychoanalysis* [1959–60], trans. Dennis Porter. London: Routledge, 1988.
- *Seminar VIII: Transference* [1960–61], trans. Cormac Gallagher, unpublished manuscript.
- *Seminar XI: The Four Fundamental Concepts of Psychoanalysis* [1963–64], trans. Alan Sheridan. London: Penguin, 1977.
- *Seminar XII: Crucial Problems for Psychoanalysis* [1964–65], trans. Cormac Gallagher, unpublished manuscript.
- *Seminar XIII: The Object of Psychoanalysis* [1965–66], trans. Cormac Gallagher, unpublished manuscript.
- *Seminar XIV: The Logic of Fantasy* [1966–67], trans. Cormac Gallagher, unpublished manuscript.

Knox Peden
Introduction: The Fate of the Concept

The first half of this volume is made up of essays that engage with various theoretical, historical, and political aspects of the *Cahiers pour l'Analyse* and its legacy in European thought; the second contains interviews with participants in the endeavour as it unfolded in the 1960s at the École Normale Supérieure in Paris. This difference of genre results in a striking discrepancy. Taken together, the essays make a case for why such a demanding set of texts deserves some measure of our attention today. By contrast, the interviews present the journal as stemming from a conjuncture that was unique in its political and institutional conditions and that is consequently unrepeatable in its specifics. The sentiments range from the dismissive to the enthusiastic, sometimes within the same interview, but, with the notable exception of Alain Badiou, the editors of the *Cahiers* generally emphasize the degree to which their effort belongs to the past. As a result, the implicit insistence on the journal's contemporary resonance that informs the book's first part is offset in the second by a focus on its essentially historical quality.

This generic discrepancy is not surprising, however, but is simply emblematic of the fact that theoretical disputes shaped by exceptional historical circumstances often possess a value that transcends those circumstances. Assessing these disputes thus requires a kind of balancing act between historical contextualization and conceptual extraction. For example, when Martin Jay published the first history of the Frankfurt School in 1974, he was criticized for the 'elegiac' tone of his account of the early years of the Institute for Social Research and his claim that its moment had 'now irrevocably passed'.[1] Dispensing with overzealous comparisons between the Weimar Republic and the American one of the 1960s and 70s, Jay nevertheless recognized that an assessment of Frankfurt School ideas in their historical gestation might give those ideas added value in the present precisely by illuminating those aspects that were irreducible to context. The *Cahiers pour l'Analyse* confronts us with a similar challenge, given that the journal occupies a historical position at a double remove. Politically, its contents were generated prior to the events of May 1968 and the sequence that followed. Theoretically, it exemplifies a commitment to 'high structuralism' prior to the shift to poststructuralism

---

1   Martin Jay, *The Dialectical Imagination: A History of the Frankfurt School and the Institute of Social Research, 1923–1950*, second edition (Berkeley: University of California Press, 1996), xiv.

that was virtually coterminous with structuralism's arrival in the Anglophone context.[2]

A wide array of factors clearly distinguishes the Frankfurt School from the *Cahiers pour l'Analyse*. One is a multigenerational endeavour that emerged from the experiences of revolution, Nazism, war, and exile; the other was a student-led experiment conducted amidst the *Trente Glorieuses* at one of Paris's most elite institutions. But the very ephemerality of the latter risks obscuring its significance, as well as the fundamental ambition it shared with the former: to unite the discourses of Marx and Freud in a more general theory of experience and subjectivity. To be sure, 'lived experience' was a derided term within the *Cahiers*, as was any notion of the subject that might be confused with the 'imaginary' experiences of an 'ego' or 'consciousness'.[3] But like the progenitors of Critical Theory, the members of the Cercle d'Épistémologie – the editorial collective responsible for the *Cahiers pour l'Analyse* – believed that combining Marx and Freud's efforts might yield a comprehensive theory that could identify both the structural mechanisms of ideological mystification and the practical mechanisms by which one might seek to evade them. If a keyword on this score for the Frankfurt School was 'critique', for the editors of the *Cahiers* the key concept was none other than a prominent target of Frankfurt School 'critique': in a word, 'science'.

The valorization of science (and in particular science as a formalized discourse) that pervades the *Cahiers pour l'Analyse* was most immediately a result of the combined influence of Louis Althusser and Jacques Lacan. Indeed, in the complementarity between the Marxist philosopher and the renegade psychoanalyst we find what is most specific about the *Cahiers'* effort to unite these discourses. After all, the thinkers in question were decidedly Althusser's Marx and Lacan's Freud. Althusser himself lamented the paucity of serious Marxist thought in France prior to his own example, and lauded Lacan as 'the first thinker who has assumed the theoretical responsibility of giving to Freud veritable concepts worthy of him'.[4] In other words, if, notwithstanding its breadth of reference and international impact, the Frankfurt School occupies a privileged place as a regional phenomenon within German intellectual history, with the *Cahiers pour l'Analyse* we encounter historically

---

2   For an overview of the political, institutional, and intellectual contexts surrounding the advent and end of the *Cahiers pour l'Analyse* see Peter Hallward, 'Theoretical Training', CF1.

3   See below, François Regnault, 'All of a Sudden, Psychoanalysis'. Jacques Rancière would target this derision in *Althusser's Lesson* [1974], trans. Emiliano Battista (London: Continuum, 2011): 'Our privileged situation allowed us to make science the only important thing and to push everything else – the petty academic, financial, or sexual grievances of students – into that realm of illusion known in our discourse by the term *lived experience (le vécu)*' (42).

4   Althusser, FM, 26–27; Althusser, *Freud and Lacan: Writings on Psychoanalysis*, trans. Jeffrey Mehlman (New York: Columbia University Press, 1999), 148.

German discourses being appropriated, mediated, and in the event transformed by French intellectual traditions. The distinction that Michel Foucault established at the heart of twentieth-century French thought between a 'philosophy of experience' and a 'philosophy of the concept' has become a staple, if not a cliché of introductions to the field.[5] And yet, what is often overlooked in the discussions of this heuristic, not to mention the way it has been parsed by other thinkers before and since,[6] is that Foucault predicates this scission within French thought upon a more fundamental one between historically 'German' and 'French' responses to Kant's question: 'What is Enlightenment?'. This question was grounded in the attempt to understand the relation between the ostensible universality of 'reason' and the manifestly historical quality of its emergence.

According to Foucault, whereas German thinkers in Kant's wake were primarily concerned to track the historical advent of reason in the domain of the 'social', French thinkers from Auguste Comte onward focused their attention on the historical rationality of science. In Foucault's clipped assessment, the Germans from Feuerbach to Weber, by way of Marx and Nietzsche, had 'one central problem, the religious experience as it related to the economy and the state'.[7] By contrast, it was ultimately the French concern for the 'regional' fields of science, dedicated to 'the formation of a rational power against a background of traditional experience', that subtended the true 'hotbeds of philosophical elaboration'.[8] This option for the 'regional' culminated in the pluralism of French philosophy of science in the twentieth century, with Gaston Bachelard's focus on physics and chemistry, Jean Cavaillès's on mathematics, and the expertise of Georges Canguilhem, the subject of Foucault's essay, in biology and medicine serving as the foremost examples. In the end, despite being united by a distrust of phenomenology's 'irrationalism', Critical Theory and French philosophy of

---

5   Michel Foucault, 'Life: Experience and Science' [1985] in *Aesthetics, Method, and Epistemology*, ed. James D. Faubion (New York: The New Press, 1998), 465–478. Foucault's 'dividing line' is 'one that separates a philosophy of experience, of meaning, of the subject, and a philosophy of knowledge, of rationality, and of the concept. On one side, a filiation which is that of Jean-Paul Sartre and Maurice Merleau-Ponty; and then another, which is that of Jean Cavaillès, Gaston Bachelard, Alexandre Koyré, and Canguilhem' (466). For two recent deployments of Foucault's frame, see Giuseppe Bianco, 'Experience vs. Concept? The Role of Bergson in Twentieth-Century French Philosophy', *The European Legacy*, 16:7 (2011), 855–872 and Knox Peden, 'Descartes, Spinoza, and the Impasse of French Philosophy: Ferdinand Alquié versus Martial Gueroult', *Modern Intellectual History*, 8:2 (2011), 361–390. Foucault's heuristic also sets the organizational terms for *French Philosophy since 1945: Problems, Concepts, Inventions*, eds. Étienne Balibar and John Rajchman (New York: The Free Press, 2011), xvii–xxiii.

6   For variations on the historical contours of this 'scission', see Louis Althusser, 'The Philosophical Conjuncture and Marxist Research' [26 June 1966], HC, 5; Alain Badiou, LW, 7–8; and Elisabeth Roudinesco, *Philosophy in Turbulent Times*, trans. William McQuaig (New York: Columbia University Press, 2008), 31.

7   Foucault, 'Life', 468.

8   Ibid., 469.

science were distinctive for Foucault in that the former was haunted by the 'ghost of Luther' and the latter by the 'memory of Descartes'.[9]

Foucault's countervailing dualisms – between the subject and the concept within French thought, and more broadly between a German commitment to the 'social' and a French investment in the 'scientific' – help us to identify the *Cahiers pour l'Analyse* not only as a fascinating document of 'French Theory' and a crucial prolegomenon to post-Althusserian political thought, but also as a key chapter in the history of French rationalism and its relationship to other continental philosophical traditions. Marx famously wrote in *The Poverty of Philosophy* that 'it is the bad side that produces the movement that makes history, by producing a struggle'.[10] After years in which the writings of Marx and Freud were variously mediated by vitalism, idealism, and humanism, Althusser's students wilfully adopted the 'bad side' of an adamantine formalism to struggle against the spiritualist currents that provided a welcome reception to phenomenology in France[11] and, in their view, obscured what was most revolutionary in the 'theoretical practices' of Marxism and psychoanalysis.

Above all, the *Cahiers pour l'Analyse* promoted a 'philosophy of the concept' that sought to articulate a viable concept of subjectivity, theretofore one of the chief concerns of French phenomenological existentialism and a target of Althusser's anti-humanism. But, in a sense, the journal was also an effort to produce a 'scientific' answer to a set of historically 'social' questions, and the result, strewn over ten issues, was a kind of renovated Comteanism shorn of optimism in light of the 'suspicious' discourses of Marx and Freud. Lest 'scientific' be confused with dogmatic, it must be noted that Foucault's argument concerned precisely the historical quality of French philosophy of science as a constitutively incomplete project given the constitutive incompleteness of its object: 'science'. In this regard, Althusser's heralding of science was less a return to a bygone positivism than the resurgence of a rationalism only briefly eclipsed during existentialism's heyday in France. Likewise, Lacan's novel consideration of the relationship between the 'concept' and 'practice' bears a patent kinship with similar positions in French epistemology. To appreciate the impact of this tradition on Althusser and Lacan's teaching, and by extension the *Cahiers*, it will be helpful to consider how the 'philosophy of the concept' as a theoretical stance was itself conditioned by

9   Ibid., 469. For examples of the Frankfurt School antipathy to phenomenology, in both its Husserlian and Heideggerian guises, see Theodor Adorno, *Against Epistemology: A Metacritique* [1956], trans. Willis Domingo (Oxford: Basil Blackwell, 1982) and Adorno, *The Jargon of Authenticity* [1964], trans. Knut Tarnowski and Frederic Will (London: Routledge, 2003).

10   Karl Marx, *The Poverty of Philosophy* [1847], chapter 2.1 (Beijing: Foreign Languages Press, 1966), 116.

11   Cf. Jacques Bouveresse, 'To Get Rid of the Signified'.

the arrival in the interwar years of a rival, and distinctively 'German' philosophical project: phenomenology.[12]

I 'A PHILOSOPHY OF THE CONCEPT'

Althusser's debt to French epistemology has been widely noted, not least by Althusser himself (FM, 32). Among the myriad notions he borrowed from this tradition, perhaps the most famous was Gaston Bachelard's concept of the 'epistemological break', which Althusser used to describe both the moment that Marx took leave of the ideological humanism of his youth for the science of *Capital*, as well as the moment that any given subject moves from the terrain of ideology to the discourse of science *tout court*. More fundamentally, Jean Cavaillès's clarion call, penned in 1944, and which stated that 'it is not a philosophy of consciousness but a philosophy of the concept that can yield a doctrine of science',[13] was a clear source of inspiration for Althusser's effort to 'construct' or 'produce' the key concept of the 'mode of production' in *Reading Capital* (RC, 101). Althusser's relentless affirmation of the 'concept' as such went hand in hand with his derision toward the nominally ideological specimen 'consciousness'. But in certain respects, Althusser's Marxist programme was a particular instance of a broader effort to philosophically recalibrate rationalism in the wake of 'the crisis of European sciences'[14] that troubled thinkers in the interwar years. Faced with the unappealing options of abandoning science to its political instrumentalization, or instead taking shelter from its impasses and implications in a return to the 'lifeworld' of a more primordial or 'originary' experience, French philosophers of science developed an ethic of extensive philosophical engagement with science in its most current and demanding forms.[15]

The ethos sloganized in the 'philosophy of the concept' can be gleaned from the words of Georges Canguilhem that served as an epigraph to each issue of the *Cahiers*:

---

12   On the French reception of phenomenology in the interwar years, see Stefanos Geroulanos, *An Atheism that is Not Humanist Emerges in French Thought* (Stanford: Stanford University Press, 2010), 37–206 and Ethan Kleinberg, *Generation Existential: Heidegger's Philosophy in France, 1927–1961* (New York: Cornell University Press, 2005), 47–154.

13   Jean Cavaillès, *Sur la logique et la théorie de la science* [1946] (Paris: Vrin, 1960), 78.

14   Cf. Edmund Husserl, *The Crisis of European Sciences and Transcendental Phenomenology* [1954], trans. David Carr (Evanston, IL: Northwestern University Press, 1970).

15   In this regard, Jean-Toussaint Desanti should be added to Foucault's list. At the moment of the *Cahiers*, Desanti was preparing his major philosophical work *Les Idéalités mathématiques: Recherches épistémologiques sur le développement de la théorie des fonctions des variables réelles* (Paris: Seuil, 1968), a book which in many ways constituted a resumption of Cavaillès's attenuated project.

> To work a concept [*travailler un concept*] is to vary its extension and comprehension, to generalize it through the incorporation of exceptional traits, to export it beyond its region of origin, to take it as a model or on the contrary to seek a model for it – to work a concept, in short, is progressively to confer upon it, through regulated transformations, the function of a form.[16]

The original context of this injunction was a discussion of Bachelard's *La Philosophie du Non* (1940) that Canguilhem published in 1963. Following upon *La Formation de l'esprit scientifique* (1938), Bachelard's book promoted a rationalist philosophy suitable to the material realities of modern scientific practice. Opposed to the effort to ground science in a phenomenological description of lived experience prior to the mediating tools – conceptual or material – of experimentation, Bachelard argued that a philosophy of science must, in effect, adhere to the open-ended and transformative nature of the scientific enterprise. The philosophy of the 'No' was not to be construed as a mere will to negation, nor as the quest for an *a priori* dialectic subtending fleeting particularities. The 'No' was simply a methodological directive against the illusory comforts of our spontaneous experience of the world. 'In sum', Bachelard wrote, 'science instructs reason. Reason must obey science, the most evolved science, the evolving science. Reason does not have the right to overvalue an immediate experience. On the contrary, it must put itself in equilibrium with the most richly structured experience. In all circumstances, the *immediate* must give way to the *constructed*.'[17]

Bachelard's critique of the immediate applied to any philosophy that sought to endow subjective experience with a foundational status for rationalism, and Husserl's late efforts to ground scientific rationality in our experience of the 'lifeworld' were no doubt a target of Bachelard's critique.[18] For his part, Cavaillès levelled a similar charge against Husserl when he wrote, 'lived impossibility and distinct actualization are the last instances of phenomenological analysis.'[19] Moreover, in phenomenology, 'the foundation of all necessity is this "I can do no other" of the eidetic variation, which, however legitimate it may be in itself, is an abdication of thought.'[20] For Cavaillès, as for Bachelard, phenomenological

---

16   Georges Canguilhem, 'Dialectique et philosophie du non chez Gaston Bachelard', *Revue Internationale de Philosophie* 66 (1963), 452.

17   Gaston Bachelard, *La Philosophie du Non* (Paris: PUF, 1940), 144.

18   Husserl, *The Crisis of European Sciences*. Published posthumously, this volume reproduced many of the contents of Husserl's lectures and publications from the 1930s.

19   Cavaillès, *Sur la logique*, 76. On Cavaillès's relationship to Husserl see David Webb, 'Cavaillès, Husserl, and the Historicity of Science', *Angelaki*, 8:3 (2003), 59–72. For a helpful general account of Cavaillès's thought see Hourya Sinaceur, *Jean Cavaillès: Philosophie Mathématique* (Paris: PUF, 1994).

20   Cavaillès, *Sur la logique*, 77. The 'eidetic variation' is a reference to the principle of the phenomenological or 'eidetic' reduction which 'brackets' the contingent properties of an object – be it an ideal mathematical object or a sensible one – so as to perceive its most essential property or *eidos*, i.e. that which makes the object what it is.

recourse to the 'lived' put a halt to the essentially generative quality of scientific thought. The eidetic variation is an 'abdication of thought' because it misrepresents what actually happens in mathematics, tethering its procedures to the contingencies of a subject rather than a rational necessity that inheres in it as a discourse. In Husserl's project, Cavaillès saw the resurgence of the same solipsism that marred Kant's account of transcendental subjectivity. If consciousness is the very source of the rules that it uses to apprehend the world, then in what sense, or indeed by what other lights, can we validate its judgments? Cavaillès's primary concern was to develop a 'theory of science' that granted science full rights, that did not reduce its objects, mathematical or otherwise, to mere reflections or emanations of 'consciousness' itself, but recognized their status as immanently rational entities.

In the end, Cavaillès's essay gives us no account of the content of the 'philosophy of the concept' that is supposed to replace the maligned 'philosophy of consciousness', which partly explains why the former served as such a provocative slogan for a later generation. Nevertheless, we gain a sense of what Cavaillès intended by comparing his claims with those of his friend and colleague, Albert Lautman. In *Being and Event,* Badiou describes the loss of Cavaillès and Lautman, both of whom were executed by the Nazis, as a veritable 'tragedy' for French philosophy.[21] And indeed the arguments of these philosophers of mathematics prefigure the efforts of Althusser and Lacan, not to mention the contents of the *Cahiers pour l'Analyse,* in suggestive ways. Committed to an in-depth engagement with mathematics, Cavaillès and Lautman believed genuine theoretical insight emerged solely via the navigation of formalized discourse and its interstices.

Despite their intellectual proximity, at issue between Cavaillès and Lautman was whether or not Heidegger's philosophy could be productively integrated into a rationalist philosophy of science. For Cavaillès, science was not to be 'considered as a simple intermediary between the human mind [*esprit*] and being in itself, equally dependent on both and lacking its own reality, but rather as an object *sui generis*, original in its essence, autonomous in its movement.'[22] Cavaillès's primary philosophical problem was, in a word, the *history* of mathematics. Whereas histories of the experimental sciences could avail themselves of phenomenological descriptions of empirical space (as in Bachelard's work for example)[23] mathematics was a wholly immanent discourse whose truth content was not dependent upon something like 'empirical' proof. Be that as it may,

---

21   Badiou, BE, 482; cf. Étienne Balibar and Yves Duroux, 'A Philosophical Conjuncture', CF2, 175. Badiou also laments the death of the mathematician Jacques Herbrand, who died in an accident during a hiking expedition in 1931.

22   Cavaillès, *Sur la logique*, 21.

23   Cf. Bachelard, *The Poetics of Space* [1957], trans. Maria Jolas (Boston: Beacon Press, 1962).

mathematics had a history, which meant that whatever truths it did produce had to emerge in time. In Cavaillès's view, Georg Cantor introduced fundamentally new mathematical knowledge with his theory of transfinite numbers, and the task of a properly philosophical account was to track the emergence of Cantor's ideas out of the set of discursive constraints inherent in the mathematics that preceded his effort without regarding those ideas as simply prefigured in antecedent instances.[24] Throughout his abbreviated career, Cavaillès was insistent that any properly philosophical account of mathematics and its history had to remain wholly immanent; mathematics was not the expression of something other than itself – e.g., 'being' or 'consciousness' – but was indeed '*sui generis*'. As he wrote to the Catholic personalist philosopher Étienne Borne in 1930, 'to reduce philosophy to a simple description, or a recognition of the exterior is to renounce philosophizing. Outside rationalism, I believe that philosophy can only be self-defeating.'[25]

Recourse to the 'exterior' was not an option. Whatever rationality there was in mathematics lay wholly in the operations of mathematical discourse itself. In this regard, Cavaillès was more Spinozist than Platonist. The material of mathematical notation was not the sensible incarnation of intelligible forms; rather, this material was the rational form in itself. 'Mathematical activity is an object of analysis and possesses an essence; but like a scent or a sound, it is itself.'[26] By contrast, for Lautman the concern was less for mathematical activity on the model of a scent or a sound, but, to stick with the simile, what this activity was the 'scent' or the 'sound' *of*. A committed Platonist, Lautman considered 'Ideas' as always in excess of their concrete actualization. The task of a philosophy of mathematics was to articulate the relationship between this rhapsodic wealth of Ideas and their instantiation in mathematical concepts or 'solutions'. The novelty of Lautman's approach – and where he departed from Platonism – was to see this relation as a two-way street. Here, his key reference was Heidegger, who allowed Lautman to conceive of the dialectic of Ideas as an 'ontological' phenomenon and the concrete solutions that constituted mathematical discourse as their 'ontic' correlate. Mathematics was a privileged discourse for Lautman, as it was for Cavaillès, but for Lautman this privilege lay in the access it provided to a higher domain. In a letter to the mathematician Maurice Fréchet, Lautman remarked as follows:

In sum, while Cavaillès searches in mathematics itself for the philosophical sense of

---

24   This was the subject of Cavaillès's minor doctoral thesis, *Remarques sur la formation de la théorie abstraite des ensembles* [1937], reprinted in *Oeuvres complètes de Jean Cavaillès*, ed. Bruno Huisman (Paris: Hermann, 1994), 221–374.

25   Cited in Hourya Sinaceur, 'Philosophie et Histoire', in *Jean Cavaillès Résistant, ou la Pensée en actes*, eds. Alya Aglan and Jean-Pierre Azéma (Paris: Flammarion, 2002), 220.

26   Cavaillès, 'Mathématiques et formalisme' [1949] in *Oeuvres complètes de Jean Cavaillès*, 664.

mathematical thought, this sense appears to me rather in the connection of mathematics to a metaphysics (or Dialectic) of which it is the necessary extension. It
constitutes the matter closest to Ideas. It seems to me that this is not a diminution
for mathematics. It confers on it, on the contrary, an exemplary role.[27]

Aiming for an immanent perspective, Lautman nonetheless maintained a
methodological and arguably metaphysical distinction between the dialectical
'Idea' and the conceptual 'solution', one that he likened to Heidegger's distinction between the 'concern' or the 'question' and the 'response'.[28]

Indeed, Lautman insisted upon the Idea's essential 'ontological anteriority'
to the concept's existential solution, thereby opening a gap between aspects of
mathematical thought wherein a philosophy of mathematics might make its
entry. After reading Lautman's arguments for this position, Cavaillès expressed
his disagreement in no uncertain terms:

> Heidegger vigorously rejects the opposition between essence and existence and
> wouldn't like that you even seem to be comparing him with Plato. I'd thought before
> that you allowed an immanence of ideas to their mathematical actualization. This
> doesn't seem to be the case now, at least if you go with Heidegger. Too bad – but you
> might be right in the end.[29]

The last lines of Cavaillès's *Sur la logique et la théorie de la science* note that the
'generative necessity' one finds in mathematical science 'is not that of an activity, but a dialectic',[30] a choice of words that suggests Lautman's impact on his
own thought. Still, the contrast with 'activity' indicates that, for Cavaillès, this
dialectic was wholly immanent to science itself, and its truth content was not
dependent upon the activity of mediating subjects.

The Second World War terminated Cavaillès and Lautman's discussion, so
determining the sense of Cavaillès's oracular conclusion must remain a matter
of conjecture. But their dispute, nascent as it was, nevertheless provides us with
a way to historically and conceptually situate the tension between Althusser and

27   Albert Lautman, *Mathematics, Ideas and the Physical Real* [2006], trans. Simon Duffy
(London: Continuum, 2011), 224. This volume contains virtually the whole of Lautman's published
writings, and several key pieces of correspondence. The crucial document for Lautman's engagement with Heidegger is 'New Research on the Dialectical Structure of Mathematics' [1939],
195–219.

28   Ibid., 203. Lautman's consideration of the movement from Ideas to solutions as one
wherein 'the virtual is transformed into the real' (203) will prove crucial to Gilles Deleuze's efforts
throughout *Difference and Repetition* [1968], trans. Paul Patton (New York: Columbia University
Press, 1994).

29   'Lettres inédites de Jean Cavaillès à Albert Lautman', ed. Hourya Benis-Sinaceur, *Revue
d'histoire des sciences* 40:1 (1987), 123–124.

30   Cavaillès, *Sur la logique*, 78.

Lacan's positions that would inform the *Cahiers pour l'Analyse*. To simplify, Cavaillès was insistent upon the internal nature of scientific discourse, which required no appeal or reference to an exteriority, be it a site of ontological pleni-tude or an empty void, in order to proceed. This was the vision of science that Althusser promoted. For Lacan, by contrast, as he argued in the *Cahiers'* inau-gural article 'Science and Truth' (CpA 1.1), scientific discourse was permanently conditioned by the lack at its root, a peculiar exteriority whose function *within* discourse was not unlike the recurrent presence of Lautman's 'Dialectic' amidst the operations of mathematics. Haunted by the 'miscognition' at its source, science proceeded in a state of ideological mystification, 'suturing' the lack at its origin in order to maintain the 'truth' of consistent discourse. Jacques-Alain Miller developed this point at length in 'Suture (Elements of the Logic of the Signifier)' (CpA 1.3) and Alain Badiou rejected it in his 'Mark and Lack: On Zero' (CpA 10.8).

If we can detect ascending formal similarities amidst the pairings Lautman/ Cavaillès, Lacan/Althusser, and Miller/Badiou, one discrepancy is striking nevertheless. For Lautman and Cavaillès, the concern was exclusively science. For Miller and Badiou, the dispute also concerned social and political practice, and the relation of science, as a practice, to this broader field. In this generaliza-tion of the problematic, we see the mark of Althusser and Lacan's influence, and their efforts to draw from technical assessments of scientific practice lessons about the relation between conceptual thought and practice *tout court*. What's more, in the distinction between Lacan and Althusser, with the former hewing closer to Lautman's regard of scientific discourse as essentially derivative of a more fundamental truth and the latter sharing Cavaillès's convictions regarding the adequacy of scientific discourse in itself, we can perhaps discern the impact of Lacan's sympathies to Heidegger, which were much greater than Althusser's.[31] But whereas Lautman and Cavaillès were united by a common concern to provide a philosophical account of the mathematical sciences that nevertheless pulled in opposite directions, the difference between Lacan and Althusser was predicated upon a shared investment in the practical and pedagogical value of formalized discourse.

Like Althusser, Lacan had a specific investment in thinking the relationship between the 'concept' and 'practice'. Indeed, concepts *qua* concepts were central to this period of his teaching, as signalled by the title of the seminar, delivered in 1964, that had the most proximate impact on the Cercle d'Épistémologie: *The Four Fundamental Concepts of Psychoanalysis*. There Lacan makes clear that the concept is to be conceived as a mode of praxis: 'What is a praxis?', he asks. 'It is

---

31   In the early 1950s, Lacan met Heidegger and translated his commentary on Heraclitus, 'Logos' for his review *La Psychanalyse*. See Roudinesco, *Jacques Lacan: Outline of a Life, History of a System of Thought*, trans. Barbara Bray (New York: Columbia University Press, 1997), 219–232.

the broadest term to designate a concerted human action, whatever it may be, which places man in a position to treat the real by the symbolic' (S11, 6). Following upon this provisional definition, Lacan then distinguishes science and religion in practical terms: religion seeks, science finds. This distinction suggests that what is essential to science is that its results cannot be prefigured, a conviction shared by Cavaillès. And yet, concepts are tools that are clearly designed for some end, some 'symbolic' purchase on the 'real'. Despite its equally determined and determinate capacities, the concept alone is nevertheless insufficient for Lacan, as it was for Lautman. Lacan writes, 'If the concept is modelled on an approach to the reality that the concept has been created to apprehend, it is only by a leap, a passage to the limit, that it manages to realize itself' (S11, 19). This gap demarcates the field of psychoanalysis as a practice. 'For what the unconscious does is to show us the gap through which neurosis recreates a harmony with the real – a real that may well not be determined' (S11, 22).

With these claims, Lacan occupies a peculiar position as at once an inheritor of the disputes within French epistemology and as the theoretician of the desire that subtends this tradition. In other words, Lacan attempts to conceptualize the desire to conceptualize as an effort that is integrally doomed to inadequacy. More specifically, by explicating the way in which the concept's purchase on the 'real' is only achieved through a 'passage to the limit', Lacan also thematizes the constitutive incompleteness of the 'philosophy of the concept' as a more general project that is unable to 'complete' itself as a consistent discourse without abandoning the very terms of its own consistency as an incomplete project. The engagement with analytic philosophy that one finds in the *Cahiers* should not be overestimated. Nevertheless, the conceptual relation between Lacan and Gödel's teachings on this score is, while something less than perfect symmetry, something more than mere analogy.[32]

As Lacan famously remarked: 'the real can only be inscribed on the basis of an impasse of formalization' (S20, 93). This phrase only makes sense if formalization is regarded as something equally practical and conceptual.[33] And where French rationalism does ultimately steer closer to analytic philosophy than German dialectics in the pages of the *Cahiers pour l'Analyse* is in the recognition that the impasses that structure our cognitive and practical relation to the world are a result not of 'History' as a metaphysical domain that contains such impasses within it, but rather of the discursive and symbolic overlays brought to bear on the incipient worlds that thought confronts. Indeed, Althusser's claims

---

32   Cf. CpA 1.3, 10.5 and 10.8.

33   N.B. that Lacan's claim is different from the more familiar gloss it receives in Badiou's *Theory of the Subject* as 'the real is the impasse of formalization'. Badiou's version makes for a better slogan, but at the price of shifting the register from that of discursive practice ('can only be inscribed on the basis of') to the ontological ('is'). Badiou, TS, 23. The discursive will regain some of its rights in *Being and Event*. Cf. Alain Badiou, 'Theory from Structure to Subject', CF2.

that history is a 'process without a subject' and that scientific knowledge 'is the historical result of a process which has no real subject or goal(s)' (ESC, 56) are only scandalous to one who holds a metaphysical view of history; these are basic methodological principles for the empirical historian or scientist.

But the scandal of Althusserianism was precisely to produce a Marxism decoupled from Hegelian metaphysics and its humanist avatars. The inconsistency of the project lay in Althusser's inability to articulate how individuals were any less the vessels or *Träger* of broader forces in a structural totality than in an expressive one. If its practical implications were obscure, the concept of the structural totality did have the virtue of insisting on the rights of reason to assess that fractured totality, rather than serve as yet another vehicle for its expression. Lacan for his part rejected a metaphysically hypostatized 'ego' to which subjects were doomed to adjust their efforts. Likewise, Althusser's demystification of 'History' was also an effort to wrest a practice of (intellectual) freedom from the realm of (metaphysical) necessity. With the critical force of a deliberately austere formalism averse to metaphysical hypostatization in view, it becomes easier to appreciate that Althusserian science did not bridle a generation with a resurgent dogmatism – despite the rhetorical efforts of many of Althusser's students to meet the challenge – but instead infused French rationalism with new vigour and a new critical brief. Left to its own devices, 'History' had resulted in catastrophe: colonialism, Nazism, world war, and Stalinism. The 'retreat' to science was experienced as the 'advance' of rational thought against History's irrational drift.[34] In his reflections on this moment, Jean-Claude Milner conveys a sense of the enthusiasm that permeated Althusser's seminar room and the conviction that French had become 'the natural language of the concept'.[35] After the travesty of Nazism, German had abrogated its status as the standard bearer of philosophical discourse and, with the onset of the Cold War, English seemed even further enthralled to 'market forms'.[36] By the 1960s, the time for French rationalism had come.

II THE VIRTUES OF INCOMPLETENESS

Milner also remarks, however, that the content of this enthusiasm amounted to a 'mirage'. And indeed, French rationalism seemed to go just as quickly as it had come. The authors of the *Cahiers* took leave of theoreticism for various forms of practice. Populisms proliferated in the 1970s; transgression became a matter of

---

34   Althusser's project is most explicitly formulated in such terms in the lecture from his 'Philosophy Course for Scientists' titled 'Du côté de la philosophie', omitted from the published version of this course, but reproduced in Althusser, *Ecrits philosophiques et politiques*, vol. 2 (Paris: Stock/IMEC, 1995), 265–310.

35   Jean-Claude Milner 'The Force of Minimalism', CF2, 244.

36   Ibid.

principle. Althusser dismantled the elaborate constructions of *For Marx* and *Reading Capital* with alternately self-serving and self-defeating 'self-criticisms'. Lacan's teaching moved from formalist strictures to increasingly baroque explorations of topological space. Lévi-Strauss's anthropology steered ever closer to parochialism. Derrida's deconstruction found a wider berth in the Anglophone world, and entered into renewed dialogue with the phenomenology and religious philosophy that provided its earliest conditions.[37] Foucault ultimately insisted on his distance from structuralism, donning the mantel of Nietzschean genealogy before focusing his efforts ever more narrowly on historical descriptions of various technologies of government and the self. Eventually, the combined forces of political circumstance and intellectual probity rendered structuralism obsolete.

The chapters that follow attempt to overturn this summary judgment, which reproduces a variation on the standard epitaph for French structuralism. A guiding principle of our effort has been to restore the *Cahiers pour l'Analyse* to its rightful place in twentieth-century French intellectual history. By reconsidering the field through the prism of the journal, familiar names and apparently exhausted debates acquire a new lustre. Patrice Maniglier shows how the effort to provide a formal account of subjectivity's emergence in various domains remains worthwhile, and how Miller, Milner, and above all Lévi-Strauss, provide us with still useful tools for generating such an account. Edward Baring sheds new light on Derrida's trajectory, by recovering the critical elements of his relation to Althusserianism at the very moment that he seemed closest to the Althusserians in his critique of phenomenology and Lévi-Strauss's putatively Rousseauist naturalism. My contribution seeks to establish the lasting impact of the Cercle d'Épistémologie's critique of Foucault on his later thinking regarding the 'subject'. Tracy McNulty and Adrian Johnston each in different ways help us read the *Cahiers pour l'Analyse* as a crucial document in the history of Lacanian psychoanalysis as both a clinical practice and research programme. Peter Hallward's assessment of Badiou's earliest philosophical articles illuminates the paradoxical consistency of Badiou's trajectory, and as a result also provides us with novel ways for thinking about the relation between theory and practice in the present.

The section of essays begins with François Regnault's account of how the effort to think structure and subject together was first experienced on the ground and ends with Slavoj Žižek's assessment of the dispute between Miller and Badiou as presenting today's political militants and philosophical practitioners with a conflict that awaits resolution. The resolution may need to wait further still, for it is our hope that the contents of this volume will serve, alongside Volume One and the website devoted to the project, as an invitation to

---

37   Cf. Edward Baring, *The Young Derrida and French Philosophy, 1945–1968* (Cambridge: Cambridge University Press, 2011).

others to pursue research into this pivotal chapter in twentieth-century French thought. For when we consider the breadth of coverage in the journal itself – from the history of political thought, to the modern sciences, to the modernist novel – the coverage in this volume is shamefully narrow. Apart from the journal's extensive engagement with the texts of modern logic and psychoanalysis, the volume also fails to address the key contributions of Michel Pêcheux. In addition to being foundational for his later work in discourse analysis,[38] Pêcheux's articles in the *Cahiers*, published under the pseudonym Thomas Herbert, stand as arguably the most comprehensive attempt of the period to produce, as one title has it, a 'general theory of ideologies'.[39]

Deficiencies aside, the main goal of this project has been to do the recovery work necessary for others to develop their own assessments of the *Cahiers pour l'Analyse* and its legacy. In pursuing the balance between an insistence on both historical contextualization and contemporary currency, perhaps we approach the sense of the 'generative necessity' that Cavaillès described as a 'dialectic' that would not be metaphysical and would require no halting appeals to 'consciousness'. The rational progress that Cavaillès called for requires the willed recovery of the very discourses that oblivion threatens to erase for us. The 'philosophy of the concept' introduced in Cavaillès's essay was but a sketch, an incomplete project brutally interrupted by a murderous regime. The efforts of the Cercle d'Épistémologie were interrupted by a politics of a different sort. The perennial interruption of the project seems to fortify its tenacity. If, as Adorno wrote, 'the whole is the untrue', then perhaps what truth there is in the *Cahiers pour l'Analyse* bears some relation to the project's manifest incompleteness, though whether it is 'in spite of' or 'because of' this incompleteness, is unclear. The fate of the concept remains undetermined.

---

38   See in particular Michel Pêcheux, *Automatic Discourse Analysis* [1969], eds. Tony Hak and Niels Helsloot, trans. David Macey (Amsterdam: Rodopi, 1995).

39   Thomas Herbert, 'Réflexion sur la situation théorique des sciences sociales et, spécialement, de la psychologie sociale' (CpA 2.6) and 'Pour une théorie générale des idéologies' (CpA 9.5).

François Regnault
Structure and Subject[1]

We were structuralists, we believed in science, we were not humanists.

Was it possible to reconcile these three positions? This is what I will undertake to analyze.

It seems to me that this was possible thanks to a new theory of the subject. This is what I will undertake to demonstrate.

I STRUCTURE

Structuralism, in the form that it took in the late 1950s, and in the form that young students of literature and philosophy could encounter it, without asking themselves where exactly it came from, was slowly to render phenomenology, the dominant philosophy of the day, empty and obsolete. Phenomenology retained consciousness as its main category. It was all about consciousness in those days, about lived experience, about intention, about perception.

And then suddenly the unconscious and structure crept in, 'on tip toes' (*à pas de colombe*, as Nietzsche would say). Logic, which had survived in the guise of formal logic as a scholastic remnant, now regained its immemorial rights, augmented by, that is to say re-founded by, the great mathematicians and logicians of the twentieth century: Russell, Frege, Gödel. Mathematics could claim to be of interest to philosophers once more, if only as a means of formalization – a formalization of arithmetic, of geometry, as well as of syntax and language: Hilbert, Peano, Carnap. The sciences themselves, which had been considered as a general category in the lifeless form of 'scientific method', with Claude Bernard as their guardian angel, now powerfully reasserted themselves at the centre of philosophical concerns, reinforced by the gravity of epistemological problems, or the guarantee of the History of the sciences. There was Gaston Bachelard, on the one hand, whose concepts were easy to grasp for non-specialist philosophers (though he himself knew his science perfectly well). On the other hand there was Alexandre Koyré, whose history of the sciences returned us to Galileo and Newton, and to mathematical

---

1   This text was first presented at the 'Concept and Form' conference, organized by the Centre for Research in Modern European Philosophy on 21 and 22 May 2009; the programme is online at http://fass.kingston.ac.uk/activities/item.php?updatenum=1428. Translated by Cécile Malaspina, revised by Peter Hallward.

physics. Georges Canguilhem, meanwhile, who had always applied himself with rigour to the domain of natural history, biology and medicine, introduced us to the formation and history of scientific concepts, such as, for instance, the concept of the reflex.[2]

I remember that at the time the very notion of structure – which was starting to receive enough attention to warrant becoming the object of a class at the École Normale Supérieure in 1960–61 given by the eminent specialist of Logic, Jules Vuillemin (who later became a Professor at the Collège de France) – had seemed somewhat opaque to me, especially since Vuillemin insisted that it made hardly any sense outside the domain of algebra. But we soon discovered that Claude Lévi-Strauss had established its credibility in 1949, in his book on the kinship relations of societies that were then still called primitive;[3] that psychoanalysis, as taken up by Dr. Jacques Lacan, contained structural considerations, if only in Freud's two topographies; and that Marxism, finally, soon to be renewed by Louis Althusser, was putting structure in a commanding place at the centre of the field that Marx had himself inaugurated as the critique of political economy.

Your average student in philosophy towards the end of the 1950s, however, would have had hardly any opportunity to learn about Russell and Gödel, while the names of Marx and Freud remained marginal, at the borders of the discipline. The unconscious was considered to be at most a factor of general psychology, while superstructures were dismissed as strata of a suspect economic theory. I haven't forgotten that, for other reasons (less philosophical than epistemological), a philosopher such as Bertrand Russell himself had little consideration for Marx or Freud, as far as their scientific claims were concerned. This, however, was not a critique that we were able to take on board at the time that we became structuralists.

So we believed in 'Science', even if (as I'll explain in a moment) some of us emphasized the plurality of the sciences. We even believed in a certain scientific ideal, and at the time some of us (notably Jean-Claude Milner) began to distinguish between the differentiated concepts of *ideal science* and *the ideal of science*, with the Cartesian, or Spinozist, sentiment that *Science* or the sciences, including mathematics, were a guarantee of truth that could and should inspire philosophy, far from any descriptions of consciousness and the indefinite uncertainties of lived experience.

I am talking here about the beginnings of the *Cahiers*, without forgetting that Alain Badiou, for example, who soon joined us, was competent in mathematics,

---

2   Georges Canguilhem, *La Formation du concept de réflexe aux XVII et XVIII siècles* (Paris: PUF, 1955).

3   Claude Lévi-Strauss, *Les Structures élémentaires de la parenté* (Paris: PUF, 1949); *The Elementary Structures of Kinship*, trans. J.H. Bell, J.R. von Sturmer, and Rodney Needham (Boston: Beacon Press, 1969).

as his subsequent work has always shown, and that we later made up some ground by publishing, in our last issues, Boole, Cantor, Gödel and Russell!

II SCIENCE

As far as science is concerned, it seems to me that two differences, or *différends*, inspired us. Since we were fairly ignorant of the Anglo-Saxon tradition, including Karl Popper, we referred instead, in part, to Gaston Bachelard and to his concept of *epistemological cut* or *rupture*. After the ideological errings or wanderings that generally precede the advent of a new science (which he referred to as 'epistemological obstacles'), Bachelard explained, such a science would constitute itself on an entirely different basis, inaugurating a new programme of research, even if some remainders and fictions that had preceded this science often continued to inhabit it, sometimes for long periods of time – for instance the so-called *phlogistic* fluid, the fire that supposedly animated bodies and justified their interactions, only disappeared with the creation of 'chemistry' by Lavoisier, when his theory of simple bodies came to ruin this fiction.

I took it upon myself, at the time, to develop an entire theory of epistemological *rupture* (for instance the birth of Galilean physics), and of the recastings or remouldings [*refontes*] (another of Bachelard's terms) which this same science might encounter in the course of its history – for instance, the science of physics brought by Newton to its classical perfection, followed by the remoulding of the concepts of physics by Einstein and the theory of relativity. I went as far as to turn this theory into a kind of formal system, of a somewhat scholastic kind, which could be applied to all the sciences, thereby establishing a sort of circle whereby what would qualify as sciences would be those disciplines or knowledges that conformed to this schema.[4]

This is indeed how Althusser sought to found Marxist political economy, relying in particular on a text by Friedrich Engels which compared Marx's discoveries in economics (of surplus value and other things) to the foundation of chemistry by Lavoisier.[5]

This theory did not develop without a certain idealism with regard to science, granting it a kind of closure on itself, an imperviousness to those ideological preconceptions that might contaminate it, an intrinsic purity and a field

---

4   TN: See François Regnault, 'Dialectic of Epistemologies', CpA 9.4. Cf. Regnault, 'Qu'est-ce qu'une coupure épistémologique?', lecture of 26 February 1968, given as part of the 'Philosophy Course for Scientists' organized by Louis Althusser at the École Normale Supérieure; notes on this lecture were published as 'Définitions', in Michel Pêcheux and Michel Fichant, *Sur l'histoire des sciences* (Paris: Maspero, 1969).

5   Friedrich Engels, preface to Karl Marx, *Capital* vol. II, http://www.marxists.org/archive/marx/works/1885-c2/choo.htm.

of truth, a purity which I doubt that we – though this *we* no longer exists – would still maintain.

To be more precise, it seems to me that Popper's theory of *falsification,* whereby a science by definition involves a degree of precariousness, and also Feyerabend's theory, which ruins any apodictic certainty in science, would both put profoundly in question Bachelard's problematic, which, despite the clarity of its detailed descriptions, was too formal in its generalizations. What I have since read by Imre Lakatos, *The Methodology of Scientific Research Programmes*,[6] has convinced me that every science indeed inaugurates what he calls a research programme, but that there is nothing to ensure that this programme should be eternal, or that it should always preserve its inaugural foundations.

We believed above all in 'Science [La *Science*] in the modern sense' when psychoanalysis gave us an occasion for its affirmation. We might say that psychoanalysis arrived gloriously among us when in early 1964 Louis Althusser invited Lacan, who had just been thrown out of Sainte-Anne (the mental asylum where he had previously taught and presented his cases), to the École Normale Supérieure at rue d'Ulm, where we were students (and where the *Cahiers pour l'Analyse* came into being). There Lacan, in the name of Freud and in the name of psychoanalysis more generally, and in opposition to the so-called human sciences (essentially psychology and sociology), presented *Science,* with a capital 'S', as a unique discipline, bearing an absolute singularity, one that Lacan identified, roughly speaking, with mathematized physics. Science was thus open to mathematization and also closed in on itself, or, according to the concept he put forward, foreclosed. In other words, science performed a radical foreclosure of the realities from which it cut itself loose in order to come into being, thus rejoining the idea of an epistemological cut. But Lacan leaned less on Bachelard than on the great historian of the sciences, Alexandre Koyré. Koyré, in his exhaustive and minutely detailed historical studies of the birth of mathematical physics in the seventeenth century, had described most of the conceptual movements, the obstacles, errors and forays, the mistakes and surprises and moments of genius of this history, as it developed from Galileo to Newton via Copernicus, without however drawing a general theory of science from it. Koyré was keen to avoid coming too close to the sovereign theories or doctrines of *Wissenschaft* peculiar to German philosophy after Kant: Hegel, Schelling, Fichte, philosophies for whom science exceeds what we ordinarily call (empirical) science.

Similarly, philosophers like Jules Vuillemin, Georges Canguilhem himself and, I believe also Michel Serres – who had come to the École Normale to teach an *agrégation* class on Leibniz (1961–62), some years before the publication of

---

6   Imre Lakatos, *The Methodology of Scientific Research Programmes*, 2 vols. (Cambridge: Cambridge University Press, 1980).

his illuminating *Système de Leibniz*[7] – preferred in truth this History of the sciences to our or should I say 'my' portable epistemology.

All in all it was also in order to avoid a *Wissenschaftslehre* that Althusser – who sought to eliminate the difference assumed in the Communist Party between bourgeois science and proletarian science, and who attempted to turn Marxist economics into a science like any other – admitted that there was a plurality of sciences, materialist figures or forms of scientificity, but not Science [*La Science*], not Science with a capital 'S', a matter of general scientificity or the concern of a general philosophy. Althusser dismissed as idealist any attempt to establish or have recourse to such a Science. Althusser also held that philosophy, since it found it difficult to apply the sovereign Eleventh Thesis of Marx on Feuerbach ('the philosophers have hitherto only interpreted the world in various ways; the point is to change it'), ought rather to content itself with being a theoretical practice – a praxis like others – and not an interpretation of the world or of the sciences.

The debate might itself have seemed somewhat scholastic: there is not *one* science, there is only the *plurality* of sciences. Fine. For there to be a plurality of sciences, however, they still had to correspond to an idea of science. There had to be a certain idea, albeit one inspired by the actual sciences, without substituting for them science in itself.

But the debate did not seem scholastic to our Lacanian eyes, however, because the Lacanian proposition of *La* Science, of science in an absolute sense, was founded on his theory of the subject, or at least on the experience that psychoanalysis had of psychosis. Remember Freud's formula concerning Schreber: there is, in the *Verwerfung* of President Schreber a foreclosure of reality, but (as Freud also wrote to Jung) 'I prevail where the paranoiac fails', for according to Freud science operates like psychosis, by excluding a reality for which it substitutes the object it constructs, which is its real.

As Jacques-Alain Miller put it in his 'Action of the Structure', 'the closure proper to science therefore operates a redistribution between a closed field, on the one hand, of which one perceives no limit if one considers it from the inside, and a foreclosed space. *Foreclosure* is the other side of closure. This term will suffice to indicate that every science is structured like a psychosis: the foreclosed returns under the form of the impossible.'[8]

The falling of bodies, as explained by Galileo: it is only when he *forecloses* (excludes) the form of bodies, their weight, their density, their colour, etc., that he can formulate a law which concerns only the relation of spaces and the time that it takes a body to cross these spaces. Reality is the form of bodies. Reality is

---

7   Michel Serres, *Le Système de Leibniz et ses modèles mathématiques*, 2 vols. (Paris: PUF, 1968).

8   Jacques-Alain Miller, 'Action de la structure' [1964], CpA 9.6:102–103.

friction [*La réalité, ce sont les frottements*]. The impossible, which is the real, is the real of this fall, which in classical physics repeats itself . . . imperturbably. In Lacan's own words, which I believe have stayed with all of us: 'the impossible is the real'.

'How then', continues Miller, 'is such a discourse possible, a discourse which only takes orders from itself, a flat discourse, without unconscious, adequate to its object? [. . .] This closing of scientific discourse should not be confused with the suture of non-scientific discourse, because it actually expels lack, reduces its central exteriority, disconnects it from every other Scene. Thought from within the field it circumscribes, this closing [*fermeture*] will be given the name: *closure* [*clôture*].'[9]

Perhaps there was, regarding science, and also more generally, a certain Platonism amongst the four or five of us [involved in the formulation of the *Cahiers*], as suggested by Jean-Claude Milner's text entitled 'The Point of the Signifier', which retraces the genera of being in the *Sophist* in order to conclude: 'A formal system is thereby constituted, and the ways it might be interpreted can now be specified. How can we not read, in their double dependence, being as the order of the signifier, the radical register of all computations and set of all chains, also as "one" of the signifier, unity of computation, element of the chain? And non-being, as the signifier of the subject . . .'[10]

III SUBJECT

The greatest *différend* between us and 'the others' concerned the subject. It served as a shibboleth between psychoanalysis and materialist philosophy, between Lacanians and Althusserians, between Althusser's process without subject and the procedures of the barred subject, between the logic of the signifier and a certain scientific positivism. This is how Lacan launched into the opening lecture of the seminar he gave in 1965–66 at the École Normale Supérieure, reading a text which was immediately published in the first issue of the *Cahiers pour l'Analyse*: 'Shall we say that we established the status of the subject in psychoanalysis last year? We went so far as to develop a structure that accounts for the state of splitting [*refente*] or *Spaltung* where the psychoanalyst detects it in his praxis.'[11]

It must be admitted that this subject has always appeared hard to handle and rather strange to philosophy, and even more so to general psychology. In fact, far from being a unity, a centre, a power of synthesis, it is divided, split [*refendu*]. It is the effect of the signifier, or rather of two signifiers, such that 'the

---

9   Miller, 'Action de la structure', CpA 9.6:102.
10   Jean-Claude Milner, 'Le Point du signifiant', CpA 3.5:77–78.
11   Lacan, 'La Science et la vérité' [1965], CpA 1.1:7; E, 855/726.

signifier represents the subject for another signifier'. In other words, all you need are two signifiers side by side in order to produce the effect of the subject: it is in the interstice of the two, but also disappears there, such that they miss or lack it. I will remind you of the simplest example: you go to see someone, a friend, and you are surprised to find yourself at their door with your own key in hand, ready to enter their house. 'How silly I am!', you say to yourself. Well! The subject of the unconscious is this subject, unknown by you, immediately effaced, which, for an instant, allowed you to glimpse . . . And it is up to you to interpret it: 'I am breaking into the other's home, I am at home with the other, etc.' The first signifier: my key; the second: his or her lock!

Lacan had the audacity to draw his subject from Descartes' *Cogito*: 'I think therefore I am'. It became, by an interpretation: 'I think: "therefore I am"', and then, via a topological transformation: 'I am where I do not think, therefore I think where I am not'. For Lacan this is the price that must be paid in order for the subject of psychoanalysis to be at the same time the foundation of science.[12]

One could separate and then join, or disjoin, the linguistic version from the topological version: this is what Jacques-Alain Miller did in a 1984 lecture, when he opposed two different and even in a sense contradictory interpretations, by Lacan, of the cogito. The first style of interpretation is his interpretation of the *punctual* and *evanescent* cogito, and the second style of interpretation is the topological cogito, or, once more, the *erratic* and *heterotopic* cogito.

Lacan had thus posited the cogito both as axiom and as consequence: 'To say that the subject upon which we operate in psychoanalysis can only be the subject of science may seem paradoxical.'[13]

The Cartesian cogito reworked by Lacan is also the cogito which, rather than have extraordinary thoughts like the idea of God, the idea of absolute infinity, etc., has instead as its thoughts the unconscious thoughts of hysterics. Hysterics suffer from unconscious thoughts, and it is with reference to such thoughts that Lacan seeks to impose the Cartesian cogito. As a result the Cartesian cogito becomes the source of the subject of psychoanalysis and is torn away, by the same token, from philosophy. 'If therefore', says Jacques-Alain Miller in 'Action of the Structure',

> against the philosophy of structuralism, we require a notion of subjectivity, this subjectivity will figure not as regent but as subject [*sujette*]. Although it is required by representation, this subjectivity is not required to occupy the position of a foundation, with the function of a cause. Its gap or deficiency distributes its conscious being at each of the levels induced by the imaginary in structured reality; as for its

---

12   TN: cf. *Cogito and the Unconscious*, ed. Slavoj Žižek (Durham: Duke University Press, 1998).

13   Lacan, 'La Science et la vérité', CpA 1.1:10; E, 858/729.

unity, it depends on its localization, its localization in the structuring structure. The subject in the structure thus retains none of the attributes of the psychological subject, it escapes from the latter's definition, and is never stabilized between the theory of knowledge, morality, politics and law.[14]

Those who refused to grant us this subject, be they materialists or 'spiritualists', also refused to accept the anti-humanism that followed from it.

IV ANTI-HUMANISM

When I speak of humanism I am not, or barely, thinking of that of the Renaissance, of Montaigne or Erasmus, which remains, to say it swiftly and without saying much: a great thing. Doesn't it? What is at issue, fundamentally, concerns the consequences of the Cartesian movement itself, when in the *First Meditation* Descartes puts everything in doubt and thus declares that he does not know what a man is. The cogito begins with this reduction of the body, which was to become such a problem for all post-Cartesian philosophy. In the same way, we might say that 'around us' there gathered, in a shared anti-humanism, Lacan, coming from Descartes, Althusser, coming from Marx, and Foucault, coming from Nietzsche. We've already looked at Lacan. For Marx, 'it is not the consciousness of men that determines their being, but on the contrary it is their social being that determines their consciousness'; as a result man becomes nothing more than the carrier of this function, and the ideas he has or makes correspond to his social being. Singular social being ruins universal Man. Marx replaces him, at least for a while, with humanity, which 'sets itself only such tasks as it can solve'.[15] That the notion of humanity itself poses some problems is a question we will have to leave aside for now; it is being posed today, I think, insofar as no-one speaks of humanity any more: we speak only of the global Market (in its Marxist version) or of the World (including its *alter-mondialiste*, or idealist, version: 'another world is possible'). As for Foucault I shall only recall the end of his *Archaeology of Knowledge* (1969), where he evokes all those who have been overcome by the modern proliferation of discourses, their displacements and their incessant transformations, and who find themselves being told, against the notion of Man to which they still cling, that: 'Discourse is not life: its time is not your time; in it, you will not be reconciled to death; you may have killed God beneath the weight of all the things you have said; but don't imagine that, with all that you are saying, you will make a man that will live longer than he.'[16]

---

14   Miller, 'Action de la structure', CpA 9.6:97–98.

15   Marx, Preface to *A Contribution to the Critique of Political Economy* [1859], http://www.marxists.org/archive/marx/works/1859/critique-pol-economy/preface.htm.

16   Michel Foucault, *The Archaeology of Knowledge* [1969], trans. A.M. Sheridan Smith (NY: Random House, 1972), 211.

With respect to this point we ought to have developed a differential analysis of the concepts of *knowledge* [*savoir*] and of *discourse*, which were treated in a variety of ways by different authors, in relation to science or to History; and also, as a corollary, the concepts of *genealogy* (in the *Cahiers pour l'Analyse*) and of *archaeology* (in Foucault).

This equivocation on the nature of the subject lasted for a long time, because the subject in Lacan's sense is one of a kind. This subject appeared when Lacan transferred it from Cartesianism to psychoanalysis, thereby inventing the possibility that the Cartesian *cogito* could lend its meaning and direction [*sens*], or rather its structure, and in any case its gravity, to the subject as understood by Freud – this *Ich* that appears in the third of the *New Introductory Lectures on Psychoanalysis*: '*Wo Es war, soll Ich werden.*' Confronted with this subject, the materialists raised their eyebrows in an apparently Spinozist fashion, preferring Spinoza's axiom 'man thinks' to Descartes' 'I think'. In doing so they joined up with all those who subsequently accused us, particularly after the events of 1968, of having fallen for all kinds of inhuman causes. At which point the call went out, in the name of an intermittent humanism, for a return to the subject, as if we had not done everything we could, working alongside Lacan, to introduce its name and its structure to philosophy. But the Lacanian subject, tenuous, punctual and evanescent, etc., did not seem, unconsciously, to fit the bill for those who wanted to restore the subject, that is to say the good old notion of consciousness affirmed by phenomenology or spiritualist (if not idealist) philosophy – that consciousness that was so hatefully tossed aside by structuralism, materialism and anti-humanism.

Let us conclude this point with a Lacanian formula that I value a great deal: 'The *I* and the *ego* separate and overlap in every particular subject.'[17]

CONCLUSION

These questions undoubtedly continued to inspire our investigations for a long time (and perhaps they still do), and they might even have been refined and resolved had the events of 1968 not interrupted the run of things. At the time we were preparing, or rather envisaging, an issue on God. Why God? No doubt as a point of view, a perspective on the whole of these investigations, inasmuch as God, the sovereign concept of philosophy and present in most philosophical systems, but also the sovereign illusion denounced by Marxism and by psychoanalysis, was able to contain the supreme différend that might divide us from ourselves. We had even obtained an (unprecedented) promise for a text on this question by Maurice Blanchot, the author of *The Most High* [*Le Très-Haut*].[18]

---

17   Lacan, 'La Chose freudienne', E 418/348tm: 'Le *je* et le *moi* se séparent et se recouvrent en chaque sujet particulier'.
18   Maurice Blanchot, *Le Très-Haut* (Paris: Gallimard, 1948).

In the end it was perhaps God, why not, or History, if you believe in it, or a singular event, which stopped us; and since everyone had 'moved on to politics', a politics dominated by what were called 'revolutionary slogans' and revolutionary words, the *Cahiers* were interrupted without a word![19] Better this than what happens to those journals that endure in dullness and routine, or that slide into ugly conflicts, and slowly collapse.

The *Cahiers pour l'Analyse* thus died of an external cause, which is a perfectly Spinozist outcome, and should have pleased us well, since we were all Spinozists – a little, a lot, passionately . . . or not at all!

---

19   TN: The original French reads: 'En somme Dieu, pourquoi pas, ou l'Histoire, si vous y croyez, ou un événement singulier nous en empêchèrent, et comme tout le monde était "passé à la politique", et une politique où domina ce qu'on appelait "la phrase révolutionnaire", les *Cahiers* s'interrompirent sans phrase!'

CHAPTER TWO

Patrice Maniglier
Acting Out the Structure

Structuralism is commonly understood to have dismissed subjectivity as a rele-vant dimension of the human experience and as a source of meaning in general, in a context still dominated by Husserl's transcendental idealism. If indeed meaning only emerges from oppositional relations within a system, how could the subject be at the origin or even have any particular authority over what he or she says? If structuralism is understood in this way, then the re-emergence of subjectivity as a central theoretical concern in the mid 1960s might likewise have been understood as a symptom of the fading of structuralism as a domi-nant intellectual orientation.

This is certainly a diagnosis shared by the young students of Althusser and Lacan who edited the *Cahiers pour l'Analyse*. In 'Action of the Structure' (CpA 9.6) (which though only published in the penultimate issue of the *Cahiers*, in 1968, was actually written in 1964, serving to outline the 'research programme' at issue throughout the journal) they clearly argued both that structuralism actually needs a theory of subjectivity, and that this theory requires a reworking of the concept of structure which will have to go beyond the conceptuality inherited from structural semiotics. Following Lacan, Jacques-Alain Miller named this reworking the 'logic of the signifier'.

In this article, I would like to take this attempt seriously, but I also want to assess its rather mixed results. To this end, I will first come back on the motivations and meaning of such an endeavour, and defend its relevance in the context of structuralism itself, as well as for philosophy in general. I will then consider the solutions that were proposed forty years ago, in the *Cahiers*: for reasons I hope will become clear, I think the famous concept of 'suture' construed by Jacques-Alain Miller failed to give a convincing account of this logic. In a third section, therefore, I will propose an alternative concept of structure, one that will draw on a reconsideration of the conceptuality of structural semiotics which the *Cahiers* group, in my view, was too quick to overlook; in particular I will draw on insights formulated by Lévi-Strauss regarding the structure of myth which, contrary to what is commonly believed, aimed at grasping the essential, formal – structural! – incompleteness of symbolic systems. Such a movement backwards in history is all the more interesting in that, as I will show in my fourth section, it is precisely these speculations by Lévi-Strauss about the structure of myth that prompted Lacan to believe, as he wrote later, that 'structuralism [. . .] allowed us to elaborate logically [. . .] the subject caught up in a constituting division' (E, 856/727). I hope to show how a better awareness of the historical context of structuralism may help to perceive both the significance and the limitations of the work undertaken in the *Cahiers pour l'Analyse*. I also hope this will help in the development of alternative solutions to the problem of the relation between structure and subjectivity, solutions that differ from those formulated in the *Cahiers*, and that still remain very influential today in particular through the work of Ernesto Laclau and Slavoj Žižek.[1]

I STRUCTURAL ONTOLOGY AND THE TROPICAL SUBJECT

In 'Action of the Structure' (CpA 9.6), Miller gives at least one compelling argument as to why structuralism should account for the emergence of subjects as necessary effects of the systems which seem to exclude them. Indeed, by defining symbolic systems merely as sets of codetermined entities, structuralism 'prohibits itself from saying anything' about any aspect of the 'relation that the subject entertains with its speech', and, as a consequence, relegates comprehension of actual human action to the most traditional sorts of philosophical anthropology.[2] It may be the case, for instance, that anything I say must be predetermined as a possibility within the linguistic system that I share with my community – but the *fact* that I said it, and said it in this particular context, to this particular person, is an essential part of its actual *meaning*, which can be distinguished from the structural dimension of the 'signified'. Everything that structuralism was deemed to undermine – subjectivity, context, reference, practice – can then come back at another level, the level of *use*.[3] It suffices to read Paul Ricoeur's defence of hermeneutics against the structuralist challenge to perceive the strength of this argument.[4] Therefore, if structuralism is indeed to dislodge subjectivity from its privileged position at the origin of meaning, it cannot content itself with a concept of structure as a *condition* for meaningful

---

1   Ernesto Laclau and Chantal Mouffe, *Hegemony and Socialist Strategy* (London: Verso, 1985); Slavoj Žižek, *The Sublime Object of Ideology* (London: Verso, 1989).

2   'When structuralist activity rejects temporality and subjectivity from the neutralized space of the cause, it obliges itself to guarantee its already-constituted objects by referring them back to the categories of "social life", "culture", "anthropology", if not to biology, or to mind [*l'esprit*]. It makes an illegitimate appeal to linguistic structuralism: the latter, by opening its field of analysis through preliminary exclusion of any relation that the subject entertains with its speech, prohibits itself from saying anything about it. As long as the *alteration* brought about by this exclusion of the speaking subject is not annulled, linguistic structures do not apply beyond their region of origin' (Jacques-Alain Miller, 'Action of the Structure', CpA 9.6:95).

3   'Use' here refers not so much to the Wittgensteinian problematic as to the Saussurean distinction between *langue* and *parole*, which was later generalized by the Danish linguist Louis Hjelmslev as a distinction between 'system' and 'use'.

4   See Paul Ricoeur, 'Structure, Word, Event', *The Conflict of Interpretations: Essays in Hermeneutics*, ed. Don Ihde (Evanston: Northwestern University Press, 1974).

events (this very sentence is possible only because it belongs to the structured set of all the possible alternative sentences which could have been used in its place), it must construe it as a *cause* (the system is such that it determines its own actualization: I must write this sentence *because* of those I could have written). There must be something in the structure itself which sets it into *action*. Far from being a complete, self-sufficient, immanently codetermined world of virtualities, overlooking the actual world and coding it from above, a structure must contain a principle of actualization into partial, incomplete views, such as particular speech actions.

Now, the subject which is expected to emerge as an effect of a structure cannot, by definition, be the self-determined entity so dear to the philosophical tradition. It must be, as Lacan had it, constituted through its own division. This means that the very relation it has to itself must be rooted in its impossibility of coinciding with itself. This may sound like an odd definition of subjectivity. But it must be remarked that it is also a perfectly classical one: from Hegel to Sartre, passing via Kierkegaard and Heidegger, the subject has long been defined either as an impossible being that is what it is not and is not what it is, or one for whom identity and difference are identical, a paradoxical entity which is at the same time a given and a task, an 'ecstatic' term which cannot stand (in) itself, etc.

This helps to illuminate the significance of the *Cahiers* in the longer history of philosophy. Indeed, the rationale for such a paradoxical definition of subjectivity has to do with the problem of the relation between *being* and *subjectivity*. Does it make sense to say that 'I' *am*? The problem can be rephrased from the standpoint of a very simple question: is it possible to apply the category of truth to the subject of knowledge itself? If nothing is true about the subject but what the subject endorses, there seems to be no difference between that which appears to him and that which is indeed the case about him. But, on the other hand, it seems difficult to understand in what sense anything can be true about the subject, without the subject ascribing it to itself. If it is true for instance that, behind the illusions of consciousness, there operate only blind forces, this may imply that the very idea of subjectivity is wrong – but not that there is anything which *I* should acknowledge about myself of which I was not aware. Sartre made this case against the objectivist interpretation of Freud: why should *I* feel concerned by those wishes (that appear through psychoanalysis to be at the origin of my symptoms and dreams) if they are nothing but rough facts, simple data of the world, to which I could refer from outside, as if I was other than myself?[5] What reason do I have to consider them as 'mine'? Why should I

---

5   'I am the Ego, but I am not the Id. I hold no privileged position in relation to my unconscious psyche. [. . .] I stand, in relation to my Id, in the position of the Other' (Jean-Paul Sartre, *Being and Nothingness: An Essay on Phenomenological Ontology*, trans. Hazel E. Barnes [London: Routledge, 1956], 50–51).

assume these wishes as my *own*, more than, say, the ones of the analyst? And if I don't assume them, can the analytic cure still be effective?

The *Cahiers pour l'Analyse* inherited Lacan's solution to this dilemma, which is to define the subject as a paradoxical entity. Such a subject can only constitute itself as being different from itself: its very identity is to escape itself. In the *Four Concepts of Psychoanalysis* (1964), through which our young *normaliens* discovered Lacan's teaching first-hand, Lacan explicitly raises the question of the ontology of the subject, and proposes that the kind of entities in which the subject realizes itself have the strange property of being 'evasive', 'elusive', self-erasing, that is, ultimately, of having the being of an event rather than a thing.[6] Such are, for instance, slips of the tongue. Through them, I betray the truth about me. But the important point is that this truth is such that it cannot be simply acknowledged and endorsed; it only *exists* at the very instant of the surprise, of the betrayal.[7] Truth about me happens, but does not really subsist; it is a matter of what happens, not of what is; it belongs to the ontology of the event rather than to an ontology of substance.

This implies that the truth about the subject cannot be expressed in a simply *descriptive* form, as a more or less 'correct' assertion. It can only be said in a *figurative* or indirect way: it always points or alludes to something else. It is not a matter of fact, but rather a poetic figure. Indirect does not mean, though, that instead of, for instance, calling a cat 'a cat', I call it the 'shadow guest of the house', while you understand that I nonetheless have a cat in mind. The stylistic or poetic figure rather points at something which cannot be designated as such. If I say 'We are such stuff as dreams are made on and our little life is rounded with a sleep', there is no way to extenuate the meaning of this sentence through any descriptive comment. It may be true, or it may not, but it cannot be judged as the 'correct' or 'incorrect' description of a fact. Such is subjective truth. This is the reason why subjectivity can only escape in the form of slips of the tongue, symptoms and dreams: because it is precisely nothing other than these slippages, qua slippages. The truth about the subject is not so much in the meaning of the dream as in the endless process of associations, that is, in the substitutions of signs which constitute the interpretation.[8]

An old joke about slips may illustrate this point. 'A psychoanalyst having

---

6   'Ontically, then, the unconscious is the elusive' (Jacques Lacan, S11, 32). 'The gap of the unconscious may be said to be pre-ontological [. . .,] it does not lend itself to ontology. [. . . It] is neither being, nor non-being, but the unrealized' (30–31).

7   'Impediment, failure, split. In a spoken or written sentence something stumbles. Freud is attracted by these phenomena, and it is where he seeks the unconscious. There, something other demands to be realized – which appears as intention, of course, but of a strange temporality. What occurs, what is *produced*, in this gap, is presented as *the discovery* [*retrouvaille*]' (S11, 28).

8   This is why Freud can say that the dream-work is the 'essence of dreaming' (Sigmund Freud, *The Interpretation of Dreams*, trans. James Strachey [Harmondsworth: Penguin Books, 1976], 650); cf. Žižek, *The Sublime Object of Ideology*, 14.

breakfast with his wife, instead of asking: "Darling, would you kindly hand me the sugar pot?", lets out: "Why did you ruin my life, you bitch!?'" Of course this is an impossible 'slip'. But think of the situation in which this same man comes back home one evening, having made up his mind to ask her for divorce, and simply says: 'Hello darling, would you like a cup of tea?' The point is that we must not suppose that the truth of the subject is that he, 'objectively', whether he acknowledges it or not, wishes to get rid of his wife, as if this wish was just a fact – but rather that his way of asking something from her is itself to reproach her for their entire life together, and that, *conversely*, his very way of reproaching her is also 'merely' to ask her for a domestic service . . . In other words, the truth about the subject is not 'either one interpretation or the other', but the displacement by which one *is* also the other, whereby love is hate and hate is love – and this is why it can be grasped only through figures.

To designate the paradoxical nature of the subject, Lacan famously coined the term 'split subject', which he characterized as follows: 'I am thinking where I am not, therefore I am where I am not thinking'.[9] This does not mean, though, that I am somewhere else, but rather that *I am nothing other than this very displacement*. The truth about the subject can only be expressed through *tropes*. The Lacanian subject is essentially tropical.

Now, the question is: how should the concept of structure be reworked so that such a paradoxical entity can be understood to emerge as a necessary consequence of its own nature? What does the expression 'logic of the signifier' designate, ultimately? Miller and his collaborators present it as a theory of the *form* of all symbolic systems or processes. More precisely it is a sort of abstract machine or a symbolic automaton that can model the workings of all symbolic phenomena (including itself, of course). But how should we define symbolic processes? It may be tempting to define them as that which conveys meaning, but we would then teleologically subordinate them to meaning, and in that case would have to refer them to a pre-structural understanding, which is precisely what Miller wanted to avoid. The virtue of the structuralist definition of the sign, however, is that it enables definition not by its function, but rather by its way of *being*, i.e. by its ontology. If we can say that different things – say, languages, political ideologies, mythologies, fashion, etc. – are indeed symbolic phenomena, this is not based on any pre-understanding of either the notion of meaning or of their function, but simply because they can be described and modelled as *systems of differential and positional entities*. The theory of 'structure' in general can in this sense serve as the ontology of symbolic systems.

Now, this of course implies that there *are* symbolic systems in the world (natural languages, popular mythologies, etc.). But these systems don't simply emerge just like that, from anywhere. We can make the following hypothesis:

---

9   Lacan, E, 517/430.

symbolic systems are produced by the workings of some blind symbolic function (which we can imagine as a function of the brain) which processes pertinent sets of data and extracts from them differences by mapping these differences onto another set of differences. The powerful idea in structuralism is precisely that 'meaning' has nothing to do with somebody trying to say something about something, as in the traditional model of predication; meaning is rather the consequence of some reverse mapping of one set of differences onto another one, and vice versa, a mapping carried out by some blind automatic function, which we will call the symbolic function. This process unwittingly elicits symbolic systems.

We can now rephrase the problem in more precise terms: the guiding idea here is that the new kind of objectivity introduced by the structuralist reworking of the 'cultural sciences' may enable us to account for the emergence, in this thoroughly 'objective' world, of subjects as effects. If we can successfully argue that, in each and every symbolic system (as defined above) there is at least one term that is included by the very manner in which it is excluded, that is, a possibility which at the same time is its own impossibility, then we would have shown that symbolic systems cannot constitute themselves without implying a subject in the psychoanalytic sense. How so? Because we have seen that the authentic definition of a subject is not as a positive entity, but rather as a term that only exists in the form of a *being-displaced*, as the impossibility of coinciding with itself.

Understood along these lines, I sympathize enthusiastically with this structuralist project. But I will now explain why I am not convinced by the solutions given to this problem in the *Cahiers* themselves. They are not the only available solutions. I have tried to show elsewhere that this question was indeed the matrix of many of the most important works undertaken in recent French philosophy, referring to the work of Alain Badiou, Michel Pêcheux, Étienne Balibar, or Jean Petitot.[10] But I will limit myself here to the best-known models of the 'logic of the signifier': those provided by Jacques-Alain Miller and, in an alternative version, by Jean-Claude Milner.

II WHAT'S WRONG WITH 'SUTURE'?

There is no need to repeat here the details of Miller's argument in 'La Suture' (CpA 1.3). It's enough to recall that Miller equates the Lacanian subject (in its relation to the chain of signifiers) with zero in its relation to the natural numbers (1, 2, 3 . . .), as defined by Frege in his *Foundations of Arithmetic*. According to Frege, the constitution of the ordered series of successive numbers implies one

---

10   See Patrice Maniglier, 'The Structuralist Legacy', in *The History of Continental Philosophy*, vol. 7, *After Poststructuralism: Transitions and Transformations*, ed. Alan Schrift and Rosi Braidotti (London: Acumen, 2010).

term (i.e. zero) which refers to an object that is 'impossible' (an object non-identical to itself) but that nonetheless operates in the series of numbers as that which links each one to its successor. In the same way, for Miller the subject is a condition for the constitution of a signifying chain even though it cannot be designated by any particular sign, but only surfaces in the displacements it imposes on (all) other signs: it only exists between two signs, just as each natural number subsumes both *n* objects and *n+1* numbers (since it includes zero which must be counted as a number but not as an object).

The first remark I would like to make is that it is quite odd, in this context, to refer to Frege rather than Saussure, and to arithmetic rather than linguistics, in order to provide a general theory of the form of language which would imply the emergence of a subject. Are we supposed to be constituted as subjects only through our use of numbers *per se*? Is it because we are capable of counting that we become subjects? In truth, the very status of Miller's analogy is unclear. Is it supposed actually to represent the way all discourses function? Taken literally, this would imply that each discourse can be construed as a sort of arithmetic series . . . This seems untenable, of course. It would mean that all speech can be represented by the series of natural numbers. In other words, there would be just one structure in the world. But since this is not true even for the set of arithmetic theorems, I doubt it is true for ordinary language . . .

Or, on the contrary, is this just an example of the way 'suture' works in one particular field of human life – in this case, arithmetic? Shall we read Miller's text as a 'symptomal' reading of Frege's logical account of arithmetic, which shows that even numbers are conditioned by the kind of symbolic mechanisms which Freud uncovered? In other words, is it because we are subjective (i.e. suturing, traversed by unconscious drives) creatures that we are indeed capable of arithmetic? But then in that case it would be clear that the way zero functions in arithmetic does not really *explain* the emergence of subjectivity; it is rather the other way round. The question remains: what are we to make of the 'logic of the signifier' itself? It would be unsatisfying to settle for an interpretation that reduces the function of this logic to one of clarifying the nature of the operation through which the subject exists in every structural domain by appealing to a mere analogy: this interpretation would fall prey to a sort of vicious circle, since the 'logic of the signifier' would be elucidated by appealing to one of its symptoms, i.e. to what it precisely should elucidate.

A final and in my view decisive objection is that Frege's account of arithmetic draws from a particular semantic theory, one that happens to be incompatible with structural semiotics, since in perfectly traditional fashion it appeals to *reference*, moreover to reference understood according to the logic of extension. It is precisely because numbers are supposed to be concepts which *refer* to objects, that we can construe the concept of an object 'non-identical to itself'. Even apart from the fact that this logic is incompatible with the kind of structuralism which

Lacan seemed to draw on (for instance regarding the notion of entities constituted only of differences which cannot be construed within an extensional logic), it is clear that it cannot be *the* 'logic of the signifier'. Such a logic would have to describe the most fundamental way by which signs can be constituted or meaning can happen in the world; but the experience of suture requires that we are already able to signify things through concepts and make reference to them. There would then be a still more fundamental theory of the sign than the one which lays claim to the grandiose title of a 'logic of the signifier'.[11]

It is clear that we will not find in Frege's logic of arithmetic the logic of the signifier proper. We must therefore look for it somewhere else. Miller himself tried later to provide such a logic that would not appeal to any sort of referentialist theory of sign, one that would only rely on a structural definition of the sign, in a short text entitled 'Matrice'.[12] But I would like here to focus on a similar but simpler attempt made later by Jean-Claude Milner, in a retrospective presentation of the project underlying the *Cahiers pour l'Analyse*. In his book, *Le Périple structural* (2002), Milner advances a strikingly simple syllogism to explain why every symbolic system necessarily implies an element which can be called a subject.

(1)   Each property of any term in a symbolic system implies the existence of another term.

This is so because each property is differential: for instance, the phoneme /p/ can be said to be 'voiceless' (in the phonological sense) not because of any intrinsic positive feature of all its realizations, but because there exists a term (in English) from which it is distinct with regards to this feature: /b/.

(2)   There is at least one property that is common to all terms: their being differential.

But, since there cannot be any property without there being another term, each term in a symbolic system can only be said to be differential because there exists at least one term which supports this property. Now the conclusion is obvious:

(3)   In each and every symbolic system, there must exist at least one term which is different from itself.

---

11   It may be worth recalling that Badiou, in his 'Marque et manque' (CpA 10.8), made a similar objection to Miller's uncritical endorsing of Frege's referentialist definition of signs. But, of course, at that time Badiou opposed to it a purely formal theory of signs and tried to prove that arithmetic did not need Frege's semantics.

12   Jacques-Alain Miller, 'Matrice', *Ornicar?* 4 (1975), reprinted in Miller, *Un Début dans la vie* (Paris: Gallimard, 2002), 135–144.

Indeed, this term is also differential, but it has this property only because it differs from itself. This, of course, is the subject. 'Allowing that any structural term as such is non-identical to oneself, the subject is the term of the chain which supports the [property of being] "not-identical to oneself" of any term of the chain.'[13]

It may be worth recalling that this emphasis on the notion of differentiality was already at the core of Milner's reading of the *Sophist* in the third volume of the *Cahiers* (CpA 3.5). Indeed, Milner argues there that the three first genres of the *Sophist* – Being, Movement, and Rest – are selected because of their 'formal properties', that is, because they can be defined as distinct instantiations of one oppositional trait: mixture or non-mixture [*mélange/ non-mélange*] (cf. CpA 3.5:74). While Being can mix with either Movement or Rest (in the sense that it can be attributed to one or the other), Movement and Rest cannot mix with one another (nothing can be said at the same time to be in movement and at rest). The single oppositional trait 'mixture or non-mixture' can only be deployed through *three* terms and not only two, one of which can mix with each of the others, and two which cannot, while the identity of each term is oppositional.

Milner then shows that the further couple 'Same' and 'Other' must be introduced to complement this oppositional system: while Being is compatible with Movement, it is nonetheless different (something can be said both to be and to be in movement, without equating being with movement). But this system reveals itself to be unbalanced. The paradox of Being is that it is defined by its differential property of mixing with any other term, but it cannot be posited as such without all the other ones falling into 'non-being': Being *is* (or is only itself) inasmuch as everything which can be is not (i.e. it has something that none of the other terms have); and conversely, anything is inasmuch as Being is not or not purely and merely itself (i.e. it is always also something else: a mobile, a chair, a cat . . .).[14]

This has an embarrassing consequence: there must exist one term which is the impossibility of all the other ones. This 'term' would be Non-Being. Non-Being is not really a distinct term, but rather it is both what Being is when any other term is said to be, and what all the terms are together when Being is affirmed for itself.[15] The oppositional system must elicit a term which cannot be differentially situated within the system itself: it has no place.[16] It is not a sixth

---

13   Jean-Claude Milner, *Le Périple structural* (Paris: Seuil, 2002), 165.

14   'So even *that which is* is not, precisely insofar as the others are, since, not being them, it is one thing, namely itself, and on the other hand, it is those others, which are an indefinite number' (Plato, *Sophist*, 257a, in Milner, 'Le Point du signifiant', CpA 3.5:75).

15   'It is the abyss which erases all terms ("the others are not")' (CpA 3.5:76).

16   'In the series that must be unfolded to support the opposition of mixture and non-mixture, non-being has no assigned place, other than those points of inflection [*fléchissement*]

term, but rather what turns one into the other. Its identity is purely operational: it is what is repeated each time a term is posited as existing, and, at the same time, what annuls all the terms together in order to posit Being as a term.

Milner concludes that, behind the apparent oppositional system of the 'genres' of being, we find the operational and alternating chain of the signifier (Being) and the subject (Non-Being). But, instead of the referentialist framework of Frege, we reason here from a purely differentialist conception of the sign. The 'logic' articulating the subject with the signifier is a result of the positing of a differential ontology. This is why Milner writes, rather timidly: 'It is as if we are in possession of a logic capable of situating the formal properties of any term submitted to an operation of fission' (CpA 3.5:78). I contend that this is that logic of the 'fissured element' which he later simplifies, in the syllogism of *Le Périple structural*.

Now, why am I not satisfied with this syllogism? First, because I suspect a mere fallacy: why should the property of 'being differential' be abstracted as such, as if it was another property different from 'being different from this or that'? To say that signs are differential is not to say that they are something *on the top* of being voiceless, strident or long: it is rather to say something about these 'properties' themselves, i.e. about *any* property understood in the structuralist sense. Besides, I can see no reason why there should exist only one term which instantiates the differentiality of terms in general: for instance, 'voiceless' is true for the phoneme /p/ in relation to /b/, but also for /t/ in relation to /d/. Therefore, even if it made sense to say that all the terms in a symbolic system have the property of being differential on top of all the other properties, I cannot see why they would not be so in relation to each of the terms from which they differ.

But even if the reasoning were valid, it does not seem to be more workable than Miller's. It would imply, for instance, that a phonological system, being as it is a set of differential entities, must as such contain a subject. As it happens, Jakobson, in a famous article (from which Lévi-Strauss drew his concept of floating signifier or zero symbolic value),[17] tried to show that, in French, the mute 'e' is precisely a term which belongs to the French phonological system not because it would bear any particular distinctive feature which would oppose it to any other sign, but because it is simply opposed to the *absence* of sign as such: it has, as its sole property, the property of being a sign, and this is why it is silent though operating in the phonological chain. But would it make any sense to say that through the silent 'e' we, French native speakers, are constituted as subjects? Probably not.

---

where the limiting shape [*cerne*] shows itself to be passage' (CpA 3.5:75).

17   Roman Jakobson, 'Notes on the French Phonemic Pattern' (1945), *Selected Writings. Vol. I: Phonological Studies* (The Hague - Paris: Mouton 1971), 426ff.; cf. Claude Lévi-Strauss, *Introduction to the Work of Marcel Mauss*, trans. Felicity Baker (London: Routledge and Kegan Paul, 1987), 64.

It emerges from this discussion that one striking feature of these conceptu-alizations is their incapacity to provide a plausible account of the symbolic systems in which a subject is indeed revealed to itself in the same movement that it escapes itself. At best, they provide a sort of metaphor of the operations that a structural theory of subjectivity should account for. This is how we can interpret their use in film theory by Stephen Heath, Jean-Pierre Oudart, and the team of *Screen* in the seventies, for instance, or in the theory of ideology by Ernesto Laclau and Chantal Mouffe, later expanded by Slavoj Žižek: the notion of suture may be helpful to isolate particular features in different domains, but these have nothing in common other than an analogical functioning. These concepts of structure cannot be generalized to each and every symbolic system without giving rise to absurdities. Does this mean that the 'logic of the signifier' is nothing but a mirage typical of that sixties-style heat which cools rather quickly when we inspect it more closely? Or is there a way at least to outline the possibility of such a logic which would be both general and capable of account-ing for the kind of subjects that we are? I would like to sketch in the following sections an alternative logic of the signifier, one which will rely more closely on empirical semiotics through the work of Claude Lévi-Strauss himself, while preserving the original intuitions of Miller and Milner about the relation between the symbolic and the subject.

III AN ALTERNATIVE LOGIC FOR THE ACTION OF THE STRUCTURE:
LÉVI-STRAUSS AND THE OPENNESS OF SYMBOLIC SYSTEMS

It may seem odd if not simply paradoxical to think of looking to Lévi-Strauss for such a logic. Nothing seems to be more unlikely to provide a theory of the *action* of the structure than the pretension to find, behind the variety of myths or the set of kinship rules, what mathematicians call *groups*, as Lévi-Strauss is supposed to have done.[18] The definition of a group implies that, given a series of operations, whatever operation is combined with another one, the result will always be an operation already defined in the group. In other words, the very

---

18   See for instance the definition of the structure propounded in Lévi-Strauss's *Structural Anthropology* (New York: Basic Books, 1963), 279: 'First, the structure exhibits the characteristics of a system. It is made up of several elements, none of which can undergo a change without effect-ing changes in all the other elements. Second, for any given model there should be a possibility of ordering a series of transformations resulting in a group of models of the same type. Third, the above properties make it possible to predict how the model will react if one or more of its elements are submitted to certain modifications. Finally, the model should be constituted so as to make immediately intelligible all the observed facts.' There is actually only one example in the general body of Lévi-Strauss's work of such an attempt to formalize a cultural phenomenon in terms of algebraic groups – the annex written by André Weil in *The Elementary Structures of Kinship* on an Australian kinship system (André Weil, 'On the Algebraic Study of Certain Types of Marriage Laws [Murgin System]', in Lévi-Strauss, *The Elementary Structures of Kinship* [London: Eyre & Spottiswoode, 1969], 221–229).

concept of group means that you cannot get out of the group by using only operations internal to the group.

But this would be only a very partial account of the concept of structure which is actually at work in Lévi-Strauss. On the precise matter of groups, here is what Lévi-Strauss himself writes in the final section of *The Naked Man*, the last of the four volumes of the *Mythologiques*, alluding to a passage from the previous volume (*The Origin of Table Manners*) in which the concept of group was used:

> We saw then that myths or variants of myths were arranged like Klein groups including a theme, the contrary of a theme, and their opposites. [. . .] But we also saw that these groups were not independent of each other, that none was self-sufficient as an entity of its own right, as it would appear to be if it could be envisaged from a purely formal angle. Actually, the ordered series of the variants does not return to the initial term after running through the first cycle of four: as through an effect of slippage, or more accurately an action comparable to that of the gear-change of a bicycle, the logical chain is jolted loose and engages with the initial term of the immediately interlocking group, and the process is repeated right through the end.[19]

It is quite striking that a modest bicycle mechanism appears to be a more accurate model of structure than algebra. It shows that there is something odd in the kind of totalities symbolic structures preside over, something which forces us, in order to complete each and every group, to appeal to another group, and then to yet another one. The consequence is that, even if each mythical theme or variant must be defined by its position in a system of oppositional transformations, its identity will always be *wanting*, it will be *overdetermined*, in the technical sense that this word has in the work of Sigmund Freud. Freud used the concept of overdetermination to say that every element of our dreams belongs not to one but to many non-homologous networks of associations. Likewise, we can see here that to determine the precise position of any given theme, we have to go through an endless series of interlocking groups which leap from one to another.

Far from being an isolated case, proper to this particular group of myths, or even proper to mythical thought in general, Lévi-Strauss considers this formal process of co-structuration as the true form of any symbolic process. He writes, immediately after the previous passage: 'Transformations of this kind constitute the basis of all semiology.' We can easily understand why: a sign is something which stands for something else; it is twofold, signifier and signified, and must

---

19   Claude Lévi-Strauss, *The Naked Man: Introduction to the Science of Mythology, Volume IV*, trans. Doreen Weightman (London: Jonathan Cape, 1981), 650.

be determined at the intersection of at least two levels of determination (two networks). If it was possible to lock any of these layers of the system into itself, then this layer would become independent, and would not refer to anything else; it would then be possible to extract the form of the system, without appealing to anything else. This situation does indeed exist, but it is only typical of *formal systems*, in which the interpretation of the group – say, a group defined by the operation of addition – in a given set of entities (whether these be stones or buffalos or sticks or abstract units . . .) is constrained by the formal properties it has to instantiate, but nonetheless completely contingent vis-à-vis the sort of things they are. The semantics of a formal system, in other words, is independent from its syntax. This is the reason why Lévi-Strauss always rejected the assimilation of structural analysis to a mere reduction of cultural facts to formal logics: actual symbolic structures are *not* independent from their semantics.[20]

Symbolic structures, therefore, far from being self-sufficient totalities independent in their own right and overlooking human subjectivities, are essentially incomplete and, therefore, can never be entirely objectified. Lévi-Strauss says it very simply in *The Origin of Table Manners*: 'Far from being separate from the others, each structure conceals an imbalance, which can only be corrected through recourse to some term borrowed from the adjacent structure.'[21] This is why, as Lévi-Strauss puts it in the introduction of the first volume of the *Mythologiques*, their analysis must remain 'interminable'.[22] Indeed, the effort to reconstitute the system of the variants of a myth must necessarily borrow from another myth, of which it is necessary to reconstitute the system of variants, but which will in its turn appeal to another myth, and so on. This is exactly the way the enormous work of the *Mythologiques* is written: Lévi-Strauss starts with one myth, called the myth of reference, and tries to reconstitute the system of variants to which it belongs. But in order to do so, he must introduce a variant which only appears as a transformation of the myth he is interested in according to *another* transformational system, thus obliging him to reconstitute this second one, and the relation it may have with the former. But since this second system also requires the same procedure, the study of one myth implies more and more myths, and finally extends to the entire corpus of the two Americas, substantiating the hypothesis that there may be just one very complex structure to all the myths of the continent as a whole.

Lévi-Strauss sometimes formulates this structural condition in terms which

---

20   See in particular Lévi-Strauss, 'Structure and Form', in *Structural Anthropology, Volume Two* (Chicago: University of Chicago Press, 1976), 115–145.

21   Lévi-Strauss, *The Origin of Table Manners: Introduction to the Science of Mythology, Volume III* (London: Jonathan Cape, 1978), 358.

22   Lévi-Strauss, *The Raw and the Cooked: Introduction to the Science of Mythology, Volume I* (London: Jonathan Cape, 1970), 6.

cannot but echo the ones which defined the very idea of the 'logic of the signi-fier'. It is particularly the case in the article entitled 'Of Mythical Possibility'. He first suggests, as he often does, that every symbolic system can be construed as a problem space, i.e. a way for a group of people or a population to raise a prob-lem, the different codetermined signs then appearing as alternative solutions to a single problem. Then he adds:

> A population devotes several versions of one of its myths to examining various possibilities, except for one that would contradict the facts of the problem confront-ing the group. It therefore leaves a lacuna in the range of possibilities, allowing a neighbouring group, which is not faced with the same problem, to take over the myth and fill the empty square – but only on the condition of deflecting this myth from its original goal and even profoundly altering its nature.[23]

Thus, if a symbolic system must be understood as a set of codetermined possi-bilities, these systems necessarily include one possibility which is at the same time the impossibility of the system itself, i.e. not only an alternative option within the same system, but also the possibility of an alternative system of alter-natives. In every system of signs, there is one sign which is included but only in the mode of its being excluded, a sign which is at the same time necessary in order to complete the system, but that is itself meaningless in this very system, or, even worse, that is the irruption of another form of rationality, of another way of making sense of the world. This clearly should evoke the very definition of the subject as an essentially displaced, 'tropical', entity.

It seems therefore reasonable to think that, if we are looking for a concept of structure which shows that the very kind of systematization which is at work in symbolic life is marked by an essential incompleteness which elicits a subjec-tive effect, we would do better to look for it in such an account of the working of actual symbolic systems like myths and languages, rather than follow Miller's recourse to Frege's logicization of arithmetic, or Milner's recourse to vague conceptual syllogisms.

As it happens, Lévi-Strauss himself propounded a quasi-formal presenta-tion of this sort of system. It is known as the 'canonical formula of the myth'. It was proposed as a kind of anticipatory conclusion to the article 'The Structure of Myth'; Lévi-Strauss then seemed to leave it to one side, but the formula slowly reappeared and it was eventually presented, in his last books,[24] as the very form of symbolic thought. It has since triggered a large literature, full of subtle or

---

23   Lévi-Strauss, *The View from Afar* (Oxford: Blackwell, 1985), 161–162tm.
24   See in particular Lévi-Strauss, *The Jealous Potter*, trans. Bénédicte Chorier (Chicago: University of Chicago Press, 1988), which is a sustained illustration of the analytic virtues of the canonical formula.

confused commentaries, enthusiastic or disparaging assessments, impressive or vague applications, which have been in part reviewed by Lucien Scubla in his book *Lire Lévi-Strauss*.[25] Here is the formula:

$$F_x(a) : F_y(b) \approx F_x(b) : F_{a-1}(y)$$

I will come back to it, below. But my hypothesis here is that such a formula (as long as we do not mistake it for an algorithm, and that we take it for what it was in Lévi-Strauss' mind, that is, as a way of visualizing a certain kind of systematization, a certain type of relations between elements, in short as the *image* of a concept)[26] is indeed a good candidate for the position of a 'logic of the signifier'. Of course, I cannot really substantiate this suggestion within the limits of this article. But, my real motive for introducing it here is that it happens to have been precisely from this theory of myth that Lacan himself drew his intuition that the structuralist theory of symbolism may show that subjectivity in a truly Freudian sense could be understood as an effect of symbolic mechanisms. While it seems hard to see how Miller's and Milner's 'formalization' could be applied to actual subject-processes, our canonical formal has already been applied to at least one particular case, moreover by Lacan himself, in his reading of Freud's famous analysis of the Rat-Man, with which I will conclude.

IV CASE-STUDY: LACAN AND THE LOGIC OF THE RAT-MAN

The possibility of applying the methodological concepts developed by Lévi-Strauss about myths to psychoanalytical materials was suggested to Lacan when he read two articles later included in the *Structural Anthropology* collection.[27] The first one is 'The Effectiveness of Symbols', where Lévi-Strauss propounds that neurosis must be understood as an 'individual myth'. Lévi-Strauss' idea can be paraphrased in the following way: if neurotics are trapped in their history and compelled to repeat a recurring schema, it is not because of events that in themselves might have a traumatic character, but rather because a 'constellation' of elements in a situation suddenly precipitates into something like a myth, in the sense that the elements of this situation are put into relation in such a way that the system cannot stabilize itself and never ceases to 'interpret' itself into every given situation, as a sort of signifying grid compulsively applied. Here we see that, if Žižek is right to argue that, for Lacan, a structure always implies a traumatic (i.e. unsymbolisable) kernel, he is wrong firstly to believe that

---

25   Lucien Scubla, *Lire Lévi-Strauss: le déploiement d'une intuition* (Paris: Odile Jacob, 1998).

26   See Lévi-Strauss, *Paroles Données* (Paris: Plon, 1984), 13.

27   Lévi-Strauss, *Anthropologie structurale* (Paris: Plon, 1958); *Structural Anthropology*, trans. Claire Jacobson and Brooke Grundfest Schoepf (New York: Basic Books, 1963).

structuralism does not want to know anything about the unsymbolizable, and secondly to believe that anything can be traumatic in and by itself; it becomes so precisely because its position (i.e. its external relations to other elements in the situation or to other events in the history of the subject) actualizes certain specific features.[28] In other words, it is traumatic because it triggers an endless symbolic process, as if the attempt to make sense of it could never end, not because it would be too rich in itself (or too poor, as the notorious notion of a 'lack in itself'), but because of the very structure of the symbolic network in which it occurs. The interesting idea, here, is that the psychological problems we have are not just a matter of fact (as if there was a conflict between the necessities of social life and the imperatives of individual drives); they are constituted by the very way we make sense of the world. We create our own problems; they are not given to us.

The second text is 'The Structural Study of Myth', where Lévi-Strauss lays the foundations for what will soon become the main field of his application of structural methodology, the study of myth. This text greatly impressed Lacan, precisely because it makes it clear that the logic of myth is such that, though each variant of a myth must be understood as but one stage in a group of transformations, this group is worked through by an impossible closure. The function of the myth as a symbolic system is not to make sense of the world in a perfect way, but rather to conceal the impossibility of making sense of it (i.e. to conceal the incompleteness of symbolic systems) by establishing an analogy between two incompatible polar terms, for instance life and death on the one hand, and agriculture and hunting on the other. The first contradiction is mediated by the second one, because it bears a peculiar analogy with it. 'Since the purpose of the myth is to provide a logical model capable of overcoming a contradiction (an impossible achievement if, as it happens, the contradiction is real), a theoretically infinite number of slates will be generated, each one slightly different from the others. Thus, the myth grows spiral-wise until the intellectual impulse which has produced it is exhausted.'[29]

It is the peculiarity of the analogical reasoning at work in myth which Lévi-Strauss tries to grasp by introducing the 'canonical formula of the myth':

---

28 'The traumatizing power of those situations stems from the fact that at the moment when they appear, the subject experiences them immediately as living myth. By this we mean that the traumatizing power of any situation cannot result from its intrinsic features but must, rather, result from the capacity of certain events, appearing within an appropriate psychological, historical, and social context, to induce an emotional crystallization which is moulded by a pre-existing structure. In relation to the event or anecdote, these structures – or, more accurately, these structural laws – are truly atemporal' (Lévi-Strauss, 'The Effectiveness of Symbols', in *Structural Anthropology*, 202).

29 Lévi-Strauss, 'The Structural Study of Myth', in *Structural Anthropology*, 229.

Finally, when we have succeeded in organizing a whole series of variants into a kind of permutation group, we are in a position to formulate the law of that group. [. . .]

$$F_x(a) : F_y(b) \approx F_x(b) : F_{a-1}(y)$$

Here, with two terms, *a* and *b*, being given as well as two functions, *x* and *y*, of these terms, it is assumed that a relation of equivalence exists between two situations defined respectively by an inversion of *terms* and *relations*, under two conditions: (1) that one term be replaced by its opposite (in the above formula, *a* and *a-1*); (2) that an inversion be made between the *function value* and the *term value* of two elements (above, *y* and *a*).

This formula becomes highly significant when we recall that Freud considered that *two traumas* (and not one, as is so commonly said) are necessary in order to generate the individual myth in which a neurosis consists.[30]

The reference to Freud's theory of the double nature of the trauma shows that it is not an isolated event which can be traumatizing, but rather the kind of twisted relations that it bears with another event, which it echoes, not by repeating it as in a formal homology but by transforming it in a way which then makes it impossible for it not to be endlessly repeated.

These two ideas prompted Lacan to try to apply this intuition to a particular case of neurosis studied by Freud, the case of the 'Rat-Man'.[31] He presented his conclusion in a little-known text (which he didn't republish in his *Écrits*), entitled, with a nod to Lévi-Strauss, 'The Neurotic's Individual Myth'.[32]

Lacan starts by reaffirming his commitment to psychoanalysis as an exercise confronted with the problematic notion of 'subjective truth'. 'Analytic experience is not definitely objectifiable. It always implies the emergence of a truth that cannot be said.' He then turns to the concept of myth, in search of an account of this 'emergence'. 'Myth is what provides a discursive form for something that cannot be transmitted through the definition of truth.'[33] In other words, myth is the language of the tropical subject.

In his structural interpretation of Freud's case, Lacan tries to show that the powerful effect of the father's story on the son's life is not due to the fact that the son had too repressive a father, who would have repressed too violently his masturbating habits and incestuous drives, but on the contrary to the fact that there was an intrinsic semiotic instability in the familial story, which made it

30   Ibid., 228.

31   Freud, *Notes Upon a Case of Obsessional Neurosis [1909]*, SE10: *Two Case Histories* ('Little Hans' and the 'Rat Man').

32   Jacques Lacan, 'The Neurotic's Individual Myth', *Psychoanalytic Quarterly* 48 (1979), 405–425. As its editor Jacques-Alain Miller notes, Lacan's '"The Neurotic's Individual Myth" was given as a lecture at the Philosophical College of Paris, organized by Jean Wahl, late Professor at the Sorbonne. The text was distributed in 1953 without the approval of Dr. Lacan and without his corrections' (405).

33   Lacan, 'The Neurotic's Individual Myth', 406.

necessary for it to be variously repeated, over and over again. There are two episodes in the history of the father which have been put in a relation of twisted analogy by the blind symbolic function of this poor symbolic animal that becomes the Rat Man. First, he knows that his father, once, at the time he was a young soldier, gambled the money of the regiment for which he was responsible, and lost it. He could not reimburse the money, and was then saved by a friend, who lent him the money and saved his honour. It is not clear, though, whether the father reimbursed his friend. And second, the subject knows that his father was in love with a poor woman, but then decided to marry his mother because she was wealthier and more respectable.

We therefore have a structure with four terms, and two different kinds of substitution. The father has been substituted by the friend in order to be able to substitute the poor woman by the rich woman. There are two debts which he did not reimburse, a debt of honour and a debt of love. Because he remained in debt to the former, the father was not able to honour the latter. In an article published in 2006, the psychiatrist Juan Pablo Lucchelli interpreted this relation using the canonical formula of the myth.[34] The relation that the father has to the army is to the relation he has to the friend the same as the relation he has to the poor woman is to the relation he has to the rich woman (i.e. the future wife). In both cases, the one was substituted by the other.

1. THE FAMILIAL COMPLEX

Father	Wife
Friend	Poor woman

The problem is that it is because the friend took the place of the son's father that the rich woman could take the place of the poor woman, i.e. would occupy the place of his mother. The analogy conceals an asymmetry under a parallelism: one column *conditions* the other; the system is unbalanced.

This imbalance appears at the next generation. For Freud makes it clear that the illness really started when the subject found himself in the same position as his father, at a point when he too was in love with a woman (whose reputation made her difficult to marry) and was told by his family that he had to marry one of his cousins instead. Following the paternal pattern, repetition of the established structure should require the father to take the position which was occupied for him by his friend, while the debt the subject owes to his father would force him to renounce the young lady and marry his cousin:

---

34   Juan Pablo Lucchelli, 'Le Mythe individuel revisité', *L'Information Psychiatrique* 82 (2006), 155–158.

2. 'NORMAL' REPETITION

Subject	Cousin
Father	Lady

The problem is that (because of his old unpaid debt) the father has no legitimate right to ask his son to obey him: the only one entitled to ask would be the friend who replaced him. In other words, the very condition which puts the father in the position of asking his son to do something is also what makes it impossible for him to do so. It is thus the splitting of the father figure into two which makes it impossible for the child to situate himself unequivocally in the structure, but which also pulls him subjectively into the structure, or rather, which enables the structure to be the formal condition for his emergence as a subject.

Here comes the supernumerary twist which is so characteristic of symbolic formations. The subject is himself in the army. He receives new glasses by the post. He is informed by a cruel lieutenant (who has made a great impression by telling him about a Chinese torture which consists in introducing rats into the anus of the victim) that one of his fellow officers paid for the shipping, and that he has to reimburse him. He happens to know that this is not the case, and that, in truth, it was the lady in charge of the Post office who trusted him and paid for him. But he feels compelled nonetheless to do exactly what the lieutenant told him, and tries to imagine impossible schemes to have the money circulate in such a way that both the officer and the lady at the Post office can receive the money – so much so that he ends up taking a train back to Vienna and consults Doctor Freud . . . The truth is that, in terms of the family structure, the subject has positioned the cruel lieutenant in the place of his father and therefore feels compelled to obey him blindly, even though (or, rather, *because* he knows that) he has no grounds for obeying him. Besides, he has unbearable fantasies in which he introduces rats into the anuses of both his father and his beloved.

The structure of the father's history thus repeats itself in the following table:

3. NEUROTIC REPETITION

Subject	Cousin
Cruel Lieutenant (*Spielratte*)	Lady

The key to this substitution is a signifier: in German, *Spielratte* designates a frantic gambler, as his father was, while it also evokes the torture with the rats told by the cruel lieutenant. We can summarize the complex symbolic play by saying that the son fantasizes that the punisher must himself be punished, and in the worst way. He says to his father something like: 'You pretend to give me orders, but I know that you don't have right on your side: you are a usurper

– and I am a rat – I will gnaw my way up your ass . . .' This is why Lacan insists that the real matrix of neurosis is not the triadic oedipal schema where one would find only a sort of external conflict between the Law, embodied by the father, and Desire, embodied by the Mother, but rather a quaternary schema where the split in the Law itself is concealed but also re-enacted by the split in the objet (good/bad object), thus making it impossible for the subject either to find a clear and simple position inside the structure or simply to get out of it. He can only respond to this situation by trying to cope with or to displace it, by producing an endless series of symbolic formations which it would be interesting but time-consuming to consider in more detail.

There is much more to say about this analysis, of course. But the point is just to illustrate the thesis that it is the very way we make sense of the surrounding world which determines the symbolic tasks we have to undertake, symbolic tasks meaning here an endless participation in displaced positionings or tropes. The position of the subject is defined by the nature of the transformations which are necessary to conceal the irreducible imbalance in the original structure, while reproducing it at another level; at the most general level, this reproduction proceeds according to rules which are nothing but the laws of symbolic thought, laws that Lévi-Strauss tried to formalize through his 'canonical formula' of myth. In Lacan's own words: 'The original constellation that presided over the birth of the subject, over his destiny, I would almost say his prehistory, specifically the fundamental family relationships which structured his parents' union, happens to have a very precise relation, perhaps definable by a transformational formula, with what appears to be the most contingent, the most phantasmatic, the most paradoxically morbid [aspect of] the case.'[35] The repetition is therefore not motivated by the fact that the original symbolic system is too perfect to allow for any escape, but on the contrary by the fact that it cannot be completed without being *varied* once again at the next generation. The subject is nothing but this slippage from one system to another without which the system could not be completed. It emerges in a symbolic world which Lacan called, in his famous Rome Discourse, 'transindividual'.[36]

Now, that Lacan had in mind here the canonical formula is clear from the way he describes the relation between the neurotic structure and the familial one: 'Within the fantasy developed by the subject, we observe something like an exchange of the outside terms of each of the functional relations' – which is exactly the definition of the canonical formula.[37] He almost quotes Lévi-Strauss's claim that the function of the whole structure is to conceal the original imbalance:

---

35   Lacan, 'The Neurotic's Individual Myth', 409.
36   'The unconscious is that part of concrete discourse qua transindividual, which is not at the subject's disposal in re-establishing the continuity of his conscious discourse' (E, 258/214).
37   Cf. Lacan, 'The Neurotic's Individual Myth', 413.

'Everything happens as if the impasses inherent in the original situation moved to another point in the mythic network, as if what was not resolved here always turned up over there.'[38] Although the relation between Lacan's concept of split subjectivity and Lévi-Strauss's canonical formula has been overlooked by almost all the commentators of Lacan (Lucchelli is the only exception, to my knowledge), Lacan himself made it entirely explicit, following a lecture given by Lévi-Strauss (later republished in *Structural Anthropology* under the title 'Structure and Dialectic'):

> As Lévi-Strauss is aware, I tried, almost immediately and I daresay with consider-
> able success, to apply his grid to the symptoms of obsessional neurosis, and more
> specifically to the admirable analysis Freud gave of the Rat-Man case, in a lecture I
> precisely entitled 'The Individual Myth of the Neurotic'. I was even able to formalize
> strictly the case according to a formula given by Claude Lévi-Strauss, by which an
> *a*, associated initially with a *b*, while some *c* is associated with a *d*, happens to
> exchange, at the second generation, its partner with the other one, but not without
> an irreducible residue remaining in the form of a negativization of one of the four
> terms, which imposes itself as correlative to the transformation of the group. I
> would say we might find here the sign of a sort of impossibility of any total resolu-
> tion of the problem posed by the myth. The upshot is that we might explain the
> myth as a way of showing us how to put into the signifying form of an equation a
> problematic which must by itself necessarily leave something open, a problematic
> that answers the insoluble by signifying insolubility, with its projection [*sa saillie*]
> reproduced in its equivalences, which furnishes (this would be the function of the
> myth) the signifier of the impossible.[39]

I hope it is now apparent that Lacan, contrary to his followers then and now (that is, from Miller to Žižek), was aware that the concept of structure offered by Lévi-Strauss, far from formalizing this projecting but immanent and self-sufficient symbolic order from which subjects were excluded, implied the elici-tation of an entity which at one and the same time belonged to the system but forced it out of itself, a term which was nothing other than an endless (self-) displacement: the subject is constituted by these elements which cannot be actualized as such, but which are still necessary to the very completion of the system, i.e. its completion as a necessarily incomplete system. The key of the issue is precisely not to oppose the notion of system and that of incompleteness: it is because incompleteness is here a defining feature of the kind of systematiza-tion which characterizes symbolic thought, that we cannot enter any symbolic

---

38   Ibid., 414.
39   Lacan, 'Intervention après un exposé de Claude Lévi-Strauss à la Société Française de Philosophie', in *Le mythe individuel du névrosé* (Paris: Seuil, 2007), 105–106.

world without being constituted as subjects in the sense of the classical philosophical tradition, i.e. as elements whose very identity implies an endless figurative slippage.

I realise, of course, that even so sketchy a conceptualization of structure does not leave unaffected the conceptualization of that subject which emerges in it. There is no room for articulating these consequences in detail here, but I can point out at least one of them: the subject now appears to be less the signifier of the impossible than the point of articulation between different symbolic universes. To be a subject means to be at the limit of many symbolic systems. It is not the relation to the *absolutely* unspeakable that defines the position of a subject, but the relation to the *relatively* unspeakable, as it is endlessly reworked throughout the series of transindividual symbolic re-systematizations, like the one articulating in the example of the Rat-Man the system of the father with that of the son. These systems are related to one another by 'subjective' elements, that is, the elements in which the imbalance of the structure manifests itself. In other words, such a notion of subjectivity would be inseparable from the fact of cultural or historical variation.[40]

But my goal here was only to defend the central insight that presided over the foundation of the *Cahiers pour l'Analyse*, and to suggest that, while the answers given forty years ago may be found wanting in some respects, there may still be good reasons for thinking that the project of a 'logic of the signifier' remains more than a mirage glimpsed through a mid-sixties haze. Formulation of such a 'logic' remains a valuable undertaking. In 1967 Gilles Deleuze concluded his famous article 'How Do We Recognize Structuralism?' with a clear allusion to the work done by the *Cahiers pour l'Analyse* after Lacan and Althusser, writing prophetically that the redefinition of subjectivity was at the same time one of the 'most obscure' criteria of structuralism and the one in which its future was at issue.[41] This future remains our present.

---

40   Lévi-Strauss suggests this quite clearly in his *Introduction to the Work of Marcel Mauss*, where he defines subjectivity as the indefinite possibility of self-objectification, which is to say, in his view, of self-estranging. 'The subject itself – once the object-subject distinction is posited – can be split and duplicated in the same way, and so on without end, without ever being reduced to nothing' (31–32).

41   Gilles Deleuze, 'How do we Recognize Structuralism?', in *Desert Island and Other Texts (1953–1974)*, ed. David Lapoujade, trans. Michael Taormina (New York: Semiotext(e), 2004), 192.

CHAPTER THREE

Edward Baring
Derrida, Lévi-Strauss, and the *Cahiers pour l'Analyse*; Or, How to Be a Good Structuralist

'Structure, Sign, and Play in the Discourse of the Human Sciences', Derrida's presentation to the 1966 Johns Hopkins Structuralism Conference, has played a determinative role in the Anglo-American reception of his work.[1] Read as a critique of Lévi-Strauss's ethnographic nostalgia, the Baltimore talk helped construct a peculiarly resilient genealogy for deconstruction: Derrida as patricidal heir to the structural anthropologist. But a closer look at the initial context of Derrida's analysis suggests that Lévi-Strauss, a scholar in a different field and at a different institution, may not have been the main interlocutor in this essay. For Derrida first broached the question of Lévi-Strauss's anthropology much closer to home, in an article published one month earlier in the *Cahiers pour l'Analyse*. In this academic milieu, Derrida's complaint that Lévi-Strauss unjustifiably privileged primitive societies was hardly the most noteworthy aspect of his text, for this criticism was already common currency amongst contributors to the journal. Derrida's analysis was scandalous, rather, because of the way in which he deployed this critique and used it as an occasion to intervene in the debates of the Cercle d'Épistémologie.

I THE *CAHIERS* AND LÉVI-STRAUSS

With respect to the central concern of the *Cahiers pour l'Analyse* – an exploration of the relationship between Marxism and psychoanalysis – the students who published there did not present a unified philosophical front. They were divided according to the *différend* represented by the two dominant intellectual forces at the journal: Althusser and Lacan. And yet, despite this doctrinal split, they found common ground in their reading of Lévi-Strauss. Members of both sides attacked Lévi-Strauss's naturalism and criticized his suggestion that the study of primitive societies might provide privileged access to the underlying biological structure of the human brain.

Though Lévi-Strauss consistently rejected biological accounts of the incest

1   This paper has been significantly improved thanks to the advice and suggestions of Angus Burgin, Peter Gordon, Katja Günther, Peter Hallward, Knox Peden, Dan Shore, Judith Surkis, and the participants at both the New York Consortium for Intellectual and Cultural History and the European History Workshop at the Minda de Gunzburg Center of European Studies, Harvard University.

taboo or instinctual explanations of social and cultural practices, he argued that certain structures were basic and common to all humans. While in so-called 'hot' or civilized societies, these structures were obscured beneath the turmoil of movement and change produced by social differentials (like heat differentials in a steam engine), in 'cold' or primitive societies the basic building blocks of cultural structures were clear to see; primitive societies were windows into Man's soul.[2] Further, at moments in his work, and particularly in two books from 1962, Lévi-Strauss suggested that these basic structures reflected brain biology. As he wrote in *Totemism Today*, the homology of differences required for totemic systems was 'the lowest common denominator of all thought [. . .], an original logic, the direct expression of the structure of the mind [*esprit*] (and behind the mind, doubtless, of the brain).'[3] Elaborating in the contemporaneous *Savage Mind*, Lévi-Strauss asserted that the biological grounding of cultural phenomena did not demean them. Instead the fact that culture could be explained by nature demonstrated the richness and fecundity of biology, what one might call a transcendence of matter.[4]

For the editors of the *Cahiers*, Lévi-Strauss's nostalgia for primitive society and the naturalist impulses that it facilitated marked a betrayal of structuralist principles. Lévi-Strauss sought to understand all cultural structures by privileging a limited number of social and cultural forms, grounding his structuralism in a 'psychology' of primitive peoples. In doing so he ignored the possibility that these forms were themselves the effect of more fundamental processes, whether of the unconscious or of history in all its complexity.

Lacan refrained for the most part from criticizing Lévi-Strauss, the man who had first introduced him to Saussure's linguistics. But, in his seminar from 1964–5, Lacan suggested that Lévi-Strauss's *pensée sauvage* did not fully account for the Freudian unconscious: while Freud's analysis of desire moved beyond psychology, Lévi-Strauss's structuralism remained at that level (S11, 13). Lévi-Strauss's structures were the structures of the imaginary ego, whereas Lacan was more interested in the structures that produced it: the structures of the unconscious. As Lacan suggested in 'Science and Truth', published in the first volume of the *Cahiers*, Lévi-Strauss, though describing structures sanctioned by this 'subject of science' – the 'crucially important mark of structuralism' – placed too little emphasis upon it (CpA 1.1:7–12; E, 855–860/727–731). Instead of describing the structuring effects of this subject, Lévi-Strauss relied excessively on a theory of the 'transcendence of matter', thinking that

---

2   See Claude Lévi-Strauss, *Conversations with Claude Lévi-Strauss*, ed. G. Charbonnier (London: Cape Editions, 1969), 26–42.

3   Lévi-Strauss, *Le Totémisme aujourd'hui* (Paris: Presses Universitaires de France, 1962), 130.

4   See Lévi-Strauss, *The Savage Mind*, trans. Rodney Needham (Chicago: University of Chicago Press, 1966), 22, 247–248.

cultural structures could emerge out of (albeit reconceptualized) biological and chemical reactions.[5]

This argument was reiterated by Lacan's new *normalien* students in the *Cahiers*. Jacques-Alain Miller criticized Lévi-Strauss for ignoring 'subjectivity', and thus constructing an ideological object, the object of *méconnaissance* found in 'social life', 'culture', 'or even the biology of the mind', while missing the deeper structures of the unconscious (CpA 9.6:95–99). Even less dedicated Lacanians, such as the psychoanalyst André Green, criticized Lévi-Strauss for merging the cultural and the natural. Though, according to Green, Lévi-Strauss in his early work saw 'rule and law [. . .] as the limit of natural phenomena, the frontier of the human [. . .] one gets the impression that this barrier and this limit are now pushed back to the structure of the human brain.'[6] The rooting of essential structures in brain biology rendered Lévi-Strauss open to the charge that he denied the specificity of humanity, hoping to find a *single* explanation for the diverse 'processes of matter, of life, of the psyche, and of society'.[7] Green suggested that the attempt to ground such structures in the human brain blinded Lévi-Strauss to the deeper structuring effects of the Oedipus complex.

While the Lacanians in the *Cahiers* refused Lévi-Strauss's naturalism because it obscured the workings of the subject of the unconscious, Althusser and many of his students criticized it because it preserved a residual humanism (read subjectivism) that they wanted to expunge fully: the charge was thus deployed for two diametrically opposed arguments. According to Althusser, Lévi-Strauss's privilege of 'cold' societies was just the reverse racism of ethnologists, 'sons of the colonial conquest who, to assuage their bad consciences, discover that the primitives are "men" at the dawn of human civilization'.[8] Lévi-Strauss had unjustifiably promoted one type of society to the status of an archetype, declaring it suited to man's inherent nature. For this reason Lévi-Strauss's humanism was ideological, even if his reasoning denigrated rather than promoted his own society. Further, by presenting modern society as a corruption of this primitive model, Lévi-Strauss had aligned himself with Marxist humanism, which urged the liberation of 'Man' from his alienation in capitalist society, and which Althusser had combated in the Communist Party. Althusser argued that Lévi-Strauss and his 'epigones' 'claim to be representatives of Marx, while misrecognizing him'.[9]

---

5   CpA 1.1:25; E, 874/742, referring to Lévi-Strauss, *The Savage Mind*, 248.

6   André Green, 'La Psychanalyse devant l'opposition de l'histoire et de la structure', *Critique* 194 (July 1963), 651.

7   Green, 'La Psychanalyse devant l'opposition de l'histoire et de la structure', 652.

8   Louis Althusser, 'On Lévi-Strauss', in HC, 22tm.

9   Althusser 'On Lévi-Strauss', 19–20tm. Althusser referred in particular to the passage in Claude Lévi-Strauss, *Anthropologie Structurale* (Paris: Plon, 1958), 364–375.

Instead, Althusser asserted, we should move beyond the ideological object of '*la pensée sauvage*' to study the broader social and economic structures that grounded it. As he elaborated, primitive structures of kinship were not immediate reflections of brain biology, but rather relations of production intimately related to different modes of production. In prematurely asserting the 'object' of his science, mistaking certain societies for natural forms, Lévi-Strauss had falsely appealed to an ideological and thus distorting universalism.[10] Because all societies were complex and overdetermined, the classification of one as 'natural' could only be the manifestation of an author's subjective commitments, which in turn could be elucidated by structural analysis.

This criticism of Lévi-Strauss even stretched beyond those of Althusser's students who were closely involved with the *Cahiers*. The recent *agrégé*, Pierre Macherey, who kept a certain distance from the *Cahiers* project,[11] nevertheless attacked Lévi-Strauss's formalism in similar language. Like the others, he argued that Lévi-Strauss's structures remained at the level of the psychological, the concrete study of the mind: 'structure is thought in its relationship to an intention (which it produces, or of which, on the contrary, it is the product), it is thus the object of a *psychology*, but not of a veritable *logic*.'[12] Macherey wanted to move beyond this ideological object of man, to discover the social and economic structures of which this conception of 'man' was merely an effect. Discussing literary criticism, Macherey asked whether it might be possible to propose not merely an '*art de lire*' but rather a '*critique positive*', which would reveal the conditions of the work's production. Such a critique would reach beyond the structure of the work itself, to inscribe it in the social and economic structures of its age. It was not about finding the latent discourse, but rather about revealing the conditions that structured a discourse in the first place, often by their absence: 'if there is structure, it is not to be found deep or hidden in the book: the book belongs to it, without containing it'.

Despite diametrically opposed visions of structuralism – either hoping to reintroduce or expel the subject – Lacanians and Althusserians produced parallel criticisms of Lévi-Strauss. Both focused their attacks around Lévi-Strauss's reference to brain biology and cited the same passage from *The Savage Mind* as damning evidence. Praising the 'scientificity' that Lévi-Strauss brought to the study of social structures by deploying the methods and language of structuralist linguistics, philosophers at the ENS criticized him for naturalising particular social and cultural structures, a classic gesture of ideology. The nature/culture distinction mapped for many onto the signified/signifier distinction that structuralist linguistics had asserted. Just as structural linguistics refused any

---

10   Althusser 'On Lévi-Strauss,' 27–29.
11   See Étienne Balibar and Yves Duroux, 'A Philosophical Conjuncture', CF2.
12   Pierre Macherey, *Pour une théorie de la production littéraire* (Paris: Maspero, 1966), 177.

referential relationship between a signifier and a signified, so too one should refuse claims that certain cultural structures were direct reflections of the natural state. When Lévi-Strauss suggested that some sort of base code for these structures could be found in the biology of the human brain, he contravened the strict separation between signifier and signified, symbolic and real, the object of knowledge and the real object, that for them was so central to the method. Criticizing this move, then, became a shibboleth for rigorous structuralists at the ENS.

II ROUSSEAU: ALTERNATIVE ORIGINS FOR STRUCTURALISM

The concentration of criticism on what was essentially a relatively minor and undeveloped part of Lévi-Strauss's work is perhaps surprising. Lévi-Strauss did not consider the hypothesis that cultural structures were rooted in the brain at length. As he began the substantive section of *The Elementary Structures of Kinship*: 'even if the incest prohibition has its roots in nature it is only in the way it affects us as a social rule that it can be fully grasped.'[13] Lévi-Strauss deferred the task of investigating the rise of language out of the 'structure of the human brain' to the biologist, chemist, or philosopher. As he explained, 'this is no longer an anthropological problem. All the anthropologist can do is say to his colleagues in other branches of study that the real question is the question of language. If you solve the problem of the nature and origin of language, we can explain the rest: what culture is, and how it made its appearance; what art is and what technological skills, law, philosophy and religion are. But it is not within the scope of anthropology to rend the veil.'[14]

While the hypothesis was peripheral to Lévi-Strauss's work, shunted to one side for disciplinary and methodological reasons, it was nevertheless indicative of deeper commitments. The importance of Lévi-Strauss's naturalism to the broader ethical concerns that motivated his ethnological project can be seen in his analysis of Jean-Jacques Rousseau. In 1962, the 200th anniversary of the publication of Rousseau's *Social Contract*, and the 250th anniversary of his birth, Claude Lévi-Strauss claimed him as the founder of ethnography. Rousseau's 1764 *Second Discourse* was in Lévi-Strauss's words, 'the first treatise on general anthropology in the French canon.'[15] Rousseau had rejected the Cartesian *cogito* that was 'imprisoned by the hypothetical evidences of the self', arguing instead that 'when one proposes [. . .] to study man, one must learn to cast one's glance afar; one has to begin by observing the differences in order to discover the properties.'[16] In looking

---

13   Lévi-Strauss, *The Elementary Structures of Kinship*, trans. James Bell (Boston: Beacon Press, 1969), 29.

14   Lévi-Strauss, *Conversations*, 153–155.

15   Lévi-Strauss, *Totémisme*, 142.

16   The quotation comes from Rousseau's 'Essay on the Origin of Languages,' in Jean-Jacques

to foreign societies to learn about our own, Rousseau put 'the other before the self'.[17] Further, Rousseau's analysis took him to the first human groups before the invention of metallurgy that were relatively free of the inequality that plagued societies after it. This distinction as expressed in the *Second Discourse* matched Lévi-Strauss's own between 'hot' and 'cold' societies.[18]

Lévi-Strauss argued that Rousseau's analysis revealed a natural man built for society, and thus unthinkable outside of it.[19] As he elaborated, 'if it is possible to believe the demonstration of the *Discourse* – that a threefold passage (from nature to culture, from feelings to knowledge, from animality to humanity) occurred with the appearance of society – it can only be by attributing to man, even in his primitive state, an essential faculty which moves him to get over these three obstacles.' This faculty, pity, allowed the identification of the self with the suffering other, whether animal or human.[20] Like the incest taboo in Lévi-Strauss's *Elementary Structures of Kinship*, pity seemed to break down the distinction between culture and nature, both by being the natural condition for the former, and by promoting the identification of man and beast.

But if the earliest societies privileged pity and identification, later developments would upset the natural harmony. Rousseau described a demographic expansion in the early life of Man that injected social and cultural diversity into the human race, as different groups adapted to different environmental conditions.[21] When that variety began to be recognized, the initial identification that had led to society was trumped by a sense of difference, first between human and non-human, then between groups of humans themselves. The ever-increasing attempts at differentiation, the turn towards distinctions and social hierarchies that Lévi-Strauss had found so distasteful in 'hot' societies, built on the recognition of difference with which Man had first separated himself from other living things.[22] Divisions between 'us and them' were mere echoes of the original sin, where man cut off culture from nature and humans from other forms of life. The assertion of the nature/culture divide, to which many of the *normaliens* were so attached, was for Lévi-Strauss the source of immorality.

Lévi-Strauss recognized, however, that Rousseau would not follow him all the way in his analyses. In *The Savage Mind*, Lévi-Strauss again made his claims about the heritage of ethnography in Rousseau's thought. But he

---

Rousseau, *The Discourses and Other Early Political Writings*, ed. Victor Gourevitch (Cambridge: Cambridge University Press, 1997), 266.

17   Lévi-Strauss, *Structural Anthropology* II, trans. Claire Jacobson (New York: Basic Books, 1976), 36–37.

18   See also Claude Lévi-Strauss, *Tristes Tropiques* (Paris: Plon, 1955), 421–425.

19   Lévi-Strauss, *Tristes Tropiques*, 423.

20   Lévi-Strauss, *Structural Anthropology* II, 37–38.

21   Rousseau, 'Second Discourse', in *The Discourses and Other Early Political Writings*, 161–163.

22   Lévi-Strauss, *Structural Anthropology* II, 40–41. See Rousseau, 'Second Discourse', 74–79.

suggested that Rousseau had not gone far enough in breaking down the distinction between nature and culture.[23] While Rousseau thought we could learn about Man by studying other societies, and emphasized an essential pity that drove Man's identification with all forms of life, 'this first enterprise opens the way for others which Rousseau would not have been so ready to accept and which are incumbent on the exact natural sciences: the reintegration of culture into nature and finally of life with the whole of its physico-chemical conditions'.[24] For Lévi-Strauss, the nature/culture distinction was an uncriticized residue in Rousseau's theory.

At the ENS, under the influence of Louis Althusser, a very different interpretation of Rousseau was current, one that emphasized his compatibility with *Cahiers* structuralism. For Althusser, the most important aspect of Rousseau's work was his absolute distinction between nature and culture. This central insight, however, was obscured because Rousseau continued to use the language of his contemporaries, including the 'state of nature', 'contract', and 'civil state'. Such language gave the impression that Rousseau hoped to uncover a factual origin for society, and informed the nostalgic moment in Rousseau's work: the desire to seek 'Man' in the purity of primitive societies.[25] Commenting on Lévi-Strauss's own nostalgia, Althusser stated that it was 'Rousseau's old myth [. . .] resuscitated by the bad conscience of ethnologists'.[26]

Althusser quickly added that this was only part of Rousseau's project, and acknowledged that he 'says many *other* things that are great [*géniales*]'. For despite the constraints of the language he used, Rousseau had taken a big step forward in the history of philosophy. Previous philosophers had contaminated their analyses of the state of nature with presuppositions drawn from the social realm: with Locke this was the retrojection of the civil state; with Hobbes it was the retrojection of the state of war.[27] As Althusser summed up, 'all the ideology of the Enlightenment thought that the interior essence of history was the development of reason, which is to say that men were philosophers before being men.' Such an analysis of the past only served to justify the rationality – and thereby the society – of the present.[28] It was for Althusser a circular logic, modern reason creating a specular image of itself in the state of nature as a form of self-validation, just as humanist philosophies constructed their vision of Man to legitimate particular societies.[29] By universalizing a very particular and

23   See also Lévi-Strauss, *Le Totémisme aujourd'hui*, 144.
24   Lévi-Strauss, *The Savage Mind*, 247.
25   Louis Althusser, *Politique et histoire de Machiavel à Marx* (Paris: Seuil, 2006), 301.
26   Althusser, 'On Lévi-Strauss,' 21.
27   Althusser, *Politique et histoire*, 303.
28   See Rousseau, 'Second Discourse', 65.
29   See also Althusser, *Psychanalyse et sciences humaines* (Paris: Livres de Poches, 1997), 93–94.

subjective form of reason and society, the Enlightenment analysis of the state of nature strayed into ideology.

Rousseau, on the other hand, recognized the inescapability of this circle, that no presentation of the state of nature could be free of ideological implications. Though noting those aspects of Rousseau's theory that troubled the distinction between culture and nature, including pity, Althusser was insistent that the rise of society was reliant upon what society itself produced.[30] Society was dependent upon language, and yet language, as the institution of signs by convention, already required society: '[society] must have preceded its cause, for that cause to have been born.'[31] Because no logical process could explain this development, according to Althusser, Rousseau was compelled to resort to 'accidents' to explain the jumps in the history of man. In his analysis of the origin of society, Rousseau postulated two discontinuities, one separating the state of nature from the '*jeunesse du monde*' and the other between this society and the state of the social contract, caused either by natural catastrophes, or the accidental discovery of metallurgy. The emphasis on such accidents to break the circular logic that had plagued previous accounts of the origin of society showed that Rousseau had made significant progress in overcoming the ideological arguments of his predecessors. If ideology could be defined as the nostalgia for societies falsely regarded as natural, then scientific thought would emphasize the absolute heterogeneity of nature and culture.

While Lévi-Strauss emphasized Rousseau's commitment to pity, and hoped to radicalize his thought to show how the nature/culture division could be broken down, for Althusser the judgment was reversed; pity, a residue of the metaphysical language that Rousseau could not escape, was overshadowed by his efforts not to confuse the cultural and the natural. To purge the remaining ideology implicit in Rousseau's descriptions of the state of nature and the nostalgia that was concomitant with it, Althusser argued that this old metaphysical language must be rejected. Just as Lacan had freed Freud from his biological metaphors, and Althusser himself had rescued Marx from the concepts of classical political economy, one could free Rousseau from the ideology inherent in eighteenth-century philosophical concepts by constructing a new scientific language.

Despite Alain Grosrichard's effort in 'Gravité de Rousseau' (CpA 8.2) to provide a counterweight to Althusser's relentless focus on the 'discrepancies' in Rousseau's thought, the latter's reading effectively became ENS orthodoxy.[32] In

---

30   Althusser, *Politique et histoire*, 310.

31   Ibid., 306.

32   Unlike Althusser's narrow reading of the *Social Contract*, Grosrichard's essay focuses on Rousseau's oeuvre as a whole in order to show how its theoretical and literary elements perform a delicate balancing act with one another, one that mirrors the precarious relationship between nature's tendency toward equilibrium and the cultural or symbolic tendencies that drive the subject toward disequilibrium.

an article for the volume of the *Cahiers* devoted to Rousseau, Althusser's student Patrick Hochart emphasized the same elements as his teacher: 'we must absolutely safeguard the independence and irreducibility of the two levels, one cannot attribute to the foundational level any tendency to develop in the direction of morality; for the foundation to have the sense of a rupture, it is necessary that the foundational level be pure and that nothing in it should call for the constitution of a political body' (CpA 8.3:69). For Hochart too, the necessity of a complete rupture was grounded upon the circular logic required for the creation of a society: a social group as the necessary condition for the production of the laws that would form society. According to Hochart, to break this circle, abolish 'the divorce between nature and convention', and explain the origin of society, Rousseau was compelled to resort to theology, a divine lawgiver. The necessity of such an exorbitant recourse was testament to the initial rigour of Rousseau's distinction (CpA 8.3:84).

The debate over interpretations of Rousseau's work – the choice between the apparently mutually exclusive nature/culture distinction and nostalgia for primitive societies – had become a privileged centre-point for discussions of Lévi-Strauss's structuralism at the ENS well before the foundation of the *Cahiers* in 1966. In a presentation to a 1962–3 ENS seminar on structuralism, Pierre Macherey discussed the origin of language in Condillac and Rousseau, especially the latter's essay *On the Origin of Language*. While Condillac had traced the origin of language back to nature, seeing it as the internal development of a 'natural' and isolated man, as expressed in his metaphor of the statue, for Rousseau the absolute difference between nature and culture made the idea of a natural origin of language impossible.[33] As Macherey put it 'there are no absolute premises, no *immediate givens* of the understanding, no "savage mind" [*pensée sauvage*]'.[34] In language that recalls Althusser's case for overdetermination as a structural concept, Macherey stated that Rousseau figured language as the product of a dialectical relationship between several processes, not a simple origin that could be located in history.

Macherey asserted that 'Lévi-Strauss did not read Rousseau in Rousseau, but only the ideological background or horizon': despite a declared debt to the Genevan theorist, Lévi-Strauss followed Condillac's example instead. In doing so, according to Macherey, Lévi-Strauss's work 'arrives at a *mechanist materialism* in the exact tradition of the eighteenth century; the mechanical production of elementary symbolisms ([. . .] reflection of the brain's structure)'.[35] It was his misreading of Rousseau, his overemphasis on the ideological elements of Rousseau's thought,

---

33 Condillac's statue was discussed in his *Treatise on Sensations* (1754), describing the natural genesis of the senses and then of reason.

34 Pierre Macherey, 'L'Origine du langage', in IMEC archives, ALT2. A40-02.01, folder 3, sheet 9.

35 Pierre Macherey, 'L'Origine du langage', sheet 9.

that induced Lévi-Strauss's biological reductionism. Read more carefully, Rousseau's theory should lead away from simple origins, to uncover a more complex theory of history and language that resembled Althusser's.

Macherey's argument is similar to that of another *normalien*, Jean Mosconi, in his October 1966 contribution to the *Cahiers pour l'Analyse*.[36] Mosconi began his analysis by criticizing 'modern anthropology's reactivation of a characteristic gesture of the philosophy of the eighteenth century: that by which, to explain the genesis and functioning of individual thought, one is constrained to return to a first origin of culture' (CpA 4.2:53). Seeing a precedent in Rousseau, Lévi-Strauss wanted to reach beyond the 'diversity of social organizations' to 'find in them, rejecting artifices and accidents, an unchanging and universal base'. But, according to Mosconi, this goal was stymied by the distinction between nature and culture. The absolute 'break [*coupure*]' between nature and culture meant that 'no proximity to nature could make primitive societies preferable' (CpA 4.2:55).

And since it was to Rousseau that Lévi-Strauss turned, Mosconi dedicated the majority of the article to an explanation of 'origins' in Rousseau's thought. Unlike Condillac's isolated man in the metaphor of the statue, which developed considerable practical understanding by itself, Rousseau's man only developed as a species. Thus whereas for Condillac reason was already latent in nature, its development necessary, for Rousseau the social element in the rise of reason was irreducible. Here Mosconi referred to the Althusserian circle: language and society were both necessary for the other's development, a circle that could only be broken by fortuitous events (CpA 4.2:67). Lévi-Strauss's attempt to seek a natural form of thought, read in primitive culture, derived from a faulty interpretation of Rousseau.[37]

Dividing between a good and a bad Rousseau – the good that asserted the absolute division between nature and culture, and the bad which retained a certain nostalgia for man in his 'natural' state – the *normaliens* attacked Lévi-Strauss for seizing on the wrong elements. Lévi-Strauss betrayed structuralism, they argued, when he nostalgically turned to primitive society, and hoped thereby to uncover structural constants that would allow the naturalization of culture. Such an error could be rectified by returning to a more scientific reading of the originary father, Jean-Jacques Rousseau, jettisoning his moment of ideology and reformulating his most important insight in a new scientific language.

---

36   Indeed Mosconi cited Macherey as an influence at the start of the essay.

37   Mosconi did however see Lévi-Strauss's analysis of music, which contradicts his analysis of primitive thought by marking an absolute break with nature, as showing important continuities with Rousseau's work. See CpA 4.2:86–88. In this sense Mosconi preferred the musical metaphor in the overture to *The Raw and the Cooked* to the earlier analyses of culture, say in *Totemism Today* or *The Savage Mind*.

III NOSTALGIC DISTINCTIONS: DERRIDA READING LÉVI-STRAUSS

Derrida, in the same 1966 edition of the *Cahiers pour l'Analyse* as Mosconi's paper, published his own intervention, 'Nature, Culture, Writing: The Violence of the Letter From Lévi-Strauss to Rousseau'.[38] Derrida's analysis centred on a chapter of *Tristes Tropiques*, where Lévi-Strauss recounted how he had taught a Nambikwara chief to write. As Derrida noted, Lévi-Strauss had always associated the 'hot/cold' distinction with the presence or absence of writing; he had even changed the name of his chair at the EPHE from 'Religions of Primitive Peoples' to 'Religions of Peoples without Writing Systems'.[39] It was writing that allowed the institution of social hierarchies and violence that were typical of 'civilized' societies. The Nambikwara for Lévi-Strauss was a 'cold' society without writing, and when Lévi-Strauss taught the chief to write, the insidious effects of social 'warming' were soon visible. According to Lévi-Strauss, the chief 'immediately understood its role as sign, and the social superiority that it confers' (OG, 125/CpA 4.1:34).[40]

In terms comparable to Althusser's criticism, Derrida argued that Lévi-Strauss's assertion of the Nambikwara's initial purity demonstrated reverse ethnocentrism, keeping the same categories and distinctions (society without writing) as earlier imperialistic thought, but just reversing the value judgment (114/22). The colonial disdain for primitive societies became with Lévi-Strauss an unwarranted nostalgia for a better way of life. For Derrida, as for Althusser, this primitivism gave the lie to Lévi-Strauss's declared Marxism. Derrida reprimanded Lévi-Strauss for taking primitive societies out of the Marxist paradigm, declaring them free from any form of exploitation (118–120/26–29).

According to Derrida, elements in Lévi-Strauss's own work seemed to threaten his analysis. The reaction of the chief showed that writing was not as alien a concept to the Nambikwara as Lévi-Strauss thought, that though they might not have had writing *'au sens courant'*, they already had the means to understand it; it could not have been entirely foreign to them (123/32). For Derrida, writing broadly understood, and hence also violence and exploitation, had already existed in Nambikwara society before Lévi-Strauss arrived. The introduction of writing in a narrow sense did not mark a significant rupture, nor did it shake social and cultural structures to the core.

If writing in a broad sense was already present amongst the Nambikwara

---

38 The paper later formed a central chapter of *Of Grammatology*. I will cite from the English translation in *Grammatology* (OG); when applicable, page references within the *Cahiers pour l'Analyse* will follow those of the book. When necessary, I will note points where the text in the book differs from the original article.

39 François Dosse, *History of Structuralism* vol. 1, trans. Deborah Glassman (Minneapolis, 1997), 13. See Lévi-Strauss, *Tristes Tropiques*, 317–318.

40 Lévi-Strauss, *Tristes Tropiques*, 314–318.

and they were not essentially different from later societies, then Lévi-Strauss's declaration of primitive exceptionalism, resulting from his metaphysics of presence, was 'ideological' (120/28, 131/41, 168). Just as for Althusser ideological thinking privileged or 'centred' a particular moment that was really the product of a structure like any other, so too for Derrida the metaphysics of presence was the trace of the trace, the forgetting that origins too are worked over by the structure of différance.

The central argument of Derrida's paper – the criticism of Lévi-Strauss's nostalgic presentation of primitive societies – seemed to put him on the side of the Althusserians. But this appearance was deceptive. In his analysis of Rousseau that acted as a frame for the paper, Derrida edged closer to Lévi-Strauss's understanding, emphasizing the role of pity.[41] The latter half of *Of Grammatology*, which discusses Rousseau at length, but which was only published in 1967, stressed the centrality of 'supplementarity' in Rousseau's theory, especially the 'Second Discourse'. 'Supplementarity,' according to Derrida, simultaneously asserted and effaced the distinction between nature and culture. Culture was a supplement, a necessary addition to make up for the inadequacies of the origin; in Émile's education 'culture or cultivation [. . .] must supplement a deficient nature' (146). Similarly, human pity, which Lévi-Strauss had classed a natural form of sociability, required the supplement of society. As Derrida described it, pity was 'that fundamental affection, as primitive as the love of self, which unites us to others naturally' (105/11). In contrast to the Althusserians, Derrida argued that in Rousseau's theory, culture was posited as an internal necessity for nature; the nature/culture distinction could not be absolute.[42]

But a supplement could also mean an unnecessary addition, perhaps even a dangerous one. Rousseau, for all his advances, remained caught by logocentric metaphysics and so resisted the idea that nature, the absolute origin, could be inadequate or could *need* to be supplemented. To preserve the purity of nature, Rousseau had to argue that the rise of culture could not be attributed to any internal cause, any natural insufficiency, but was the result of a catastrophe. Appealing to the second meaning of supplementarity, Rousseau argued that culture imposed itself on a virgin nature; it was an unwelcome corruption. As Derrida wrote, 'the concept of origin or of nature is nothing but the myth of addition, of supplementarity annulled by being purely additive. It is the myth of the effacement of the trace' (167). Rousseau's ideological and nostalgic appeal to a pure and whole nature meant denying that it had to be supplemented by

---

41   Derrida's suggestion that the *Essay on the Origin of Languages* was compatible with the *Second Discourse* attempted to show, against the Althusserians, that his analysis of pity also manifested a process of supplementarity there. See OG, 171–194.

42   See also Derrida, *Margins of Philosophy*, trans. Alan Bass (Chicago: Chicago University Press, 1982), 144–147.

culture. The two had to be rigorously separated. Nostalgia and the *coupure* were not as opposed as the Althusserians imagined.

The presentation allowed for a new interpretation of Lévi-Strauss's relation to Rousseau, a comparison articulated through their analyses of writing. For Derrida, Rousseau's antipathy towards writing, and his desire to divide it cleanly from speech, was the clearest sign of his allegiance to the nature/culture split (98–100). Rousseau's depiction of speech as the immediate presence of meaning was the prototype for the absolute purity of nature, the appeal to an unquestionable ground.

As Derrida's analysis of the 'Writing Lesson' had shown, Lévi-Strauss participated in the same logocentric tradition (101–107/7–12). Despite his resistance to the nature/culture opposition, Lévi-Strauss's distinction between 'hot' and 'cold' societies, with and without writing, merely reinscribed it at another level. In refusing to allow an internal development of primitive societies, he hoped to keep them pure and make the division between hot and cold absolute. The jump from 'cold' to 'hot' societies was structurally similar to Rousseau's jump between nature and culture; it was only possible through a catastrophe or outside influence, the chance arrival of a careless ethnologist. Lévi-Strauss's nostalgia for primitive societies was of a piece with the assertion of their distinction from the civilized, just as Rousseau's nostalgia for the state of nature necessitated, according to Derrida, the assertion of the nature/culture distinction. Lévi-Strauss had not effaced the nature/culture opposition, as the contributors to the *Cahiers* had thought; he had merely shifted it.

When Derrida showed that, contrary to common belief, Lévi-Strauss's nostalgia implied an assertion of absolute ruptures, he aligned the father of structuralism with the *Cahiers* philosophy. The rapprochement raised the question of whether the *normalien* criticism of Lévi-Strauss's nostalgia might be equally applicable to the *Cahiers* project. The concerted efforts of the Cercle d'Épistémologie to rid analyses of culture of any natural contamination might have its own ideological implications, indicating a parallel nostalgia for a pure unadulterated science.

While Derrida's interpretation of Rousseau suggested that the Cercle d'Épistémologie's criticism of Lévi-Strauss's naturalism could be turned against them, his analysis of writing provided the details of the argument. Most contributors to the *Cahiers*, as we shall see, placed writing on the side of science, focusing on its epistemological benefits, in particular its formalism and indifference to subjectivity. Lévi-Strauss, on the other hand focused on the negative aspects of writing, and thus refused to accept writing as the ground of science. In his analysis, writing's function was 'sociological [. . .] rather than intellectual' (127/36).

Lévi-Strauss argued that writing broke up the self-presence of the 'crystalline' social group, becoming a technique of oppression. And though Derrida disagreed with the excessively limited and ethnocentric presentation of writing that guided these analyses, he did not object to their substance. Indeed, in what must have been a very bold move in the highly politicized ENS, Derrida admitted that différance, his neologism that described the essential structure of writing, was itself the condition of capitalization and class division:

> It has long been known that the power of writing in the hands of a small number, caste, or class, is always contemporaneous with hierarchisation, let us say with political différance; it is at the same time distinction into groups, classes, and levels of economico-politico-technical power, and delegation of authority, power deferred [*différée*] and abandoned to an organ of capitalisation [. . .]. This entire structure appears as soon as a society begins to live as a society, that is to say from the origin of life in general, when, at very heterogeneous levels of organisation and complexity, it is possible to *defer presence*, that is to say *expense* or consumption, and to organize production, that is to say *reserve* in general (130–131/40–41).

Derrida agreed, at least in part, with Lévi-Strauss's analyses of the dangerous effects of writing: it disrupted the supposed self-presence and identity of the social group. But crucially he maintained with the Cercle and against Lévi-Strauss that it was also a necessary condition for science (128–131/38–41). Derrida's central intervention was to suggest that you could not have one without the other; différance or writing was the common root of both social injustice (hierarchies, economic oppression, and violence) *and* science. To the question 'is there a knowledge, and, above all, a language, scientific or not, that one can call alien at once to writing and to violence?' Derrida responded in the negative (127/36–37).[43] When other contributors to the *Cahiers* tried to exclude the non-self-identity of différance from science, they were being just as ideological as Lévi-Strauss had been when he had tried to exclude différance from primitive societies.

IV SIGNIFIERS, MARKS, AND TRACES

Though he never addressed Jacques-Alain Miller's 'Suture' or Alain Badiou's 'Mark and Lack' directly, it is worth considering how the ideas expressed in Derrida's *Of Grammatology* profoundly challenged the central presuppositions of these two bookend essays from the *Cahiers pour l'Analyse*. Both sides of the *Cahiers* divide, whether demanding or rejecting a subject of science, wanted to reduce non-self-identity – either through the suture or through

---

43   In Althusser's reading notes on Derrida's essay, he remarked that Derrida wasn't sufficiently attentive to the differences of violence. Lévi-Strauss was only talking about class violence, not violence in general. The corollary of this would be that the violence of writing and class violence could be distinguished, which would save science from an intimate connection to ideology. See IMEC archives, ALT2. A58–02.03, sheet 4.

foreclosure – and make the formal the site of the identical. For Miller, the preservation of self-identity was the necessary condition for a viable concept of 'truth' (CpA 1.3:43), whereas for Badiou self-identity was what shielded the integrity of scientific discourse from ideological representations of it from the outset (CpA 10.8:156–157).

In his reading of Frege's *Grundlagen der Arithmetik*, Miller argued that 'zero' was the mark of a lack, the self-identical sign '0' standing in for the lack of an object conforming to the concept 'non-self-identical'. But since the mark '0', unlike the thing it signified, was self-identical, it could be counted; with the '0' the non-self-identical was stitched up or 'sutured'. It was this process that lay behind Frege's construction of the integers: Frege's method demonstrated that the constant 'suturing' of the 'non-identical' was the necessarily repressed condition for arithmetic, a 'logic of the signifier' underlying all mathematics.

In Badiou's contribution, he vehemently rejected Miller's analysis, which provided resources for reintroducing the Lacanian subject of science, and with it the trappings of ideological *méconnaissance*, into structuralist discourse. Badiou elaborated a stratified conception of formal logic, comprising the levels M_1, M_2, and M_3. At the first level were the marks, the 'absolutely raw material of the logical process', which 'is supplied by a particular sphere of technical production: writing' (CpA 10.8:151–152). These could be joined together to form finite sequences or 'expressions'. At the level of the second mechanism, these expressions were judged to be well- or ill-formed. Only at the level of the third mechanism (M_3), could these expressions be judged to be derivable or non-derivable.

This framework allowed Badiou to re-interpret the mark 'o'. *Pace* Miller, it did not stand in for the non-self-identical object excluded from mathematics, the 'mark of a lack', but rather was the 'lack of a mark', the absence of any mark 'x' to fulfil a particular expression like $\sim I(x,x)$ (x is not identical to x). Badiou argued that, while $\sim I(x,x)$ failed at the level of 'derivability' (M_3), judged syntactically (at the level of M_2) it was a well-formed expression. And this meant that it remained firmly ensconced in the realm of self-identical marks (defined by M_1). While Miller thought that the '0' was the sutured non-self-identical thing, in Badiou's presentation the world of 'things' was never in question; marks could only refer to other marks. As he asserted, 'logic, as a machine, lacks nothing it does not produce elsewhere' (CpA 10.8:151). In attempting to recast arithmetic as dependent upon a 'logic of the signifier', where 'things' were represented, even as lacking, Miller had given merely an ideological representation of science, an (admittedly rather complex) referential account wedded to concepts of truth and the real (150).

Derrida would have agreed with the thrust of Badiou's analysis here, as is clear both in his criticism of Lévi-Strauss's nostalgia and in his analysis of writing. The signified of writing, what is present in absence there, is not a 'thing', something existing in the world, but rather it is also a signifier (speech), another trace. The appeal to an outside, a pure state of nature, or a primitive society, even an absent or excluded one, was the classic gesture of metaphysics that Derrida wanted to deconstruct. Thus Derrida like Badiou remained resistant to this notion of truth, because it was governed by the idea of a reference outside the system of signifiers (OG, 10).

But even if Derrida's analysis seems to endorse Badiou's argument over Miller's, he would have been very resistant to the confidence of Badiou's account of science. Badiou took as an axiom that the marks produced in his system were self-identical. $\sim I(x,x)$ was a non-derivable expression, because non-self-identity had been 'foreclosed' at the level of syntax. The sorting of propositions according to whether they complied with syntactical rules relied, according to Badiou, on the self-identity of every mark. As Badiou explained, 'what is not substitutable-for-itself is something radically unthought, of which the logical mechanism *bears no trace*' (CpA 10.8:157).

But it was precisely such claims that Derrida had challenged in his work. As he suggested in *Writing and Difference*, because 'logic obeys [. . .] the principle of identity', it relies on 'the founding expression of a philosophy of presence'.[44] Despite his rejection of referential systems, Badiou's absolute reliance on the self-identical mark was a sign that he too participated in metaphysics; in short his presentation of mathematics was ideological, and in more than the narrow Althusserian sense.

Derrida discussed this question at greater length in his 1967 book, *Speech and Phenomena*. Though Badiou's work is generally very critical of phenomenology, Derrida's reading of Husserl seems pertinent to Badiou's own analysis in 'Mark and Lack'. Derrida's book was explicitly a discussion of Husserl's *Logical Investigations*, but its argument was focused by Husserl's claims in the *Formal and Transcendental Logic*.[45] In the first part of this 1929 text, Husserl had described a formal system that, like Badiou's, was stratified. Corresponding to Badiou's strata, Husserl elaborated the elements of formal logic, whose combinations were sorted depending on whether they were non-sensical (*unsinnig*) or not (in Badiou's language, M_2), and then contradictory (*widersinnig*) or not (M_3). And like Badiou, Husserl had insisted upon the self-identity of these expressions. As Derrida related, for Husserl, no matter how we might say or write a word, its meaning did not change: 'it must remain the *same*, and be able to be repeated as such, despite and across the deformations which the empirical event necessarily makes it undergo.'[46]

But for Derrida this self-identity of the signifier (or in Badiou's terms, the

---

44   Derrida, *Writing and Difference*, 207.

45   See Edward Baring, *The Young Derrida and French Philosophy 1945–1968* (Cambridge: Cambridge University Press, 2011), chapter 7.

46   Derrida, *Speech and Phenomena*, trans. David Allison (Evanston: Northwestern University Press, 1973), 50.

mark) was dependent upon the underlying non-self-identity of différance. Though the mark was 'ideally' self-identical, each empirical version was not: 'x' was not identical to another 'x' written elsewhere. Rather each material signifier was merely a 'representation' (*Vorstellung*) of the ideal one, related to the self-identical x by the process of signification. As Derrida elaborated in *Of Grammatology*, it is only because two material marks x_1 and x_2 both differ from all other marks a, b, c, d, etc. that they can be identified (OG, 326–327n.17). Thus whereas Badiou suggested that $x \neq x$ could only be classed as non-derivable at the level of the 'calculi of identity' because scriptural non-self-identity has already been foreclosed at the level of syntax, Derrida argued that the non-self-identity of writing was a necessary condition for the construction of identity on which formal logic relied. Because identity was always built upon a non-identity, Badiou's attempt to foreclose non-self-identity in the construction of logic was structurally similar to Lévi-Strauss's attempt to expel the non-self-presence of writing from primitive societies.

In this sense Derrida leant towards Miller. Though Miller conceived of the signifier as marking the 'lack' [*manque*] of a non-self-identical object, at least he recognised that mathematics was dependent on a movement of signification, on a non-self-identity that it could not accept. Derrida implicitly allied deconstruction with Miller's 'logic of the signifier' in his 1966 presentation 'Freud and the Scene of Writing'. Asserting that the suppression of writing uncovered in the deconstruction of logocentrism was a 'repression, not forgetting', Derrida repeated the formulation that Miller had used for the *méconnaissance* of the 'logic of the signifier' in the 'logic of the logician'.[47] In confirming that différance, like the logic of the signifier, was repressed in science, Derrida endorsed Miller's claim that the formal contained a constitutive non-self-identity that foreclosure could never fully exclude. Badiou wanted to draw on the benefits of writing, its formalism, without recognizing the 'différance' that was at work at its core, while Miller argued that science relied on the suturing of this différance. Both depended upon what Derrida saw as the metaphysical appeal to absolute self-identity, which resembled Lévi-Strauss's ideological nostalgia for a pure primitive society.

If Derrida never openly addressed the *Cahiers* texts, he did reject the methodological underpinnings of their criticism of Lévi-Strauss in a chapter placed just after the revised *Cahiers* piece (OG, 157–64). Though like the *normaliens*, Derrida refused simple 'commentary' upon an author's intentions (a 'psychology') and rather hoped to 'produce' a 'signifying structure', he was unwilling to see the text as the effect of deeper forces, whether in history or of the subconscious. This was the context for his famous, and much misunderstood, assertion

---

47   Derrida, *Writing and Difference*, 196; cf. CpA 1.3:39, where Miller had used the phrase deliberately to mark a distance between his and Derrida's work.

that '*il n'y a pas de hors-texte* [there is nothing outside of the text]'. The drive to find some ultimate ground for a text in economic or psychoanalytic structures over-emphasized their stability. Since, according to Derrida, everything was structured like a text (its meaning was never inherent, but produced by 'differential references') the broader structures to which the Althusserians and Lacanians turned were just as provisional and unstable as the textual or psychological structures they hoped to ground there. We should not leave the text to seek a more secure ground – since no such security exists – but rather 'remain within the text,' and work through its tensions and aporiae (158–9). Though affirming the ideological nature of Lévi-Strauss's naturalized structures, Derrida denied that the Cercle d'Épistémologie could do any better.

Derrida's reading of Lévi-Strauss and deployment of the *normalien* criticism of his nostalgia allowed him to challenge the validity of a *coupure* between nature and culture, a *coupure* that undergirded the distinction between ideology and science. He criticized Lévi-Strauss's ideological nostalgia not because it threatened to dissolve culture into nature, but because it did the opposite, re-establishing the duality. For this reason, despite all his criticisms of the older man's structuralism and the complaints of its residual logocentrism, Derrida approved of Lévi-Strauss's attempt to break down the nature/culture distinction. As the ultimate litmus test of the debate, Derrida cited the key passage from *The Savage Mind* that his students had attacked: when Lévi-Strauss suggested that cultural structures could be the result of physico-chemical reactions in the human brain, Derrida did not criticize it as a sign of unrepentant ideology, but asserted instead that at this moment Lévi-Strauss was 'putting a strain on the boundaries and working toward [the] deconstruction' of metaphysics (OG, 105; CpA 4.1:10).

V AFTER STRUCTURALISM?

In a letter to the *Cahiers pour l'Analyse* published in 1967, Lévi-Strauss responded angrily to Derrida's paper. The vehemence of Lévi-Strauss's text is strange given the relative restraint of Derrida's criticism in comparison to that of the others in the *Cahiers*. The reaction can be traced to two sources. If Derrida's text was not the most critical, it was the most prominent of the *Cahiers* readings of the anthropologist; Lévi-Strauss responded to the teacher and not his students at the ENS. But Lévi-Strauss's antipathy also followed from the internalist character of Derrida's critique, in which Lévi-Strauss's own words were used to undermine the narrative he wanted to tell. Lévi-Strauss criticized Derrida for treating him as a philosopher ('isn't scrutinizing my texts with the care that would be better justified if they came from Spinoza, Descartes, or Kant, just playing a philosophical farce?') and suggested that Derrida had handled 'the excluded third with the delicacy of a bear. Doubtless the Nambikwara are both good and bad, and the treachery which accompanied the arrival of writing is only a form of which they already practised other aspects'. Further, Lévi-Strauss explained that his use of Rousseau was purely strategic, that he would 'resort to whatever schema from the philosophical tradition that has fallen into the public domain, if it could help me make my contemporaries see, in a language that is accessible to them, the unique flavour of a way of life, an institution, a belief, a group of representations [. . .]. I reply thus at the same time to the insidious question, asked somewhere in a note, as to whether the ethnologist wants to be an engineer or a *bricoleur* [handyman]' (CpA 8.5:89–90).

Lévi-Strauss had introduced the concept of the *bricoleur* in his 1962 *Savage Mind*, suggesting that the mythmaker had to rely on the fragments of cultural codes lying around him to create new myths; he could not, like the engineer, tailor-make his tools and language. But Derrida's suggestion that Lévi-Strauss might be a *bricoleur* was not 'insidious'. To read it as such would be to conflate Derrida's argument with that of the Althusserians and Lacanians he was trying to engage. In labelling Lévi-Strauss a *bricoleur*, Derrida argued that Lévi-Strauss recognized the limitations of his discourse, the potential failure of his science, and the necessity of relying on old and ill-fitting concepts, most particularly the nature/culture opposition. Derrida's criticism was aimed not at an anthropologist at the Collège de France, but rather at his own colleagues and students at the ENS and particularly at the editors of the *Cahiers*, who believed that it was possible to be an 'engineer' and create a new self-identical language from scratch, thereby rescuing science from ideology. The engineer was more an Althusserian than a Lévi-Straussian myth.

At the 1966 Johns Hopkins Structuralist Conference, Derrida further developed his point and, perhaps responding to Lévi-Strauss's reaction, brought the question of the *bricoleur* to the centre of his discussion. Lévi-Strauss, Derrida suggested, wanted to leave the Western metaphysical tradition, but did not make the traditional metaphysical error of thinking he could do so without its resources. In particular, Lévi-Strauss continued to use the nature/culture distinction methodologically even as he recognized the 'impossibility of giving it credit', and here again Derrida made reference to the much maligned passage in *The Savage Mind*.[48] According to Derrida, Lévi-Strauss was a *bricoleur*, like the mythmaker, making the best of the materials that lay around even if they were not perfect for the task. In thus bringing attention to the 'mytho-poetic' nature of his work, Lévi-Strauss had recognized its limitations.[49] His suspicion of the nature/culture distinction and his embrace of *bricolage* only further proved that Lévi-Strauss had confronted the central problem of metaphysics: there was no firm place outside of metaphysics on which to build a science.

---

48   Derrida, *Writing and Difference*, 284–285.
49   See especially the 'Overture' to Lévi-Strauss, *The Raw and the Cooked*.

The language of Derrida's endorsement is also significant. He asserted that, by continuing to use the discredited nature/culture distinction, Lévi-Strauss had taken a step towards the abandon of 'all reference to a centre, to a subject, to a privileged reference, to an origin or an absolute *arché*'.[50] The phrase recalls the Cercle d'Épistémologie's own attempts to break with ideology.[51] But whereas for Althusser and his students the rejection of the centre and the subject could only arise through a renunciation of existing conceptual frameworks, now for Derrida it was precisely this renunciation that was in question. The de-centred approach was best represented by *bricolage*, the knowing reliance on an old inadequate language.

Derrida approved of Lévi-Strauss's efforts and sided with the anthropologist against the Cercle d'Épistémologie. But just as before, Lévi-Strauss's gesture was limited by his logocentrism. There were two possible causes for the failure to produce a totalizing science, or, as Derrida phrased it, 'two interpretations of interpretation'. At times in Lévi-Strauss's work, he implied that there could be no absolute science of myth, because of an irreducible 'play' in the system.[52] For Derrida, 'play' was the always-possible substitution of elements in a structure. Due to this play, no analysis would ever be final, because the system continually transformed itself and mutated. A totalizing comprehension was impossible, even of a finite set. Accepting the centrality of play, Derrida asserted, would be a joyful act, forgoing the desire to pin down a structure that was always on the move, in a moment of Nietzschean dance.[53]

But at certain points in his writings, Lévi-Strauss suggested that his work was limited because of a lack of empirical evidence. As Derrida showed, despite railing against empiricism, all of Lévi-Strauss's texts were presented as empirical arguments; as long as one had not collected the totality of data points, there was always the possibility that a new and determinative fact would be discovered to overthrow previous theories. This was why Lévi-Strauss's conclusions would always be provisional. The uncertainty of his scientific theory would be merely a result of Lévi-Strauss's own limitations, the necessarily unfinished nature of his research. Understanding the totality was impossible because there were too many elements to collect.[54]

In this interpretation, the underlying and hidden structures were

---

50   Derrida, *Writing and Difference*, 285. In rejecting the idea of the centre, Derrida again picked up on Althusser's language.

51   See amongst others Althusser's 'Three Notes on the Theory of Discourses,' in HC 50–54 and 77.

52   Derrida, *Writing and Difference*, 289. Derrida saw hints of this type of play in Lévi-Strauss's discussion of 'mana' in his *Introduction to the Work of Marcel Mauss,* and in the references to games in his *Conversations, Race and History* and *The Savage Mind*.

53   Derrida, *Writing and Difference*, 292.

54   In the earlier text, Derrida had been clearer that this interpretation of interpretation was implicit within *bricolage* (OG, 139).

represented as stable and they would only change as the result of external shocks and chance ruptures.[55] Though Lévi-Strauss recognized that play disrupted presence, he still saw play as a *fall* from presence, from an ultimate grounding structure, which he worked to uncover in a moment of 'Rousseauian' nostalgia. Certainty and stability were out of reach, but by shifting the blame for this uncertainty from the structures themselves onto the scientist, Lévi-Strauss preserved for himself the impossible dream of a definitive science.

Rousseau or Nietzsche? Both recognized the lack of certainty, the impossibility of absolute truth. But whereas the former saw it as a loss to be recouped, if never fully, the second lived it as a liberation. In Derrida's eyes, Lévi-Strauss recognized the impossibility of a pure science better than the Cercle d'Épistémologie did. Lévi-Strauss's error was to make this impossibility contingent, impossible for finite man, not essential to the system itself. This error was perhaps inevitable. In a final paragraph added for the 1967 edition, Derrida suggested that one could not choose between the two interpretations of interpretation: the Rousseauian nostalgia for a forgotten purity or the Nietzschean affirmation of the absence of grounds. Rather both showed themselves to be absolutely necessary. The contributors to the *Cahiers* had defined metaphysics as both the ideological appeal to a secure ground outside of the structural system of signifiers *and* what had dominated all prior philosophical discourse. But Derrida suggested that the two conspired against the philosopher; the attempt to escape metaphysics, to step outside of the tradition, was the metaphysical gesture *par excellence*.

Even as Lévi-Strauss bridled at Derrida's criticism, Derrida was, as we saw, kinder to him than most of the other 'structuralists' at the ENS and beyond. Derrida's criticism focused on Lévi-Strauss's nostalgia, as did theirs, yet he defended Lévi-Strauss's rejection of the nature/culture distinction and embraced Lévi-Straussian *bricolage* as a means to escape ideology. And from the perspective of his students and colleagues, this was the truly scandalous aspect of his project; Derrida the 'post-structuralist' was most radical when he agreed with Lévi-Strauss.

---

55 Derrida, *Writing and Difference*, 292.

CHAPTER FOUR

Knox Peden
Foucault and the Subject of Method

Shortly after Michel Foucault's death in 1984, Alain Badiou published an obituary in *Le Perroquet* that pointed to an unexpected filiation between the former's recent investigations into Graeco-Roman sexuality and the latter's philosophical efforts.[1] Badiou wrote that he was 'personally moved' by Foucault's reintroduction of the category of the subject in his courses of the 1980s and went on to explain why this was such a pleasant surprise: 'For the only conformism that one could detect in Foucault – a conformism established and maintained by almost all recognized French philosophers – was that, at least in his theoretical writings, he tried to avoid Lacan.'[2] Foucault's hostility to psychoanalysis has become something of a truism, chiefly because of its treatment in *The History of Sexuality* as one variant, albeit an exemplary one, of confessional discourse. His rejection of structuralism and its linguistic and psychoanalytic bases in the 1970s also leads one to think that Foucault's thinly veiled approbations of Lacan in *The Order of Things* were but fleeting instances of anti-humanist solidarity.[3] But Badiou's remarks suggest that Foucault's final writings might register a kind of belated recognition of the value of some of Lacan's claims and positions. And if Badiou is 'personally moved' by this belated recognition, this also suggests that there might be a personal history behind it.

In addition to being one among several partisans of Lacano-Althusserianism whom Foucault invited in 1969 to staff the new experimental university in Vincennes, Badiou was one among these same partisans who put a series of pointed methodological questions to Foucault in volume nine of the *Cahiers pour l'Analyse*. Foucault's 'Response to the Cercle d'Épistémologie' (CpA 9.2), published in the same volume, would serve as a template for *The Archaeology of Knowledge* published several months later.[4] What's more, Foucault apparently

---

1   This chapter greatly benefited from the responses of my colleagues in the Centre for the History of European Discourses at the University of Queensland. Special thanks as well to Tom Eyers and the Interdisciplinary Project in the Humanities at Washington University in St. Louis.

2   Alain Badiou, *Pocket Pantheon*, trans. David Macey (London: Verso, 2009), 123–124.

3   On Foucault's turn away from these elements, see Joan Copjec, *Read My Desire: Lacan against the Historicists* (Cambridge: MIT Press, 1994), 4–5. On psychoanalysis as a 'counter-science', alongside Lévi-Strauss's ethnography, to the 'human sciences', see Foucault, *The Order of Things* (New York: Random House, 1970), 373–387.

4   An uncredited translation of the 'Response to the Cercle d'Épistémologie' is reprinted in Foucault, *Aesthetics, Method, and Epistemology*, ed. James D. Faubion (New York: The New Press, 1994). In-line references will be to this volume and the original pagination in the *Cahiers pour l'Analyse*. Foucault, *The Archaeology of Knowledge*, trans. A.M. Sheridan Smith (New York: Random House, 1972), hereafter AK.

entrusted the 'pruning' [*élagage*] of this manuscript to Badiou in November 1968.[5] As virtually any survey of Foucault's work attests, this book served as a hinge between the archaeology of his early works and the genealogy of his writings in the 1970s.[6] The English translation gives this transitional quality dramatic form, since it includes Foucault's inaugural lesson to the Collège de France as an appendix. Here the theoretical strain of the preceding text subsides in 'The Order of Discourse', where the nascent emphasis on discursive practice finds firmer grounding in Foucault's turn toward a kind of discursive voluntarism centred on the 'will to truth'.[7]

Complemented by Foucault's newfound sense of political engagement, the genealogical reconstruction of this will culminated in *Discipline and Punish*, the key work of this period.[8] And yet, soon after publishing this volume, Foucault began to complicate its theses in his courses. Moving from a problematic of discipline to one of sovereignty, Foucault recognized that he could no longer think of subjectivity purely in terms of disciplinary 'subjection'. Rather, the thematics of biopower required a thinking of subjectivity as a negotiated terrain, one that involves a complex set of relations gathered in the space between one's capacity to be subjected and one's capacity to be free as a subject.[9] In other words, Badiou's endorsement in 1984 of Foucault's 'return' to the subject risks underestimating the degree to which the problematic of the subject within a wholly structured field – be it structured by epistemes or disciplinary apparatuses – was a periodically resurgent concern *throughout* Foucault's oeuvre.

This punctual continuity in Foucault's project is at once fitting and ironic given his proclivity for the discontinuous, but it is also the privileged site of Foucault's equally theoretical and historical connection with the *Cahiers pour*

---

5   Foucault, *Dits et écrits, 1954–1988*, eds Daniel Defert and François Ewald, vol. 1 1954–69 (Paris: Gallimard, 1994), 33.

6   Hubert Dreyfus and Paul Rabinow, *Michel Foucault: Beyond Structuralism and Hermeneutics*, 2nd edition (Chicago: University of Chicago Press, 1983) and Gary Gutting, *Michel Foucault's Archaeology of Scientific Reason* (Cambridge: Cambridge University Press, 1989). Despite his assessment of *The Archaeology of Knowledge* as 'written too early and too hastily', Paul Veyne also described it as 'an awkward and brilliant book in which the author achieved full awareness of what he was doing and took his theory to its logical conclusion', to wit 'to dispense with "things"'. The former judgment is found in Paul Veyne, *Foucault: His Thought, His Character*, trans. Janet Lloyd (Cambridge: Polity Press, 2010), 84; the latter in 'Foucault Revolutionizes History', trans. Catherine Porter, in *Foucault and his Interlocutors*, ed. Arnold I. Davidson (Chicago: University of Chicago Press, 1997), 146.

7   Foucault, *L'Ordre du discours* (Paris: Gallimard, 1971) appears under the title 'The Discourse on Language', trans. Rupert Swyer in AK, 215–237.

8   Foucault, *Discipline and Punish: The Birth of the Prison*, trans. Alan Sheridan (New York: Pantheon Books, 1978).

9   For a helpful discussion of this transition, see Michael C. Behrent, 'Liberalism without Humanism: Michel Foucault and the Free-Market Creed, 1976–1979', *Modern Intellectual History*, 6:3 (2009), 539–568. The key courses are *Security, Territory, Population* and *The Birth of Biopolitics*, ed. Michel Senellart, trans. Graham Burchell (New York: Picador, 2007 and 2008).

l'Analyse. More than the superficial veneer of structuralism, what made Foucault's work an object of interest for the Cercle d'Épistémologie was the common concern to develop a methodology that avoided any appeal to the transcendental, be it phenomenological ground or synthetic consciousness. The desire for 'analysis' was integrally connected with the desire to have a theory of the subject that was consistent with such a method's disavowals of the transcendental. And though the questions put to Foucault chiefly concern his putatively non-synthetic method, they equally bear on the conceptual conundrum of a non-synthetic subject. In fact, the subject of method is precisely the site in which, to exploit the pun, the concepts of 'subject' and 'method' become intertwined. For asking how Foucault's method 'works' without an appeal to a transcendental principle ensuring its purchase is another way of asking what kind of subject is in play in the deployment, and the presumptions, of this method.

By returning to Foucault's exchange with the Cercle d'Épistémologie with a focus on these intercalated themes, we gain insight into the relation between two heterogeneous discourses in recent French thought that can be broadly grouped under the signifiers 'Foucauldian' and 'Lacanian'. Despite the differences that divided Foucault and Lacan, their projects were in fact much closer than their respective adherents might care to allow.[10] Briefly stated, this proximity was a result of each thinker's desire to develop a discourse that would displace the philosophical concept of the 'subject', and yet retain critical purchase on the post-Kantian phenomenon conventionally described as 'subjectivity'. The centrality of this agenda to Lacan's teaching is obvious; indeed, his psychoanalytic enterprise has been described as an exemplar of 'antiphilosophy'.[11] For Foucault, the situation is more problematic, precisely because his use of the 'subject' in his writings and courses of the 1980s harbours an array of equivocal tendencies. *The Hermeneutics of the Subject* (1981–2) alone addresses myriad triangulations among the self, the individual, and the subject.[12] But this conceptual triangulation is itself grounded in the binary and more fundamentally historical relation between 'subject' and 'truth' as respectively practical and discursive conventions. Conventional or not, the 'subject' nonetheless plays the role of an agent in Foucault's thought of this period, an agent endowed with the capacity to mediate relations, and not least the relation that is Foucault's main concern at this point: the care of the self.

With this relation in view, the practical/discursive correlate of subject/truth

---

10   For a rare attempt to show how Foucault and Lacan's projects can complement one another, see Charles Shepherdson's chapter 'History and the Real: Foucault with Lacan' in his *Vital Signs: Nature, Culture, Psychoanalysis* (London: Routledge, 2000), 153–185.

11   Badiou, 'Antiphilosophy: Plato and Lacan' in *Conditions*, trans. Steven Corcoran (London: Continuum, 2008), 228–247.

12   Foucault, *The Hermeneutics of the Subject: Lectures at the Collège de France, 1981–1982*, ed. Frédéric Gros, trans. Graham Burchell (New York: Picador, 2005).

maps onto another, that between spirituality and philosophy. The subject's spiritual (practical) exercises are what provide it with access to the (discursive) truth of philosophy.[13] For Lacan, the relationship involved in one's accession to truth is historically transcendental, though not invariant, since it has the advent of post-Galilean science as one of its primary conditions,[14] and is best described by a distinctive blend of psychoanalytic and formalist discourse. For Foucault, this relationship is thoroughly historical, and best described via the techniques of an agnostic empiricism. But the question remains whether this empiricism is not predicated upon a more basic conceptual armature that retains a kind of minimal transcendentalism that allows for its multiple applications. In *The Use of Pleasure* (1984), Foucault remarks near the end of his introduction that 'there is a whole rich and complex field of historicity in the way the individual is summoned to recognize himself as an ethical subject of sexual conduct.'[15] If the summoning occurs in different ways throughout history, what nevertheless appears to transcend this historicity is the fact of summoning itself. The fundamental self-relation constitutive of this 'summoning' to subjectivity, the assumption of one's place as subject that formed the guiding thread of Foucault's historical investigations of the 1980s, was arguably the object of Lacan's life's work.

Foucault apparently once conceived of volume one of *The History of Sexuality* (1976) as 'beat[ing] on Lacan by arguing the opposite of what he says.' But according to other testimony, 'Foucault's relation to Lacan was less polemical than commonly believed. He was very sensitive to Lacan's asceticism, which he considered to be parallel to his own [. . .]. He even agreed with Lacan about ethical questions, which is to say that he would respect psychoanalysis insofar as it established an ethic. And that was what Lacan was looking for.'[16] Although various contingencies of Foucault's career, chief among them his encounters with Peter Brown at Berkeley and Pierre Hadot in Paris, led to his engagement with the ancients, the wager of what follows is that the conceptual content of Foucault's assessment of this material bears a patent historical and theoretical debt to Lacanianism most generally and the *Cahiers pour l'Analyse* more specifically.

The demonstration of this point will require a sustained engagement with the details of Foucault's exchange with the Cercle in volume nine of the journal and its continuation in *The Archaeology of Knowledge*. For the goal is not to develop a quasi-psychoanalytic claim that Foucault repressed the truth of this encounter only to witness its return more than a decade later. Nor is it my intention to put forth a metaphysical claim that enshrines the transhistorical truth of

13   Ibid., 15.

14   See in particular Jacques Lacan, 'Science and Truth' (CpA 1.1:7–28; E, 855–877/726–745).

15   Foucault, *The Use of Pleasure*, trans. Robert Hurley (New York: Random House, 1985), 32.

16   Both quotations, the first from Pierre Nora and the second from François Ewald, come from François Dosse, *History of Structuralism, Volume 2: The Sign Sets, 1967-Present*, trans. Deborah Glassman (Minneapolis: University of Minnesota Press, 1997), 339.

the Lacanian subject making its way against all obstacles, including those of Foucauldian genealogy. Instead, the argument is predicated upon a set of convictions concerning the constructive effects of intellectual dialogue and the historical tenacity of concepts and conceptual arrangements that, for a variety of reasons, ultimately prove compelling. In his challenging essay on 'The History of Theory' Ian Hunter writes: 'When sciences and philosophies encounter limits and restrictions, these typically arise not from apositive relations of their formalizations but from concrete obstacles and rivalries they meet in contested cultural and institutional spaces.'[17] What follows attempts to demonstrate a complementarity of historical objects in the very space where Hunter argues for a contrast of historical methods, and is based less on a concession to dialectical historiography than on an appeal to the plausibility of historical circumstance. In a word, the institutionally contested critiques and claims of the Cercle d'Épistémologie left their mark on Foucault, such that he would return to them after his efforts to provide archaeologies of knowledge and genealogies of power manifestly encountered a series of apositive limits. In the end, it is perhaps not too metaphorical to suggest that Foucault returns to this set of critiques to pursue more directly the implications of his own historical method for a non-metaphysical thinking of the subject as a self-relation that presupposes a lack of self-identity, that is, for considering that method in light of the attenuated endeavour that was the *Cahiers pour l'Analyse*.

I THE ILLUSIONS OF FORMALIZATION

Among the questions the Cercle d'Épistémologie put to Foucault, one in particular stands out for its prophetic quality:

> If one were to call an author's historicity his belonging to the episteme of his epoch and 'finitude' the name that an epoch – notably our own – might give to its own limits, what relations or non-relations, according to Foucault, might obtain between this historicity and this finitude? (CpA 9.1:7).

This is also the central question put to Foucault by Hubert Dreyfus and Paul Rabinow in their classic study of his work, and further developed in Béatrice Han's incisive philosophical assessment in *Foucault's Critical Project: Between the Transcendental and the Historical*.[18] A key task of *The Order of Things* was to establish the historicity of epistemes, and to show that epistemes by and large determine the horizons of intellectual activity for an epoch. If such is the case,

---

17   Ian Hunter, 'The History of Theory', *Critical Inquiry* 33:4 (Autumn 2006), 102.
18   Dreyfus and Rabinow, *Michel Foucault*; Béatrice Han, *Foucault's Critical Project: Between the Transcendental and the Historical*, trans. Edward Pile (Stanford: Stanford University Press, 2002).

and if, notwithstanding the rumblings of a nascent epistemic transition, the 'episteme' in which Foucault's own effort must be located bears the signal mark of finitude, then are we not led to conclude that the emergence of the concept of the historicity of epistemes has the specific episteme of finitude as its historical condition? What the Cercle detects in Foucault is a kind of bait and switch whereby affirming the historical in place of the transcendental serves ultimately to make the historical operate as a transcendental condition at the level of method. The accuracy of this assessment is conceded by Foucault himself in his recourse to the admittedly 'barbarous' concept of the historical *a priori* in *The Archaeology of Knowledge* (127). Despite Foucault's antipathy to the Kantian figure of the empirico-transcendental doublet, his own method remains within a Kantian horizon to the extent that it is designed to establish the at once historical and discursive quality of epistemes as 'conditions'. That Foucault, like Deleuze, seeks out the conditions of the actual rather than the possible makes the effort no less post-Kantian as a result, for the appeal to 'conditions of X' is the gesture *par excellence* of transcendental philosophy.[19] Foucault's own turn to genealogical description was, at least in part, an effort to take leave of this conundrum. Opting for the 'gray, meticulous, and patiently documentary' is a way to avoid the temptation to perform a transcendental deduction that grants metahistorical meaning to the *dispositif* in question.[20]

The editors of the *Cahiers pour l'Analyse* were acutely sensitive to this pitfall in Foucault's archaeological method, which likewise remained unresolved in the efforts toward a 'philosophy of the concept' delineated by Jean Cavaillès, a common influence for Foucault and the Cercle d'Épistémologie on this score.[21] The Cercle's engagement with a variety of formalist discourses sprung from their desire to see if it was possible to maintain a discourse in which the reciprocity between the conditioning and the conditioned could be thought without an appeal to some ground or instance extrinsic to the relation. This problem has taken many forms in the history of philosophy. Limiting ourselves to those instances most germane to the *Cahiers pour l'Analyse*, we note a recurrent

19   See Gilles Deleuze, *Difference and Repetition*, trans. Paul Patton (New York: Columbia University Press, 1994), 69: 'It is in this direction [of the simulacrum, as emblem of difference in itself] that we must look for the conditions, not of possible experience, but of real experience'. Cf. Foucault's remark: 'what I mean by [*historical a priori*] is an *a priori* that is not a condition of validity for judgments, but a condition of reality for statements' (AK, 127).

20   Foucault, 'Nietzsche, Genealogy, History', in *The Foucault Reader*, ed. Paul Rabinow (New York: Pantheon Books, 1984), 76. According to Dreyfus and Rabinow, the '*dispositif* is distinguished from *episteme* primarily because it encompasses the non-discursive practices as well as the discursive' (121).

21   See Jean Cavaillès, *Sur la logique et la théorie de la science* (Paris: PUF, 1946). For helpful assessments of Foucault's debts to Cavaillès, see David Hyder, 'Foucault, Cavaillès, and Husserl on the Historical Epistemology of the Sciences', *Perspectives on Science* 11:1 (2003) 107–129, and David Webb 'Cavaillès and the historical *a priori* in Foucault', in *Virtual Mathematics: The Logic of Difference*, ed. Simon Durry (London: Clinamen Press, 2006), 100–117.

conjugational variation: Spinoza's *natura naturans/naturata*, Cavaillès's *sens posant/posé*, Jacques-Alain Miller's *structure structurant/structuré* (CpA 9.6) and François Regnault's *raison raisonnante* (CpA 9.4), with its implied double *raison raisonnée*. In Kantian terms, these pairings of active and past participles could each be translated into the relation between the transcendental (the conditioning) and the empirical (the conditioned). In the terms of post-Fregean logicism, we might translate the relation as one between function and term. Indeed, Miller's claim that the 'lack of a lack is also a lack' (CpA 9.4:102) is not merely an instance of Lacanian obscurantism. It is also a well-argued conclusion which demonstrates that, within a given discursive field, the function on a term is also a term within that field. So if a term is lacking, then that lack *qua* function becomes a term upon which other functions operate. This structure receives its most comprehensive elaboration in the *Cahiers* in Jean-Claude Milner's 'The Point of the Signifier' (CpA 3.5), wherein the vacillating nature of 'being' as at once function and term in Plato's *Sophist* is demonstrated, as is the corresponding vacillation of 'non-being', which is stymied ultimately, or 'sutured' rather, by Plato's refusal to grant 'non-being' its status as term.[22]

This relation between function and term is central to the questions that the Cercle put to Foucault, and in particular the 'New Questions' that would only be answered in *The Archaeology of Knowledge*. In his initial response, they write, 'the statement is conceived as an *element* in a system and as an *event* of enunciation. In fact, the 'Response' explicates the principle of reading the statement as element [. . .] all the while leaving us to understand that a principle of the statement as event also exists. [. . .] However, are there actually *two* principles of reading? And what would be the second's articulation upon the first? In fact, the event, since it is always inscribed in a configuration, and related to the system of its conditions, seems to be nothing but an element' (CpA 9.3:43). This vacillation between element and event in terms of the Foucauldian 'statement' [*énoncé*] is the homologue of Miller and Milner's efforts in the *Cahiers* to think of the subject as an alternating function and term in discursive sequences. But in the Cercle's view, this relation is conspicuously under-theorized in Foucault's work; the attention devoted in *The Archaeology of Knowledge* to establishing the regularity of the enunciative modalities that determine the 'dispersion' of the subject amidst the recurrent binary of discursive events and elements will attempt to address this precise point (54). Nevertheless, the Cercle has already keyed in to the fact that Foucault's effort to develop an empiricism of 'rules' is, in addition to being contorted in its conception, not sufficiently vouchsafed by an explanation of how discursive events occur and become elements in turn. In other words, Foucault's

---

22   For a fuller discussion of Milner's argument and its place in the *Cahiers*, see Knox Peden, 'The Rights of the Imaginary: On Jean-Claude Milner', *S: Journal of the Jan Van Eyck Circle for Ideology Critique*, Vol. 3 (2010), 115–136.

efforts to articulate the relation between the regulation and the regulated always wind up articulating the qualities of regulated 'elements', leaving the appeal to the process or 'event' of regulation with little more than rhetorical substance.

The 'Response to the Cercle d'Épistémologie' that provoked this incisive question is an exemplary Foucauldian document. Deploying what would become a familiar trope in later writings, Foucault had responded to pressure on the philosophical implications of his claims with a focus on method. Rather than confront this hard kernel of post-Kantian philosophy directly, Foucault questions the assumption of the *Cahiers* that such a problem could be resolved, or even needs to be resolved, with a comprehensive theory of discourse. Foucault's displacement of the problem onto new terrain involves several steps. For the bulk of the document, he avoids the conditioning/conditioned conundrum captured in the Cercle's question on historicity and finitude by limiting himself to the field of pure description. This allows Foucault to enumerate the concepts that will come to be central to *The Archaeology of Knowledge*, e.g. discursive events, discursive formation, positivity, and finally knowledge itself. With this edifice constructed, Foucault concludes with 'Several Remarks' that will be omitted from *The Archaeology of Knowledge* but which speak directly, and critically, to the *Cahiers pour l'Analyse*.

After insisting that no science – and not least mathematics – can be taken as a model for our assessment of all the others, Foucault speaks to the virtues of his descriptive method: 'It is possible [. . .] to situate a certain number of legitimate descriptions of scientific discourse in their possibility, but also to define them in their limits. Descriptions that are directed not toward knowledge as an instance of formation but to the objects, forms of enunciation, concepts, and, finally, to the opinions to which they give rise' (328–9/CpA 9.2:36–7). The descriptive method defines knowledge not as an insight into the 'instance of formation' – a fitting summary of the *Cahiers* agenda – but rather to 'objects, forms of enunciation, concepts, and [. . .] opinions' as just so many given historical objects. Forestalling critique of his naïve empiricism, Foucault then warns against the '*doxological illusion*' that 'sets forth description as the analysis of the conditions of a science' (329/37). Beyond empiricism, this critique would apply to multiple variants of phenomenology as well as vulgar Marxist assessments of nominal 'sciences' as reducible to their ideological conditions.

On this score, Foucault agrees with his interlocutors and lends credence to their efforts to combat the illusions of doxology. But in the next paragraph, he turns his sights on the heart of their project:

> But it is necessary to be wary of what we could call the *formalizing illusion*: i.e., of imagining that these laws of construction are at the same time and with full rights the conditions of existence; that concepts and valid propositions are nothing more than the giving of form to a primitive experience, or the result of working over

concepts and propositions already in place. [. . .] The formalizing illusion elides knowledge (the theoretical network and enunciative repartition) as the site and law of the formation of concepts and propositions (330/37–8tm).

In the trivializing of 'working over concepts [. . .] already in place' one hears the echoes of the *Cahiers* epigraph containing Canguilhem's instructions for how 'to work a concept'. Foucault is criticizing the efforts at extrapolation and transferral underway in the *Cahiers*, suggesting that their relentless quest for a determinant form prior to knowledge leads them into the cul-de-sac of transcendental 'conditions of existence' as well. What is more, concepts cannot be lifted wholesale from one discourse and deployed in another, no matter how extensively they might be 'worked'. Against this conception, Foucault proffers the notion of 'regional analysis', which might be used to define 'the domain of objects for which a science is intended' (330/38tm). With his turn to the 'regional', Foucault introduces a need for disparity rather than uniformity, and here his critique becomes more robust.[23] 'There is an illusion that consists in the supposition that science is grounded in the plenitude of a concrete and lived experience', he writes. Again, he concedes his agreement with the *Cahiers* critique of phenomenology. 'But it is equally illusory', he continues, 'to imagine that science is established by an act of rupture and decision, that it frees itself at one stroke from the qualitative field and from all the murmurings of the imaginary by the violence (serene or polemical) of a reason that founds itself by its own assertion' (331/38tm). Without using the term, Foucault is criticizing the fundamental idealism of the *Cahiers* agenda. Their relentless focus on the determinative qualities of form, and especially the form that is thoroughly rationalized discourse, eliminates the necessary distance between science and experience that makes science possible. 'If, in a general way, science refers to experience and yet detaches itself from it, it is not a matter of univocal determination, nor of a sovereign, constant, and definitive break' (331/39).

Here we see Foucault making an appeal to the historical, albeit in a distinctively Foucauldian sense. History in itself knows no breaks, only continuous dispersion or a kind of disparate continuity. To speak in terms of 'breaks' is to tarry with the kind of ontological discourse that Foucault is, in this instance, keen to avoid. But Foucault leaves himself open to critique in the next breath, when he claims that the distance between science and experience 'has its

---

23   Cf. Louis Althusser's effort in his 'Three Notes on the Theory of Discoures' (HC, 33–84),which likewise sought to develop a sequence of 'regional theories'. The crucial difference between Foucault and Althusser is that the latter still conceived of his theory of regional theories as, precisely, a 'general theory of discourse'. It is this assumption of the terms of 'general theory' that Foucault struggles to avoid; whether this avoidance is scrupulous or not is precisely what is at issue. For an alternative view, which suggests it was precisely Foucault's effort to develop a general theory of 'rules' in *The Archaeology of Knowledge* that accounts for this work's status as a misguided hiatus between the descriptive enterprises of his early and later periods, see Ian Hunter, 'From Discourse to *Dispositif*: Foucault and the Study of Literature', *Meridian* 10:2 (1991), 36–53.

principle in the morphology of the referential' (331/39tm). The principle that accounts for the distance between science and experience – which Foucault takes to be a historical fact as much as a theoretical norm – is 'the morphology of the referential', i.e. the changing form of that to which science refers. But lest Foucault fall into the philosophical abyss opened here, he reasserts the rights of 'knowledge' to determine the space in which the two terms – science and experience – are separate and relate to one another.

Nevertheless, this reference to 'the morphology of the referential' is a remarkable concession to empiricism, however tacit, and it is one that the Cercle pounces upon in their 'New Questions'. They open with pressure on the circularity of Foucault's method. 'At the fundamental level he distinguishes as "the referential", the set of statements to be studied has no other unity than that of the very law that regulates the dispersion of the "different objects or referents" that this set "puts in play", which means: the law defines what defines it' (CpA 9.3:41).[24] In his response's opening invocation of discontinuity as at once 'the object and instrument' of historical research, the Cercle detected a collapse into the hermeneutic circle. They explicate the consequences in their next question, which concerns Foucault's concept of the 'rule of formation'. Foucault insists that 'the system of a set of statements must be capable of forming solely the statements that are actually produced, and no others in addition, or in their stead' (CpA 9.3:42). But they seize on the equivocation between Foucault's transcendental appeal to 'rules' and his apparently modest commitment to historical description. For why is the 'rule of formation', once identified, exhausted by its historical actuality? If it truly is a 'rule of formation', why indeed can it not be deployed elsewhere? They cite Martial Gueroult's magisterial reconstruction of Cartesianism and its capacity to respond in a Cartesian way to questions that Descartes did not, and historically could not, encounter.[25] In other words, if the 'rule of formation' does not retain some sort of unity or coherence that might be transmissible beyond its concrete instantiation, then it is difficult to grasp what qualifies it as a 'rule'.

The Cercle's pressure on Foucault's project corrodes its unifying principles, and the heralding of dispersal throughout *The Archaeology of Knowledge* is the result. As if anticipating this manoeuvre, and developing their critique of the equivocal nature of the statement as at once element and event, they turn in conclusion to Foucault's insistence on the lack of coherence within historical discourses, i.e. their manifestly disparate character, which serves as Foucault's methodological point of departure:

---

24   Cf. Dreyfus and Rabinow on the results of *The Archaeology of Knowledge*: 'the strange notion of regularities which regulate themselves' (84).

25   Martial Gueroult, *Descartes' Philosophy Interpreted According to the Order of Reasons*, 2 vols. [1953], trans. Roger Ariew (Minneapolis: University of Minnesota Press, 1984/1985).

Taking this one step further, would the abandonment of the principle of coherence entail as a consequence the genuine independence of the 'non-discursive event'? And do we not have to suppose that each time an event is taken up again as a statement and serves as an element in the set of knowledge, there is an irreducible remainder that limits the claims of a 'pure description of the facts of discourse', and which necessarily implies an articulation of knowledge upon that which it cannot integrate? (CpA 9.3:44).

Here the Cercle points the way toward a methodological exit, latent within Foucault's own arguments, from a narrow focus on discourse toward a more capacious set of historical *dispositifs*. The prophetic quality of these questions has already been noted, which makes the Cercle's final question all the more striking: 'After the "Response to the Cercle d'Épistémologie", the question arises: where does Foucault stand now, in relation to Freud, and to Nietzsche?'

II THE LIMITS OF FORM

Foucault's work throughout the 1970s will provide the answer to this last question. Taking leave of the problematic of the historical 'unconscious', which provided some of the rhetorical underpinning to *The Order of Things*, Foucault will develop a method of genealogy inspired by Nietzsche in his historical investigations of power and its apparatuses. As noted, this turn is already manifest in Foucault's opening lesson to the Collège de France, where the introduction of the concept of 'the will to truth' indicates the development of a voluntarist epistemology indebted more to Nietzschean irony than the anemic structuralism of discourse analysis. *The Archaeology of Knowledge* nevertheless remains a central document in Foucault's oeuvre, not simply as an instrumental step in Foucault's turn to genealogical description, but rather as a site wherein the Cercle's critiques of Foucault's project gain their deepest traction. In his effort to answer their charges he winds up ultimately affirming their validity and in particular that of the inchoate theory of subjectivity underpinning them. Béatrice Han is correct to note that Foucault's turn to the subject in his final works is in many respects a return to the concerns of this earlier period, a kind of resumption of thinking through the post-Kantian problematic.[26] But the return is neither arbitrary nor wholly internal to Foucault's intellectual development. Rather, it results from a dialogic exchange in which the limitations of Foucault's method were presented to him alongside avenues for their overcoming. In his effort to articulate an alternative to the univocal concept of form promulgated by the

---

26   In addition to Han, *Foucault's Critical Project*, see her essay 'The Analytic of Finitude and the History of Subjectivity', trans. Edward Pile in *The Cambridge Companion to Foucault*, 2nd edition, ed. Gary Gutting (Cambridge: Cambridge University Press, 2005), 176–209.

editors of the *Cahiers* based in a kind of formal pluralism, Foucault effectively demonstrates that that very pluralism presupposes a concept of split subjectivity that makes a cognitive assessment of the relation among forms, not to mention their historical transformation, possible.

To show that this is the case requires us to read *The Archaeology of Knowledge* against the grain in certain respects, but the aim remains to gain a better understanding of how precisely the hermeneutics of the subject provides a belated salve to the hermeneutic circle that aggravates this earlier effort. Indeed, the Cercle's focus on the 'rule of formation' made clear that Foucault's own claims presupposed a unifying principle that belied the disparity of his data, and this despite Foucault's own warnings against the illusion of privileging a singular determinate form. But if Foucault's claims on this score are unsatisfactory in the 'Response', in his book they are even more so.

The problem is most acute in Foucault's attempt to clarify his concept of 'discursive formations' in the chapter of that name. Distancing himself from structuralist synchronism, he writes:

> A discursive formation, then, does not play the role of a figure that arrests time and freezes it for decades or centuries; it determines a regularity proper to temporal processes; it presents the principle of articulation between a series of discursive events and other series of events, transformations, mutations, and processes. It is not a temporal form, but a schema of correspondence between several temporal series (74).

The vicissitudes of grammar compromise Foucault's effort to avoid singular form in favour of a plurality of formations. 'Form' may not be singular, but unfortunately all of its alternatives are: *a* regularity, *the* principle of articulation, and most striking, 'not a temporal form, but a schema of correspondence'. Proffering a schema in place of a form does not solve the problem. But Foucault persists several paragraphs later in his critique of all variants of *Lebensphilosophie*: 'Behind the completed system, what is discovered by the analysis of formations is not the bubbling source of life itself, life in an as yet uncaptured state; it as an immense density of systematicities, a tight group of multiple relations' (76). Here regularity meets with density, and the principle and the schema are joined by the group.

Although Foucault leaves his more pointed barbs about formalizing illusions out of *The Archaeology of Knowledge*, there is at least one instance where he takes direct aim at the Lacanian enterprise as it was expressed in the *Cahiers*. Moving away from the problematic of the 'historical unconscious', Foucault maintains that in the description of statements one avoids recourse to 'the secret presence of the unsaid' (110). The liability of invoking such a secret presence is that it tends toward making the 'unsaid' the same 'unsaid' in virtually all occasions. By contrast, the ostensibly 'hidden elements' of a discourse depend on 'the enunciative modality' itself. Effectively cataloguing articles from the

Cahiers, Foucault insists: 'we know that the "unsaid", or the "suppressed", is not the same – either in its structure or in its effect – in the case of a mathematical statement, a statement in economics, an autobiography or an account of the dream' (110). Foucault concedes that there may indeed be a *lack* that accompanies each of these modalities. 'But one should not confuse, in its status or in its effect, the lack that is characteristic of an enunciative regularity and the meanings concealed in what is formulated within it' (110).

In effect, Foucault renders lack banal and thereby saps it of its talismanic properties. There is a lack accompanying each discursive modality; indeed, lack plays 'a role in the determination of its very existence'. But using lack to criticize appeals to deeper meaning comes to naught when that lack itself is imbued with a surfeit of meaning. Lack may be a technical concept in Miller's logic of the signifier, but it is also an existential concept laden with pathos. Beyond this pathos, and perhaps despite it, lack plays a crucial role in the concept of structural causality underpinning the *Cahiers pour l'Analyse*. For Lacan, the problematic of the 'cause' is only invoked in situations in which something does not work or function smoothly (S11, 17–28). Ultimately, for Lacan, lack and cause are not simply equivocal; they are almost equivalent. Miller's 'Action of the Structure' argued for lack's causal role in producing this 'action'. Like the missing piece that causes the Jenga tower to collapse, it is the lack within a structure that sets it in motion. But just as Foucault questions the appeal to singular lack that would explain the 'action' of any given 'structure', he is also committed to avoiding recourse to any singular explanatory principle that explains the move from one episteme or discursive formation to another. Foucault expressed his antipathy to the 'break' in his 'Response', which did not stop the Cercle from continuing to exert pressure on the knotted circularities of his method. But here the skein becomes exceptionally tight:

> [Discourse] is made up of a limited number of statements for which a group of conditions of existence can be defined. Discourse in this sense is not an ideal, timeless form that also possesses a history; the problem is not therefore to ask oneself how and why it was able to emerge and become embodied at this point in time; it is, from beginning to end, historical . . . (117).

The paradox of Foucault's effort to avoid a single formal principle of explanation is captured in that final phrase: 'it is, from beginning to end, historical'. To paraphrase: it is absolutely historical. In refusing to appeal to a transcendental invariant – whatever form it might take – Foucault nevertheless makes history itself an invariant, a fount of permanent change that, as opposed to language for example, serves as discourse's most fundamental condition. Typically, the appeal to history is made to ensure the possibility of change, indeed the manifest reality of change. But though Foucault's invocation of the historical in such terms sanctions a multitude of empirical descriptions, his method lacks conceptual traction insofar as it fails to articulate how conceptual transformations take place in something that is 'from beginning to end, historical'.

It is in his chapter on the 'historical *a priori*' that Foucault takes tentative steps toward the resolution of this problem. Hammering the point, he insists again that statements are dispersed, that they constitute a 'non-coherence, in their overlapping and mutual replacement, in their simultaneity, which is not unifiable, and in their succession, which is not deductible' (127). But Foucault then establishes a remarkable contrast: 'in short, [this *a priori*] has to take account of the fact that discourse has not only a meaning or a truth, but a history, and a specific history that does not refer it back to the laws of an alien development'. Foucault shared with the *Cahiers* the critique of phenomenological efforts to find 'meaning' in history. Here, however, he separates history not simply from meaning, but from truth as well. The history of a discourse and the truth of a discourse are distinct questions and as such they require different kinds of responses. Althusser and Lacan, each in his own way, had maintained that the revelation of truth was the goal of their discursive practice, not truth in a theological sense, to be sure, but rather one tied to method and specifically a method of manifestation. Althusserian science would allow 'true ideas' to be formulated about the class struggle as a historical phenomenon; Lacanian psychoanalysis would broker a traversal of the fantasy that would reveal – however fleetingly – the truth of lack, or the lack as truth, of subjectivity. By contrast, especially with Althusser, Foucault's history of various sciences was never an exercise in debunking. It might not even be going too far to say that Foucault's method displayed a manifest indifference to the truth of discourses; it was precisely this nonchalance that accounted for its scandal. But at the end of the day, this position has a potentially striking ethical payoff, one argued for in the chapter on the historical 'a priori'. For 'the *a priori* of positivities is not only the system of a temporal dispersion' – we are told for the umpteenth time – 'it is itself a transformable group' (127).

And yet, as many commentators have noted, nowhere in *The Archaeology of Knowledge* is it ever explained how the transformation of this group might take place.[27] What would be its agent? Its mechanisms? Foucault's writings up to this point had made it clear that change was possible, even a historical necessity. Indeed, for all its putative synchrony and exquisite tableaux, *The Order of Things* is arguably a book *about* moments of transformation, when one episteme collapses via the formation of a new one. But Foucault had always been

---

27   In addition to Dreyfus and Rabinow, *Michel Foucault*, and Han, *Foucault's Critical Project*, see Peter Dews 'Foucault and the French Tradition of Historical Epistemology' in Idem., *The Limits of Disenchantment: Essays on Contemporary European Philosophy* (London: Verso, 1995), 39–58. For Gary Gutting, this aspect of AK is an asset, given that archaeology is precisely 'a method of concrete historical analysis, not of general social scientific or philosophical theorizing' (Gutting, *Michel Foucault's Archaeology of Scientific Reason*, 287).

reluctant to do more than describe these transformations; it would seem as if his rejection of dialectics and teleology limited him to the recounting of contingent events and a catalogue of their results. It is altogether striking, then, to find Foucault returning to this notion of the 'transformable' in the original preface to volume two of *The History of Sexuality*,[28] a book which, along with its sequel, stands out as the most historically restricted and purely descriptive of all Foucault's writings. In this text, Foucault enumerates the principles on which his work has been heretofore based. He names the first 'the irreducibility of thought', the notion that thought itself is a practice with its own forms and ways of being; the second principle claims that 'this thought has a historicity that is proper to it'. Foucault correlates these two principles with the two main prior phases of his writings up to that point, with the archaeological period under the heading of the first, and the genealogical under the second.

Finally, however, Foucault describes the third principle or 'axis' as that which constitutes 'any matrix of experience: the modality of relation to the self'. But in the preceding pages, he described it somewhat differently:

> There is a third and final principle implied by this enterprise: an awareness that criticism – understood as an analysis of the historical conditions which bear on the creation of links to truth, to rules, and to the self – does not mark out impassable boundaries or describe closed systems; *it brings to light transformable singularities*. These transformations could not take place except by means of a working of thought upon itself; that is the principle of the history of thought as critical activity.[29]

The Archaeology of Knowledge treated the 'transformable group' as a kind of limit concept of the historical *a priori*, one that could be registered and recorded, but whose inner workings could not be adequately articulated. To do so would have required too much of a concession to the intercalated thematics of structural causality and sutured subjectivity being developed in the *Cahiers*. In his final writings, however, Foucault returns to the same point, but now provides its mechanism. The critical task of a history of thought, i.e. Foucault's own endeavour, is to bring transformable singularities to light. But the very method by which that 'bringing to light' is achieved is based upon a 'modality of relation to the self'. In *The Hermeneutics of the Subject* the transformable singularity goes by the name of the 'event in thought', and as Arnold Davidson remarks, 'when

---

28   The 'Preface to *The History of Sexuality, Volume II*' contained in Rabinow, *The Foucault Reader*, 333–339 is not the same document that serves as the Introduction to *The Use of Pleasure*. The editorial notes to *Dits et écrits*, volume 4, state that the text used in the Rabinow volume was the 'first version' of the introduction, which Foucault abandoned, deciding to use instead an article titled 'Usage de plaisirs et techniques de soi', *Le Débat* 27 (November 1983), 46–72, as a general introduction for all the remaining books of the series (*DE*, vol. 4, 578, 539).

29   'Preface to *The History of Sexuality, Volume II*', 335–336, emphasis added.

Foucault speaks of the idea of the care of the self as an "event in thought", we cannot help but hear in these words an invocation of some of the most original dimensions of his own philosophical practice.'[30]

To demarcate the forms that constitute one's selfhood as transformable requires an antecedent formal thinking of the 'self' as a site of non-identity in which two terms relate, for transformation presupposes relation. But to think the self in this way – which is the fundament of Foucault's 'philosophical prac-tice' at this point – in order to provide a historical assessment of the care of the self is in itself already an exercise in that care.[31] Foucault has taken the nominal demerit of his project revealed to him by the Cercle d'Épistémologie – in a word its circularity – and made of it his method's virtue. But in accepting this circu-larity and thinking through its implications, Foucault has effectively ceded the basis of the *Cahiers* critique. He was unambiguous on this point in one of his final interviews. Asked for clarification concerning the substantial quality of the subject, Foucault replied that the subject 'is not a substance: it is a form and this form is not above all or always identical to itself'.[32]

III FOUCAULT AND LACAN

This minimal conception of the subject as a non-self-identical form was one of the guiding threads of the *Cahiers* enterprise. It was also, not coincidentally, one of the main themes of Lacan's teaching in his first years at the ENS in the seminars that provided much of the inspiration for the Cercle d'Épistémologie. Though the editors of the *Cahiers* would themselves disperse in the wake of May 68, Lacan in a sense continued the critique of Foucauldian disparity on their behalf. In the opening lesson of his seventeenth seminar in November 1969, Lacan makes explicit reference to Foucault's position. At issue is the relation of the signifier of the subject – S_1 – to the extant signifiers among which it intervenes, nominated S_2:

> I am talking about those signifiers that are already there, whereas at the point of
> origin at which we place ourselves in order to establish what discourse is about,

---

30   Foucault, *The Hermeneutics of the Subject*, xx–xxi.

31   See the closing lines of 'Preface to *The History of Sexuality*, volume, II': 'I also reminded myself that it would probably not be worth the trouble of making books if they failed to teach the author something he hadn't known before, if they didn't lead to unforeseen places, and if they didn't disperse one toward a strange and new relation with himself. The pain and pleasure of the book is to be an expe-rience' (339). In the text that ultimately served as the 'Introduction' to *The Use of Pleasure*, Foucault is more acerbic on this point: 'As for those for whom to work hard, to begin and begin again, to attempt and be mistaken, to go back and rework everything from top to bottom, and still find reason to hesitate from one step to the next – as to those, in short, for whom to work in the midst of uncertainty and apprehension is tantamount to failure, all I can say is that clearly we are not from the same planet' (7).

32   Foucault, 'The Ethic of Care for the Self as a Practice of Freedom' (Interview, 20 January 1984) in *The Final Foucault*, ed. James Bernauer and David Rasmussen (Cambridge: MIT Press, 1991), 10.

discourse thought as the status of the statement [*l'énoncé*], S_1 is the one to be seen as intervening. It intervenes in a signifying battery that we have no right, ever, to take as dispersed, as not already forming a network of what is called knowledge [*savoir*] (S17, 13).

Here Lacan ventures a direct rebuttal of *The Archaeology of Knowledge*, published several months earlier. The battery of signifiers in which a subject intervenes – in which a subject necessarily intervenes, simply by virtue of being a subject of language – can never be taken as dispersed. Rather, it is always already formed, or structured. Lacan's riposte to Foucault need not be read in an ontological register, or even a psychoanalytic one. Most basically, it is a methodological point about how to conceive of the subject in its linguistic being, or, to use Foucault's language, as an instance of practice, discursive or otherwise, in relation to the myriad other instances of linguistic being or practice it confronts.

This disagreement is the ironic sign of how close Lacan and Foucault are on this issue. For despite his multiple hats as psychoanalyst, pedagogue, and guru, at root Lacan was himself a thinker of discursive practice, i.e. of the question of how concepts and descriptions result in material effects. In his first ENS seminar he asked: 'What is a praxis? [...] It is the broadest term to designate a concerted human action, whatever it may be, which places man in a position to treat the real by the symbolic' (S11, 6). But Lacan's point, *pace* the Foucault of *The Archaeology of Knowledge*, is that this 'real' is always laden with the symbolic forms that have already been used to 'treat' it. And to take these symbolic forms as purely disparate, lacking all structure, is to misrecognize the forms in which one is embedded and their constitutive relation to that embedded 'self'.

Access, be it cognitive or practical, to this relational form, presupposes a dualism within the subject itself. In his first seminar at the ENS, Lacan delivered his clearest exposition of how the subject is constitutively split, between a subject of enunciation – the subject who says 'I' – and the subject of the statement, the 'I' that is said and carried forward in discourse. This abstract formulation then receives exemplary content in Lacan's discussion of Descartes in 'Science and Truth' (CpA 1.1), the inaugural article of the *Cahiers*. Here Lacan effectively translates the 'subject of the enunciation' into the Cartesian 'I think' and the 'subject of the statement' into the 'I am'. Around this same time, however, Lacan published a commemorative piece on Merleau-Ponty in which he came dangerously close, in the Cercle d'Épistémologie's view, to reconciling these Cartesian 'subjects' in a foundational unity. In his response to their concerns published in volume three of the *Cahiers*, Lacan is unequivocal:

At a crucial point of the Cartesian *askesis*, precisely the one I am invoking here, consciousness and the subject coincide. It is holding that privileged moment as exhaustive of the subject which is misleading [...].

It is, on the contrary, at that moment of coincidence itself, insofar as it is grasped by reflection, that I intend to mark the site through which psychoanalytic experience makes its entrance. At simply being sustained within time, the subject of 'I think' reveals what it is: the being of a fall. I am that which thinks: 'Therefore I am', as I have commented on elsewhere, noting that the 'therefore', the causal stroke, divides inaugurally the 'I am' of existence from the 'I am' of meaning.[33]

Two things are particularly striking about this passage. Most obvious is the reference to *askesis*, a concept that will become central to Foucault's lessons on the self in the 1980s. Of more fundamental importance, however, in light of Foucault's remark in 1984 that a subject is a form that 'is not *above all* or *always* identical to itself', is Lacan's claim that the 'privileged moment' of the coincidence – i.e., the fleeting identity – of the 'I think' and 'I am' is not 'exhaustive of the subject'. What Lacan and Foucault both recognize is that, were the subject to be identical to itself at all times, the possibility of change and transformation would be foreclosed. The obverse is then true by implication; the subject's capacity to be transformed relies upon the rift within it that makes self-relation possible. The error or tragedy of a phenomenological or transcendental conception that privileges instances of self-identity is that it sanctions the permanence of a given state of affairs (or 'battery of signifiers') and consequently renders opaque the 'transformable singularities' that structure it. Christian Jambet points us toward the proximity of Lacan and Foucault's critical positions on this score when he makes a theoretical point, a propos of spiritual exercises, that expresses equally the view of both authors: 'The matter and the form of the experience intersect at the point where a subject exists; yet this subject can only be the 'blind spot' of the forms of knowledge [*savoirs*] which validate it.'[34] The 'blind spot', the 'point', the rift – all of these are metaphors for the same paradox of self-relation that is constitutive of subjectivity; they simultaneously highlight and obscure the possibility of subjective transformation. In this regard, it is not coincidental that Lacan argues that the process whereby the subject emerges is itself best grasped as a 'metaphor', one that results in the 'assumption' of one's place in a signifying chain. This process of 'assumption', which Lacan first articulated in the late 1950s, makes for an uncanny conceptual fit with the figure of a 'summoning' toward one's subjectivity that was Foucault's concern in the 1980s.[35]

---

33   CpA 3.1:6. See as well Lacan's remark in Seminar II: 'If this *I* is in fact presented to us as a kind of immediate given in the act of reflection by which consciousness grasps itself as transparent to itself, for all that, nothing indicates that the whole of this reality – and it is granting quite a bit already to say that we come to a judgment of existence – would be exhausted by this' (S2, 6).

34   Christian Jambet, 'The Constitution of the Subject and Spiritual Practice: Observations on *L'Histoire de la sexualité*' in *Michel Foucault: Philosopher*, ed. François Ewald, trans. Timothy J. Armstrong (London: Routledge, 1992), 242.

35   The key text wherein Lacan develops this argument is 'The Instance of the Letter in the Unconscious, or Reason since Freud' (E, 493–528/412–39). For more on 'metaphor' see 'Metaphor/

The second paragraph of Lacan's response is also pertinent because it explicitly articulates the disjuncture internal to the subject in terms of causality, the 'causal stroke'. In their 'inaugural' division from one another, the subject of existence and the subject of meaning are irreducible to one another, which means that the subject of existence, despite its continuous 'fall' can, via the 'praxis' that Lacan calls for, enact transformations in the subject of meaning upon which it 'works'. Realizing the truth of this 'fall' – the insubstantiality of the subject in its nominal interiority – was for Lacan the condition for genuine work on the subject of meaning. Foucault, for his part, recognized this in full clarity, giving Lacan pride of place in his opening lesson of *The Hermeneutics of the Subject*:

> Lacan tried to pose what historically is the specifically spiritual question: that of the price the subject must pay for saying the truth, and of the effect on the subject of the fact that he has said, that he can and has said the truth about himself. By restoring this question I think Lacan actually reintroduced into psychoanalysis the oldest tradition, the oldest questioning, and the oldest disquiet of the *epimeleia heautou*, which is the most general form of spirituality.[36]

In the next breath, Foucault goes on to express his misgivings over the fact that psychoanalysis remains mired in a problematic which conceives of the subject's relation to truth as a matter of knowledge rather than practice, work, or indeed 'care'. But if a cursory glance at Lacan's seminars shows that knowledge and practice are in no way opposed, it is also clear that Foucault considers Lacan's thought to be irreducible to the historical reality of psychoanalysis as an institution. In a later session, an auditor presses Foucault on the proximity of his claims to Lacan's. He responds that the only two contemporaries who have posed the question of the subject's relation to truth are Heidegger and Lacan, and that he considers himself more indebted to the former than the latter. Foucault allows, however, that the extent to which elements of his approach

---

Metonymy' on the *Concept and Form* website, http://cahiers.kingston.ac.uk/concepts/metaphor-and-metonymy.html. In light of this complementarity between 'summoning' and 'assumption', see Jacques-Alain Miller's remark that the subject Foucault was concerned with in the 1980s had not been Lacan's concern since 1957, in Miller, 'Michel Foucault and Psychoanalysis' in *Michel Foucault: Philosopher*, 62. This schema also bears obvious resonances with Althusser's concept of 'interpellation', as developed in Althusser 'Ideology and Ideological State Apparatuses: Notes toward an Investigation' [1970], trans. Ben Brewster, in LP.

36   Foucault, *The Hermeneutics of the Subject*, 30. Lacan's privileged place in this lesson is obscured by a historical contingency. At the outset, Foucault states that for each two-hour meeting of the course he will spend the first hour on general conceptual themes and focus on a text in the second. But Foucault begins the 'second hour' of the first course meeting by saying that he had gone over time in the first, so that he needed to say a few more words before turning to the texts. The last item on his agenda before he turns to the *Alcibiades* is this set of remarks about Lacan.

come from Lacan is not for him to say.[37]

Foucault's distancing from Lacan in the same course in which he privileges him lends credence to Badiou's judgment concerning the vestiges of Foucault's conformism on this score. But the point of the preceding discussion has not been to demonstrate that Foucault and Lacan ultimately say the same thing, nor that they have the exact same conception of subjectivity and its place in the domain called 'history'. Indeed, Jacques-Alain Miller would maintain in 1988 that, at best, Foucault's explication of the subject ran parallel to Lacan's, in its opening from sexuality onto the problematics of subjectivity and selfhood *tout court*. In Miller's view, Foucault's late efforts to take leave of the thematic of 'desire' for that of 'pleasure' betrayed a utopian longing to escape the ubiquitous castration of the modern world.[38] Miller, as the executor of Lacan's pedagogical estate, obviously has a vested interest in affirming its superlative value against alternative models. But for our purposes it is the proximity of the alternatives that is of marked historical interest.

For our primary goal has been to make clear the role which a certain Lacanian problematic, mediated by the Cercle d'Épistémologie, played in illuminating certain limitations of Foucault's method and the paths by which they might be circumvented. Disparities no doubt persist. And it is ironic that the most crucial disparity between them is perhaps best expressed in philosophical terms. In the last instance, the conception of the subject that one finds in the *Cahiers pour l'Analyse* and in Lacan's teaching of the period is one wherein the subject's advent can be coded as an instance in which contingency becomes necessity. By contrast, Foucault's historical method was committed to ensuring that contingency always remains contingency, that we never mistakenly take as necessary that which we can demonstrate to be historically contingent. For Lacan, then, the ego's imaginary experience of subjectivity is a necessary illusion; for Foucault, by contrast, it is at best an illusory necessity. But perhaps in the end, these countervailing metaphysical encodings of the subject matter much less than the minimal, and ultimately practical agreement that subtends them, and that also makes for one of the most striking legacies of the *Cahiers pour l'Analyse*: that there are subjects, and that they are the privileged sites where the work of transformation begins and eventually takes place.

---

37   Ibid., 188–189.
38   Miller, 'Michel Foucault and Psychoanalysis', op. cit., 63. For a demonstration of just how opposed to the psychoanalytic concept of 'desire' Foucault was, see Wendy Grace 'Faux Amis: Foucault and Deleuze on Sexuality and Desire', *Critical Inquiry* 36 (Autumn 2009), 52–75.

CHAPTER FIVE

Tracy McNulty
Desuturing Desire: The Work of the Letter in the Miller–Leclaire Debate

One of the most influential assessments to date of the *Cahiers pour l'Analyse* is that of founding co-editor Jean-Claude Milner, who in his 1995 book *L'Œeuvre claire* associates the *Cahiers* with what he calls the 'first classicism' of Jacques Lacan. According to Milner, this period of Lacan's work culminates in the publication of the *Écrits* in 1966.[1] Lacan's first classicism constitutes the progressive and nearly systematic development of the programme articulated in his Rome Discourse of 1953,[2] where the new science of structuralist linguistics is reinterpreted to prove that structuralist analysis is legitimate for objects other than language, and notably for the subject of psychoanalysis, who is thereby equated with the subject of science (102, 111). The focus here is on the signifying chain as the 'most minimal instance of structure' (102), expressed in the dictum that 'the signifier is what represents a subject for another signifier' (105).

Although Lacan neither embraced nor disavowed the *Cahiers* explicitly, Milner sees its ultrastructuralist project as the distillation of the important properties of this period (111), and therefore also of the impasses that led to its eventual displacement. An especially important limitation of the *Cahiers* and of the 'first classicism' in general, he argues, is the lack of any rigorous distinction between the signifier and the letter. While the two notions are enunciated separately, they are also used almost interchangeably (119). The subsequent elaboration of the letter minimizes the significance of the signifier, and of structure more generally inasmuch as the theory of the signifier is its foundation.

Beginning around 1970, Milner maintains, the first classicism is displaced by a new phase in Lacan's work, defined by its concern with the literality of mathematics, with mathematical formalization *à la lettre*. The disappearance of structuralism in 1968 means that what appeared to be the emergence of a new science was in fact a false emergence; now a single foundation remains, literalization (121). Following Bourbaki, Lacan equates it with mathematization: 'Mathematical formalization is our goal, our ideal. Why? Because it alone is

---

1   Jean-Claude Milner, *L'Œuvre claire: Lacan, la science, la philosophie* (Paris: Seuil, 1995), 111. Subsequent citations will be given in the main text.

2   Jacques Lacan, 'The Function and Field of Speech and Language in Psychoanalysis' in E, 237–322/197–268.

matheme, that is, capable of transmitting itself integrally' (S20, 108).[3] In this 'second classicism' it is the knot (and specifically the Borromean knot) that comes to be emblematic of the function of the letter, displacing the theory of the signifier that dominated in the first. This is because, in Lacan's words:

> The nature of mathematical language, once it is sufficiently isolated in terms of its requirements of pure demonstration, is such that [. . .] if one of the letters doesn't stand up, all the others, due to their arrangement, not only constitute nothing of any validity but disperse. It is in that respect that the Borromean knot is the best metaphor of the fact that we proceed only on the basis of the One (S20, 128).

The Borromean knot is formed of three interconnected rings; if any one is severed, all are set free. It articulates the logical interdependence of the real, the symbolic, and the imaginary, especially insofar as these together express three dimensions of the fantasy. For Milner, it follows that the Borromean knot 'opens, in the proper sense of the term, the royal road of psychoanalysis in its relation to modern science,' giving its full force and confirmation to the matheme. The result is that the theory of structure now appears to be relevant only for a consideration of the symbolic, and is absorbed into the regional theory of the 'S' ring of the Borromean knot (146). Because the signifying chain is the 'most minimal instance of structure' (102), the corollary is that the chain is itself local to the problematic of 'structure', and in turn of the symbolic. More broadly, then, Lacan's second classicism represents a displacement of the *chain* by the *knot* as the core articulation of the subject of psychoanalysis.[4]

For Milner, therefore, the achievements of the second classicism mean that 'the *Cahiers pour l'Analyse* is no longer admissible' (145). The entire project retroactively appears as nothing more than an archaeological stratum in the development and dissemination of a particular phase of Lacan's thought with no enduring theoretical significance for what follows.

To appreciate this assessment, we have to understand what Milner means when he advances that the theory of 'structure' – and the 'chain' that articulates it – is relevant only for a consideration of the symbolic. This claim effectively collapses 'structure' with the problematic of repression, and more specifically with the sense Lacan gives to the Freudian concept of 'primal repression' (*Urverdrängung*): the subject's alienation in language by the signifier of identification or 'unary trait' that simultaneously represents and represses it. His argument supposes a particular reading of Lacan's 1960 paper 'The Subversion of the

---

3   Cited by Milner, *L'Œuvre claire*, 123.
4   In characterizing the knot as the 'royal road of psychoanalysis', Milner is no doubt referring to Freud's famous description of the dream as the 'royal road to the unconscious'. His argument therefore makes an implicit equation between the signifying chain and the dreamwork, and implies that both are superseded by the knot.

Subject and the Dialectic of Desire in the Freudian Unconscious', which for Milner emblematizes the treatment of the subject under the first classicism. There Lacan writes that the unary trait 'alienates this subject in the first identification that forms the ego-ideal' by 'filling in the invisible mark the subject receives from the signifier' (E, 808/684). It follows that 'the fantasy is really the "stuff" of the *I* that is primally repressed, because it can be indicated only in the fading of enunciation' (E, 816/691). In collapsing the theory of the signifier with the problematic of primal repression, Milner's gloss makes the signifier synonymous with the unary trait.

This is only one dimension of the signifier, however. Its other dimension is precisely the letter, or what Lacan calls the 'invisible mark the subject receives from the signifier'. Willy Apollon defines the letter as 'the writing of the subject's division, since its inscription supports the first signifier of subjective identification by articulating as a body that part of the organism whose jouissance must make way for the signifier of the Other.'[5] In Lacan's terms, it marks the alternation between 'what never ceases *not* to be inscribed' (the jouissance lost to the speaking being) and 'what never ceases *to* be inscribed' in its place, the insistent return of a deadly jouissance around this failure.

While Milner is right that many of the psychoanalytic contributions to the *Cahiers* do not take up the problem of the letter, his own analysis approaches the letter primarily in terms of formalization and transmission, and as a result fails to address the clinical stakes of the letter for Lacan and its importance for the clinic of the symptom. This clinical dimension, which prevents the letter from being reduced to a signifier, also implies a more complex understanding of the signifier itself. Milner's assessment of the 'first classicism' as concerned primarily with the 'S' ring is inadequate to account for the clinical dimension of psychoanalysis, where it is impossible to work with the signifier apart from the real (jouissance) and the imaginary (the ideal ego). The three are always and inevitably linked, and the question is how. In failing to consider the inseparability of these registers as an essential feature of the analytic experience, Milner offers an impoverished account of the symbolic that fails to do justice even to the earliest and most structuralist teachings of Lacan. It supposes a static or merely descriptive understanding of the symbolic (as the fact of the subject's rejection from language) that precludes any consideration of the signifying chain as a *construction* leading to the traversal of the fantasy. There is thus no evaluation of what Jacques-Alain Miller, in the ninth issue of the *Cahiers*, describes as the 'action of the structure' (CpA 9.6), its effectivity or transformative potential.

More broadly, therefore, Milner's argument is limited by its failure to consider the clinical context in which the theory of the signifier (and the knot)

---

5   Willy Apollon, 'Psychanalyse et littérature: Passe et impasse,' *L'Universel, perspectives psychanalytiques* (Québec: GIFRIC, 1997), 263.

is elaborated. To some extent this limitation also applies to the *Cahiers* more generally. What is often missing, both in Milner's assessment and many contributions to the journal, is a fuller consideration of the transference, and more broadly of the logic and temporality of the analytic experience. In this respect, both lag well behind Lacan's work of the same period. But this temporal disjuncture is pertinent to any assessment of the historical and theoretical relation between the *Cahiers* and Lacan's teaching. For while Lacan's interest in 'literalization' does come to displace the paradigm of structuralist linguistics, it does not follow that he opposes literalization or the letter to the problematic of the chain. Instead, literalization goes to the heart of the chain's structure and function. Lacan's subsequent interest in the knot as a 'monstration'[6] certainly represents a period of intense exploration of the possibilities of mathematical formalization, which displaces the linguistic paradigm of the 1950s and 1960s. The emphasis now is on construction, or the possibility of a non-intuitive or non-imaginary approach to the subject of the unconscious. This interest in monstration, however, in no way displaces the importance of the signifying chain as the site of elaboration of the knowledge of the unconscious. To the contrary, it raises the question of what, precisely, *is* monstrated by the signifying chain: not in the 'symbolizations' it proffers, but in the 'invisible mark' to which it leads.

Indeed, Lacan's interest in the problem of the knot – and the Borromean knot in particular – first emerges as a way of thinking about the operation of the signifying chain under transference. While Milner tends to identify the problematic of the knot with the seminars and essays dating from 1972 and later, Lacan's first discussions of the Borromean knot date back to 1954, and it is a frequent motif in his seminars of the 1950s and 1960s. Throughout this period, the knot is invariably linked to the problem of the transference. In 1956 Lacan first uses 'knot' to describe the navel of the dream, the unrepresentable kernel to which the dreamwork leads (S3, 260); in 1957, he describes the structure of the signifying chain as a chain of rings (S5, 30–31). The interest in the knot does not displace the signifying chain, therefore, but represents a further elaboration of its stakes and function. In the years immediately preceding the publication of the *Cahiers*, Lacan identifies the Borromean knot with the formations of the unconscious, and ultimately with the logic of the transference itself (S11, 129–131).

In my view, therefore, Lacan's growing investment in the knot marks a terminological rather than a conceptual shift. The introduction of the neologism *chaînoeud* ('linknot') in 1976 makes clear that the knot does not displace the chain in Lacan's theory, but that the two are understood as structurally

---

6   Lacan's first discussion of the knot as a 'monstration' of the real dates from 1975 (Seminar XXII, Session of March 11, 1975), but the notion of 'monstration' is arguably implicit in Seminar XX (1972–73).

homologous.[7] Technically speaking, of course, the so-called Borromean 'knot' is itself a chain: it articulates several different threads or links, while a knot is formed by a single thread. The knot is thus nothing more than an elaboration of the chain's structure and function: one that points to the particularity of the signifying chain and the impossibility of reducing it to a logic of signification or meaning, or even for that matter to language. In Lacan's words, the Borromean knot 'can serve us by representing a metaphor that is so often used to express what distinguishes the use of language – the chain metaphor' (S20, 127). That the signifying chain is a knot (and the knot a chain) means that its elements are not linked by logical subordination, sense, or latent meaning, and that it cannot be equated with any number of terms or concepts potentially invited by chain as 'metaphor', for example with a series, concatenation, or progression.

While there's no denying that many of the contributions to the *Cahiers* privilege what Milner calls the 'symbolic register' (or more accurately the mechanism of primal repression) in the way they approach the logic of the signifier, this is not a wholly generalizable position. Milner's monolithic view of the *Cahiers* 'project' is challenged by the very first issue, which includes both Jacques-Alain Miller's seminal essay 'Suture' (CpA 1.3) (which seems to stand in for the *Cahiers* as a whole, in Milner's assessment) and Serge Leclaire's vigorous critique of it in 'The Analyst in His Place?' (CpA 1.4). Their debate raises a number of fundamental questions, among them the function of the letter and the stakes of 'literalization' in the Freudian clinic. These exchanges no doubt played a crucial role in pushing Lacan to further specify how the logic of the signifier in psychoanalysis (the elaboration of the signifying chain under transference) differs from the operation Miller calls 'suture', which describes the repression of the subject from discourse by the place-holder that substitutes for it. In Lacan's own work, this distinction will be developed through the theory of the four discourses (of the master, the university, the hysteric, and the analyst) in his 1969–70 seminar *L'Envers de la psychanalyse* (S17). But the authors of the *Cahiers* are also exploring this problem in their own ways. This essay will focus on the exchanges between Miller and Leclaire, with an emphasis on the contributions of Leclaire.

One of only a handful of clinical contributors to the *Cahiers*, Serge Leclaire (1924–1994) was an early analysand and disciple of Lacan who played an important role in the French psychoanalytic movement. He stood with Lacan after his excommunication from the *Société française de psychanalyse* in 1963, and in the years following the publication of the *Cahiers* played the leading role in founding the Department of Psychoanalysis at Paris VIII–Vincennes. Although he was not a member of the *Cahiers* editorial board, Leclaire contributed more texts (six in total) than any other author. Three of these are

---

7   See the session of 13 January 1976 (S23, 47–59).

summaries of his 1965–67 seminar at the École Normale Supérieure, 'Compter avec la psychanalyse' (CpA 1.5, 3.6, 8.6), which was attended by several of the figures associated with the journal: Miller, Milner, Alain Grosrichard, Jacques Nassif, and Michel Tort. Though older than his interlocutors, Leclaire was, like them, a young man near the beginning of his career when he penned these essays; his first book, *Psychanalyser* (based in part on his contributions to the *Cahiers*), would not be published until 1968.[8]

But while Leclaire is not yet a major theorist and never produces a piece for the *Cahiers* that is as original or influential as Miller's 'Suture', his contributions offer a dynamic engagement with the more structuralist contributions of other authors, putting them to the test of the clinic and demanding that they respect the constraints of the analytic experience. Leclaire is the first author in the *Cahiers* to offer a properly clinical account of the signifying chain and its function. His most important claim is that Lacan's account of the signifier is a translation and development of what Freud calls the 'unconscious concept of castration'. This equation tells us that the signifier is not an element of language, but an 'unconscious element' constituted by the 'anchoring of a letter in a movement of the body' (CpA 5.1:14). The corollary is that a signifying chain cannot be thought apart from the body, localized in the erogenous zones that the drive detaches from the organism and inscribes in the logic of the fantasy. More specifically, Leclaire's contribution to the *Cahiers* project will be to show that the function of the signifying chain in the analytic experience has a unique status that is not adequately captured by Miller's analysis of suture.

Leclaire's contributions are not taken into account in Milner's later judgment of the *Cahiers* project, with respect to neither the scientific pretensions of structuralism (Leclaire being sceptical about its clinical pertinence) nor to the problematic of the letter (where Leclaire is already closer to what Milner identifies with the second and third periods of Lacan's thought). They undermine Milner's attempt to periodize Lacan's thought, and suggest that the most crucial distinction is not between different chronological periods in his work, but between clinical and non-clinical elaborations of his theory of the signifier – i.e. between clinical and 'philosophical' approaches to the theory of the subject at stake in Lacanian conceptions of the signifier and the letter.

I REFUSING SUTURE

Miller's wager in 'Suture' is precisely that the logic of the signifier need not be approached from within analysis, since the subject of the unconscious asserts itself in every discourse from which it is excluded. Miller defines suture as 'the

---

8   Serge Leclaire, *Psychoanalyzing: On the Order of the Unconscious and the Practice of the Letter*, trans. Peggy Kamuf (Stanford, CA: Stanford University Press, 1998).

relation of the subject to the chain of its discourse'. It both 'figures there as the element which is lacking, in the form of a place-holder' and refers to 'the general relation of lack to the structure of which it is an element, inasmuch as it implies the position of a taking-the-place-of' (CpA 1.3:39). His argument proceeds through a demonstration borrowed from Frege, in which the position of a zero defined as lacking its own identity is shown to condition the serial constitution of numbers. Miller's central claim is that the position of this zero-as-lack is 'sutured' by the zero number, which stands in for its absence in the series of numbers: 'it is this decisive proposition that *the concept of not-identical-with-itself is assigned by the number zero* which sutures logical discourse' (44). Miller develops the implications of these opposed treatments of zero for psychoanalysis by positing that zero corresponds to the misrecognized place of the subject: 'what is there to stop us from seeing in the restored relation of the zero to the series of numbers the most elementary articulation of the subject's relation to the signifying chain?' (47).

In 'The Analyst in His Place?', Leclaire offers an impassioned rebuttal to Miller that focuses on his treatment of three key terms: 'subject', 'lack', and 'chain'. While Miller considers the subject through the lens of repression (as what is simultaneously called forth and rejected in discourse), Leclaire offers a clinical consideration of the subject of the analytic experience, the analysand who enters into the transference to construct an unconscious knowledge.

Leclaire concedes that the crucial point in any discourse is the point of suture. In listening to the patient's discourse, the analyst seeks to discover 'what has been fixed for him as a point of suture' (CpA 1.4:52). Clinical experience sheds further light on the relation of lack to the structure, however, by revealing that the lack at stake in 'suturation' (or repression) is invariably the 'difference-with-oneself' – or castration – 'that imposes itself [. . .] in the face of the irreducibility of sexual reality' (52). This emphasis on castration narrows and renders more precise the stakes of the 'not-identical-with-itself' in Miller's argument. As an example Leclaire cites a passage from Freud's 'Wolf Man' case, which invokes the notion of an 'unconscious concept' in relation to the problematic of castration. At stake is a unity, a concept, but one whose particularity consists in gathering together a series of 'indifferent little things' – the faeces, the child or the penis, a finger, the tip of the nose – that are not identical, but united only by their susceptibility to being separated from the body, and therefore to be lacking (51). It confronts us with 'the concept, the reality of a thing not-identical to itself' (52).

A purely logical approach to 'suture' fails to account not only for the mode in which the subject encounters lack, however, but for the function of lack within the trajectory of an analysis as well. Unlike the 'chain of discourse', the transference foregrounds the structuring function of lack. It supposes a *different relation to the signifying chain*, which leads to the traversal of the fantasy rather than its repression. This is the significance of Leclaire's most important claim, that the analyst 'is the witness to the radical difference between a sutured desirer and one who refuses to be sutured, a not-suturing, a desiring-not-to-be-sutured' (52). The 'desirer who refuses to be sutured' is one who follows the signifying chain to the castration to which it leads, who encounters the truth of an object not identical with itself, and who assumes this lack as the condition of its desire.

The work on the letter will be crucial to this desuturing. Miller and Leclaire both develop the importance of the letter in Lacan's 'Subversion of the Subject', but each approaches it in different terms. For Miller, 'piercing suture demands that one traverses what a discourse explicates of itself, that one distinguishes, from its sense, its letter' (CpA 1.3:40tm). In the terms of his reading of Frege, the 'zero lack' is the 'letter' that must be distinguished from the 'unary trait' of the 'zero number'. However, Miller's essay leaves undeveloped how the 'letter' of a discourse might be distinguished from its 'sense' where psychoanalysis is concerned. Conversely, Leclaire introduces the possibility of 'pinpointing' (E, 816/691–692) the subject of the unconscious by locating the 'invisible mark' it fills in, the site of the letter's 'anchoring' in the body.

II THE SIGNIFIER AS SUPPORT FOR DESIRE: FREUD'S 'WOLF MAN' CASE

In 'The Elements in Play in a Psychoanalysis: Freud's Analysis of the Wolf Man', in volume five of the *Cahiers*, devoted to Freud, Leclaire attempts to elaborate this procedure through a reading of the celebrated case. The essay begins by recalling how the psychoanalytic signifier differs from the linguistic signifier, which Leclaire describes as a 'psychic entity with two faces': a combination of two elements, signifier and signified, that together constitute the sign. As used by Lacan, however, the signifier cannot be considered as an element derived from the problematic of the sign, but rather as a fundamental element constituting the nature and truth of the unconscious (CpA 5.1:11). The signifier is the 'representative of an impossible identity', and its structuring principle is absence (12).

Leclaire credits Miller with elaborating 'the central paradox of the Lacanian signifier', that 'the trait of the identical represents the non-identical, from which can be deduced the impossibility of its redoubling, and from that impossibility the structure of repetition as the process of differentiation of the identical' (12). He also cites Milner's 'The Point of the Signifier' (CpA 3.5), which advances that the signifying order develops as a chain wherein 'the term that transgresses the sequence, situating as a term the founding authority of all terms, calls the one to be repeated as term transgression itself, an agency that annuls every chain' (12).

Even as they shed light on the signifier's function, however, Leclaire stresses that neither author can explain how the psychoanalyst distinguishes a given signifier. While any element of discourse *may* be a signifier, the psychoanalyst must be able to differentiate between signifiers, to privilege some over others. Leclaire warns against 'the error of making the signifier no more than a letter open to all meanings,' and argues that '*a signifier can be named as such only to the extent that the letter that constitutes one of its slopes necessarily refers back to a movement of the body*. It is this elective anchoring of a letter (gramma) in a movement of the body that constitutes the unconscious element, the signifier properly speaking' (14).

The remainder of the essay attempts to elaborate this claim through a detailed reading of the Wolf Man case. Leclaire begins by identifying what he holds to be the first 'major signifier' in the case: 'opening' [*ouverture*]. 'Opening' links the celebrated wolf dream ('the window opens by itself') to the memory of the primal scene (his eyes opened suddenly to see the parents engaged in coitus), but also to the symptom of infantile anorexia (which Leclaire translates as a 'precocious enjoyment of the possibility of not opening his mouth'), the terror provoked by the sight of a butterfly opening and closing its wings, and the various openings in the body that will be implicated as erogenous zones. We can infer from these examples that the signifying chain is composed of a very restricted number of signifiers, each of which relates to a dream, a significant childhood event, a symptom, and an erogenous zone. This last point is particularly important for Leclaire: 'Around the signifier "opening", we already glimpse a multitude of possible determinations, all linked to the awakening of a sensitive zone of the body: the mouth, the eyes, the ears' (15). What they reveal is that the signifier 'is a body as much as a letter' (16). It follows that 'opening', as a signifier, 'can in no way be abstracted from a movement of the body so as to become the *concept* of opening' (16). In stripping the signifier of its sensual agency to make it function as a concept, Leclaire argues that 'we lose precisely what makes psychoanalysis possible, the access to the economy of the drives, to the dimension of desire as such, to the very order of the unconscious' (16).

'Opening' corresponds not merely to an orifice or cut in the body, therefore, but to the alternation between identity and non-identity. It reveals that its reference to a movement of the body 'is curiously the most ungraspable dimension of the signifier' (12), in that the 'opening' to which it attests

is not essentially the movement in its recordable materiality (what is an ear that opens?) [. . . but] this *experience of pleasure or displeasure*, an ungraspable difference apprehended at the very moment of its dissipation; the very experience of this 'the same—not the same' that one discovers in the final analysis when one interrogates the truth of desire. I say therefore that *the signifier is constituted by a letter (gramma) to the extent that it refers back intrinsically to a movement of the body as the ungraspable difference* of a 'same—not the same' (17).

While the importance he accords to the signifier 'opening' might seem to depart from Freud's method, Leclaire argues that it demonstrates quite well the 'floating attention' that allows the analyst to separate a signifier from the patient's discourse. As an example he cites the different stages of Freud's dream analysis. Immediately after enumerating a list of fragments ('a real event – dating from long ago – looking – immobility – sexual problems – castration – the father – something terrible'), a list that has neither the rigour of a signifying chain nor the coherence of a discourse, 'Freud proceeds with admirable assurance to the nodal signifier of the dream: "the window opens by itself." At this moment the analysis opens onto a new dimension, the question of the primal scene and its impasses' (16).

While the 'nodal signifier' of opening does refer back to the primal scene, it is not related to the latent dream thoughts ('sexual problems – castration – the father'). It represents the dreamer, whose eyes open suddenly to observe the scene that will confront him with an unassimilable reality, the deadly jouissance implied in the mother's anal penetration (and castration) by the father. To push Leclaire's reading a bit further, we might say that 'opening' is the signifier of the effraction implied in the subject's encounter with the death drive (an effraction that is not metaphoric, but inscribed in a zone of the body as a transgression of its surface). While the 'question of the primal scene' is related to the dream thoughts enumerated in the initial list, therefore, it also goes further: to the logic of the fantasy that structures the patient's relation to the death drive, the undue jouissance inscribed in the letters of the body as symptoms.

Leclaire's treatment of the signifier can thus be understood in part as an attempt to distinguish the signifying chain from the dreamwork, or to claim that the latter does not exhaust the former. The signifier is not simply any element of the dream, for example the words or images 'selected' by the dreamwork according to the metaphoric and metonymic principles of condensation and displacement, which articulate the manifest dream content to the latent dream thoughts via a process of distortion. Hence it is striking that 'wolf' is not a 'major signifier' for Leclaire, despite the frequency with which it returns in the patient's dreams and associations and the numerous childhood memories, dreams, and symptoms it articulates by means of the metaphoric process of condensation. While these correspondences reveal a great deal about the latent thoughts behind the dream (castration anxiety, fear of the father), they do not tell us anything about the 'letter slope' of the signifier, its 'elective anchoring in the body'. 'Opening', on the other hand, does not establish a correspondence between the window and the eyes so much as offer (in the image of the open window) a graphic representation of what Leclaire describes in his seminar as the 'hole' left by the 'transgression of the body's surface', where the fantasy will henceforth be situated (CpA 1.5:68). In Lacanian terms, we could say that the signifier's repetition does not found equivalences at the level of sense, but stages the repetitive (non)inscription of jouissance in the letters of the body.

In claiming that 'a signifier can be named as such only to the extent that the letter that constitutes one of its slopes necessarily refers back to a movement of the body' (CpA 5.1:14), Leclaire introduces an understanding of the letter different from what we find in Miller. While both agree that the signifier has two dimensions or 'slopes', the unary trait and the letter, they define the latter very differently. In the discussion following Leclaire's seminar in the third issue of the *Cahiers*, Miller expanded upon the argument of 'Suture' by noting that while the definition of the signifier as a 'unary trait' is there to designate the 'minimal trait of sense', the letter is the 'materiality of the signifier', the 'unsigni-fied of the signifier', an 'irreducible non-sense' (CpA 3.6:95). This material 'non-sense' need not necessarily be conceived in relation to the body, however, since it could also be phonic or graphic – or, as in the case of Frege, formally excluded on ontological grounds as incompatible with the dimension of truth. The 'letter' is the zero as lack, rendered 'numerable' by the signifier as unary trait. Leclaire on the other hand – while he adopts Miller's formulation that 'the trait of the identical represents the non-identical' to describe the function of the unary trait – departs from him in arguing that the letter is the site where the surface or limit of the body is transgressed by the order of discourse. In the language of his seminar, the letter 'incarnates' the signifier, inasmuch as the cut 'brings forth the zero of lack *and* the polarizing one of the trait', the 'conjunction between the dehiscence of the un-oriented surface and the separation of a piece of the body that orients it' (CpA 1.5:68).

This point is made explicit as the essay continues, with Leclaire maintaining that the next 'link' in the chain is the signifier 'tearing' [*déchirure*], which articu-lates the tearing of the caul at birth, the foxes in the associations to the wolf dream whose tails have been torn off, the hallucination in which the patient sees his own cut finger hanging from a piece of skin, the dream of a man who tears the wings off a wasp, and finally the tearing of the 'veil' that separates him from the world when he is able to pass stool following an enema. Freud himself links the two signifiers when he observes that 'the tearing of the veil is analogous to the opening of the window, to the opening of the eyes' (CpA 5.1:17). In Leclaire's reading, Freud's use of 'analogy' must be read not as an invocation of conceptual equivalence or identity, but as an apprehension of the literal dimension of these two nodal signifiers. In Lacan's terms, we could say that while 'opening' is the signifier of the effraction (of the body by jouissance), 'tearing' is the signifier of castration. 'Opening' and 'tearing' have a 'literal' quality in the precise and restricted sense Lacan gives to the term when he speaks of mathematical formalization and the Borromean knot:[9] literal because not amenable to

---

9   In Seminar XX, Lacan develops this literality in relation to the letter's status as 'assem-blage': 'Set theory bursts onto the scene by positing the following: [. . .] Let us put together objects of thought, as they are called, objects of the world, each of which counts as one. Let us assemble

substitution.[10] With respect to Lacan's later characterization of the knot as a 'monstration', which for Milner comes to emblematize the stakes of 'literalization', we might say that Leclaire's intervention is precisely to argue that the 'letter slope' of the signifier is a *monstration* of castration, and not a metaphor or concept of castration. 'Veil', on the other hand, seems to function as the unary trait that supports the formation of the ideal ego in the fantasy of seduction.

What can we then learn about the question of difference from the Wolf Man's attempt to 'install a caesura' so as to accede to the 'reality' of the cut of castration? Leclaire maintains that the concept of difference can only be founded on a signifier, which differs from a concept in that the signifier, in its letter, cannot be abstracted from its anchoring in a movement of the body. He notes that Milner, in 'The Point of the Signifier', had proposed the unitary term of 'fission' as a signifier of difference, thereby grouping together – so as to emphasize their formal homology – the splitting of the subject, the expulsion of the object *a*, and the division of being and non-being. For Leclaire, however, it is the psychoanalytic term of 'castration' that fits best, and that ought to be preserved. Castration is implied in 'tearing', as well as in the many terms from the case commentary – separation, rejection, splitting – that suggest analogies with the major terms of Lacan's theory.

More importantly, 'castration' invites us to think of Freud's use of this word in relation to the loss of the penis, and his rejection of any conceptual extension of the signifier of castration that would 'detach' it from its somatic reference. (Conversely, Milner's use of 'fission' as a signifier of difference scrupulously avoids any reference to the body as the site of inscription of this division. In 'fission' he chooses a molecular metaphor belonging to the physical world, which supposes a 'natural' unity that can only be split artificially through the application of an external force.) In Leclaire's gloss, 'every separation, cut or loss, whatever it may be (even and especially that of parturition) necessarily refers back to the time of conception, to the phallus; and the phallus, as master signifier, cannot be other than lost with respect to the efficacy of sexual difference' (CpA 5.1:28). Above all, it is in relation to castration that Freud first introduces the notion of an 'unconscious concept' that Leclaire reads as the

---

these absolutely heterogeneous things, and let us grant ourselves the right to designate the resulting assemblage by a letter. That is how set theory expresses itself at the outset, that theory [. . .] I mentioned last time in relation to Nicolas Bourbaki. [. . .] [The authors] are very careful to say that letters designate assemblages. Therein lies their timidity and their error – letters *constitute* (*font*) assemblages. They don't designate assemblages, they *are* assemblages. They are taken as (*comme*) functioning like (*comme*) these assemblages themselves' (S20, 47–8).

10   The letter is inaccessible to sense not because it is negative (as in the negative characterization of the object that tends to dominate Miller's discussion of the zero), but because it is excessively positive. While Miller emphasizes the exclusion of the non-identical, and thus the failure of inscription ('what never ceases *not* to inscribe itself'), Leclaire's reading suggests that the positive side – 'what never ceases *to inscribe itself*' (on the body) is equally important.

prototype for Lacan's theory of the signifier. In Freud's words, 'the faeces, the child, the penis therefore constitute a unity, an unconscious concept – *sit venia verbo* – the concept of a little thing that can be detached from the body' (26–27).

The example of the child is especially important for Leclaire, since it shows that this detachment is not only a loss, but the condition of emergence of a subject of desire. The birth of a child entails a literal separation of a part of the mother's body that culminates in the existence of another sexuated human body. This is what links castration to the phallus as a signifier of difference. If the phallus 'is the signifier par excellence of impossible identity' (28), it is because there is no subjectivity without the loss of identity, 'the movement of separation, of differentiation, in which the signifier of castration finds a necessary dimension of its somatic anchoring' (27). As the object of his mother's desire, Leclaire hypothesizes that the Wolf Man 'found himself identified [. . .] in a kind of short-circuit with the very object of his quest, the phallus'. It follows that 'to reopen this cycle, to free himself from his blissful identification with the object of his mother's desire, is really the condition of his being able to access castration himself, to enter into the order of the signifier, of impossible identity' (29).

Where Freud maintains that the Wolf Man simultaneously *is* a penis (for the mother) and *desires* the penis (of the father), Leclaire in essence reads these two dimensions of the fantasy as expressing the conflict between an identification with the *signifier as unary trait* (which sustains the ego ideal only at the cost of alienating the subject's position), and the quest for the *signifier of difference* that sustains the desire of the divided subject. In trying to 'find the father's penis [. . .] in the mother's body', in other words, the Wolf Man is really searching for the *phallic signifier* that would allow him to break with the fantasy staging that makes of his 'whole body' a *penis* for the mother. In Lacan's terms, the phallus is above all the signifier of the effects of the signifier; and the first effect of the signifier is desire.[11]

In Freud's treatment of the case, Leclaire argues, 'the phallus gets lost in the game' of his virtuosic elaboration of the primal scene (40). To illustrate his argument he turns to another pivotal moment in the Wolf Man case, when the patient recalls being seized with terror as a child when a striped butterfly he was pursuing alighted on a flower and began opening and closing its wings. Leclaire claims that Freud missed an occasion to conclude the cure when he cut short the analysis of a dream that occurred in response to this memory: 'A man was tearing the wings off a Wasp.' In recounting the dream the Wolf Man introduces a slip, substituting *Espe* for *Wespe* (Wasp). When Freud points to his slip, the Wolf Man volunteers that 'Espe' is a homonym for his own initials, 'S' and 'P'.

---

11   Cf. Lacan, 'The Signification of the Phallus': 'For the phallus [. . .] is the signifier that is destined to designate meaning effects as a whole, insofar as the signifier conditions them by its presence as signifier' (E, 690/579).

Leclaire therefore concludes that the Wolf Man is himself the mutilated Wasp of the dream, and that 'the man' who tears off the wings is none other than Freud himself. The dream is thus a demand for castration addressed to Freud, express- ing the patient's 'most profound desire': to be torn away from the mother, cut loose from the signifier that substituted itself for the phallus, and allowed to accede to castration (37–38).

III FROM THE SIGNIFIER TO THE LETTER OF THE BODY

In interpreting the wasp dream as a quest for symbolic castration, Leclaire offers a richer understanding of the signifying chain than Miller's 'chain of discourse' does. While the latter was defined by the simultaneous evocation and rejection of the subject by the unary trait that takes its place, the signifying chain elabo- rated under transference supposes a different logic: a working backward from the unary trait to the letter, or to the 'invisible mark' the unary trait fills in. In the terms of Leclaire's earlier distinction between a 'sutured desirer' and 'one who refuses to be sutured', we might say that the operation of 'suture' corre- sponds to the 'fantasy of the veil' and the wish to re-enter the mother's body, while 'refusing to be sutured' corresponds to the quest for castration, the desire to have a man 'tear his wings off'.

It is striking, however, that this operation seems to unfold for Leclaire entirely at the level of the signifier. While he understands the elaboration of the chain as engaging the letter, or the 'elective anchoring' of the signifier in the body, this anchoring is often treated primarily as a confirmation of the identity of the so-called 'nodal signifiers', or as a point of intersection of the imaginary and the symbolic dimensions of the signifier and the fantasy: the place of the real is for the most part not addressed. While 'tearing' as a signifier certainly elucidates the stakes of the 'unconscious concept of castration', and the necessity of 'losing a little piece' of the body so as to accede to castration, it doesn't really engage the letter properly speaking. With 'tearing', as with '*Espe*', Leclaire never really gives us more than an ideational representation of the *corps morcelé*, the 'real' body fragmented by the drives. His argument tends to privilege the work on the signifier to the exclusion of the symptom, which alone allows for a locali- zation of the subject of the drive.

Remarkably, Leclaire never says a word about what Freud considers to be the key to the case, the symptom of constipation. It is in relation to this symp- tom that the patient uses the formulation to which Freud and Leclaire alike give so much weight: that the world was 'enveloped by a veil' that was only 'torn' when the faecal matter passed through the intestine, briefly allowing him to see the world with clarity. When the case reaches an impasse where the Wolf Man's dreams and associations are no longer moving the analysis forward, Freud, in an effort to reopen the transference, promises to cure his patient's constipation within a prescribed period of time. He then writes with satisfaction that the patient's 'bowel began, like a hysterically affected organ, to "join in the conversation", furnishing a response to the analyst's questions there where the signifiers of the dream were unable to (SE17, 76). At this point a new phase of the transference begins, in which the response of this 'letter of the body' – the bowel as the erogenous zone implicated in the fantasy of the primal scene – functions to confirm or refute the accuracy of the fantasy's construction. The faeces lodged in the bowel literalizes the position of the Wolf Man himself within the fantasy, with the pleasurable stimulation of the bowel by the faecal column confirming his identification with the mother's position in the primal scene.

In appealing to the symptom itself to elucidate the subject's position in the fantasy, Freud isolates the clinic of the symptom as a distinct phase of the analysis that cannot be assimilated to the construction of the signifying chain. Although the symptom is certainly linked to the chain through the 'tearing of the veil', the work on the letter of the body is distinct from the work on the signifier. It brings forth for the first time the identification with the mother's position in the primal scene, which cannot be isolated – much less constructed – by means of the signifying chain. The clinic of the symptom involves a direct interrogation of the jouissance inscribed in the letters of the body, which intervenes where the signifier fails. This emphasis is radicalized by Lacan when he makes the clinic of the drive – and the errant jouissance it unleashes – the centre of his practice. In 'Subversion of the Subject', he writes that

> it is difficult to designate that subject anywhere as subject of a statement – and therefore as articulating it – when he does not even know he is speaking. Hence the concept of the drive, in which the subject is designated on the basis of a pinpointing that is organic, oral, anal, and so on, which satisfies the requirement that the more he speaks, the further he is from speaking (E, 816/691–692).

In the Wolf Man case, the subject 'speaks' from the bowel, where his position is 'pinpointed' by the constipation that literalizes his position in the fantasy.

Inviting the bowel to 'join in on the conversation' goes well beyond claiming that 'a signifier is a body as much as a letter'. It supposes the exhaustion of the signifying chain, the lack internal to the chain inasmuch as it abuts – but cannot inscribe – the real. Lacan speaks of an 'inherence of a (-1) in the set of signifiers', which is due to the fact that there is no signifier for the jouissance that marks the place of the subject.[12] This (-1) means that the signifying chain is necessarily incomplete. Lacan writes that the lack at stake in the barred A is 'a

---

12   This (-1) occurs whenever a proper name is pronounced, since as opposed to the proper name from which I am absent, 'I am in the place [. . .] called Jouissance' (E, 819/694).

lack inherent in the Other's very function as the treasure trove of signifiers', precisely 'insofar as the Other is called upon (*chè vuoi*) to answer for the value of this treasure [. . .] in terms of the drive' (E, 818/693).

This answer does not result in a completed narrative or full reconstruction, however: the symptom 'stages' the subject's position in the fantasy without inscribing it within signification. The symptom is a product of the transference that attests to its status as a 'knot' that articulates (without rendering into sense) the different dimensions of the fantasy: imaginary (the election implied in being veiled, and therefore existing as a phallic object for the mother), symbolic (separation/castration, the 'tearing of the veil'), and real (jouissance, the symptom). This knotting is precisely what is at stake in the concept of the object *a*. In Lacan's words,

> A common characteristic of these objects as I formulate them is that they have no specular image, in other words, no alterity. This is what allows them to be the 'stuff' or, better put, the lining – without, nevertheless, being the flip side – of the very subject people take to be the subject of consciousness. For this subject, who thinks he can accede to himself by designating himself in the statement, is nothing but such an object [. . .]. It is to this object that cannot be grasped in the mirror that the specular image lends its clothes (E, 818/693).

In the Wolf Man case, we might say that the 'veil', as the unary trait supporting the specular image, 'lends its clothes' to the 'non-specular object' that the Wolf Man is, the piece of faeces lodged in the mother's bowel. Leclaire deals (at least implicitly) with the 'veil' as support for the ideal ego, the 'specular image'. But he never addresses the real object exposed by the tearing of this veil. Leclaire emphasizes the imaginary and symbolic dimensions of the fantasy to the exclusion of the real, and in the process loses sight of the letter whose causal connection to the elaboration of the signifying chain his reading had sought to elaborate.

The continuity of Lacanian theory lies in its clinical perspective, and this is an oft-forgotten part of the *Cahiers*. It is most evident in the contributions of Leclaire, and in particular his rejoinders to Miller's overweening emphasis on the logic of the signifier. Its limitations notwithstanding, Leclaire's treatment of the relationship between the signifier and the 'letter of the body' directly anticipates the work of the later Lacan, with its focus on knots and inscription. *Pace* Milner, his contributions allow us to understand that this turn is not the result of a simple 'failure' of the first classicism, but a development out of the already evident dependency of the signifier on the letter.

CHAPTER SIX

Adrian Johnston
Turning the Sciences Inside Out: Revisiting Lacan's 'Science and Truth'

Nobody could accuse Jacques Lacan of modesty. The title of his contribution to the inaugural January 1966 issue of the *Cahiers pour l'Analyse* promises to address not one but two immense issues in the space of a single article-length intervention. 'Science and Truth' (CpA 1.1) was originally delivered on 1 December 1965 as the opening session of his thirteenth annual seminar on 'The Object of Psychoanalysis'. In order to set the stage properly for an examination of its argument, a little background is required.

Lacan's title might lead a psychoanalytically-inclined reader to expect yet another disquisition rehashing the recurrent debates about whether or not psychoanalysis can and should be qualified as somehow scientific. Both the brief write-up of the eleventh seminar as well as the back cover of the 1973 Seuil edition of it succinctly announce a 'radical' reframing of these debates, shifting emphasis away from the question 'is psychoanalysis a science?' and toward the question 'what would a science that included psychoanalysis have to be like?'[1] Of course, Lacan does not hesitate on a number of occasions to air his views in response to the former question. But his most interesting and important speculations regarding the sciences and scientificity, speculations arguably still of great interest and import today after the passage of over forty years, do not hint at how psychoanalysis must change in adapting itself to the methods and results of the extant versions of the experimental physical sciences, even though this standard approach is frequently adopted by those in the analytic field who are anxiously concerned to gain legitimacy through recognition and acceptance from the established empirical sciences. Rather, Lacan turns the tables, reversing the standard approach, to ask instead: how must the sciences change in order to take account of everything that is revealed in the theory and practice of analysis? Similarly, in the opening session of the eleventh seminar, he muses that 'psychoanalysis [. . .] may even enlighten us as to what we should understand by science, and even by religion' (S11, 7). Analysts should not reduce themselves to being mere suppliants with respect to the scientists and their institutionally supported (and well-funded) authority.

---

1   Jacques Lacan, 'Les Quatre Concepts fondamentaux de la psychanalyse: Compte rendu du séminaire 1964', in *Autres écrits*, ed. Jacques-Alain Miller (Paris: Seuil, 2001), 187.

'Science and Truth' can be interpreted as a strange transitional text moving back and forth between the two questions raised for Lacanian psychoanalysis by science, i.e., 'is psychoanalysis a science?' and 'what would a science be that included psychoanalysis?' On the one hand, the essay makes several appeals to the theoretical paradigm of structuralism, seeming to imply that a structuralist version of analysis would qualify as strictly scientific in a certain sense (a sense related to the history of modern science according to the French historian and philosopher of science Alexandre Koyré, upon whom Lacan explicitly relies).[2] On the other hand, although these appeals to structuralism betray a continuing preoccupation with the issue of whether or not psychoanalysis is some sort of science, many other instances in 'Science and Truth' testify to the unfolding of something more than a claim of scientific status for analysis. In 1964, in the second session of his twelfth seminar, Lacan had already acknowledged 'the difficulty of establishing a psychoanalytic science', since analytic theory and practice tend to defy capture by scientific formalization.[3] As is well known, one of Lacan's favourite formal sciences is topology, upon which he draws extensively, especially in his 1970s seminars, and we may be entitled to read 'Science and Truth' as an attempt to delineate a twisted, multifaceted topological space simultaneously conjoining and disjoining psychoanalysis and the various sciences. This nuanced, subtle delineation – in it, neither domain is simply collapsed into the other, although points and areas of overlap are highlighted – might well be the most fertile aspect of Lacan's 1965 musings on scientificity.

Before tracing the more complex topology of the psychoanalysis-science link in 'Science and Truth', I will address its less complicated appeals to structuralism as a means to broaden the scope of the term 'science' (beyond familiar accepted images of the empirical sciences) so as to include psychoanalysis. Early on in this essay, Lacan repeats a gesture familiar from his 1950s-era 'return to Freud', one that presents Freud as a post-Saussurean structuralist *avant la lettre*. However, whereas Lacan's 1950s coupling of Freud with Saussure draws primarily from the early Freud of the first topography (particularly from such analytically foundational writings as *The Interpretation of Dreams*, *The Psychopathology of Everyday Life*, and *Jokes and Their Relation to the Unconscious*), the 1965 characterization of Freud as a proto-structuralist makes reference to the later Freud of the second topography inaugurated with 1923's *The Ego and the Id*:

---

2   Lacan, 'La Science et la vérité', CpA 1.1:7; 'Science and Truth', trans. Bruce Fink, E, 855–856/726–727 (subsequent references appear in parentheses in the main text, with the French *Cahiers* page numbers followed by Fink's English edition of Lacan's *Écrits*).

3   Lacan, S12 (unpublished typescript), session of 9 December 1964.

The doctrinal revamping known as the second topography introduced the terms *Ich*, *Über-Ich*, and even *Es* without certifying them as apparatuses, introducing instead a reworking of analytic experience in accordance with a dialectic best defined as what structuralism has since allowed us to elaborate logically: namely, the subject—the subject caught up in a constituting division (CpA 1.1:8/727).

An inflection subsists in this quotation signalling a distance between Lacan and classical French structuralism (as epitomized by someone like Claude Lévi-Strauss) despite his apparent reliance upon it in this essay. In order to discern this inflection, we need to remember that Lacan's subject, the 'barred S' ($) split in its very (non-)being, is not reducible to the positivity of one, two, or all three of the psychical agencies distinguished in Freud's second topography (i.e., id [*Es*/*ça*], ego [*Ich*/*moi*], and superego [*Über-Ich*/*sur-moi*]). Rather, Lacanian subjectivity is tied to the quasi-insubstantial negativity of intra-psychical rifts, namely, the tension-ridden gaps between the different sectors and functions of the psyche *qua 'parlêtre'* (speaking being). Although the negativity of this subject-as-$ would not exist without the positivity of these psychical agencies (as themselves conditioned and shaped by signifiers and images), it nonetheless remains irreducible to them insofar as it circulates amongst them as their conflicts and clashes between one another.

The structuralist 'logic' Lacan has in mind in this context, a logic capable of capturing both temporality and dialectics, is not that of an orthodox, textbook version of a structuralism privileging static synchrony at the expense of kinetic diachrony, but is closer to the temporal logic he first struggles to sketch in his 1945 text 'Logical Time and the Assertion of Anticipated Certainty.'[4] Perhaps what Lacan values most about structuralism is its pronounced anti-humanism. At first, he associates an anti-humanist rendition of subjectivity with science – 'all humanist references become superfluous in science, the subject cutting them short' (CpA 1.1:9/728). This assertion is promptly and forcefully reiter-ated – 'There is no such thing as a science of man because science's man does not exist, only its subject does' (11/730). In his only other contribution to the *Cahiers*, appearing in its third issue and entitled 'Responses to Students of Philosophy Concerning the Object of Psychoanalysis', Lacan again insists that 'in point of fact, psychoanalysis refutes every idea heretofore presented of man.'[5] In 1970, during a question-and-answer conversation with auditors in front of the Pantheon, he bluntly states, 'the discourse of science leaves no place for man'

---

4   Lacan, 'Logical Time and the Assertion of Anticipated Certainty: A New Sophism', E, 197–213/161–175.

5   Lacan, 'Réponses à des étudiants en philosophie sur l'objet de la psychanalyse', CpA 3.1:12; Lacan, 'Responses to Students of Philosophy Concerning the Object of Psychoanalysis', trans. Jeffrey Mehlman, in *Television/A Challenge to the Psychoanalytic Establishment*, ed. Joan Copjec (New York: W.W. Norton and Company, 1990), 114.

(S17, 147). Of course, a significant red thread running through 'Science and Truth' and related to these remarks consists in Lacan's conjoined efforts, first, to connect the birth of modern science via Galileo's mathematization of the experimental study of nature with the emergence of the modern subject *à la* Descartes' *cogito*; and second, to demonstrate that these connected events of the early seventeenth century are historical conditions of possibility for the advent of Freudian psychoanalysis itself, with its distinctive conception of subjectivity. Although I will address these efforts in 'Science and Truth' in passing below, they won't be the focus of this intervention.

In line with Koyré, Lacan considers mathematical formalization to be essential to scientificity in its modern sense. Related to this, he warns, in 'Science and Truth', about 'what has been trumped up about a supposed break on Freud's part with the scientism of his time.' Against this view, he contends,

> it was this very scientism – which one might designate by its allegiance to the ideals of Brücke, themselves passed down from Helmholtz and Du Bois-Reymond's pact to reduce physiology, and the mental functions considered to be included therein, to the mathematically determined terms of thermodynamics (the latter having attained virtual completion during their lifetimes) – that led Freud, as his writings show, to pave the way that shall forever bear his name (CpA 1.1:9/728).

Lacan immediately adds: 'I am saying that this way never sheds the ideals of this scientism, as it is called, and that the mark it bears of the latter is not contingent but, rather, remains essential to it' (9/728).

Lacan's stress on the mathematical side of the 'scientism' endorsed by Freud throughout his work is indispensable for his own purposes. Freud himself remains focused on the more biological side of his psycho-physicalist influences conveyed to him through his early training in neurology; he never entirely leaves by the wayside his formative relations with this field. However, Lacan's structuralist-tinged 'return to Freud', drawing on cybernetics, formal logic, game theory, knot theory, and topology as well as Saussurean linguistics (CpA 1.1:8/727, 12/730–731), prefers to emphasize the deeper Galilean undercurrents connecting the nineteenth-century psycho-physicalism colouring Freudian psychoanalysis to the modern regulative ideal according to which the degree of scientificity is directly proportional to the degree of mathematization of the area under consideration. To cut a long story short, Lacan, in 'Science and Truth', proclaims yet again his fidelity to a psychoanalysis that is scientific precisely in the sense of grounding itself on a mathematical-type formalism liquidating the humanist image of individual persons in favour of an anti-humanist theory of subjectivity-beyond-the-ego, a subjectivity decipherable through the matrices of combinations of differentially co-determined signifying units distributed simultaneously in synchronic and diachronic dimensions (this being one of the several things referred to in this mid 1960s context by Lacan's use of the phrase 'the subject of science') (8/728, 10/730, and passim). But, as I will argue in a moment, perhaps the biological facets of Freud's scientism, which Lacan tosses aside as a superficial vitalist shell hiding a core mathematical kernel, ought to be re-examined in a different, new (post-)Lacanian light.

Referring to the same passages quoted above, Jacques-Alain Miller observes that 'in this sense, psychoanalysis can be considered as the manifestation of the positive spirit of science in a domain which has been specially resistant to the conceptual grasp of science.'[6] In other words, as Lacan and many of his interpreters (including Serge Leclaire, another key psychoanalytic contributor to the *Cahiers*)[7] regularly maintain, Freudian analysis properly understood is not an obscurantist mysticism celebrating the unconscious as a dark underbelly, an irrational depth of primordial profundities forever evading the grasp of scientific-style reason's secular reflections. If anything, psychoanalysis shares in the *Weltanschauung* of scientific modernity and the Enlightenment insofar as it pursues a hyper-rationalist project that attempts, loosely speaking, to discover logic in the ostensibly illogical, reason in apparent unreason, and method in manifest madness. Furthermore, like mathematized modern science, it also eschews positing any sort of deep meaning at the real material base of being.

Seemingly in resonance with his recourse to modern science as involving an anti-humanist, mathematizing formalism, Lacan proceeds to mention examples of specific sciences in which portraits of humanity are effaced. 'A case in point,' he writes, 'is game theory, better called strategy, which takes advantage of the thoroughly calculable character of a subject strictly reduced to the formula for a matrix of signifying combinations' (CpA 1.1:12/730). If this formalism alone is what garners a scientific status for structuralism generally and structuralist psychoanalysis specifically, then, as Lacan admits here, subjectivity (i.e., the subject of science, including the subject of an analysis constitutively indebted to modern science) is indeed entirely dissolved into the networked structures of trans-individual symbolic orders. Such a structuralist paradigm, as Jean-Claude Milner describes it, amounts to a non-mathematical-but-literal (i.e., formally symbolized) dissolution of the non-formalizable qualities of humans as objects of investigation, echoing the Galilean privileging of primary (i.e., quantitative) over secondary (i.e., qualitative) properties in the scientific observation of material bodies.[8] But, passing without delay to the example of linguistics, the

6   Jacques-Alain Miller, 'Elements of Epistemology', trans. L.S. Rodríguez, in *Lacan and Science*, ed. Jason Glynos and Yannis Stavrakakis (London: Karnac Books, 2002), 155.

7   Serge Leclaire, 'Note sur l'objet de la psychanalyse: Séminaire à l'École Normale Supérieure, mars 1966', CpA 2.5.

8   Jean-Claude Milner, *L'Œuvre claire: Lacan, la science, la philosophie* (Paris: Seuil, 1995), 92–95, 98; cf. Milner, 'De la linguistique à la linguisterie', in *Lacan, l'écrit, l'image*, ed. L'École de la Cause freudienne (Paris: Flammarion, 2000), 8.

discipline of origin for structuralism and the key 'scientific' partner of analysis in Lacan's Saussure-inflected 'return to Freud', Lacan indicates that the subjectivity he is concerned with theorizing is not simply the subject *qua* fully subjected to the constellations and movements of formally delineable representational units. 'The case of linguistics is subtler as it must take into account the difference between the enunciated and enunciation, that is, the impact of the subject who speaks as such (and not of the subject of science)' (12/730–731).

Lacan's distinction between the subjects of enunciation and utterance serves to clarify that the former in particular (which consists of much that eludes formally delineable structures, including multifaceted affective and libidinal dimensions) is different from 'the subject of science', itself associated with the *cogito*. As Bruce Fink helpfully explains, the Cartesian skeleton of the subject of the unconscious is an 'unsaturated' subjectivity posited at the hypothetical level of metapsychological theory, whereas the subject dealt with in clinical practice is a subjectivity 'saturated' by concrete affective and libidinal contents, permeated by drives, desires, fantasies, *jouissance*, and so on.[9] The subject of the utterance, insofar as it is constituted on the basis of chains of concatenated signifiers differentially co-determining each other within the contexts of enveloping webs of larger batteries of signifiers forming surrounding symbolic big Others, looks to be amenable to treatment by game-theory-variety reductive formalism. And yet, it too cannot be equated straightforwardly with the symbolically subjected subject, the passive puppet or plaything of (to use Hegel's terms) the 'objective spirit' of autonomous signifying systems. Why not? Simply put, the subjects of enunciation and utterance are bound together in an oscillating dialectic of entangled, bi-directional influences making it such that they cannot actually be handled separately from one another.

Soon after these references to game theory and linguistics, Lacan turns to topology, reaching for one of his favourite topological objects: the Möbius strip (CpA 1.1:8/727). He employs this object to underscore and complicate the demarcation between subjectivity and scientificity – 'structuralism [. . .] ushers into every "human science" it conquers a very particular mode of the subject for which the only index I have found is topological: the generating sign of the Möbius strip that I call the "inner eight".' He then proposes that 'the subject is, as it were, internally excluded from its object [*en exclusion interne à son objet*]' (12/731). The image of the Möbius strip, both in 'Science and Truth' and elsewhere, is brought into association with, among other topics, the distinction between 'knowledge' [*savoir*] and 'truth', a distinction bound up, especially in

9   Bruce Fink, 'Science and Psychoanalysis', in *Reading Seminar XI: Lacan's Four Fundamental Concepts of Psychoanalysis*, ed. Richard Feldstein, Bruce Fink, and Maire Jaanus (Albany: State University of New York Press, 1995), 64; cf. Fink, *Lacan to the Letter: Reading* Écrits *Closely* (Minneapolis: University of Minnesota Press, 2004), 127–128, 185.

this 1965 presentation, with Lacan's interrelated readings of Descartes' philosophy, this philosophy's framing of subjectivity as *cogito*, and the genesis of the break with pre-modern 'science' via Galileo's mobilization of mathematics as the language of nature (as the physical universe) (7–8/726–727).

At this juncture, I want to underline the following: Lacan's structuralist innovations of the mid 1960s (which already anticipate a kind of poststructuralism) trace a convoluted topology of subjectivity such that psychoanalysis, although having been made historically possible by the advent of mathematized modern science and its subject (the *cogito qua* subject of science) with Galileo and Descartes, now peels away from such scientificity. As Alain Lemosof puts it, 'if the subject is the correlate of science, it's a correlate which is [. . .] absolutely antinomic to science.'[10] Using one of Lacan's own neologisms, one might say that the subject, as psychoanalysis conceives of it, is 'extimate' (i.e., an intimate exteriority as an internal exclusion, a foreign void at the heart of the familiar) with respect to the sciences of post-Galilean/Cartesian modernity.

Lacan frequently speaks of science as involving the *Verwerfung* of foreclosure (S7, 130–131), a 'successful' paranoid psychosis,[11] primal repressions of the truths upon which its knowledge rests, fetishist-style disavowal (*Verleugnung*) of that which defies treatment by its methods motivated by blindness to the ideological mechanisms enveloping and supporting it, and a death-drive-like compulsion toward knowledge at all costs.[12] This recourse to the vocabulary of psychopathology unambiguously serves to advance the thesis that the sciences presuppose yet simultaneously exclude from consideration specific faces and/or types of subjectivity illuminated by psychoanalysis; that is to say, the sciences have an unconscious of sorts in the form of their defensively occluded foundational bases. Expressed in Lacanese, these disciplines 'suture' such subjectivity (CpA 1.1:12/731). In the last sentence of his 'Responses to Students of Philosophy Concerning the Object of Psychoanalysis', Lacan, referring to a structuralism (or, again and more precisely, to his own brand of structuralismbeyond-structuralism) that formally outlines the limits of its own formalizations, closes by remarking that 'psychoanalysis as a science will be structuralist, to the point of recognizing in science a refusal of the subject.'[13] Years later, in the twenty-third seminar, Lacan returns to and summarizes much of the preceding by insisting that the divided subject ($) of analysis 'puts in question science as such' (S23, 36).

One moment in 'Science and Truth' in particular reveals how, in this pivotal

10   Alain Lemosof, 'L'Objet de la psychanalyse (1965–1966)', in *Lacaniana: Les séminaires de Jacques Lacan, tome 2, 1964–1979*, ed. Moustapha Safouan (Paris: Fayard, 2005), 111.

11   Lacan, 'On a Question Prior to Any Possible Treatment of Psychosis', E, 576/480.

12   Lacan, 'Science and Truth', CpA 1.1:19/737–738, 25/742, 28/744–745; Lacan, 'Allocution sur l'enseignement', in *Autres écrits*, 302; cf. S16, 238–240; S17, 104–106.

13   Lacan, 'Responses to Students of Philosophy', 13/114.

essay, Lacan's attention begins to be turned toward the question 'what would a science that included psychoanalysis have to be like?' At this point, he indicates that science will have to change in order to accommodate 'the object of psychoanalysis', namely the *objet petit a* as inextricably intertwined with the subject-as-$ in the structural logic encapsulated by the 'formula of fantasy', whose Lacanian 'matheme' is $ ◊ a:

> And let me remind you that while, certainly, to now pose the question of psychoanalysis' object is to re-raise a question I broached upon first mounting this rostrum – that of psychoanalysis' position inside or outside of science – I have also indicated that the question probably cannot be answered without the object's status in science as such being thereby modified (CpA 1.1:14/733).

Generally speaking, in Lacanian theory, the barred subject and object *a* co-implicate each other in the form of fantasies as fundamental formations of the unconscious. This co-implication between the subject and object of fantasy invariably entails one or more schematizing incarnations of conjunction (∧), disjunction (∨), and relative positions of being greater than (>) or less than (<), with the 'lozenge' of the *'poinçon'* (◊) designating all of these possible permutations fleshed out by various fantasies of union or fusion, rejection or abandonment, domination or mastery, submission or slavery, and so on. Lacan, in 'Science and Truth', clearly maintains, first, that $ is extimate *qua* 'internally excluded' from the sciences of modernity (structuralist sciences too), and, second, that *a*, the fantasy-correlate of $, can be digested by the sciences only if they themselves are transformed in the process.

Fink makes reference to the passage quoted above on a couple of occasions.[14] He claims that, 'science itself is not yet capable of encompassing psychoanalysis. Science must first come to grips with the specificity of the psychoanalytic object. [. . .] Lacan's view is that *science is not yet equal to the task of accommodating psychoanalysis*.'[15] This claim, and those of Lacan it echoes, can be construed in several manners, especially depending upon how one understands 'science' here. Recourse to the distinction between what the French (and Lacan, albeit with grave reservations) call the 'human sciences' (i.e., both the humanities and social sciences, and including structuralist versions of these as well as what Lacan designates as 'conjectural sciences' (CpA 1.1: 11–12/732–733), an example of which would be game theory) and the physical sciences (i.e., physics, chemistry, biology, etc.) is mandatory here. As for the so-called human sciences, an obvious way in which the psychoanalytic conception of the

---

14   Fink, *The Lacanian Subject: Between Language and Jouissance* (Princeton: Princeton University Press, 1995), 140; cf. Fink, 'Science and Psychoanalysis', 64.

15   Fink, *The Lacanian Subject*, 140.

unconscious creates profound difficulties for these disciplines is that it under-mines a basic assumption supporting and justifying both their methods and results: the presupposition that the human subjects studied and interrogated as these disciplines' objects of investigation are willing and able to furnish investi-gators with accurate and truthful self-reports through reliance upon reflexive conscious introspection. Vast swathes of the human sciences would require radical reworking if they were to take psychoanalysis seriously. As the title of one of Lacan's best-known texts has it, the 'dialectic of desire in the Freudian unconscious' entails a 'subversion of the subject' specifically as imagined by those scientists who assume that subjectivity is exhaustively equivalent to the transparency of reflective self-consciousness, be it their own purportedly non-subjective subjectivity (along the lines of the Cartesian *cogito* as the anonymous subject of science devoid of the idiosyncrasies of particular subjectivities) or that of their objects of investigation.[16]

But what about the physical sciences? What implications would a rapproche-ment between the physical sciences and Freudian-Lacanian metapsychology generate – a rapprochement in which the interlinked subject and object of analytic metapsychology are no longer extimacies sutured by the sciences within which these intimate exteriorities have previously subsisted in internally excluded states as repressed, disavowed, and/or foreclosed? Of course, in the context of a discus-sion of psychoanalysis *vis-à-vis* these sciences, the first association that comes to mind should be Freud's complex rapport with the life sciences, that is, his frequent flirtations and multi-level engagements with biology. A contemporary assessment of Lacan's 'Science and Truth' should be framed, first and foremost, in light of the present state of the physical sciences, especially the life sciences, including the neurosciences; the remainder of what follows, therefore, will sketch the future possibilities of a new alliance in which psychoanalysis and the life sciences are reciprocally transformed through being folded into each other, such that neither is eliminated or reduced away in its specificity in the process. In the background of this project is my belief that Lacan's own mapping of the frontier between anal-ysis and the sciences of matter, after over four decades packed with momentous scientific developments, has become partially obsolete and in need of careful reconsideration in the early twenty-first century.

In 'Science and Truth', Lacan, with reference to Aristotle's four causes, empha-sizes that psychoanalysis is concerned specifically with material causality. However, the materialities in question here are the acoustic and graphic substances constitutive of pure signifiers *qua* meaningless sounds and images independent of the meaningful sign-couplings of signifier and signified – 'the

---

16   Lacan, 'The Subversion of the Subject and the Dialectic of Desire in the Freudian Unconscious', E, 671–676.

material cause is truly the form of the impact of the signifier that I define therein'
(CpA 1.1:26/743). Similarly, in his other contribution to the *Cahiers*, Lacan,
reiterating a protest he vocalizes again and again, insists that 'the least you can
accord me concerning my theory of language is, should it interest you, that it is
materialist.'[17] Soon after mentioning the notion of material causality, he
concludes that this necessitates divorcing the conception of subjectivity *à la* a
psychoanalysis tied primarily to formal apparatuses (as per structural linguistics and anthropology, conjectural sciences such as game theory, various
branches of mathematics, etc.) from anything having to do with the life sciences.
'Conveyed by a signifier in its relation to another signifier, the subject must be
as rigorously distinguished from the biological individual as from any psychological evolution subsumable under the subject of understanding' (26/743).
Lacan's conclusion warrants critical re-visitation today.

One could go so far as to assert that Lacan's odd materialism centred on the
'material cause' of 'the impact of the signifier' – the word 'impact' (*incidence* as
an effect or repercussion) clearly evokes the collision of two bodies in the form
of the acoustic and/or graphic materiality of the signifier slamming into the
physical body of the organism – requires something more in order to be truly
materialist: a scientifically well-founded explanation of how and why human
beings as living organisms can be and are transformed into the speaking beings
discussed in Lacan's own theory. Lacanianism needs a fleshed-out delineation
of what endogenously holds open the body's potentials to be exogenously
impacted and subjectified by the denaturalizing signifiers of socio-symbolic
orders. A failure or refusal to pinpoint the contingent-yet-*a priori* material
conditions of possibility for the biological emergence of more-than-biological
subjects risks allowing for (or even encouraging) the flourishing of irrational
idealisms and obscurantist spiritualisms.

Of course, in his 1965 presentation, Lacan does not have the sciences of the
brain in mind when he addresses the scientificity of psychoanalysis. However,
Lacan's relationship to things biological over the entire span of his teachings isn't
nearly as straightforward and consistent as is maintained by the widely-believed
story according to which he unreservedly purges Freudianism of all traces of bio-
materiality in favour of a thoroughly formalized and anti-naturalist metapsychology that has nothing whatsoever to do with biology and its offshoots. Both before
and after 'Science and Truth', Lacan not only calls for radically altering, based on
psychoanalytic considerations, the proto-conceptual pictures and metaphors
underpinning the notion of 'nature' in the physical sciences[18] – he also explicitly

---

17   Lacan, 'Responses to Students of Philosophy', 10/112.
18   Lacan, 'The Mirror Stage as Formative of the *I* Function as Revealed in Psychoanalytic
Experience', E, 77–78; cf. S17, 33; S21 (unpublished typescript), session of 21 May 1974. Cf. Adrian
Johnston, *Žižek's Ontology* (Evanston: Northwestern University Press, 2008), 270–273.

discusses the brain (E, 78), undeniably anticipating subsequent scientific insights into neuroplasticity, mirror neurons, and epigenetics. Like Freud before him, Lacan awaits a vindication of psychoanalysis from the life sciences as well as the formal and conjectural sciences. These still incompletely digested scientific insights signal the urgency and timeliness of revisiting anew the intersection between psychoanalysis and science. A non-reductive yet scientifically-grounded materialist theory of psychoanalytic subjectivity (one capable also of integrating key features of both dialectical materialism and existentialism) is finally foreseeable on the horizon, thanks not to further developments in pure mathematics, symbolic logic, and similar disciplines, but to empirical, experimental investigations into neural systems and evolutionary-genetic dynamics.

Several of the psychoanalytically-minded contributors to the *Cahiers* would of course be suspicious, if not entirely dismissive, of the shotgun marriage between Freudian-Lacanian psychoanalysis and the biological sciences I am arranging here. With regard to science in general, Jacques Nassif, in the ninth issue of the *Cahiers* devoted to the 'Genealogy of the Sciences', reiterates a well-worn stock assertion in French psychoanalytic circles: Freud's lifelong leanings in the direction of the physical sciences amounts to a lamentable self-misunderstanding on his part of the epistemological break he accomplishes at the turn of the century with the invention of psychoanalysis as a novel discipline unprecedented in several respects.[19] On the heels of repeating this standard downplaying of Freud's references to various things scientific, Nassif raises a problem with integrating psychoanalysis into the empirical, experimental sciences that is familiar to every school of psychoanalysis (not just Lacanian and/or French analytic orientations): the absolutely singular character of the analytic experience resists and thwarts the 'cumulative model' central to scientific knowledge (CpA 9.10:150). In other words, not only would the inherent, irreducible idiosyncrasy of each and every clinical analysis prevent the possibility of repeated experimental replications as a process crucial for and integral to post-Baconian scientific method, but according to Nassif, an impossible adding-up of unique analytic insights purportedly peculiar to incomparable subjects-of-analyses could never accumulate so much 'data' as to be enshrined in a catalogue-style encyclopaedia of 'facts' known by psychoanalysis.

Nassif's remarks warrant several responses. To begin with, Lacan's institutional experiments in his École Freudienne, inaugurated just prior to the publication of issue number nine of the *Cahiers*, with the (notorious) procedure of '*la passe*' – a kind of rite of passage from being an analysand to assuming the position of an analyst – precisely aim at, among other things, finding a way to build up a repository of transmissible knowledge (*savoir*) obtained from a countless

---

19   Jacques Nassif, 'Freud et la science', CpA 9.10:150.

multitude of unrepeatable encounters with the unconscious. What is more, Lacan seeks to do so in a manner that, like Hegel's *Aufhebung*, somehow manages to preserve-in-negation the particularity of these encounters while nonetheless simultaneously forcing them to 'pass' into the universal medium of iterable symbolico-linguistic formulations initially conveyed through testimony and subsequently conveyable through teaching within an analytic community.[20] In fact, in his 'Proposition of 9 October 1967 on the Psychoanalyst of the School', in which he first outlines the procedure of *la passe*, Lacan, *contra* what Nassif says about analysis in relation to cumulative scientific knowledge, declares regarding the proposed procedure of passage that, 'this proposition implies an accumulation of experience, its compilation and elaboration, an ordering of its varieties, a notation of its degrees.'[21] An excessive insistence on the science-defiant uniqueness of clinical analyses, in which the heart of all analyses is threatened with being portrayed as the mystical experience of an inexpressible *je ne sais quoi*, is in danger of neglecting to take into consideration (extimate) features of Freudian-Lacanian psychical subjectivity intimately involving the external mediation of the 'objective spirit' of the big Other *qua* symbolic order (i.e., trans-individual social, cultural, linguistic, institutional, etc. mediators constitutive of the *parlêtre* with its unconscious). In this vein and once again echoing Hegel, one could maintain that the notion of concrete particular analyses apart from abstract universal structures is itself the height of abstraction; or, put differently, each analysis is no doubt 'singular' but in the strict Hegelian sense, namely, an individual 'concrete universal' as a dialectical convergence/synthesis of both particular and universal constituents. Lacanian analysis consequently would be a paradoxical 'science of the singular'.

Admittedly, Lacan, right before his death, expresses reservations and regrets about *la passe* soon after having announced the 'dissolution' of the École Freudienne.[22] In line with his late-in-life renunciation of any claims to the effect that psychoanalysis is or could be scientific, he says of speaking beings with their unconsciousnesses, 'it cannot be said that even in piling up, they form a whole.'[23] He goes on to state, 'now I have a pile – a pile of people who want me to take them. I am not going to make a totality out of them. No whole.'[24] Instead of appealing to the impossibility of accumulating transmissible information upon which Nassif insists, Lacan deems his experiment in psychoanalytic training in his former Freudian school a failure precisely 'for

20   Lacan, 'Proposition of 9 October 1967 on the Psychoanalyst of the School', trans. Russell Grigg, *Analysis* 6 (1995), 10–11. Cf. S15 (unpublished typescript), session of 29 November 1967; S19 (unpublished typescript), session of 1 June 1972.

21   Lacan, 'Proposition of 9 October 1967', 10.

22   Lacan, 'Letter of Dissolution', trans. Mehlman, in *Television*, 129–131.

23   Lacan, 'The Other Is Missing', trans. Mehlman, in *Television*, 133.

24   Lacan, 'The Other Is Missing', 133.

having failed to produce Analysts within it who would be of the requisite level.'[25]

As regards Nassif's concerns, my proposal to reconsider the science-psychoanalysis relationship in Lacan's wake does not in the least bit entail trying to reduce away without remainder the singularity of more-than-bio-material subjects. I in no way attempt to lay the foundations for a 'scientific' (or, rather, pseudo-scientific) psychoanalysis in which analysands are indifferently subjected to treatment as the fungible patients of a replicable clinical framework, system, or method, a poor (and impoverished) imitation of the experimental sciences. For anyone even minimally acquainted with psychoanalysis, this would be both ridiculous and unethical. Nassif is quite right that many (although not all) facets of analysands, with their unrepeatable analyses with their chosen analysts, are difficult or impossible to replicate through representations transmissible to uninvolved third parties. But, what Nassif overlooks the need for, and what recent related developments in the neurosciences as well as evolutionary theory (with its growing appreciation of non-genetic epigenetic, behavioural, and symbolic factors in phylogenesis and ontogenesis) promise to provide, is a scientific basis explaining the non-metaphysical conditions of possibility for the immanent material genesis of exactly those sorts of beings who are at issue in analysis. Simply put, what I am heralding here is the potential for forging, at the intersection of psychoanalysis and the physical (especially life) sciences, a scientifically-backed account of the genesis and structure of subjects that come to evade the grasp of the sciences themselves (for example, Nassif's analysand-subjects). It seems to me that, in the absence of such an account, advocates of an analysis irreducible to any naturalism (of which I am one) are left with the unappealing choice between ultimately relying on either ontological dualisms or idealist epistemological agnosticism.

I can clarify and sharpen further the preceding remarks by turning attention to Leclaire's contributions to the *Cahiers*. Leclaire offers objections directly addressing the field of biology. Hence, for me, his reflections are especially topical and important to address. Very much in step with Lacanian sensibilities as (mis)understood at the time, Leclaire insists upon 'the primacy of the signifying order'.[26] Zeroing in on the place of the body in psychoanalytic metapsychology, he defines the analytic body as '*an ensemble of erogenous zones*'.[27] He describes these corporeal regions at four levels: the clinical, the structural, the topological, and the historical. In the *Three Essays on the Theory of Sexuality*, the text in which the analytic concept of erogenous zones is first introduced at length,

25   Lacan, 'The Other Is Missing', 133.
26   Leclaire, 'Le Refoulement: Séminaire à l'École Normale Supérieure, novembre 1966-mars 1967', in *Écrits pour la psychanalyse, tome 1: Demeures de l'ailleurs 1954–1993* (Paris: Seuil, 1996), 138.
27   Leclaire, 'Le Refoulement', 125.

Freud, as he does throughout his work, anchors these zones (and the libidinal economy of drives in which they feature centrally) in the anatomy of the living being, in 'somatic sources'. By contrast, Leclaire's list of four dimensions said to be relevant to an analytic handling of the sexual and affective body noticeably leaves out the dimension(s) of the biological.

Leclaire soon moves to defend and justify the exclusion of all levels having to do with biology. With detectable disdain for 'the body of the biologist', he alleges that:

> It is not necessary to ask how the erogenous body is founded in the structure of the biological body. But it is necessary to understand, on the contrary, that the biologi-cal body is constructed starting from the Signifier, that is to say, from the erogenous body. It is the biological body that it is necessary to derive from the erogenous body and not the reverse.[28]

He immediately adds: 'Psychoanalysis places the accent on the Body as an ensemble of erogenous zones. Freudianism is the accent placed on this point.' Leclaire sincerely believes 'the Signifier' literally governs from the very begin-ning 'the order of the body'.[29] It's highly doubtful that Freud himself would have agreed that this is 'Freudianism'.[30] What is more, Leclaire clearly asserts that his Lacan-inspired approach to embodiment involves a temporal-genetic dimen-sion (a dimension also prominently visible in Miller's 'Action of the Structure', CpA 9.6) that is valid not only within the register of a structuralist analytic metapsychology, but also invalidates and trumps ostensibly erroneous biologi-cal accounts of the body. He does not cautiously qualify his stance so as to indi-cate its independence from issues having to do with material geneses as discussed in non-structuralist/structuralized fields with their proper methods of inquiry; on the contrary, he makes very bold (and arguably quite false) claims about these issues, pretending to usurp a great deal of explanatory jurisdiction from other disciplines beyond the particular interdisciplinary intersections represented within the pages of the *Cahiers pour l'Analyse*. Hence, taking into account the theoretical ambitions of the *Cahiers* endeavour as represented by Leclaire's and Miller's concerns with the origins and emergence of structural facets and phenomena, such a hyper-structuralist project opens itself up as vulnerable to criticisms I will elaborate in a moment.

Stuck within the constraining parameters of a false dilemma pitting essen-tialist biology against anti-essentialist psychoanalysis in a winner-takes-all

---

28   Leclaire, 'Le Refoulement', 126.
29   Leclaire, 'Le Refoulement', 126, 127.
30   Cf. Johnston, 'The Weakness of Nature: Hegel, Freud, Lacan and Negativity Materialized', in *Hegel and the Infinite: Religion, Politics and the Dialectic*, ed. Clayton Crockett, Creston Davis, and Slavoj Žižek (New York: Columbia University Press, 2011), 159–180.

struggle, Leclaire seems to be convinced, wrongly, that the only alternative to a scientific reduction of psychoanalysis is an inverse analytic reduction of science. At one point, Leclaire appeals to Lacan's mirror stage in his account of the body.[31] Ironically, his science-versus-psychoanalysis death match stages, on the terrain of theory, a spectacle of Imaginary rivalry arising from a fundamental *méconnaissance*.

The unsatisfactory nature of Leclaire's pseudo-Lacanian idealism of the symbolic order manifests itself in stark relief when a few basic questions are posed: From where does 'the Signifier' (or, more broadly, the symbolic order) ultimately originate phylogenetically? On the ontogenetic level, what is it about the body that makes possible and inclines it toward being overwritten by signifiers coming from Others? If none of this immanently emerges from the world of matter investigated by the physical sciences, then from where does it emanate: God, *Geist*, some sort of mysterious metaphysical heaven, an utterly enigmatic X? In the face of such questions, Leclaire has two unpalatable options: either, one, espouse a Kantian-style critical idealism dogmatically asserting that such queries cannot be asked and answered in the vain hope of knowing the unknowable; or, two, endorse an uncritical idealism of the Symbolic, namely, a solipsism of the almighty Signifier. Under the sway of a certain, and sadly still commonplace, fantasy-image of Nature with a capital N (an image he attributes to biologists), Leclaire is rendered unable to envision the option of a scientifically grounded yet non-reductive materialist psychoanalytic metapsychology, one willing and able to respond to the preceding fundamental questions in a non-idealist manner.

An utterly anti-naturalist, anti-scientific materialism is no materialism at all. Any materialism worthy of the title must perform, in order to be truly materialist yet simultaneously non-eliminative, a sort of theoretical jujitsu trick, a vaguely Gödelian-style de-completion of the physical sciences. François Ansermet, reflecting on current scientific appreciations of the brain's plasticity from an analytic angle – this plasticity, of which, again, Lacan himself anticipates the discovery, enables the neurosciences to be linked with 'logosciences' such as Freudian-Lacanian psychoanalysis[32] – speaks of 'a beyond of all biologism' situated 'at the very interior of biology'.[33] Lacanian topological figurations of internal exclusions might appropriately come to mind. What is more, Ansermet invokes Lacan's own employments of topology in reference to the issue of the relation between science and psychoanalysis considered in terms of the non-antagonistic distinction between the neurosciences and the logosciences respectively:

---

31   Leclaire, 'Le Refoulement', 130.

32   François Ansermet, 'Des neurosciences aux logosciences', in *Qui sont vos psychanalystes?*, ed. Nathalie Georges, Jacques-Alain Miller, and Nathalie Marchaison (Paris: Seuil, 2002), 382.

33   Ansermet, 'Des Neurosciences aux logosciences', 381.

In effect, recent developments in the neurosciences permit advancing that it is not a matter of opposing them to the logosciences [. . .]. The non-correspondence between the biological and the psychical that the concept of plasticity tries to grasp opens onto the question of language. The neurosciences therefore open up to the logosciences, on condition of respecting their incommensurability. One cannot relate them except across a joint that one should conceive of as paradoxically disjoint. A disjoint relation: it's a topological problem that Lacan perhaps already resolved in his last constructions.[34]

What both Ansermet and I are suggesting, in Lacan's aftermath, is that the present era is more than ripe enough, considering the state of the life sciences nowadays, for approaching what Freud and Lacan each awaited: a future in which the disciplines composing the field of biology are ready to greet psycho-analysis in such a manner as to initiate a trajectory of mutual modification of these sciences and analysis, as simultaneously a theory and a practice.

Playing off an irreducible non-natural subject, portrayed as a mystery wholly inexplicable in empirical scientific terms, against the fictional straw-man caricature of a neuronal machine governed exclusively by the blind mecha-nisms of evolution and genetics, merely reinstates a version of those dualisms that rightly are so foreign to the tradition of authentic materialism. When it comes to the subjects of concern to psychoanalysis, the real challenge is to pinpoint and link up two parallel, complementary nodes of explanatory incom-pleteness within scientific and psychoanalytic discourses. A properly formu-lated neuro-psychoanalysis does precisely this. It engages in the double move of, one, supplementing Freudian-Lacanian psychoanalysis with a biological account of the material underpinnings of more-than-biological subjectivity and, two, supplementing the neurosciences with a sophisticated, systematic metapsychological theory of subjects whose geneses, although tied to brains, involve much more than bare organic anatomy. These emergent subjects also come to have significant repercussions for the bio-material bases that are the necessary but not sufficient aleatory conditions of possibility for their very existences. One can and should strive to develop a scientifically shaped (although not purely and strictly scientific) account of how human beings, defying and escaping explanatory encapsulation by the sciences, become what they are. Correlatively, a materialist psychoanalysis must be, as Lacan would put it, not without its scientific reasons, at the same time maintaining itself as a specific discipline whose objects of inquiry cannot be unreservedly absorbed without remainder into subject-less material being(s).

Lacan's attitudes toward the notion of scientificity undergo major changes

---

34   Ibid., 382.

during the course of his intellectual itinerary. In the 1950s he regularly insists that 'our discourse should be a scientific discourse' (S5, 251), but by the 1970s this ambition is abandoned and repudiated.[35] For instance, continuing to conceive of the essence of modern science under the influence of Koyré, Lacan remarks, at the end of a session of the twentieth seminar, that 'the analytic thing will not be mathematical. That is why the discourse of analysis differs from scientific discourse' (S20, 117).

'Science and Truth' is an odd text situated midway between these two extremes, both chronologically and conceptually. Lacan's contribution to the first issue of the *Cahiers* neither simply crowns psychoanalysis a science according to some already-fixed standard of scientificity nor strictly separates one discursive domain from the other. But, rather than construe this midway neither/nor as merely a transitional moment of indecision, as a wavering waiting for eventual resolution, maybe one ought to read this 1966 article in a Hegelian manner. To be quite precise, one should interpret what appears to be the temporary negative absence of a decisive insight into the psychoanalysis-science (non-)rapport as already a direct or positive revelation of this interdisciplinary link pregnant with potentials. This revelation allows for envisioning an unprecedented scenario in which a materialist metapsychology indebted to historical and dialectical materialisms attains a scientific grounding (specifically through neurobiology) and, in so doing, reciprocally acts upon this same ground, thereby delineating the immanent bio-material emergence of structures and phenomena subsequently irreducible to and partially independent of the explanatory jurisdiction of the physical sciences and these sciences' objects of research. The way forward, after Lacan and in his shadow, will involve the elaboration of a psychoanalysis through its relationships with the sciences. A moment of truth has arrived.

---

35   Lacun, S21, session of 20 November 1973.

CHAPTER SEVEN

Peter Hallward
Badiou and the Logic of Interruption

The priority of Alain Badiou's first theoretical texts, written in the mid 1960s, is to assert the self-sustaining and self-enclosed sufficiency of alternatives to ideology. Following his mentor Louis Althusser, Badiou understands ideology in terms of a subject's lived experience, a domain of illusions and of imaginary reflections of reality. The alternatives – scientific discourse (in particular mathematics) and aesthetic production (in particular literature) – offer true knowledge of their specific domain. The main task of theory, then, is to secure such knowledge against the persistent danger of ideological contamination, by defending its essential autonomy.

In this sense, a true or non-ideological discourse is one that encounters nothing other than itself. A true discourse would be one that can never be interrupted, neither by the intrusion of some external object nor by some inner gap or absence, some inner 'fault' or inconsistency that might elude articulation. A true discourse would be one whose outside – ideology, empirical reality, historical continuity, subjective experience, popular practice . . . – is conceived in such a way as to figure *exclusively* and unequivocally as outside, an outside that could never intrude into the discourse that excludes it. Insofar as the *Cahiers pour l'Analyse* set out to explore a 'general theory of discourse', Badiou's insistence on such formal self-sufficiency (in his contributions to the journal's final volumes) carries one aspect of the project to its logical conclusion, precisely as an attempt to purge this theory of its own 'inner' limit, that 'extimate' and elusive figure affirmed in its inaugural texts – the figure of the *subject*, whose place is marked by what discourse can only indicate as a gap or lack.[1]

What then happens, in May 68, is that something happens. The events of May interrupt Badiou's scientific project once and for all, both from within and without. The 'outside' overcomes, in practice, its theoretical exclusion. His project interrupted, Badiou, like the other leading figures in the *Cahiers*, quickly abandons abstract theory for concrete practice and in the following years dedicates himself entirely to revolutionary politics, before attempting, in the later 1970s, to combine the two domains in his own '*theory* of the subject'.

I want to argue here that the best way to understand the overall movement of Badiou's philosophy, in terms that account both for its inaugural

---

1   For an overview see Peter Hallward, 'Theoretical Training', CF1.

assertion and its subsequent development, is as a form of fidelity to the logic of interruption as such. What occurs in the defining stages of this movement is a conversion, after 1968, of this logic from a merely transcendent one (whereby interruption can only be thought as if stemming from a mere absence or outside) to an immanent one (such that the exception that interrupts a discourse or situation can be thought as a sort of internal excess or gap, i.e. in terms that might be affirmed by a subject). This shift will allow Badiou to reorient his philosophy in terms that embrace rather than exclude the subject of interruption as such. Badiou's philosophy acquires its distinctive shape when he is able to return to the inaugural thesis of the *Cahiers*, the thesis he himself tried to foreclose in its final issue, and find his own way of articulating the relation between subject and structure.

On the one hand, then, the moment of May 68 – for Badiou, the paradigmatic instance of what he will later conceive in more general terms as event, rupture, revolution, disruption, 'grace', and so on – indeed figures, at the level of both theory and experience, as a matter of interruption pure and simple. This aspect of Badiou's philosophy, the aspect of subject and event, has the general status of an *exception*, of an excess or supplement. It is a matter of 'supplement' not in the deconstructive sense, as the indication of an irreducible lack or 'deficiency' in the situation or discourse that is supplemented,[2] but on the contrary, as a pure addition, i.e. a pure intrusion or interruption from outside. And this is because, on the other hand, Badiou's understanding of that which is interrupted is conceived in such a way as to ensure that whatever supplements it, whatever is added or happens to it, can indeed only be understood on the basis of an interruption or addition as such (rather than as an extension, intensification or transformation of existing features of the situation, e.g. as an alteration of its fundamental tendencies, capacities, and so on). This broad conception of 'that which is interrupted' will later apply as much to the ontology he develops in *Being and Event* (1988) and the theory of appearance he develops in *Logics of Worlds* (2006) as it does to the analysis of art and science proposed in his earliest theoretical articles (1966–68), which will be my chief concern here.

Badiou's 'mature' theory of truth is essentially a theory of fidelity to a particular sort of interruption, one whose affirmation has universal and egalitarian consequences. But his philosophy is also faithful to a general theoretical perspective that obliges such interruption to be understood essentially *as* interruption, i.e. a perspective that understands reality or 'what there is' in such a way that for something new or true to happen it must happen *to* it. What takes place takes place in excess over its place. Badiou is faithful both to the

---

2   See in particular Jacques Derrida, *De la grammatologie* (Paris: Minuit, 1967), 207–211; *Of Grammatology*, trans. Gayatri Chakravorty Spivak (Baltimore: Johns Hopkins University Press, 1997), 144–147.

interruption of any self-sufficient logic, and to the presentation of such logic as self-sufficient. It is in this sense that, contrary to what readers of his most purely political 1970s writings might suspect, Badiou's later philosophy might be described as faithful both to the ultra-theoreticist work he wrote in the mid 60s *and* to the way he broke with such work in and after 68. Alone of all his contemporaries, Badiou has remained faithful to the theoretical project of the *Cahiers pour l'Analyse*, precisely in the way that he helped to interrupt it.

I FROM SARTRE TO ALTHUSSER

When Badiou left the École Normale Supérieure in the summer of 1961, already seasoned by years of campaigning against the Algerian War, he remained an enthusiastic admirer of Sartre and Sartre's effort (in his 1960 *Critique of Dialectical Reason*) to think of the relation of subject and social structure, or of freedom and constraint, from the position of the subject. Even before he left the ENS, however, Badiou was already interested in many of the new formalist projects that helped to establish the nascent 'structuralist' paradigm in philosophy and the human sciences – new axiomatic approaches to the foundations of mathematics, new work in formal logic and linguistics, the legacy of Bachelard and Koyré, Lévi-Strauss's work on kinship, and perhaps especially, Lacan – still very much a marginal figure outside psychoanalytic circles. By 1964, in the run-up to the *Reading Capital* seminar, Badiou was also reading Althusser with enthusiasm, and in the spring of 1965 he taught a broadly Althusserian course on the relation between literature and ideology back at the École Normale. By the end of the following year Badiou's shift in orientation, from Sartrean freedom to Althusser's structuring 'process without a subject', appeared definitive.

When in early 1967 Badiou joined the editorial team of the *Cahiers pour l'Analyse*, then, he joined as a *convert* to structuralism, with both the enthusiasm and the perspective that comes with conversion.[3] This is one of several important differences between him and the slightly younger *normaliens* involved with the journal, who all came of age at the ENS directly through their engagement with Althusser and Lacan. Badiou's range of reference and experience was wider than that of Jacques-Alain Miller, Jean-Claude Milner or Yves Duroux, since he had the 'good fortune', as he remembers, to have been fractionally older than the rest of his generation. Most of his younger contemporaries had 'not had the time to be Sartreans', or to engage in a political situation (like the struggle against colonialism) grasped through a Sartrean conception of commitment and principle.[4]

This first great interruption in Badiou's thought – in brief, his conversion

3   See Yves Duroux, 'Strong Structuralism, Weak Subject', CF2.

4   Alain Badiou and Bruno Bosteels, 'Can Change be Thought?', in *Alain Badiou: Philosophy and its Conditions*, ed. Gabriel Riera (New York: SUNY, 2005), 242.

from Sartre to Althusser – already defines a fundamental problem that persists in all his subsequent work. How to think both the domain of rigorously structured objectivity and the domain of absolute freedom? The first effort aligns Badiou with Plato (and Althusser), and with the formal sufficiency of mathematics; the latter aligns him with Mao (and Sartre), and an equation of reason with revolt. Can these two efforts be thought together? Yes, Badiou will come to realize, precisely insofar as one interrupts the other. They can be thought together insofar as they can be considered aspects of an irreducible duality or 'two'.[5] Subject can be thought as exception, and objective structure as that which acknowledges and indeed 'situates' a kind of 'impossible' place for that exception – i.e., in Lacanian terms, a place for that 'real' whose affirmation appears impossible or inconceivable. Again like Althusser before him, Badiou draws here on the formalist, anti-empiricist approach to science developed by Bachelard, Koyré, and Canguilhem, with the proviso that the formalizing work of conceptual construction always leaves a space for the subject it excludes. In this sense, Badiou considers, 'there is a general movement of thought' common to this generation of French philosophers, 'wherein we all agree on the fact that the world (or that which is) is arranged as a matter of formal objectivity, one that is foreign to consciousness and valid on its own terms.' It 'is precisely because this formal objectivity exists that one can search for and define the point [the gap or impasse] that exceeds it. And in this point the subject, or its possibility, takes place.'[6] Badiou has dedicated much of his later philosophy to thinking this point that is both internal to and in excess of structure, the point that can be converted from objective *impasse* to subjective *passe*.[7]

But this project too will have come as an interruption, an interruption of Badiou's ultra-formalist priorities in 1966–67. 'In 1967', he is the first to recognize,

> I was indeed at the extreme point of a strict formalism [. . .]. The fact that my thought is rooted in Platonism, which I've never denied, even when I was a convinced Sartrean, sometimes leads me to oscillate between a radical priority of the question of the Subject, on the one hand, and on the other a pre-eminence of the Idea, or of the truth, whose intelligible substructure, whose purest model, is to be found in the historical development or life of mathematics. Subjectively, for me this means that politics and mathematics constitute the two major 'appeals' on the
> ◀ side of what I call the 'conditions of philosophy', and that these two appeals are always in tension.[8]

---

5   On the centrality of 'two' as a figure in Badiou's philosophy, see Hallward, *Badiou: A Subject to Truth* (Minneapolis: University of Minnesota Press, 2003), 45–47.

6   Badiou, 'Theory from Structure to Subject', CF2, 283.

7   In *Being and Event* (1988), with a nod to Lacan, Badiou will show how the 'impasse of being-as-being' locates the '*passe* of the Subject' (BE, 469/429tm).

8   'I only came to find the conceptual form of that tension', Badiou continues, 'once I

Things will begin to fall into place when, after apparently banishing it without appeal, the neo-Sartrean domain of engagement and the subject returns, in May 68, to upset the theoretical edifice Badiou had been building in the previous years. We need then to review the construction of this edifice in more detail, before considering what suspended it.

II THE AUTONOMY OF ART

Like his younger *Cahiers* colleagues, what is at stake in Badiou's conversion to Althusserianism is the sufficiency of scientific theory as the means by which analysis can grasp a structuring dimension that remains inaccessible to those who simply experience or live its effects. Science can only proceed by overcoming the ideological obstacles that threaten its autonomy, i.e. by defending itself against interruption from the domain of non-science. Badiou's first two theoretical essays aim precisely to secure the domain of analysis from such interruption, either from without (a 'reality' or event external to it) or from within (a lack or absence that might be inaccessible to it). In art as in science, the goal is to confirm foreclosure of all that is foreign to its self-demarcating domain. As we shall see in the penultimate section of this essay, Badiou's critique of Miller in the final issue of the *Cahiers pour l'Analyse* is motivated by the same goal.

Badiou's article on 'The Autonomy of the Aesthetic Process' (APE), dated June 1965 but published in the *Cahiers Marxistes-Léninistes* in July 1966, summarizes the course that Althusser had invited him to give, that spring, at the École Normale.[9] His main concern is to show how a distinctively aesthetic process, unlike a merely ideological one, generates its own sphere or 'reality' and thus renders itself independent of anything external to it. He takes for granted Althusser's elementary categories: a 'real' element is one grasped by science, say, a particular configuration of class forces in a particular place and

---

understood that the most significant mathematical events might also provide the key to the subjective process of truths. That was the entire aim of *Being and Event* (1988), in the crossing, through the concept of genericity, of the mathematics of the pure multiple and the post-evental subjective trajectory that constructs a truth. In 1967, just before the political storm, my meditations were on the side of formal structures. For the ten years following it, I was rather on the side of political subjectivity. Philosophy really began for me after these oscillations, at the start of the 1980s' ('Theory from Structure to Subject', 280). Already, with Maoism, Badiou had 'found something that made it possible for there to be no antinomy between whatever mathematics is capable of transmitting in terms of formal and structural transparency, on the one hand, and on the other, the protocols by which a subject is constituted' (Badiou and Bosteels, 'Can Change be Thought?', 243).

9   Badiou, 'L'Autonomie du processus esthétique', *Cahiers Marxistes-Léninistes* 12–13, special issue entitled 'Art, langue: Lutte des classes' (July 1966), 77–89. Althusser originally planned to include Badiou's work on literature in his Théorie collection as a book on the 'theory of the novelistic effect (*l'effet romanesque*)' (Althusser, letter to Franca Madonia, 23 July 1966, in *Lettres à Franca (1961–1973)* (Paris: Stock/IMEC, 1998), 691; cf. 576).

time; an 'ideological' representation of such a reality is one that 'reflects' and distorts it according to positions determined by that configuration. Badiou's opening question, then, is whether the aesthetic process that produces a genuine work of art is best understood merely as one of several 'regional domains' of ideology, i.e. as one among many ideological reflections of real elements external to it, or as an autonomous process operating only on elements internal to this process itself.

Classical Marxist literary criticism, for instance Lenin's reading of Tolstoy, develops the first approach. Although it operates in ways that are no doubt convoluted and more or less inaccessible to its author himself, a literary work is supposed to reflect a real social situation, such that, in principle, the task of 'true' literature should be to reduce such convolutions to a minimum (as will be expected, for instance, of a truthful socialist realism). Badiou's contemporary and fellow Althusserian Pierre Macherey offers a more sophisticated variant of this first approach, whereby to study a work 'consists in demonstrating the relations it maintains with the historical structure' that shapes the social reality of its day.[10] Badiou applauds Macherey for recognizing that the indirect or convoluted quality of literary representation is in fact essential to (rather than destructive of) the peculiar effects it produces. Macherey shows how a text truly reflects a social reality precisely by what it *fails* to say about that reality, by the way it omits certain deplorable aspects, censors its descriptions, etc. A reader attentive to the gaps and silences in the text can thereby 'see' what subjects of the ideology itself cannot see. By rendering such absences present (as absences), by making these silences audible (as silences), this sort of Marxist literary criticism operates as a privileged domain of ideology critique.

What Badiou rejects is the assumption common to both Lenin and Macherey, that a text relates to and operates on a reality external to it (APE, 82). For Macherey, a work exists in 'an internal relation to that which is other than it, as immanent contradiction' or as 'the phenomenon of an internal difference', such that it renders 'present' i.e. visible or legible precisely 'that which holds itself in absence': insofar as all ideology reflects reality then the peculiar object of literary criticism will be the 'absence of certain reflections' in the distinctively 'broken mirror' that is a literary work.[11] For Badiou, by contrast, an aesthetic process should not be understood with reference to such an immanent alterity, i.e. in terms of gaps or absences internal to its logic (and that by interrupting this logic, thereby point to a reality external to and other than it). In Badiou's

10   Pierre Macherey, 'Lénine critique de Tolstoï', *La Pensée* 121 (June 1965), 84; republished in Macherey, *Pour une théorie de la production littéraire* (Paris: François Maspero, 1966), part two, online at http://stl.recherche.univ-lille3.fr/sitespersonnels/macherey/machereyproductionlitteraire2.html#II1; Macherey, *A Theory of Literary Production*, trans. Geoffrey Wall (London: Routledge, 1978), 112.

11   Macherey, 'Lénine critique de Tolstoï', 84/112.

view, what art creates is not a mirror, be it broken or whole, of something else. Instead, art produces its *own* reality, according to its *own* logic, to the exclusion of any outside.

Badiou accepts, of course, that 'ideology produces an imaginary reflection of reality' (APE, 81), and agrees that 'the aesthetic effect is certainly imaginary; but this imaginary is not the reflection of the real, since it is the real of this effect' (77). Moving beyond Macherey's notion that literature is ideology rendered visible (because its reflection is broken or incomplete), Badiou argues that we must conceive of the aesthetic process not as any sort of reflection or 'redoubling [of the real] but as a *reversal* [*retournement*]' of the reflecting relation between ideology and reality, i.e. as the conversion of a mere ideology into a kind of self-sufficient reality (albeit an imaginary one). If ideology produces an imaginary reflection of reality, a distinctively aesthetic process 'produces in return [*en retour*] ideology as imaginary reality. We might say that art repeats in the real the ideological repetition of this real. Nevertheless this reversal does not reproduce the real; it *realizes* its reflection' (81). In other words: ideology reflects reality but art, reversing ideology, does *not* merely reflect reality; instead it renders real or lends a sort of reality to the reflections produced by ideology.[12]

If we are to 'take its autonomy seriously' (85), Badiou continues, then by definition an autonomous art cannot merely reflect and thus depend on a reality external to it. Instead it must produce its own reality-effect, in the same way that a structuring cause generates the immanent field of its effects. By submitting them to the local 'efficacity of structural causality' (rather than the global indeterminacy of an 'expressive causality') and thus assigning them 'a place in a structure', the aesthetic process converts the elements of mere ideological reflection into an effectively self-sufficient (albeit imaginary) reality. Affirmation of the autonomy of the aesthetic process 'blocks us from conceiving it as *relation*', and consequently 'the problem of the *passage* from ideology to art cannot be formulated as such' (83). As soon as it begins, the aesthetic process *already* operates exclusively in its own self-enclosed domain, such that if ideological statements appear within it then they too will have been 'produced as ideological' by the aesthetic process itself (85). The regional autonomy (or 'regional structural causality') of the aesthetic process is such that 'the "raw material" of aesthetic production is already itself aesthetically produced.'

For this argument to work, Badiou needs a way of accounting for the incorporation of patently ideological statements within a literary text, statements like the expression of a maxim or a political opinion. In keeping with a logic that will recur in both the *Cahiers Marxistes-Léninistes* and the *Cahiers pour l'Analyse*, he

---

12   Cf. Althusser's interpretation of the 'absence of relations' at work in Bertolazzi's *El Nost Milan* (Althusser, 'The "Piccolo Teatro": Bertolazzi and Brecht. Notes on a Materialist Theatre' [1962], FM, 135ff.).

accommodates the inclusion of such 'separable ideological statements' by distinguishing between the given or structured work on the one hand and its structuring or aesthetic process on the other. A work may well include separable statements, but these will 'function in isolation' and 'owe nothing to the *structure* of the work', i.e. to its aesthetic process per se, which is the sole concern of analysis (84). Unlike a separable ideological statement that only figures in a work as external and unrelated to the process that produces it, aesthetic statements or 'generalities' are formulated as internal to the imaginary reality produced. Badiou gives as an example a sequence in Dostoyevsky's *The Demons*, in which an opinion (to the effect that suffering ennobles the person who suffers) that might be understood as a 'separable' maxim if read in isolation is in fact formulated in such a way as to require us to read it as an integral part of the narrated sequence (one that culminates in an actually noble gesture on the part of our sufferer).

The distinctive power of the aesthetic process is thus its capacity to generate an imaginary scenario (here, a compelling representation of an action) as self-sufficient, i.e. as *real*, such that 'generalities of another order cannot enter or remain' (87). The more general task of the analyst of such production will then be to determine precisely how a specific mode of the aesthetic process operates, how it forms and thus renders 'present' certain kinds of significations. (A specific 'mode of aesthetic production', Badiou suggests in his tentative conclusion, is an 'invariant and invisible structure that distributes ways of linking real elements in such a way that these elements can *function* as ideological'; his examples of such modes include the 'figurative space' of representational art, the tonal system of classical music, the metric system of ancient Greek verse, and 'the system of subjectivity in the novel' [88]).

The domain of the effects produced by an autonomous aesthetic process, in sum, can be neither hollowed out from within nor interrupted from without. Understood along these lines, art is thus 'structurally closer to science than to ideology' because, by 'realizing' or rendering-real ideology, it 'produces the imaginary reality of that which science appropriates, i.e. real-reality' (77).

III THE AUTONOMY OF SCIENCE

Unhindered by art's imaginary orientation, science itself proceeds more directly. Badiou's next article, a substantial review of Althusser's *For Marx* and *Reading Capital*, published in May 1967 under the title 'The (Re) Commencement of Dialectical Materialism' (RMD),[13] pivots on the Bachelardian assertion that, unlike ideology and the reflections of lived experience, 'science is precisely the practice that has no systematic sub-structure

---

13   Badiou, 'Le (Re)commencement du matérialisme dialectique', *Critique* 240 (May 1967), 438–467.

other than itself, no fundamental "ground"'. Whereas ideologies are concerned with the way objects are lived, represented and experienced, the 'proper effect of science – the effect of knowledge – is obtained by the rule-governed production of an object that is essentially distinct from the given object' (RMD, 443n.10, 449). In the domain of science, as Bachelard recognized, 'nothing is given, everything is constructed',[14] on the basis of an absolute and ongoing *break* with the given and the ideological. Genuine i.e. post-Galilean physics, for instance, has *no* relation with the common-sense understanding of nature associated with Aristotelian philosophy; rather than criticize or even deny the existence of nature in this sense, it has '*nothing* to say about it' (443n.9). Once Marx establishes his science of historical materialism, likewise, he is no longer required to 'invert' or 'subject to critique' the ideological categories associated with Hegel's philosophy 'for the simple reason that they are no longer encountered, they cannot be found, so much so that we cannot even refer to their expulsion, since the space of science is constituted on the basis of their radical absence' (443).

The radicality of the 'epistemological break' that establishes it allows science itself to escape reduction to a mere element of the 'super-structure' of a social order, and thus to escape the general constraint of historical determination in the usual sense. As Althusser puts it, a science 'may well arise from an ideology, detach itself from its field in order to constitute itself as a science, but precisely this detachment, this "break", inaugurates a new form of historical existence and temporality which together save science [...] from the common fate of a single history: that of the "historical bloc" unifying structure and superstructure.'[15] Badiou's main reservation regarding Althusser's effort to re-launch dialectical materialism as a general 'science of the scientificity of the sciences' (RMD, 446) is simply a concern that the project does not go far *enough* in establishing its central concepts ('structure', 'determination', 'the dominant instance of a structure', etc.) on the basis of a purely 'formal' and thus self-sufficient discipline. A general science of historical *structure*, Badiou suggests, actually requires as its foundation a 'theory of historical *sets*', to be worked out in a 'strict dependence' upon a wholly formal version of such a theory, namely mathematical set theory.[16] Badiou speculates that refinement of such a theory should allow for 'the concept of a conjuncture to be constructed' in a suitably rigorous way (463), while regretting the hasty and half-hearted character of Althusser's

14   RMD, 440n.1, citing Étienne Bachelard, *La Formation de l'esprit scientifique*, 14; cf. APE, 87n.19.

15   Althusser and Balibar, RC, 133; cf. Hallward, 'Theoretical Training', CF1, 12; Peter Dews, 'Althusser, Structuralism, and the French Epistemological Tradition', *Althusser: A Critical Reader*, ed. Gregory Elliott (Oxford: Blackwell, 1994), 124.

16   RMD, 461. Such a theory, Badiou tentatively suggests, would include a set P of places, and a set F of functions or practices, applied to these places; a subset H of F would then be 'historically representable' if its application is 'determinant' and 'structured in dominance.'

own recourse to formalization.[17] Having made only an incomplete break with philosophy and ideology, Althusser is occasionally 'blind' to their persistence in his own work; as a result the status of his general theory of science remains uncertain, torn between a neo-Kantian reconstruction of the conditions of knowledge and a neo-Spinozist theory of structuring causality (466–467).

Purged of any 'falsifiable' reference to empirical reality or experience, the only practices that might qualify as *unequivocally* scientific are indeed mathematical, in the sense exemplified by David Hilbert's formalist conception of geometry. For Hilbert, elementary geometric objects like points and lines are not ideal approximations to objects in physical space but undefined terms that conform to axiomatically asserted procedures governing their manipulation. 'If the arbitrarily given axioms do not contradict each other with all their consequences, then they are true and the things defined by them exist', with no need to verify this existence through some form of observation or experiment.[18] 'The axiomatic method', Hilbert concludes, thus 'guarantees complete freedom of investigation. To proceed axiomatically means nothing else than to think with knowledge of what one is about.'[19] In line with such Hilbertian formalism, Badiou proceeds to insist, in his contributions to the *Cahiers*, that a suitably formal mathematical logic manipulates nothing other than the 'marks', letters or symbols that it prescribes for itself, in the absence of any external relation to objects or things. 'Mathematical experimentation has no material place other than where difference between marks is manifested', and 'neither thing nor object have the slightest chance here of acceding to any existence beyond their remainderless exclusion.'[20] No more than an aesthetic process, a scientific i.e. mathematical inscription in no sense represents, reflects let alone 'imitates' an object external to it.

Although there is not space to consider it here, the same principle governs the concept of mathematical model Badiou went on to defend in a pair of lectures that were quite literally interrupted by the events of May 68.[21] As

---

17   'Althusser's whole effort is to try to achieve right away, for a discipline without tradition, something that mathematicians have been laboriously striving to obtain via the newly developed theory of Categories – a direct determination of the concept of structure, without referring to a set that underlies it' (464).

18   David Hilbert, letter to Gottlob Frege, 29 December 1899, in Frege, *Philosophical and Mathematical Correspondence*, ed. Brian McGuinness, trans. Hans Kaal (Oxford: Blackwell, 1980), 39–40; cf. Hilbert, *The Foundations of Geometry* [1899] (Chicago: Open Court, 1977).

19   Hilbert, 1922, cited in Morris Kline, *Mathematical Thought From Ancient to Modern Times* (Oxford: Oxford University Press, 1972), 1027.

20   CM, 30; CpA 10.8:156. The basic idea, as Zachary Luke Fraser notes, is that 'the material inscription of mathematical thought – its reduction to bare letters and axiomatic rules of manipulation – is a priori adequate to its essence' (Fraser, 'Introduction', CM, xxix).

21   'The story of that lecture course on the concept of the model is itself a veritable allegory of the moment. There were supposed to be two sessions: the first took place and the second didn't, because it was supposed to take place right at the beginning of May 68!' (Badiou, 'Theory from Structure to Subject', CF2, 286).

Zachary Luke Fraser explains, 'the point of interpreting a structure as a model for a theory (or interpreting a theory as the theory *of* a structure) is not to *mathematically represent* something already given outside of mathematics, but to generate a *productive interaction between already-mathematical constructions,* opening each to new, essentially experimental techniques of verification and variation.'[22] More precisely, what inclusion of the dimension of model offers here is a way to think the internal historicity of science's relation to itself. In opposition to representational conceptions of model like that offered in Lévi-Strauss's conception of kinship relations (whereby science is conceived 'as the confrontation between a real object, about which one must inquire [ethnography], and an artificial object whose purpose is to reproduce the real object, imitating it in the law of its effects [ethnology]') (CM, 10), Badiou proposes

> to call *model* the status [*statut*] that, in the historical process of a science, retrospectively assigns to the science's previous practical instances their experimental transformation by a definite formal apparatus. The category of model thus designates the retroactive causality of formalism on its own scientific history, the history conjoining object and use. And the history of formalism will be the anticipatory intelligibility of that which it retrospectively constitutes as its model.
>
> The problem is not, and cannot be, that of the representational relations between the model and the concrete, or between the formal and the models. The problem is that of *the history of formalization.* 'Model' designates the network traversed by the retroactions and anticipations that weave this history (CM 54–55tm).

Perhaps even more than the (ideological) subject, the (empirical) *object* is the primary locus of imaginary illusion and the immediate occasion for scientific i.e. Platonist distrust.[23]

IV FORM AND SUBVERSION

The essential thrust of Badiou's two contributions to the *Cahiers*, and of his early theoretical position in general, follows from his ultra-Althusserian assertion that 'science is [a] pure space, without inverse or mark or place of that which it excludes' (CpA 10.8:161). The main question at issue in the first of these contributions, 'Infinitesimal Subversion', is, as its title suggests, the

---

22   Zachary Luke Fraser, 'Model', in *Badiou Dictionary*, ed. Steven Corcoran, forthcoming.
23   As Badiou puts in 1990, defending his affirmation of a 'subject without object', 'the true does not speak of the object, it speaks of nothing but itself' (Badiou, 'Saisissement, dessaisie, fidélité', *Les Temps modernes* 531–533, vol. 1 [1990], 20). Again, 'thought is not a relation to an object, it is the *internal* relation of its real' (Badiou, *Abrégé de métapolitique* [Paris: Seuil, 1998], 37); cf. Badiou, 'On a Finally Objectless Subject' [1989], trans. Bruce Fink, in *Who Comes After the Subject?*, ed. Eduardo Cadava et al. (London: Routledge, 1991), 24–32; CM, xxxv.

abruptly 'subversive' power of scientific formalization, its capacity to interrupt and then exclude the ideological categories of continuity, quality and temporality (CpA 9.8:136). The first half of Badiou's article is concerned with the status, in any numerical system, of an empty place for a 'number' that is excluded as impossible within the limits of that system; the second half of the article explores the process whereby Abraham Robinson's non-standard analysis allows, in the domain of the standard number system, infinitesimal or 'infinitely small' numbers to come to occupy such an initially 'impossible' place, and thus render the impossible possible.[24] As with Badiou's critique of Macherey's emphasis on quasi-visible absences in the literary work, everything depends here on the way we think of this internal gap or empty place.

Consider the exemplary case of the natural number sequence, generated through repeated operations of numerical succession $(1 + 1 + 1 + 1 \ldots)$. Take any finite number n, however large: it is obviously possible, through the addition of a 'supplementary inscription' $(n+1)$, to generate a larger number, and then another, ad infinitum. Badiou's opening question concerns the place in which this unending inscription, so to speak, might come to be inscribed. If through each operation of succession number shows itself to be 'the displacement of the place where it is lacking' (CpA 9.8:118), is inscription in the place of such lack a sort of 'representation' or reflection of something external to the inscription, a sort of indication whereby the lack itself might somehow be rendered 'visible'? No, says Badiou, following Mallarmé. The endless generation of finite numbers through succession simply presupposes the blank or missing place required for its operation, such that 'it is what is written that bestows upon it its status as place of the writing that takes place.' In one and the same process, mathematical writing writes both its inscription *and* the blank space 'on which' (so to speak) it is inscribed. The space into which a further number in our sequence succeeds does not pre-exist this succession, like an inner gap in the fabric of scientific writing. There is nothing foreign, here, to this writing itself – neither object of reference nor surface of inscription. Only insofar as we assume, 'internal' to the domain of science, a space that is actually and *already* endless can we actually continue to count out an unending series of additional numbers. 'This is why the "potential" infinite, the indefiniteness of progression, testifies retroactively to the "actual" infinity of its *support*' (118).

Our domain of natural numbers is thus composed of an unending series of places that successive members of this domain come to occupy. If then we want to posit a place that is *unoccupiable* by any member of the domain, it will have to be marked by an inscription that is fully 'supplementary' to the ordinary series of inscriptions which count out this domain. Such a place will indeed be

---

24   For a more detailed account of this article see the synopsis posted on the *Concept and Form* website, http://cahiers.kingston.ac.uk/synopses/syn9.8.html.

purely external to the series. What Badiou calls an *'infinity-point* of the domain' will be a number which, by breaking the rules of the domain, can be 'forced' to occupy this 'unoccupiable empty space' (119), with the proviso that, even if it can be constructed using the mechanisms of the domain itself, such an 'impossible' number must nevertheless be constructed in such a way as to remain 'exterior' to the domain.

To illustrate this, Badiou gives the example of the simple relation of order, i.e. the relation which measures one quantity as 'greater-than' or 'lesser-than' another, applied to the domain of natural numbers. This relation allows for the construction of an unoccupiable place, i.e. the place of a number which would be larger than *all* others in the domain. This place itself is easily constructed, since the statement 'for all x, $x < y$' is a perfectly intelligible statement of the domain; it cannot be occupied, however, by any actual finite number, however large. The variable y here marks an unoccupiable place; it thus indicates the outside limit of what can be written on the basis of our 'infinity-support'. No actual number or 'constant' belonging to the system can be attributed to this place, i.e. substituted for the variable y, without contradicting the rules operative in the domain. It might seem then that there is nothing more to say: impossible is impossible, and that is all there is to it. On formalist grounds, however, there is nothing to prevent the mathematician from 'forcing' the point of impasse, and obliging the procedures operative in a domain to apply to 'precisely that which they had excluded' (120). In other words, we can simply *impose* a new constant (call it i) and define its meaning in terms of its 'occupation of this transnumeric place, positing that, for *every* number n, $n < i$.' By definition, this new number i will not then 'count' as a natural number. It will forever remain a pure addition over and beyond the domain it supplements. But if the initial procedures that generate the domain of natural numbers can be made to apply to it – if we can define a successor $i+1$ for i, and add and subtract i, etc. – then in principle there is nothing to stop us from imposing i as a previously impossible term, i.e. as an infinite number. (This is precisely what was at stake in the invention of 'irrational' and 'imaginary' numbers [123]). A similar argument, as Badiou goes on to explain in more detail, applies to the domain of the infinitely small rather than the infinitely large.

How then should we understand this version of an epistemological break, this brutal 'occupation' of a previously unoccupiable place? Since the place occupied by an infinity-point has already been marked with a variable (y), might we simply say that the variable *itself* has the immanent power, *within* the original limits of the domain, to 'occupy' the empty place? Is the potential inscription of an infinity-point thus already implicit within the actuality of the infinity-support, 'such that the true concept of the infinite would already be enveloped in the mobile inscription of x's and y's' (121)? In order to generate our new number is it enough merely to develop or stretch the existing resources of the situation? No, says Badiou, against Hegel. Mere inscription of a variable in an unoccupiable place (on the model, 'for all x, $x < y$') in no way inscribes an *actual* number or constant in that place; it attests simply to the fact that the resources of the system enable us to write or formulate 'the *impossibility* of the impossible' (122). Analysis can identify the real of a situation, but it is not possible, by remaining within the limits of the situation, to render the impossible possible.

In order to exceed the rules that limit mathematical writing to the domain it defines as possible, in other words, these rules must be interrupted by something wholly external to their domain. The 'impossible' must itself intervene and interrupt the possible. The impossible must occur as something that happens *to* the domain. Here Badiou follows Lacan's lead: for any given 'domain of fixed proofs, impossibility characterizes the real' (CpA 9.8:122). All that can be formulated of this impossibility, *within* the normal confines of the domain, is simply that it is impossible; the unoccupiable place is just that, unoccupiable, and the variable that indicates it *as* unoccupiable exhausts what can be said of it. Or to return to the terms of Badiou's argument with Macherey in 1965: the unoccupied or absent space testifies to nothing other than impossibility, and is not the indication of some hidden reality or resource that itself contributes to changing the domain. 'Non-standard' extension of the domain requires the abrupt imposition of an 'infinity-point' (i.e. a new infinite constant or number) into the impossible place. The infinity-point is imposed as a *substitute* for the variable, by asserting without mediation the *'possibility* of the impossible'. Or again, if the mere variable 'realizes [*réalise*] the difference' of a system by indicating the place of the term it excludes as impossible, the infinity-point 'irrealizes' it by including (or 'hallucinating') this term. Once included or inscribed, the new term persists in a relation of pure excess in relation to the 'standard' terms of the domain, i.e. the infinity-point for our relation of order will remain a term that is incommensurably larger than every other term in the domain. In a further confirmation of Bachelardian-Althusserian logic, the reconfiguration or 'recasting' [*refonte*] of the domain that inscription of such an exceptional point entails expands and opens it up in such a way that the 'causality' of the recasting itself is 'dissipated in its operation'. Such dissipation shows how a cause can be effaced in the 'apparatus of a structure' (CpA 9.8:132–133).

From the perspective of the initial domain itself, there is thus no more possibility of 'explaining' and justifying the impossible inscription than there is of 'deducing', to the satisfaction of those who oppose it, the fact and necessity of a political revolution. 'In science as in politics, it is the unperceived which puts revolution on the agenda' (128). It does so, however, not by helping us to understand those under-appreciated or misrecognized aspects of the situation that might lead to its 'inner' transformation, so to speak, but by identifying the point at which it might be interrupted, from without, by that which it excludes.

V MARKING THE LACK OF THE SUBJECT

Towards the end of 'Infinitesimal Subversion', referring to Hegel's contemporary Évariste Galois, Badiou expands on the general significance of his argument. It is 'by establishing oneself in the constitutive silence, in the unsaid of a domain-ial conjuncture, [that] one maintains the chance of producing a decisive reconfiguration' of this domain (CpA 9.8:128). Might we then say (with Macherey and Miller) that the task of analysis is somehow to lend voice to this silence or unsaid itself? Does the gap left by the impossible place only mark the possible place of a supplement or interruption from without – or might its status *as* gap, as lack of possibility or lack of self-identity, somehow contribute to the internal (i.e. unsupplemented) transformation of the domain? Might a gap in the discourse of science itself testify to an immanent exception to this discourse, i.e. a place for precisely that subject excluded from the Althusserian analysis of structure? No, says Badiou, following Gödel. One of the main goals of Badiou's second and last contribution to the *Cahiers*, 'Mark and Lack' (CpA 10.8), is to refute this possible line of interpretation, by reiterating once again the unconditional expulsion, from autonomous science (i.e. mathematics), of all that is external to science. This means that scientific discourse must exclude any notion of lack that is invested with the qualities of an immanent exception 'within' the domain of science, i.e. a lack invested with the dynamism of self-contradiction and self-dissociation, a lack associated with non-self-identity: it must exclude, in other words, the sort of lack or *néant* characteristic of, among other things, Sartre's theory of the subject.

Looking back at the 'basic operation' at work in the *Cahiers*, Badiou describes it as inspired by the 'idea – which also seduced me, as I've often admitted – that it's not because one engages in the most extreme formal rigour and takes up the intellectual power of mathematics, of logic, etc., that one must necessarily erase or abolish the category of the subject.'[25] What this perfectly accurate description leaves out is the fact that Badiou's seduction took place *after* the closure of the *Cahiers*, after May 68 interrupted its most emphatically formalist investigations of science and logic. His final contribution to the journal actually constitutes its most forceful argument against precisely this combination of rigour and subject, in another dazzling deployment of the former in order to secure the exclusion of the latter. As Duroux remembers, at the time of his participation with the journal Badiou rejected its founding premise, that 'subjectivity was *included* in the structure', because he rejected the whole 'theory of the structuring lack'.[26] And as Badiou himself remembers, during his *Cahiers* years, 'I was [still] freeing myself from Sartre,

---

25   Badiou, 'Theory from Structure to Subject', 278; cf. 'Can Change Be Thought?', 243–244.
26   Duroux, 'Strong Structuralism'.

existentialism and phenomenology. I would say that what first seduced me in my mathematical education was the non-subjective, the making possible of a capacity to think outside of all intentionality and subjectivity.' At this point, Badiou believed 'that if mathematics were to achieve the secrets of thought, it was because of its a-subjectivity. It seemed like a psychosis; that is to say, it was the automatism, a characteristic of the automatism of thought, a mechanical conception of mathematics, that I was concerned with in those days.'[27]

Although in a sense it was 'left behind' even before its belated publication in 1969, the argument that separates Badiou's 'Mark and Lack' (CpA 10.8) from Miller's 'Suture' (CpA 1.3) deserves to be recognized as one of the pivotal moments in the history of French structuralism. The Lacanian 'logic of the signifier' that Miller had proposed turns essentially on the representation of an irreducible lack: a signifier represents (i.e. 'sutures', treats-as-identical or counts-as-one), for another signifier, that essential lack of self-identity which is all that can be expressed of the subject.[28] In 'Mark and Lack' Badiou rejects Miller's attempt to formulate a logic that both expresses and is engendered by the subject's lack of identity with itself, in favour of a strictly formal conception of logic purged of any reference to lack, non-self-identity or subjectivity.[29] According to Badiou, in other words, Miller's logic of the signifier is not really 'logic' at all. A properly scientific logic is a wholly 'positive' process, one that – in this respect comparable to an autonomous aesthetic process – 'lacks nothing it does not produce elsewhere' (CpA 10.8:151). The pseudo-logic proposed by Miller and Lacan serves merely to blur if not to 'erase the epistemological break' by which science distances itself from the domain of ideology, i.e. the domain of the subject and lived experience. Their logic of the signifier remains a form of 'metaphysics: a representation of representation, an intra-ideological process' (151; 151n.2). The implications of Gödel's famous incompleteness theorem, Badiou adds, actually undercut rather than reinforce Miller's efforts and Lacan's gestures on this score, in effect reasserting the integrity of formalized science and restricting the 'logic of the signifier' to ideology alone.

27   Badiou and Tzuchien Tho, 'The Concept of Model, Forty Years Later', in CM, 103.

28   For more on Miller's 'Suture' see the synopsis posted on the *Concept and Form* website, http://cahiers.kingston.ac.uk/synopses/syn1.3.html, and in the present volumes, Hallward, 'Theoretical Training', CF1, and Žižek, '"Suture", Forty Years Later', CF2.

29   In RMD Badiou had already acknowledged the significance of Miller's contribution to structuralist epistemology. 'The fundamental problem of *every* structuralism is that of a term with a double function, which determines the belonging of the other terms to the structure insofar as it itself is excluded from it by the specific operation that makes it figure there only in the form of its *representative* (its place-holder [*lieu-tenant*], to use Lacan's concept).' The '*determination*, or "structurality", of the structure' is thus governed by the 'location of the place occupied by the term indicating the specific exclusion, the pertinent lack.' Badiou applauds Miller's article 'Suture' as an 'essential reference' in the conceptualization of such determination. Although 'extraordinarily ingenious', however, Badiou warns that Miller's approach is 'epistemologically inadequate' and involves a 'duplication of the structure of metaphysics' (RMD, 457n.23).

The basic argument of 'Mark and Lack' stems from its (neo-Hilbertian) 'inaugural confidence in the permanence' and self-identity or self-substitutability of logico-mathematical marks or graphemes (CpA 10.8:156). Given any mark x, i.e. any x that refers to a number or variable, logic must always treat x as strictly and unequivocally identical with itself. Badiou thus takes for granted a position that Miller associates, in 'Suture', with Leibniz and Frege (CpA 1.3:43): the articulation of scientific truth depends on the exclusion of the non-identical, with the proviso that 'the concept of identity holds only for marks', i.e. mathematical inscriptions, rather than for the 'objects' to which these marks might refer. Science as a whole 'takes self-identity to be a predicate of marks rather than of the object', a rule which applies to the *facts of writing* proper to Mathematics' as it does for the *inscriptions of energy* proper to Physics', along with the instruments used to measure them:

> It is the technical invariance of traces and instruments that subtracts itself from all ambiguity in the substitution of terms. Thus determined, the rule of self-identity allows of no exceptions and does not tolerate any evocation of that which evades it, not even in the form of rejection. What is not substitutable-for-itself is something radically unthought, of which the logical mechanism *bears no trace* [. . .]. What is not substitutable-for-itself is foreclosed without appeal or mark (CpA 10.8:157).

On the basis of this scriptural self-identity, Badiou goes on to show how the essential operation of (genuine or scientific) logic – for instance the sort of logic at work in formal propositional calculus – involves the 'separation' or distinction of statements as valid or invalid on several distinct levels, or according to several stratified 'mechanisms'. The primary level or mechanism (M_1), the mechanism of 'concatenation', produces arrangements of a discrete set of elementary marks or letters, as a sort combinatorial 'alphabet' – by way of illustration, consider for instance all the possible combinations of the letters used in the English language. At a second level, the level of 'formation' (M_2) or 'syntax', certain expressions are deemed acceptable or 'well-formed', and separated from those that are rejected as ill-formed (152); to pursue our linguistic analogy, at this second level we might distinguish between syntactically valid (though not necessarily coherent or meaningful) sequences of words, as opposed to random series of letters. The third level (M_3), the mechanism of 'derivation', will further separate sequences that can be derived or 'proved' as valid theses from sequences or statements that cannot be thus proved, i.e. from 'non-theses'. We might call this third level the domain of intelligibility or coherence, the level at which coherent expressions are distinguished from unintelligible albeit 'well-formed' strings of words.

Now whereas the distinction of well-formed from ill-formed expressions at level two is absolute and straightforward, the relation between derivable and non-derivable expressions at level three may, in any system complex enough to formulate basic arithmetical expressions, be *either* decidable or non-decidable. An undecidable statement is formulated in such a way that 'neither it nor its negation is derivable' or provable (153) – and although the details need not detain us here, Badiou proceeds to show how Gödel's demonstration of the incompleteness of any relatively complex logical system applies to this level three (M$_3$) alone. The important thing is that admission of such incompleteness or undecidability, pace Miller and Lacan, in no way threatens the self-sufficient or subject-less status of science, i.e. its exclusion of all lack or non-self-identity. No matter what is expressed of it, any mark x must itself always be identical to itself: as a sign or mark, every x must *be* and remain this same x. In other words, expression of non-self-equality at level two does not carry any ontological implications of non-self-identity at level one. It is certainly possible to express a lack of equality between x and itself, with the well-formed (though unintelligible) statement '$x \neq x$' – both $x = x$ and $x \neq x$ are legitimate expressions at level two, i.e. the level of formation, but the expression $x \neq x$ is excluded as non-derivable or meaningless from level three (CpA 10.8:158–159).

Badiou's point, against Miller, is that the expression of such non-self-equality does not threaten the identity of any variable x itself. Indeed, although it makes no sense to say it, it is only *possible* to say that 'x is unequal to x' if x necessarily remains the 'same' x in both instances. 'The mere convocation-revocation of x's non-self-identity, the shimmering of its self-differing, would suffice to annihilate the scriptural existence of the entire calculus.' In other words, we can formulate logically coherent statements of non-self-equality (on the model $x \neq x$) only if we first exclude all that is 'scripturally non-self-identical', such that 'the lack of the equal is built upon the *absolute* absence of the non-identical' (158). Miller's evocation of a non-identical and thus non-substitutable thing (i.e. a subject) is thus 'foreclosed' here in advance, 'without appeal or mark' (157).

Miller's logic of suture, like Macherey's reading of absence, is therefore condemned to apply only to the domain of ideology, i.e. to the domain of the subject considered, as much by Sartre as by Lacan, as not-identical-to-itself. For the same reason

> *there is no subject of science.* Infinitely stratified, regulating its passages, science is pure space, without inverse or mark or place of that which it excludes. Foreclosure, but of nothing, science may be called the psychosis of no subject, and hence of all: universal by right, shared delirium, one has only to maintain oneself within it in order to be no-one, anonymously dispersed in the hierarchy of orders.[30]

---

30   CpA 10.8:161–162. The 'science of psychoanalysis', consequently, can have 'nothing to say

Purged of any reference to a subject, science *qua* mathematics remains an austere 'archi-theatre of writing: traces, erased traces, traces of traces [. . .], marks indefinitely substituted for one another in the complication of their entangled errancy' (CpA 10.8:164). In terms reminiscent not only of Mallarmé, Blanchot, and Foucault, but also of the Derrida whose reflections on arche-writing had shaped most of the fourth volume of the *Cahiers* (CpA 4.1), science here prescribes a signifying movement in which 'we never risk encountering the detestable figure of Man', no more than God, Spirit or any other figure of the subject (CpA 10.8:164).

Once again, however, the exclusion of this risk indicates the point of its possible violation – the point where *philosophy* tries to intervene in science. The lack of a subject in science, i.e. its radical lack of any lack, marks the eternal 'torment [*supplice*]' of philosophy. An ideological practice, 'philosophy' figures here as the desperate effort to locate a subject (be it logos, God, revelation, man, speech . . .) at the very point, indicated by science, where every figure of the subject is proscribed in advance. 'Through science we learn that *there is* something un-sutured; something foreclosed, in which even lack is not lacking, and that by trying to show us the contrary, in the figure of Being gnawing at itself, haunted by the mark of non-being, philosophy exhausts itself trying to keep alive its supreme and specific product: God or Man, depending on the case' (163).

It is hard to imagine a more emphatic assertion of the inviolable autonomy of science as a weapon against ideology and its subject. It is all the more remarkable, then, that even before it was published this assertion had already been interrupted, not least for its author, by nothing other than an intrusion of the subject, sparked by a revolutionary though evanescent upsurge of the masses. Badiou's subsequent reorientation from scientific closure to a *philosophy* of perseverance, moreover, will involve an affirmation of the subject in precisely the place where that science had excluded it.

---

about science' *per se* precisely because it serves to analyze the 'functioning' and 'efficacy' of ideologies. Psychoanalysis helps to establish 'the laws of input and connection through which the places allocated by ideology are ultimately occupied.' It is on this basis that psychoanalysis and historical materialism might be articulated together, as a double 'determination of the signifiers' at work in lived or ideological discourse, thereby 'producing the structural configuration wherein ideological agency takes place' (162). As if to refute Badiou, Lacan would later argue, in a 1975 lecture, that 'psychosis is a trial in rigor. In this sense, I would say that I am psychotic. I am psychotic for the sole reason that I have always tried to be rigorous. This plainly takes us quite far, since it implies that logicians, who tend toward this goal, as well as geometricians, would in the final analysis share in a certain form of psychosis' (Lacan, 'Conférences et entretiens dans les universités nord-américaines', *Scilicet* 6–7 [1975], 9, cited in Peter Starr, *Logics of Failed Revolt: French Theory After May '68* [Stanford: Stanford University Press, 1995], 52).

VI AFTER THE *CAHIERS*

Badiou has never tried to downplay the force of the second great conversion experience of his life. As he was to write several years after the fact, 'I admit without any reticence that May 68 was for me, in the order of philosophy as in everything else, a genuine road to Damascus experience' (TC, 9; cf. DI, 24). 'May 1968 was for us first and foremost a formidable lesson. We felt ourselves woken up, contested, by the immense collective anger of the people [. . .]. After May, nothing is nor should be "as before".'[31] May revealed once and for all that 'it is the masses who make history, including the history of knowledge' (TC, 9). The first thing to go, then, is precisely the old Althusserian relation of science and ideology. Badiou now rejects out of hand any general 'theory of ideology' understood as an 'imaginary representation' sustaining the lived illusions of a subject. Instead, precisely because it is 'essentially reflection' or mirroring of reality, so then 'far from being an agent of dissimulation, ideology is *exactly the way things look [ce qui se voit]*', i.e. 'the material order of things', expressed from the perspective of either the exploiters or the exploited (DI, 19). In 1969 the great task is now nothing other than 'the ideological preparation of the masses', 'a vast campaign of ideological rectification, so as to guarantee the progressive preponderance of Marxism-Leninism'. Once banished to the outside of science, ideological questions have suddenly become 'questions of *life and death*.'[32]

Just as May 68 occurred as an unpredictable 'supplement' to the relatively stable state configuration of late 60s France, Badiou's successive conceptualizations of the subject have always retained an 'excessive', exceptional or supplemental status. The subject is never 'given but must be found': it isn't something one is or has so much as something one 'arrives at' (TS, 294–295/278–279). This remains the essential point, in all of Badiou's post-68 work: everything turns on the affirmation of the abrupt appearance of something that 'deregulates' the existing state of things, something 'was not there before, so that there is a supplementation, or a creation, a positive dimension, and that remains the point around which everything hangs together [. . .]. The apparition of what there isn't, that's the origin of all true subjective power!'[33] The logic of a radical 'epistemological break' is thereby preserved, precisely by applying it to the very domain it was initially formulated to foreclose: the domain of the subject. The alterity that was first excluded as pure transcendence or externality can now be incorporated as immanent excess. (And as for 'suture', it too can be recuperated,

---

31   Badiou et al., *Contribution au problème de la construction d'un parti marxiste-léniniste de type nouveau* (Paris: Maspero, 1969), 4; cf. TC, 9; LS, 178/125.

32   Badiou, *Contribution au problème*, 15, 26, 39.

33   Badiou, 'Politique et vérité' [interview with Daniel Bensaïd], *Contretemps* 15 (February 2006), 49.

through an inversion – by shifting it away from its association with the subject and lack, and thinking of it in terms of being and void).[34]

As a supplement that happens to and exceeds a pre-existing order of things, moreover, the subject must itself, over time, be supplemented. Sooner or later there must be a supplement to the supplement. That's because the subject's tendency over time is to fade away, towards reconciliation with the situation it supplements. Although the consequences of the (previously 'impossible') event unfold from within the situation it supplements, the main priority is thus 'to make sure that the initial distance established between the event and the order of the world, its law, its state, be preserved. The main danger is always that of self-dissolution under the dominant law [of the world as it is], and that the truth process fall under resignation to what there is.'[35] This is the main danger, since over time the consequences of an interruption (a 'truth-process', in the jargon of *Being and Event*) tend towards 'saturation' or exhaustion. 'Everything that is born deserves to perish, in time.'[36] In due course, then, it won't be enough to be faithful to the interruption; this fidelity must in turn be supplemented, and so in a sense must itself be interrupted, through invention of a new 'fidelity to the [old] fidelity'. The Maoist consequences of May 68 have themselves been saturated, Badiou concedes, for at least twenty years. 'Since the mid 80s, more and more, there has been something like a saturation of revolutionary politics in its conventional framework: class struggle, party, dictatorship of the proletariat, and so on.' The alternative is then either to conclude that the revolutionary sequence is simply finished (so as to 'move on with the times' and the prevailing counter-revolution), as most of Badiou's contemporaries have done, or else to affirm a new supplement. 'Fidelity to the fidelity is not a continuation, strictly

---

34   For Badiou against Lacan and Miller, 'the void is not at all the subject but rather the "object" of the procedure', void is on the side of being rather than subject (Badiou and Tzuchien Tho, 'The Concept of Model, Forty Years Later', CM, 100). In Badiou's ontology, the void of a situation, i.e. that which counts for nothing according to the criteria of a situation, is what presents its 'suture to being' per se. 'Suture' in this anti-Millerian sense marks the point of intersection between the consistent structure of a situation and the inconsistent, unpresentable multiplicity of pure being as being – leaving Badiou free to think the category of the subject in terms that interrupt the logic of its situation, an interruption that is not itself grounded in lack or the void so much as occasioned by an ephemeral supplement (a 'supernumerary' event) which indicates this void (cf. Hallward, *Badiou*, 90–93). We might say that Miller's approach allows him to think of a universal or ubiquitous subject, a subject of the signifier as such – but literally as a subject that itself counts for nothing, a subject whose 'zero' is represented as one in the movement from one signifier to another; Badiou, on the basis of an event which reveals that which counts for nothing, develops instead the theory of a subject that can come to count for everything. In a 1990 note on 'Suture', Badiou contrasts Miller's argument that number is engendered through the 'function of the subject' with his own position in which number, on the contrary, is a 'form of being', and in which non-self-identity can only be attributed to an 'event' (Badiou, *Le Nombre et les nombres* [Paris: Seuil, 1990], 36–37, 40).

35   Badiou, 'Politique et vérité', 50.

36   Badiou, 'Politique et vérité', 52.

speaking, and not a pure rupture, either. We have to find something new', and to affirm those new interruptions or events that allow us to continue in the affirmation they supplement.[37]

The subject conceived in Badiou's post-Maoist work is not simply rare and destined to saturation; it also comes to be precisely through the imposition of a *new formalization* – as a new way of formulating and thus occupying (to use the terminology of 'Infinitesimal Subversion') the position of the impossible, unoccupiable or undecidable place. In the works he published in the 1980s, unlike the works he published in the 60s and 70s, Badiou found a way of conceiving the movement of such occupation precisely by rethinking that category and position excluded as 'impossible' or unoccupiable by his own initial conception of science, i.e. the position of the subject, a subject understood now as the subject *of* inventive or revolutionary formalization itself. On this condition, Badiou can refute his initial insistence that *'there is no subject of science'* (CpA 10.8:161). With *Being and Event*, he develops an account of science in which it is not merely the domain of writing or inscription but the domain of being itself that must be *decided*, and in the most radically 'subjective' sense of the word – on the basis of a free choice, independent of all 'objective' determination or influence (i.e. as an axiom). The scientific revolutionaries of the seventeenth century, for instance, understood that to think being as being-infinite is 'necessarily an ontological decision [. . .]. What it took was a pure courage of thought, a voluntary incision into the – eternally defendable – mechanism of ontological finitism' (BE, 167/148). Pursuing the consequences of this decision, in work undertaken by the mathematicians Gödel, Cohen and Easton, Badiou can now show how 'quantity, this paradigm of objectivity, leads to pure subjectivity' and the 'almost completely arbitrary situation of a choice' (BE, 309/280).

What Badiou will do in *Being and Event* with the suspended fragments of his early formalism is thus reconstitute them in an ontological form that remains faithful to both to their original autonomy *and* to their revolutionary disruption. The only difference – but it is precisely this difference that separates Badiou's *philosophy* from his earlier scientism – is that he can now think interruption and formalization together, precisely as a logic of active, immanent, internally-excessive interruption. This allows him to uphold a fidelity to that fidelity which sustained the great formalizing projects of the twentieth century, in defiance of their apparent saturation. Against a traditional notion of form as the shaping of material or appearing of an object, what was at stake in the logic of the century was a conjunction of idea and act: formalization conceived through 'the real grip of an act' is 'the great unifying power of all the century's

---

37   Diana George and Nic Veroli, 'Interview with Badiou', *Carceraglio*, October 2006, http://scentedgardensfortheblind.blogspot.com/2006_10_15_scentedgardensfortheblind_archive.html#116103479719156657.

undertakings' (LS, 225/159–160). In the domain of science, from Hilbert to Bourbaki, Badiou can now redescribe the formalizing project as an attempt 'to reduce mathematics to its *act*', an attempt to grasp this act as 'the enunciation of the mathematical real and not an *a posteriori* form stuck onto an unfathomable material' (LS, 229/162–163). In the domain of politics, at the furthest limit of its effort, Maoism overcame the gap between objective science and subjective commitment (the gap between Althusser and Sartre) by asserting that revolt itself *is* reason.[38] There was then no longer a need to choose between scientific reason and the subject that suspends it, since revolt figured there (following Hegel) as both subject and as historical reason. Although this figure may be saturated today, Badiou's post-Maoism remains faithful to the communist Idea it inspires.[39]

This is why, when Badiou stops to remember the legacy of the *Cahiers* today, he of all its contributors is the one who remains closest to its original effort. He is 'the only one from the old team who remained faithful to the initial project'[40] – i.e. precisely that project that he, at the time, sought to refute. On the one hand, only a formalizing science indifferent to lived experience can grasp the world in its objectivity, and only the impasse or deadlock of such formalization can touch its real; on the other hand, only the interruption of an event and the subject who affirms it, in immanent exception to objectivity, can transform *impasse* into *passe*, and propose through a new formalism a genuine 'figure of universality'.[41] From Sartre to Althusser to Mao to post-Maoism: Badiou's philosophy has avoided the philosophical exhaustion evoked in 'Mark and Lack' (163) by finding a way to affirm each successive interruption as aspects of a *continuing* project.

---

38   TC, 21, cf. 15, 58; DI, 16; *Contribution au problème*, 44, 47; TS, 123–124/106.

39   See in particular Badiou, *The Communist Hypothesis*, trans. David Macey and Steve Corcoran (London: Verso, 2010); Badiou, *The Rebirth of History*, trans. Gregory Elliott (London: Verso, 2012); Bosteels, *Badiou and Politics* (Durham, NC: Duke University Press, 2011).

40   Badiou, 'Theory from Structure to Subject', 288; cf. Duroux, 'Strong Structuralism'.

41   'My fidelity to what happened in that period [of May 68 and its immediate consequences] is unshakable but it is also profound, because a large part of my philosophy in reality is an attempt fully to come to terms, including from my own experience, with what happened there and then, while at the same time explaining the reasons for remaining loyal to those events' ('Can Change be Thought?', 237).

CHAPTER EIGHT

Slavoj Žižek
'Suture', Forty Years Later

When we are dealing with great movements of ideas, their nodal points are often difficult to detect – it might be a text, a debate, an idea, or a phrase. It might also be a journal overshadowed by more popular 'masterpieces'. If we look over the large field evoked by terms like 'structuralism', 'poststructuralism', and 'deconstruction', its nodal point is undoubtedly the *Cahiers pour l'Analyse* (1966–69), the journal which stands for all that, in 'French theory', resists being incorporated into deconstruction. Although references to many great names abound in the *Cahiers* – Lévi-Strauss, Foucault, Derrida, Canguilhem . . . – what makes this particular journal a nodal point is the encounter of psycho-analysis and Marxism, or, in terms of proper names, the encounter of Lacan and Althusser. It is this encounter which counts as a true philosophical event. And, if we take a step further and ask about the focal point of the *Cahiers* themselves, it is the short debate between Jacques-Alain Miller and Alain Badiou concern-ing the notion of 'suture': Miller's seminal text 'Suture (Elements of the Logic of the Signifier)' (CpA 1.3) in the first issue and, quite appropriately, Badiou's reply, 'Mark and Lack' (CpA 10.8), in the last issue.

Their debate concerns the status of the subject, the relationship between subject (or lack) and structure, and we can say that this was *the* key problem of the entire field of 'structuralism'. Its founding gesture is to assert the differential, self-relational nature of structure in its formal purity, purifying it of all 'patho-logical' imaginary elements. Here is Lacan's classic formulation: 'It is the specific law of the symbolic chain which governs those psychoanalytic effects that are decisive for the subject, such as foreclosure, repression, denial itself – specifying with appropriate emphasis that these effects follow so faithfully the displace-ment of the signifier that imaginary factors, despite their inertia, figure only as shadows and reflections in the process.'[1]

The question is then: after this purification, is there a subject to this struc-ture? The predominant answer, at the time, was a resounding no. Even 'post'-structuralist deconstruction, with all its emphasis on gap, rupture, difference and deferral, etc., conceived the subject simply as the culmination of the meta-physics of self-presence, an entity whose self-identity was something to be dismantled (by demonstrating how its condition of impossibility is also its

---

1   Jacques Lacan, 'Seminar on "The Purloined Letter"', in *The Purloined Poe*, ed. John Muller and William Richardson (Baltimore: The Johns Hopkins University Press, 1988), 29.

condition of possibility, how the subject's identity is always-already deferred, how it has to rely on the very process that undermines it, and so on). Derrida's early analyses of Husserl's phenomenology are exemplary here: the subject's self-presence and self-identity, whose supreme and founding instance is the experience of *s'entendre-parler* (of hearing or understanding-oneself-speaking), is always-already undermined by the process of 'writing' that stands for deferral of self-identity, by the 'dead letter' in the very heart of the living spirit. Insistently valorizing the thematics of gap, rupture, deferral, lack, failure, etc., deconstruction dismisses the subject as the agent and result of the obfuscation of this lack.

So what were the positions in the *Cahiers* debate between Miller and Badiou? The ultimate reason for the breath-taking resonance of Miller's 'Suture' was that, by systematizing Lacan's dispersed statements (let us not forget that Lacan himself used the term only once, and even then only in passing), he for the first time proposed and elaborated the concept of a subject that belongs to the very 'abstract' and purely differential notion of structure. In fierce and rigorous opposition to this notion of a subjectivized structure, Badiou insists on the anonymous and asubjective nature of structure *per se*: analysis of structure offers scientific knowledge of the real, there is no lack in structure, and the place of subject should be strictly limited to the level of ideological or imaginary misrecognition, to the illusory way we live and experience anonymous structural causality.

I A BRIEF HISTORY OF SUTURE

Miller and Badiou were not the only participants in this debate. In the third volume of the *Cahiers*, Jean-Claude Milner published his 'The Point of the Signifier' (CpA 3.5), in which, relying on Miller's logic of the signifier, he proposes a brilliant interpretation of Plato's *Sophist*.[2] In breaking with an earlier, 'closed' universe of myth, ancient Greek Sophists like the ill-famed Gorgias had asserted and played upon the self-referential abyss of language which turns in its circle, lacking any external support, such that one can assert whatever one wants; there is no objective measure to the truth of our claims. Plato's main task was to deal with this new predicament, one that he

---

2   One should note here the difference between Milner's and Badiou's sustained reference to Plato, a difference focused on the status of the 'matheme' and modern science. Badiou reads Plato's Ideas as a first step towards the matheme while for Milner, a matheme is not the genuine Idea, i.e., modern science, which with its twin features of mathematical formalization and exposure to radical empirical contingency marks a radical break with the Platonic essentialist metaphysics. See Alain Badiou, 'Lacan et Platon: le mathème est-il une idée?', and Jean-Claude Milner, 'Lacan et la science moderne,' both in *Lacan avec les philosophes* (Paris: Editions Albin Michel, 1991).

experienced as a true *horror vacui*: aware that there is no return to mythic closure, he tried to control the damage by re-anchoring language in the metaphysical reality of eternal Ideas. This is why Plato's *Parmenides*, we should note in passing, in which he undertakes a self-critical subversion of his own theory of Ideas, is the closest he himself comes to being a sophist: here all variations of the relation between the signifier (One) and the real (Being), even if they are contradictory (self-contradictory and contradictory with regard to each other) are in some sense true. That is to say, each of the hypotheses of the second part of *Parmenides* can be read as an invitation to describe a specific ontological sphere within a 'crazy' pluralist ontology, such that the conclusion of these 'sophistic' logical exercises covering the matrix of all logically possible relations between Being and the One is a Gorgias-like one: nothing exists. In all his later dialogues, Plato endeavours to control this self-inflicted damage, desperately trying to draw a clear line of separation between self-referring sophistic language games on the one hand, and a true speech referring to substantial truths external to it, on the other.

The crucial dialogue in this series is the *Sophist*, in which Plato deals with the problem of non-being, trying to outline a third way between two extreme alternatives: Parmenides's assertion of the unconditional One, and Gorgias's sophistic playing with the multiplicity of non-being. Plato describes sophistry as the *appearance-making art*. Imitating true wisdom, sophists produce deceptive appearances. In their empty ratiocinations and search for rhetorical effects, they talk about things that do not exist, that are not. But how can one talk about non-being, making it appear as something that is? To formulate this question, Plato is compelled to counter Parmenides's opposite thesis, whereby 'it is impossible that things that are not are'. Things which are not (but only appear to be) also somehow 'are'. But how? Plato's answer is to define Not-Being not as the opposite of Being (i.e., not as excluded from the domain of Being), but as a Difference within the domain of Being. Negative predication indicates something different from the predicate itself (when I say 'this is not black', I thereby imply that this has any of the other non-black colours). Plato's basic solution is thus to relativize non-being, i.e., to restrict it from absolute negation of being to a relational negation of a predicate. It is in this way that a sophist can bring about a (relative) non-being and thus produce a false appearance: not by talking about absolute Nothing, but by attributing false predicates to entities.

What Plato lacks here is the full deployment of self-referentiality in such a network of relations. If the same is not different, is it then *different from difference*? And is difference the same with relation to itself (identical to itself)? Although Plato comes close to articulating this self-referentiality in his *Parmenides*, he lacked the structuralist concept of *differentiality* which defines the signifying order. The first to formulate this concept was Ferdinand de Saussure, who pointed out that the identity of a signifier resides only in the sheaf of differences (features which distinguish it from other signifiers): there is no positivity in a signifier, it 'is' only a series of what it is *not*. The crucial consequence of such differential identity is that the very absence of a feature can itself count as a feature, as a positive fact. If every presence arises only against the background of potential absence, then we can also talk about the presence of absence as such, i.e., when something does not happen, this non-happening can *also* be a positive event: it can happen that nothing happens. Recall the dialogue between Scotland Yard detective Gregory and Sherlock Holmes from 'Silver Blaze', about the famed 'curious incident of the dog in the night-time':

> 'Is there any other point to which you would wish to draw my attention?'
> 'To the curious incident of the dog in the night-time.'
> 'The dog did nothing in the night-time.'
> 'That was the curious incident.'[3]

This paradox introduces self-reflexivity into the signifying order. If the identity of a signifier is nothing but the series of its constitutive differences, then every signifying series has to be supplemented – 'sutured' – by a reflexive signifier which itself has no determinate meaning (no signified), since it stands only for the presence of meaning as such, the presence of meaning as opposed to its absence.

The first person fully to articulate the necessity of such a signifier was Claude Lévi-Strauss, in his famous interpretation of 'mana'. His achievement was to de-mystify the motif of mana, reducing its irrational connotation of a mythic or magical power to a precise symbolic function. Lévi-Strauss's starting point is that language as a bearer of meaning by definition arises in a single movement, covering the entire horizon. 'Whatever may have been the moment and the circumstances of its appearance in the ascent of animal life, language can only have arisen all at once. Things cannot have begun to signify gradually.'[4] This sudden emergence, however, introduces an imbalance between the two orders of the signifier and the signified: since the signifying network is finite, it cannot adequately cover the entire endless field of the signified. In this way,

> a fundamental situation perseveres which arises out of the human condition: namely, that man has from the start had at his disposition a signifier-totality which he is at a loss to know how to allocate to a signified, given as such, but no less unknown for being given. There is always a non-equivalence or 'inadequation'

---

3   Arthur Conan Doyle, 'Silver Blaze', in *The Memoirs of Sherlock Holmes* (1894), online at http://www.gutenberg.org/ebooks/834.

4   Claude Lévi-Strauss, *Introduction to the Work of Marcel Mauss* (London: Routledge, Kegan & Paul, 1987), 59.

between the two, a non-fit and overspill which divine understanding alone can soak up; this generates a signifier-surfeit relative to the signifieds to which it can be fitted. So, in man's effort to understand the world, he always disposes of a surplus of signification [. . .]. That distribution of a supplementary ration [. . .] is absolutely necessary to insure that, in total, the available signifier and the mapped-out signified may remain in the relationship of complementarity which is the very condition of the exercise of symbolic thinking.[5]

Every signifying field thus has to be 'sutured' by a supplementary zero-signifier, 'a zero symbolic value, that is, a sign marking the necessity of a supplementary symbolic content over and above that which the signified already contains.'[6] This signifier is 'a symbol in its pure state': lacking any determinate meaning, it stands for the presence of meaning *as such*, in contrast to its absence. In a further dialectical twist, one should add that the mode of appearance of this supplementary signifier which stands for meaning as such is non-sense – a point Gilles Deleuze develops in his *Logic of Sense* (1969). Notions like mana thus 'represent nothing more or less than that *floating signifier* which is the disability of all finite thought.'[7]

The first thing to note here is Lévi-Strauss's commitment to scientific positivism: he grounds the necessity of 'mana' in the naïve-realistic gap between the constraints of our language and the infinite reality posited as existing outside language. Like Althusser and the early Badiou, he excludes science *per se* from the dialectics of lack that generates the need for a suturing element. For Lévi-Strauss, 'mana' stands for the (futile) 'poetic' excess which tries to cover over the constraints of our finite predicament; the proper effort of science is precisely to suspend 'mana' and provide direct adequate knowledge. Following Althusser, one might claim that 'mana', understood along these lines, is an elementary operator of ideology which tries to transform a mere gap in our knowledge into the imaginary experience of the ineffable surplus of Meaning.

The next step towards 'suture' proper consists of three interconnected gestures: the *universalization* of 'mana' (the zero-signifier is not just a mark of ideology, but a feature of every signifying structure), its *subjectivization* (re-defining 'mana' as the point of the inscription of the subject into the signifying chain), and its *temporalization*. The temporality at issue here is not empirical but logical, inscribed into the very signifying structure: for Lévi-Strauss, the symbolic structure is an atemporal matrix of all possible permutations of a structure, while the radicalized 'mana' introduces into the structure an irreducible temporality; the 'floating' zero-signifier alternates endlessly between 1 and

---

5   Ibid., 62–63.
6   Ibid., 64.
7   Ibid., 63.

0, between being and non-being, the fullness of ineffable meaning and non-sense, providing the most elementary formula of what Freud called the compulsion-to-repeat. By taking the step of subjectivization, the standard Althusserian difference between science and ideology is left behind – no wonder Badiou later introduces (in his *Being and Event*, 1988) the truth-event and the subject (as the agent of fidelity to the truth-event) in terms that strangely resemble Althusser's notion of ideological interpellation as the transformation of (human-animal) individuals into subjects: the truth-event is here the big Other which enjoins the subject who recognizes him or herself in it to fidelity.

This triple gesture beyond Lévi-Strauss, a crucial step from 'mana' to 'suture', was gradually accomplished by Lacan in the 1950s and early 60s, starting with his articulation of the concept of the '*point-de-capiton* (quilting point)' – a term whose sewing reference obviously points towards the later notion of suture. As in Lévi-Strauss, the 'quilting point' sutures the two fields, that of the signifier and that of the signified, acting as the point at which, as Lacan puts it, 'the signifier falls into the signified.'[8] Recall the old Polish anti-Communist joke: 'Socialism is the synthesis of the highest achievements of all previous historical epochs: from tribal society, it took barbarism, from Antiquity, it took slavery, from feudalism, it took relations of domination, from capitalism, it took exploitation, and from socialism, it took the name . . .' A similar logic, we might say, holds for the anti-Semitic image of the Jew: from the rich bankers, it took financial speculations, from capitalists, it took exploitation, from lawyers, it took legal trickery, from corrupted journalists, it took media manipulation, from the poor, it took indifference towards washing one's body, from sexual libertines it took promiscuity, and from the Jews it took the name . . . In all these and similar cases, the 'signifier falls into the signified' in the precise sense that the name is included into the object it designates.

This, finally, brings us to Miller's text. In 'Suture', first delivered as an intervention at Jacques Lacan's seminar on 24 February 1965, Miller elevated a casual word that occurs once in Lacan into a concept designating nothing less than the relationship between the signifying structure and the subject of the signifier. Miller generates here a notion of subject without any reference to the imaginary level: this 'subject of the signifier' involves no lived experience, consciousness, or any other predicates we usually associate with subjectivity.[9]

---

8   One should note here the link between Lacan's 'quilting point' and the concept of 'point' deployed by Alain Badiou in his *Logics of the Worlds* (2006), i.e. the moment when the complexity of a situation is reduced to a simple choice of 'yes' or 'no,' when we have to decide – war or peace, attack or withdraw, accept or reject an offer . . .

9   In the later development of Lacanian theory complications arise, of course: there is a pathological 'stain' that is the subject's equivalent – not imaginary, but real, the *objet petit a*, i.e. the 'stain in the picture,' the non-signifying remainder of the signifying operation. In this way, we arrive at the four elements of Lacan's concept of discourse: the chain of ordinary signifiers (S2), the Master-Signifier (S1), the 'barred' subject ($), the object (a).

Miller's implicit starting point is Lacan's definition of the signifier as that which 'represents the subject for another signifier'. All signifiers are not on the same level – since no structure is complete, since there is always, in every structure, a lack, this lack is filled in, sustained even, re-marked, by a 'reflexive' signifier which signifies this very lack of the signifier. If we identify the subject with such lack, we can then say that the reflexive signifier of lack represents the subject for the other signifiers. If this sounds abstract, recall numerous examples from the history of science, from phlogiston (a pseudo-concept that merely betrayed the scientist's ignorance of how light effectively travels) to Marx's 'Asiatic mode of production' (another sort of negative container: the only true content of this concept would be something like 'all the modes of production which do not fit Marx's standard categorization of the modes of production').

The rest, one can say, is history. In the late 60s, the concept of 'suture' was taken over into cinema theory by Jean-Pierre Oudart.[10] In the following decade, when it was adopted and elaborated by the English *Screen* theorists, it became a global concept of cinema studies. Finally, years later, it lost its specific mooring in cinema theory and was incorporated into deconstructionist jargon, now functioning more as a vague notion rather than as a strict concept, as a term synonymous with 'closure': 'suture', in this context, signalled that the gap, the opening, of a structure was obliterated, enabling the structure to (mis)perceive itself as a self-enclosed totality of representation.

As formulated in cinema theory, the elementary logic of suture consists in three steps. First, the spectator is confronted with a shot and entranced or absorbed by it, finding pleasure in it in an immediate imaginary way. Then, in a second moment, this full immersion is undermined by the awareness of the frame as such: I realize that what I see is only a part, and I do not master what I see. I am in a passive position, the show is run by the Absent-One, the Other, who selects, frames and manipulates images behind my back. What then follows, to complete the sequence, is a complementary shot which renders the place from which the Absent-One is looking, allocating this place to its fictional owner, one of the protagonists. One passes thereby from an imaginary experience to a symbolic configuration, i.e. to a sign: the second shot does not simply follow the first one, it is signified by it.[11] In other words, in order to suture the decentering gap, the shot which I initially perceived as objective is, in the next shot, reinscribed or reappropriated as the subjective or point-of-view shot of a person within the diegetic space – in Lacanian terms, the second shot represents (i.e. positions within the diegetic space of representation) the absent

10   Jean-Pierre Oudart, 'La Suture', parts I and II, *Cahiers du Cinema* 211 and 212 (April and May 1969).

11   I rely here on the standard exposition in Daniel Dayan, 'The Tutor-Code of Classical Cinema', in *Film Theory and Criticism*, ed. Gerald Mast et al. (Oxford: Oxford University Press, 1992).

subject for/of the first shot. When the second shot replaces the first one, the Absent-One is transferred from the level of enunciation to the level of a role played within the diegetic fiction. (We can now see clearly the homology between suture in cinema and the logic of hegemony: in both cases, external difference is mapped onto the inside. In suture, the difference between image and its Absence/Void is mapped onto the intra-pictorial difference between the two shots).

Of course, such suturing procedure is rather rare in its pure form, as described here; numerous analyses have provided many examples of other, more complex forms of this elementary matrix, as well as examples that bear witness to processes in which a system of suture falls apart, no longer success-fully sustaining the appearance of a seamless continuity (in Bresson, Godard, Hitchcock, etc.).[12] What one should bear in mind is the fundamental ideologi-cal operation involved here: through suture, one way or another, the threaten-ing intrusion of the decentering Other, the Absent Cause, is 'sown up' and concealed. The trickery of the operation resides in the fact that the gap that separates two totally different levels – that of the enunciated content (the narra-tive fiction) and that of the decentred process of its enunciation – is flattened out. Enunciation is reduced to one of a series of elements that constitute the enunciated fiction, i.e. the element that functions as the stand-in for the Absent Cause of the process itself appears as one of the elements within this process. It is as if we have a Möbius strip, but deceptively rendered as one continuous surface. In Hegelese, the elementary matrix of suture functions in the same way as a 'concrete universality', i.e. as the particular element out of which one can generate, through variations, all the others, although this element itself is only rarely encountered in its purity. One of the more familiar objections to the standard notion of suture is that it misunderstands the elementary matrix of classical Hollywood narrative cinema. From this perspective, the basic ideo-logical objective isn't to reinscribe each objective shot as the subjective (point-of-view) shot allocated to a certain protagonist within the space of the narrative fiction; it's rather that each subjective (point-of-view) shot has to be firmly allo-cated to some subject *within* diegetic reality, who is presented in an objective shot. Understood along these lines, the standard procedure is rather that of first seeing the protagonist (in an objective shot) and *then*, in a complementary shot, seeing what this protagonist sees in a point-of-view shot.[13] In short, the ulti-mate threat is not that of an objective shot that might not be 'subjectivized' (i.e. allocated to some protagonist within the space of diegetic fiction), but that of a point-of-view shot which will not be clearly allocated as the point-of-view of

12   See Stephen Heath, 'Notes on Suture', *Screen* 18:2 (1977–1978), and Kaja Silverman, 'On Suture', in *Film Theory and Criticism*.

13   See William Rothmann, 'Against the System of the Suture', in *Film Theory and Criticism*.

some identifiable protagonist, and which will thus evoke the spectre of a free-floating gaze without a determinate subject to whom it belongs (i.e. the gaze of an impossible subjectivity that cannot be located within the diegetic space).[14]

At the centre of much theoretical discussion and controversy, Miller's suture thus made history; Badiou's reply (CpA 10.8), by contrast, was largely ignored, or, rather, drowned in Althusserian orthodoxy. Furthermore, soon after the *Cahiers* debate, Badiou shifted his position, introducing his own theory of the subject (first elaborated in detail in his first masterpiece, the 1982 book of the same name). In a crucial difference from Lacan and Miller, Badiou's subject is not universal (co-extensive with the structure as such, since every structure involves a lack) but *rare*, something that arises only in exceptional conditions when a truth-event disrupts the ordinary run of things. Although Badiou's notion of subject involves a reflexivity that is vaguely homologous to the reflexivity of the subject of the signifier (the site of the emergence of a subject is the 'supernumerary' element of a situation, its 'part of no part', homologous to the empty signifier), the gap that separates Badiou from Miller thus remains even after Badiou introduces the concept of subject into his philosophical system.

II THE AMBIGUITY OF SUTURE

Did then Miller 'win' the debate with Badiou? The first catch here is that the very triumph of Miller's concept of suture is inextricably mixed with the radical misunderstanding of the concept: paradoxically, what won out was a kind of perverted synthesis of the two positions, Althusser's and Lacan's. As we have already seen, what prevailed was the Althusserian notion of subject as the site of an imaginary or ideological (mis)recognition of structural necessity, and the notion of 'suture' was, in its predominant popular reception and use, interpreted as the very operator of this misrecognition. Suture, in other words, designated the operation by means of which the field of ideological experience gets 'sutured', i.e. closed in its circle, rendering invisible the decentred structural necessity. By this reading, 'suturing' means that all the disturbing traces of the radical Outside within the field of ideological experience are obliterated, so that this field is neatly 'sown up', perceived as a seamless continuity. We might illustrate the idea by considering how a large historical process is (over)determined by a complex network of 'anonymous' structural causes, but that this complexity is obfuscated when we posit a Subject (humanity, consciousness, life, God . . .) which appears to dominate and run the process.

This misunderstanding emerges when one reads suture against the

---

14   Michel Chion developed this logic with regards to voice in his *The Voice in Cinema* (New York: Columbia University Press, 1999), 17–29.

background of the conceptual couple presence/representation. This couple is in the very core of what Badiou aptly calls 'anti-philosophy', the assertion of some pure presence (of the real life of society for Marx, of existence for Kierkegaard, of the will for Schopenhauer and Nietzsche, etc.) that remains irreducible to and in excess with regard to the network of philosophical concepts and means of representation. The big motif of post-Hegelian anti-philosophy is the excess of pre-conceptual productivity or pure 'Presence' over its conceptual representation; representation is then reduced to the 'mirror of representation' (the title of one of Jean Baudrillard's early books) which reflects in a distorted way its productive ground. As Alenka Zupančič explains,

> The post-Hegelian philosophy (or, if one prefers, anti-philosophy) started off with this fundamental claim: symbolic representations which were traditionally considered as access to the truth and to the real of Being in fact alienate us from Being and deform it (or our perception of it). And classical philosophy (or 'metaphysics') was suddenly recognised as the queen of this representative misrepresentation. Indeed, if one were to name one central issue that distinguishes the rise of modern thought it is perhaps none other than precisely the issue of representation [. . .], its profound interrogation, and the whole consequent turn against (the logic of) representation. This is perhaps most perceptible in (modern) art which frontally attacked the notion of art as representation. [. . .] In politics, this also was a central issue: who represents people and how they can be properly represented? Why are some represented and some not? And what if the very idea of representation is the source of society's evils and its alienation?[15]

In so-called 'post-structuralism', the relation between the two terms is turned around, and presence itself is denounced as the illusionary result of a dispersed productive process defined as anti-presence, as a process of self-differing, etc. However, the encompassing framework remains that of production versus representation, a productive process occluded by or in the false transparency of its representation. 'Idealism' or 'metaphysics' persist as names for the enduring illusion that the circle of representation can close upon itself, totally obliterating the traces of its decentred production process. Anti-philosophy develops here its own version of the logic of 'suture': it conceives suture as the mode in which the exterior is inscribed in the interior, thus 'suturing' the field, producing the effect of self-enclosure with no need for an exterior, effacing the traces of its own production. In this way, traces of the production process, its gaps, its mechanisms, are obliterated, so that the product can appear as a naturalized organic whole.

---

15   Alenka Zupančič, 'The Fifth Condition', in *Think Again*, ed. Peter Hallward (London: Continuum, 2004), 197–198.

However, the more crucial aspect is the obverse one – there can be not only 'no interior without exterior', but also 'no exterior without interior'. Therein already resides the lesson of Kant's transcendental idealism: in order to appear as a consistent Whole, external reality must be 'sutured' by a subjective element, an artificial supplement that has to be added to it in order to generate the effect of reality, like the painted background that confers on a scene the illusory effect of 'reality'. Such is the role of *objet petit a* for Lacan: the subjective element constitutive of objective-external reality.

The matrix of an external site of production that inscribes itself into the domain of illusions it generates has thus to be supplemented: on its own, this matrix simply does not account for the emergence of the *subject*. According to the standard (cinematic) suture theory, the 'subject' is the illusory stand-in, *within* the domain of the constituted or generated, for its absent cause, its production process. 'Subject' would then be the imaginary agent that, while dwelling inside the space of the constituted phenomena, is (mis)perceived as their generator. This, however, is not what the Lacanian theory of a 'barred subject' actually involves. In the standard suture theory, the subject is that which represents, within the constituted space, its absent cause or outside (its production process), whereas the Lacanian subject can be conceptualized only when we take into account how the very externality of the generative process ex-sists only insofar as the stand-in of the constituted domain is present in *it*, i.e. only insofar as that which figures as 'interior' is present in that which figures as exterior.

The notion of reflexivity might be of some help here. To put it succinctly, 'suture' means that external difference is always an internal one, that the external limitation of a field of phenomena always reflects itself within this field, as its inherent impossibility to fully become itself. Consider the elementary example of sexual difference: in a patriarchal society, the external limit or opposition that divides women from men also functions as the inherent obstacle which prevents women from fully realizing their potential. We can see how, in this precise sense, suture is the exact opposite of the illusory self-enclosed totality that successfully erases the decentred traces of its production process. Suture means that, precisely, such self-enclosure is a priori impossible, that the excluded externality always leaves its traces within – or, to put it in the standard Freudian terms, that there is no repression (from the scene of phenomenal self-experience) without the return of the repressed.

We can now see how Lacan's definition of the signifier as that which 'represents the subject for another signifier', in its very convoluted self-referential form (whereby the *explanandum* resurges in the *explanans*), relies on a very precise rehabilitation of the centrality of representation. It relies not on representation as a secondary mirror of a primordial productive process, but on representation as something reflexively inscribed into the very represented dimension of the productive process. What this means is that the gap, the self-referentially-convoluted twist, is already operative in the 'productive presence' itself. To put it in classical Marxist terms, it is not enough to demonstrate how politico-ideological struggles are a theatre of shadows reflecting the 'true reality' of the economic process; one should supplement such demonstration with an understanding of how the politico-ideological struggle is inscribed into the very heart of the economic process itself. It is precisely this that Marx called 'class struggle', and this is why he speaks of *'political* economy'. One of the names he gives to this strange 'ideology' in the very heart of the economic process, of the 'illusion' which sustains reality itself, is 'commodity fetishism'. Commodity fetishism (our belief that commodities are magic objects, endowed with an inherent metaphysical power) is not located in our mind, in the way we (mis) perceive reality, but in our social reality itself.

III 'PSEUDO-CAUSE'

A similar ambiguity holds for Deleuze who, from *The Logic of Sense* to *Anti-Oedipus*, 'regresses' to the logic of productive presence and its re-presentation.[16] This logic, which clearly dominates the entire notional apparatus of *Anti-Oedipus* with its opposition of molecular and molar, of production and its theatre of representation, can be discerned in the radically changed status of 'pseudo-cause', one of Deleuze's key concepts. Since *Anti-Oedipus* is a study of capitalism, no wonder that the supreme example of 'pseudo-cause' is capital itself – Deleuze refers here to the well-known passage from the first volume of Marx's *Capital*, which deals with the passage from money to capital, whereby money-as-substance becomes money-as-subject, the 'abstract' universality of money (universal equivalent of all commodities) becomes 'concrete' universality of a self-mediating and self-engendering movement. In this way, the endless self-propelling circulation of the capital reaches the level of the Hegelian 'true infinity': every relation to external otherness is subsumed into a 'private relation with itself'. From this viewpoint, the 'materialist reversal of Hegel' resides in breaking this self-enclosed circle of self-mediation and to admit a radical Otherness, not engendered by the capital itself, as the source of profit: it is the 'decentred' labour force and its exploitation. In this precise sense, capital functions as a 'pseudo-cause'. It appears to engender itself, to function as a self-engendering totality, as its own cause, and this appearance obfuscates its decentred 'absent cause', the labour which produces surplus-value.

Such a formula only works, however, if we remain within the field of the opposition between presence and re-presentation. In that case, 'pseudo-cause'

---

16   For an outstanding description of this 'regression' see Peter Klepec, 'On Deleuze's Conception of Quasi-Cause', *Filozofski vestnik* 1 (Ljubljana, 2008), 25–40.

can appear as the point of 'suture' of the field of re-presentation, as the imaginary Cause which completes the self-sufficient circularity of the sphere of re-presentation and thus obfuscates its decentred real causes. But such a use of 'pseudo-cause' displaces and obfuscates its original use: Deleuze first introduced the notion of 'pseudo-cause' as the answer to a precise problem in his ontology of the virtual, namely, how to combine an unambiguous affirmation of the Virtual as the site of production which generates constituted reality with the apparently no less unambiguous statement that (as Manuel DeLanda puts it) *the virtual is produced* out of the actual.'[17] The concept of quasi-cause is that which prevents a regression into simple reductionism, by designating the pure agency of transcendental causality. We might also say that the quasi-cause is the second-level, the meta-cause of the very excess of the effect over its (corporeal) causes. This is how we should understand what Deleuze says about being affected: insofar as the incorporeal event is a pure affect (an impassive-neutral-sterile result), and insofar as something new (a new event, an event of or as the new) can only emerge if the chain of its corporeal causes is not complete, *one should postulate, over and above the network of corporeal causes, a pure, transcendental, capacity to affect.*

This is also why Lacan so appreciated *The Logic of Sense.* Is not the Deleuzian quasi-cause the exact equivalent of Lacan's *objet petit a*, this pure, immaterial, spectral entity which serves as the object-cause of desire? In the emergence of the New, something occurs which *cannot* be properly described at the level of corporeal causes and effects. Quasi-cause is not the illusory theatre of shadows, like a child who thinks he is magically making a toy run, unaware of the mechanic causality which effectively does the work. On the contrary, the quasi-cause *fills in the gap of corporeal causality.* Such a 'quasi-cause', then, is not a merely 'illusory' cause in contrast to 'real' causes. Rather, it *gives body to (or fills in) the gap in the order of real causes, and not only the gap in the order of re-presentation.*

This is what complicates the simplistic notion of 'suture' understood as the place-holder of the absent production process within the order of re-presentations. Along similar lines, Badiou proposes to situate the couple Sartre–Althusser along the axis of the Cause versus causality: while Althusser conceived the field of history as determined by a complex asubjective structural causality, Sartre opposed this reduction and focused on conscious, chosen Causes in the sense of points of reference that might motivate deliberate political subjects (like the 'Cause of the people').

Lacan also insists on a Cause as opposed to causality, although in a sense very different from Sartrean subjective engagement. For Lacan, a Cause is

17   Manuel DeLanda, *Intensive Science and Virtual Philosophy* (London: Continuum, 2002), 80.

precisely that which interrupts the regular exercise of causality, it is ex-centric with regard to the causal chain. To take a Freudian example: the normal run of our speech is determined by linguistic, psychological, etc. causalities – but when a slip of the tongue occurs and conveys an unconscious message, some ex-centric cause has interrupted the smooth exercise of causality. In this sense, the ultimate cause is for Lacan the *objet petit a*, the object-cause of desire, or even, behind and beneath it, the Cause-Thing (*la Cause-Chose*) itself. With regard to the chain of causality, this Cause is, again, a pseudo-Cause.

What this means, more broadly, is that one should leave behind any standard notion of the One (in all its different guises, through to that of a Master-Signifier) as the secondary 'totalization' of a primordially-dispersed or inconsistent field of productivity. To put the paradox in its most radical form: what we need to understand is that it is the One itself which introduces inconsistency proper. Without the One, there would have been nothing more than flat indifferent multiplicity. 'One', in other words, is originally the signifier of (self)division, the ultimate supplement/excess: by re-marking the pre-existing real, the One divides it from itself, it introduces its non-coincidence with itself.

Consequently, to radicalize things still more, the Lacanian One as the Master-Signifier is *stricto sensu the signifier of its own impossibility*. Lacan makes this point clear when he emphasizes how every One, every Master-Signifier, is simultaneously a signifier of the lack of or in the Other, i.e. a signifier of its inconsistency. So it is not only that there is Other because the One cannot ever fully coincide with itself – there is One (Lacan's *il y a de l'un*) because the Other is 'barred', lacking, inconsistent.

Everything hinges on this crucial point. The predominant deconstructionist-historicist, 'democratically-materialist' anti-philosophy extols multiplicity and abhors 'binary logic', seeing in the Two just a mirror-like redoubling of the One. Materialist dialectics, by contrast, knows that multiplicity without the Two is just the multiplicity of Ones, the monotonous night of a plurality in which all cows are black. What the anti-philosophical extolling of multiplicity can't grasp is the non-coincidence of the One with itself, the non-coincidence which makes the One the very form of appearance of its opposite. It is not only that the complexity of its situation undermines every One – much more radically, it is the very one-ness of the One, so to speak, which redoubles it, functioning as the excess over the simple one. In other words, what explodes every One from within is not a complexity which subverts its unity, but the fact that a gap or void is a part of every One. The signifier-One, the signifier which unifies/totalizes a multiplicity, is the point of inscription into this multiplicity of its own void.

In the standard space of anti-philosophy, 'excess' names the excess of productive presence over its representation, that X which eludes the totalization-through-representation. But once we accomplish the step towards the gap in the space of productive presence itself, the excess becomes *the excess of representation itself which always-already supplements productive presence.* A simple political reference can make this point clear. The Master at the centre of a social body (a King, a Leader, etc.), the One who totalizes it, is simultaneously the excess imposed on it from outside. However much the centre of power might struggle against the marginal excesses threatening its stability, there is no obfuscating the fact, visible once we accomplish a parallax shift of our view, that the original excess is that of the central One itself, or as Lacan might have put it: the One is always-already ex-timate with regard to what it unifies. The One totalizes the field it unifies by way of 'condensing' in itself the very excess that threatens this field. We encounter here the same self-relating move of the redoubled negation as in the case of the law itself as the universalized crime (or property itself as a form of theft). We pass from the excess with regard to the field of representation (the excess of that which eludes representation) to the excess of representation itself, i.e., to the representation itself as an excess with regard to what it represents.

What happened 'after Hegel', then, was not simply that the One of re-presentation was no longer able to totalize the multiplicity of present reality. What happened was something much more precise. The One (of the Master-Signifier) lost its ability to 'condense' (or, to put it in Freudian terms of libidinal investment, to 'bind') the excess, to (re)mark it, to effectively function as its stand-in, its place-holder. As a result the excess became 'unbound', a threat to the representative system in all its guises, from the rabble in politics to 'free sex' in love relations – something which was either feared and controlled or celebrated as the site of freedom and resistance:

> a spectre of excess starts haunting the society, in its different spheres; and its 'spectral' form is in no way insignificant. The Master's discourse (or, if one prefers, the authority of the One) is a social bond in which this excessive element is, if one may say so, in the 'ideal' place, in the service of the hegemonic power of the One, which reigns by *assuming* the very excessiveness of excess. What happens with the destitution of this bond is, so to speak, that the ghost of excess escapes from the bottle. This process could be said to have started with the French Revolution, to have reached its full extent in the nineteenth century, and to have continued through a part of the twentieth century. [. . .] We can say, without oversimplifying things, that virtually all serious thinkers sought to think at a maximal proximity to, if not in a direct confrontation with, this excess. A 'tarrying with the excess' thus became the most prominent figure of thought. Utopias, designed to eliminate social and other injustice, mostly proposed to achieve this by eliminating this very excess. To a certain extent, even Marx was tempted by the possibility of eliminating, once and for all, the excessive, disharmonious element of society – the element in which he himself recognized its truth, its real and its symptom.[18]

---

18   Zupančič, 'The Fifth Condition', p. 196.

This critical reference to Marx is crucial here. Precisely as Marxists, on behalf of our fidelity to Marx's work, we should discern his mistake. Marx perceived how capitalism unleashed the breathtaking dynamics of self-enhancing productivity – witness his fascinated descriptions of how, in capitalism, 'all that is solid melts into air', of how capitalism is the greatest revolutionizer in the entire history of humanity, etc. Marx also clearly perceived how this capitalist dynamic is propelled by its own inner obstacle or antagonism, such that the ultimate limit of capitalism (of the capitalist self-propelling productivity) is capital itself: capitalism's incessant development and revolutionizing of its own material conditions, the mad dance of its unconditional spiral of productivity, is ultimately nothing but a desperate flight forward to escape its own debilitating inherent contradiction. Marx's fundamental mistake was to conclude, from these insights, that a new, higher social order (i.e. communism) is possible, an order that would not only maintain but even raise to a higher degree and effectively fully release the potential of that self-increasing spiral of productivity which, in capitalism, on account of its inherent obstacle ('contradiction'), is again and again thwarted by socially destructive economic crises. In short, what Marx overlooked is that, to put it in the standard Derridean terms, this inherent obstacle/antagonism (understood as the 'condition of impossibility' of the full deployment of the productive forces) is simultaneously the 'condition of possibility' of that deployment. If we abolish the obstacle, the inherent contradiction of capitalism, we do not get the fully unleashed drive to productivity finally delivered of its impediment. Instead we lose precisely this productivity that seemed to be generated and simultaneously thwarted by capitalism. If we take away the obstacle, in other words, the very potential thwarted by this obstacle dissipates.

Therein resides Lacan's fundamental reproach to Marx, which focuses on the ambiguous overlapping between surplus-value and surplus-enjoyment. Badiou himself is ambiguous here. Although he (correctly) endeavours to re-assert philosophy against any anti-philosophical 'passion of the real', nevertheless he too remains overly indebted to the post-philosophical *topos* of representation as the mystifying mirror of the productive real.

The same basic problem arises whenever we try to understand some complex and confused empirical situation in which we find ourselves. Since we never start from the zero-point of pure pre-notional experience, we begin with the double movement of directly applying to this situation the abstract-universal notions at our disposal, and of analyzing the situation. We begin by comparing its elements among themselves and with our previous experiences, generalizing, formulating empirical universals. Sooner or later, we become aware of inconsistencies in the notional schemes we use to understand the situation. Something that should have been a subordinate species seems to encompass and dominate the entire field. Different classifications and categorizations clash, without us being able to decide which one is more 'true', etc. In our ordinary or spontaneous mind-frame, we dismiss such inconsistencies as indications of the limits of our understanding: reality is much too rich and complex for our abstract categories, we will never be able to deploy a notional network adequate to reality in all its intensity and diversity . . . But at that point, however, if we have a refined theoretical sense, we soon come to notice something strange and unexpected. We start to realize that we cannot clearly distinguish the inconsistencies of our notion of an object from the inconsistencies which are immanent to this object 'itself'. The 'thing itself', in other words, is inconsistent, full of tensions, struggling between its different determinations, and the deployment of these tensions, this struggle, is precisely what makes it 'alive'.

IV A 'FRAGMENT OF BEING'?

The problem with Badiou's post-*Cahiers* dualism of 'human animal' and 'immortal subject' is that it ignores Freud's basic lesson. There is no 'human animal', Freud tells us; a human being is from its birth (and even before) torn out from the realm of animal constraints, its instincts are 'denaturalized', caught in the circularity of the (death-)drive, functioning 'beyond the pleasure principle', etc. This is why there is no place for 'death drive' in Badiou's edifice, no place for the 'distortion' of human animality that might precede an immaculate fidelity to an event. It is not only the 'miracle' of a traumatic encounter with an event which derails a human subject from its animality: qua human, its libido is already in itself derailed. (In a step further, one should even venture that there is no animal *tout court*, if by 'animal' we mean a living being fully fitting its environs: the lesson of Darwinism is that *every* harmonious balance in the exchange between an organism and its environs is a temporary and fragile one, one that can explode at any moment; any notion of animality as a harmonious natural balance disturbed by human *hubris* is itself a human fantasy.) No wonder, then, that Badiou has such problems with the notion of (death-)drive, that he regularly dismisses it as a morbid obsession, etc.[19]

The properly dialectical-materialist alternative here is not, of course, the direct spiritualization of nature in the mode of the Romantic *Naturphilosophie*, but an immanent de-naturalization of nature. Kant already provides a guideline

---

19   Badiou's reluctance to address the death drive should be contrasted to some of the more orthodox Freudian contributors to the *Cahiers* (notably Serge Leclaire and Andre Green), who remained sceptical about the *Cahiers*' apparent push towards uncompromising formalization, and who thus emphasize drive as the (embodied) element that resists formalization. One should note here that these authors were also critical of Lacan and, especially, of Miller: what the late Lacan and Miller tried to do was precisely to radically formalize (i.e. de-biologize) drive, reading it as a purely formal 'twist' or repetitive torsion of the signifying order. See above, Tracy McNulty's contribution to this volume.

here: for Kant, 'humanizing' discipline and education do not directly work on our animal nature, forging it into human individuality. As Kant points out, animals as such cannot be properly educated since their behaviour is already predestined by their instincts. What this means is that, paradoxically, in order to be educated into freedom (*qua* moral autonomy and self-responsibility), *I already have to be free* in a much more radical, 'noumenal', monstrous even, sense. The Freudian name for this monstrous freedom, of course, is death drive. It is interesting to note how philosophical narratives of the 'birth of man' are always compelled to presuppose a moment in human (pre)history when (what will become) man, is no longer a mere animal and simultaneously not yet a 'being of language', bound by symbolic Law, i.e. a moment of thoroughly 'perverted', 'denaturalized', 'derailed' nature which is nevertheless not yet culture. In his anthropological writings, Kant emphasized that the human animal needs disciplinary pressure in order to tame an uncanny 'unruliness' which seems to be inherent to human nature – a wild, unconstrained propensity to insist stubbornly on one's own will, cost what it may. It is on account of this 'unruliness' that the human animal needs a Master to discipline him. Such discipline targets this 'unruliness', rather than the 'animal' nature in man. This insight also forms the core of Hegel's notion of madness. When Hegel determines madness to be a withdrawal from the actual world, the closing of the soul into itself, its 'contraction', the process whereby it cuts itself off from external reality, does not this withdrawal designate the severing of links with the *Umwelt*, the end of the subject's immersion into its immediate natural environs? Is it not then the founding gesture of 'humanization' itself? Was this withdrawal-into-self not already accomplished by Descartes in his universal doubt and reduction to cogito, which (as Derrida pointed out in his 'Cogito and the History of Madness'[20]) also involves a passage through the moment of radical madness?

V THE FOUR FUNDAMENTAL CONCEPTS

Badiou does offer at least an implicit reply to this question (how a distortion at the level of Being, of its animal life, opens up a space for an Event) already in his early masterpiece *The Theory of Subject* (1982), where he deploys his own four fundamental concepts – the four fundamental subjective-affective attitudes towards the Real. He opposes there two couples: the Sophoclean couple of terror and anxiety (Creon's terror, Antigone's anxiety), and the Aeschylean couple of courage and justice (Orestes' courage, Athena's justice).

Badiou supplements the 'Sophoclean' couple anxiety-superego (Antigone-Creon) with the 'Aeschylean' couple of courage and justice (Orestes-Athena).

---

20   See Jacques Derrida, 'Cogito and the History of Madness', in *Writing and Difference* (Chicago: The University of Chicago Press, 1978).

While the Sophoclean universe remains caught in the cycle of violence and revenge, Aeschylus opens up the possibility of a *new* law which breaks the deadly gridlock of violence and revenge. However, he insists that all four are necessary constituents of a Truth-Event: 'The courage of the scission of the laws, the anxiety of an opaque persecution, the superego of the blood-thirsty Erinyes, and finally justice according to the consistency of the new – these are the four concepts that articulate the subject.'[21] In Aeschylus' *The Suppliants*, for instance, a play which tackles the problem of how to deal with those who seek refuge from tyranny, what the people display is courage (to risk war with Egypt) and sense of justice (to protect the 'suppliants' from their brutal fate).

Badiou proposes here his own tetrad of the 'four fundamental concepts' of the truth-event, his own version of Lacan's four fundamental concepts of psychoanalysis. There are many deeply relevant insights to be drawn from this tetrad, from the assertion of the inevitable role of terror in emancipatory politics to the crucial distinction between heroism and justice. 'If heroism is the subjective figure of facing up to the impossible, then courage is the virtue of endurance in the impossible.'[22] Heroism without courage is constrained to a momentary pathetic suicidal gesture followed by the conformist 'sobriety' of returning to the common sense of the everyday Life; the truly difficult thing is to courageously persist in the fidelity to the Event. This tetrad allows, furthermore, for a very pertinent diagnosis of today's predicament, insofar as 'this subjective figure, whose dialectical edge is limited to that of anxiety and the superego, must always prevail in times of decadence and disarray, both in history and in life.'[23] Or, to quote Bruno Bosteels' perspicuous paraphrase: 'the Sophoclean dominant of our times can be seen as a symptom of the fact that once courage and justice are dismissed as so many illusions of dogmatic voluntarism, what we are left with are precisely only the twin dispositions of anxiety and terror, that is to say, an excessive dimension of the real as too-much that at the same time exposes the fragility and precariousness of the law qua non-law.'[24]

The problem that nevertheless persists here is double. First, is 'justice' really the term which belongs to the same series of 'emotional' responses to the encounter of a Truth? Does not locating it into this series 'subjectivize' it too much? A different possible candidate would have been *enthusiasm*, which, already in Kant, designates a subjective elevation which bears witness to the encounter of a noumenal Real. That is to say, insofar as anxiety and courage form a couple of opposites, do terror and enthusiasm not form another

---

21   Alain Badiou, *Theory of the Subject* [1982], trans. Bruno Bosteels (London: Continuum, 2009), 157.

22   Badiou, *De quoi Sarkozy est-il le nom?* (Paris: Lignes, 2007), 97.

23   Badiou, *Theory of the Subject*, 163.

24   Bruno Bosteels, 'Force of Nonlaw: Alain Badiou's Theory of Justice', *Cardozo Law Review* 29:5 (2008), 1920.

symmetrical couple? In the same way that courage can only emerge against the background of anxiety (the courage to accomplish an act which is not covered by the 'big Other'), enthusiasm can only emerge against the background of terror, as its immanent reversal – as it was, again, already clear to Kant, for whom the terror at our utter impotence in front of the unleashed violent outburst of some natural power turns around into enthusiasm when we become aware of how not even the mightiest natural violence can threaten our autonomy as free moral agents.

Second, can 'terror' really be conceived as replacing 'superego'? To put it in somewhat simplified terms, not only is terror for Badiou an unavoidable aspect of the subjective relating to a Truth, he also goes to the (political) end and insists that terror is present in *every* emancipatory politics, ironically referring to his own politics as the 'search for a good terror'. It is absolutely crucial to distinguish this emancipatory terror in both its aspects, the subjective experience as well as the exercise of power, from the superego-excesses of legal power, the excess of non-law in the very heart of the law. Whatever Creon stands for, the opportunist *Realpolitik* or the superego-excess of legal power, he definitely does not stand for emancipatory terror.

Correcting Badiou, I would like to propose a new i.e. third series of the 'four fundamental concepts of emancipatory politics': anxiety, courage, terror, enthusiasm. It was already Heidegger who developed in detail this point about anxiety: when the very base of our existence is shattered by terror, when a mere ontic fear changes into anxiety, when we are confronted with the ontological Void of our being, we are violently torn out of what Badiou calls the utilitarian-hedonist 'animal life' (and what Heidegger calls our engaged being-in-the-world). But whereas for Badiou, the experience of anxiety, of out-of-jointness, of negativity in general, is a precondition of the event, as it were its retroactive negative shadow, one should confer on it a 'stronger' autonomous role. Negativity, whose Freudian name is 'death drive', is nothing less than the primordial ontological fact: for a human being, there is no 'animal life' prior to it. In other words, a human being is *constitutively* 'out-of-joint'. Every 'normality' is a secondary normalization of the primordial dislocation that is 'death drive', and it is only through the terrorizing experience of the utter vacuity of every positive order of 'normality' that a space opens up for an event.

Where, then, do we stand today with regard to the *Cahiers* debate between Miller and Badiou? Against Badiou, we should insist on a 'universal' subject, since anxiety is co-extensive with the 'human condition', and it is this anxiety which is the site of primordial subjectivization – any subjective fidelity to a truth-event always comes after this fact. There is, however, also a crucial limitation to Miller's position, a limitation which, one might argue, is that of psychoanalysis as such. For Miller, who follows Lacan here, anxiety remains the only affect which doesn't cheat, as Freud already said. This means that there is in every political enthusiasm for a Cause an element of imaginary misrecognition, or as Miller insists, especially in recent years, politics is a domain of imaginary and symbolic identifications, and as such the domain of illusions. Such a position unavoidably culminates in a kind of cynical pessimism (which can be also masked as a position of tragic grandeur): all collective enthusiastic engagement can only end in fiasco, the truth can only be experienced momentarily, through self-blinding acts of tragic authenticity in which we 'traverse the fantasy.' These moments cannot be sustained permanently, so as a rule the only thing we can do is to 'play the (social) game', aware that it is ultimately a mere game of illusions . . .

Unlike Miller, Badiou enables us to break out of this ennobled tragic cynicism: enthusiasm is no less 'authentic' than anxiety, a collective political engagement does not *eo ipso* involve imaginary misrecognition.

This difference is absolutely crucial today – it is the difference between social death and political life, between endorsing the dominant post-political cynicism and gathering the courage for a radical emancipatory engagement.

CHAPTER NINE

A Philosophical Conjuncture:
An Interview with Étienne Balibar
and Yves Duroux

Paris, France, 6 May 2007

Peter Hallward (PH): The *Cahiers pour l'Analyse* were not your concern, Étienne, but it would be very useful to talk a little about what went on at the École Normale Supérieure (ENS) in those years, and especially in the years before the *Cahiers* were launched, i.e. before 1966. You arrived at the ENS in 1960, right?

Étienne Balibar (EB): Yes, in the autumn of 1960; I was in the same class as Yves [Duroux] and we immediately became friends. The philosophical conjuncture was shaped by the initial stages of Lévi-Strauss and Sartre's discussion on Marxism, history and structuralism; on a political level, the context was marked by the end of the Algerian war. In the student milieu, the left was completely hegemonic, and many students at the ENS quickly joined or moved towards the Communist Party. In our general assemblies that year, the main issues were always the war and the organization of demonstrations against the war. There were two groups who fought for hegemony in these assemblies: on the one hand the communists, especially the scientists, but also some students in the humanities and liberal arts, and on the other hand, people who had seceded from the Socialist Party (including Alain Badiou and Emmanuel Terray, who were roughly five years older than us) in opposition to the party's participation in the Algerian war. I thought about what to do for a while, and one day I said to Yves [Duroux] 'I'm going to join the UEC [the Union of Communist Students] because, in the end, the communists seem more serious', etc. And Yves smiled at me and answered 'I joined a month ago.'

The UEC was a very lively place, a place of non-stop arguments, an important pressure group that was highly mobilized against the war. The Communist Party (PCF) had always had trouble with its student organization and was determined to control it, in order eventually to control the UNEF [National Union of French Students]. We participated in a series of successive battles within the UEC, some in which we were in the opposition, others in which we were manipulated by the party leaders. The party leaders excelled in the art of using one dissident group against another; the main person pulling the strings was Roland Leroy, future director of *l'Humanité*.

There were three successive struggles for control of the UEC in those years. The first was the battle against the Trotskyists: Alain Krivine, who later founded the LCR [Revolutionary Communist League], had obtained great influence within the UEC because of the role he and his comrades played in fighting off Le Pen's fascist groups in the Latin Quarter, but during one of the organization's congresses various other factions united to force them out. Then there was the fight against the 'Italians', the pro-Italians, which is to say the reformist wing of the party, followed by the fight against the Maoists, the pro-Chinese. Leroy used the Maoists against the Italians very effectively.

PH: And in this context, you began studying with Althusser?

EB: In April 1961, that is, at the end of our first year at the École, Althusser published a rather erudite article in *La Pensée* (an official Communist Party journal, which nevertheless managed to avoid a stifling orthodoxy), which was entitled 'On the Young Marx'; it would eventually be the second chapter of *For Marx* (1965). It became famous for its critique of Sartre's analytico-teleological method.[1] We were very impressed. It corresponded perfectly with our philosophical preferences. Three of us went to see him (Yves, Pierre Macherey and me) and we told him 'we would really like to work with you on this, we want to read Marx, etc.' And Althusser said: 'get to work and read a certain number of texts (Marx's 1844 manuscripts, his text on the Jewish question, etc. - there wasn't any question of *Capital* yet). Come back to see me at the beginning of the next academic year, in October 62, and we'll see what we can do together.' It was obvious that he was very keen.

Althusser then set up a seminar on the young Marx for the year 1961–62 – it was an official seminar of the ENS, but open to all who wanted to come along. We were roughly 10 or 15, attending. And there, something rather unusual took shape, a special kind of collaboration. Althusser told us quite clearly that he had been thinking about certain things for a long time and that he had been waiting for this moment. Something happened, there was as a philosophical conjuncture and also a sort of personal encounter. He wanted to work in a group. The eventual outcome would be the *Reading Capital* seminar of 1964–65, which illustrated the situation perfectly: he did half of it by himself, but if the rest of us hadn't been there, he wouldn't have done anything at all.

So in 1961–62 we did a seminar on the young Marx. The following year we followed up with a seminar on 'the origins of structuralism', and the year after that, 63–64, one on psychoanalysis, mainly on Lacan. He told us: 'you cannot

1   Cf. Louis Althusser, 'Sur le jeune Marx (Questions de théorie)', *La Pensée* 96 (1961); 'On the Young Marx: Theoretical Questions', in FM, 59–63.

work if you don't study Lacan'. The aim was to keep working on the things we were interested in, but we had to take this detour through Lacan.

Yves Duroux (YD): Foucault's *History of Madness* (1961) was the point of departure for the seminar of 62–63.

EB: Yes, that's right, the first of Althusser's talks was on *History of Madness*.

YD: Althusser was convinced that it was a very important book, and he did a lot to relate this book to the question of structuralism – a term that, as such, didn't exist yet. Althusser asked each of us to prepare something – I remember that I did something on Dumézil, Jean-Marie Villégier (the future theatre and opera director) did something on structuralism in Freud, and Michel Tort gave a presentation on Lacan. Miller had just arrived at the ENS and he joined this seminar with the others; he was very young, very brilliant.

EB: Following Althusser's suggestion, Lacan came to do two small, private seminars at the École, exclusively for us. I remember that he did something he would come back to later, on the 'aphanisis' or fading of the subject, which is what he called alienation. We were five or six: Badiou and Regnault were no longer at the École, but there was Yves, me, Rancière, Miller, and then Milner. Lacan had done his homework, he'd prepared his text carefully. Then there were questions. I remember well, as a good Althusserian I asked him: 'thank you, this is very interesting – but what relation do you see with the Marxist problem of ideology?' Ideology – that was always the key word for us Althusserians, the shibboleth of Althusserianism. If I remember well, Lacan then answered, roughly: 'yes, there certainly is one, but it's not the central problem.' And this is where I would say, there was already a sort of division, not a conflict but rather a choice, a question of taste and a way of working, that separated the Lacanians from the Althusserians.

For me there was never a question, there was no doubt in my mind: I would remain with Althusser, I would work on ideology and on science, on the epistemological break, etc. But this is probably where Miller, who didn't want to break with Althusser, found a new, more interesting and more exciting teacher. And Yves, as always, maintained relations with everyone. All this crystallized later, over the course of 1965, up until the publication of the first *Cahiers pour l'Analyse* in January 66: there were Althusserian-Althusserians, there were Lacano-Althusserians, and then there were people who didn't want to be identified with a particular school. And these distinctions would be overlaid by political divisions, linked to the question of Maoism.

YD: Yes, when Lacan came to the École (the first session of his seminar at the ENS was in January 1964) he had already prepared the ground for his arrival.

Althusser too. His invitation was more than a charitable gesture following Lacan's eviction from Saint-Anne; Althusser also wanted his own strategic alliance with Lacan.[2] And we were in the middle of it all. We did those first, closed seminars with Lacan and we participated in the first seminar (Lacan's seminar XI, *The Four Fundamental Concepts of Psychoanalysis*), he gave at the ENS in 1964 – this is where you find Miller's question, which later became famous: 'what is your ontology?' The following year several of us gave presentations during the seminar itself (seminar XII, *Crucial Problems for Psychoanalysis*), which were taken up again in the *Cahiers pour l'Analyse*.[3]

To recapitulate, then: in the work on structuralism, in 62–63, there are three things that intersect – Althusser's Marx, Lacan's psychoanalysis, and Foucault. Foucault was very important too, and is too often forgotten: it's impossible to understand some declarations in the *Cahiers pour l'Analyse* without Foucault. The idea was to review potential ancestors of structuralism on the basis of Foucault, in order to show a connection of thought, to demonstrate that the label might really mean something. This connection went back through the history of philosophy, with presentations on Montesquieu and Rousseau, to arrive at Lévi-Strauss and Roland Barthes. Althusser took us to meet Barthes, we spent an evening at his place, after a conference he had given at the Sorbonne, entitled 'The Structuralist Activity'.[4] We compared them. Barthes was the first to openly declare himself as a structuralist; Foucault was much more cautious . . .

PH: . . . and he later rejected the label.[5]

YD: Yes, but in the preface to *The Birth of the Clinic*, which is one of Foucault's most 'structuralist' texts, from the spring of 1963, you can see perfectly well that he defends a 'structuralist study' of medical discourse.[6]

---

2   See Althusser, 'Correspondence with Jacques Lacan' [1963–1969], *Writings on Psychoanalysis*, ed. Olivier Corpet and François Matheron, trans. Jeffrey Mehlman (New York: Columbia University Press, 1996), 145–174.

3   These presentations were published as CpA 1.2, CpA 1.3, and CpA 3.5.

4   Roland Barthes, 'The Structuralist Activity', trans. Richard Howard, *Critical Essays* (Evanston: Northwestern University Press, 1972). According to Barthes, 'the goal of all structuralist activity, whether reflexive or poetic, is to reconstruct an "object" in such a way as to manifest thereby the rules of functioning (the "functions") of this object. Structure is therefore actually a *simulacrum* of the object, but a directed, *interested* simulacrum, since the imitated object makes something appear which remained invisible, or if one prefers, unintelligible in the natural object. Structural man takes the real, decomposes it, then recomposes it', and thereby renders it intelligible (214–215).

5   Michel Foucault, 'Foreword to the English edition' [1970], *The Order of Things* (London: Routledge Classics, 2002), xv.

6   'Is it not possible', Foucault asks, 'to make a structural analysis of discourses that would evade the fate of commentary by supposing no remainder, nothing in excess of what has been said, but only the fact of its historical appearance? The facts of discourse would then have to be treated not as autonomous nuclei of multiple significations, but as events and functional segments gradually coming together to form a system. The meaning of a statement would be defined not by the

EB: For us Foucault's preface was a crucial text; it worked out a genuine philosophical alternative to phenomenology. And it was published in Canguilhem's
collection; it marked the moment in which we began following Canguilhem's
lectures. It was simultaneously a great step forward and a masterpiece in the
tradition of French epistemology. We found an attention to language in it that
was not at all present in the phenomenologists – nor was it the same as Barthes'
Saussurean semiology.

YD: At the time, in the spring of 63, we finished our seminar on structuralism,
and I remember that for us this text – one of Foucault's great methodological
texts – confirmed our somewhat floating and slightly obscure interpretation of
structuralism. During this year, we thus drew together a certain way of working
in the history of the sciences, in the history of thought, together with a general
theory of discourse, with epistemology. We thought that we were going to
combine Canguilhem, Foucault, what Althusser said about Marx's theory, and
what Lacan said about Freud's theory.

EB: What you have to understand is, basically, that we were all, to one degree or
another, students of Althusser, students of Canguilhem, and members of Lacan's
audience.

YD: Lacan, by the way, had got hold of one of Canguilhem's articles 'What is
psychology?', which we then re-edited in the *Cahiers* (CpA 2.1). Lacan was
enthusiastic about this text.

EB: Canguilhem's article was partly directed against Daniel Lagache, who had a
psychologizing conception of psychoanalysis – and Lacan was in conflict with
Lagache, at the time when he was founding his new school, the École Freudienne
de Paris, in the spring of 1964. Lacan drew on Canguilhem to pursue his own
critique of psychology.

PH: Ok, we now have points of reference to help us think about psychology, the
human sciences, economy and history, and politics. How do you explain the
fascination with mathematics and the abstraction of mathematized logic,
already prominent in the first issue of the *Cahiers pour l'Analyse*?

---

treasure of intentions that it might contain, revealing and concealing it at the same time, but by the
difference that articulates it upon the other real or possible statements, which are contemporary to
it or to which it is opposed in the linear series of time. A systematic history of discourses would
then become possible' (Foucault, *The Birth of the Clinic* [1963], trans. Alan Sheridan [London:
Taylor & Francis, 2003], xvii).

YD: There is someone else who needs to be mentioned: Jean Cavaillès. It was the moment when people began to talk about him, and following his example, to take more of an interest in modern mathematics. It was the period in which students of mathematics at the ENS were Bourbakists, the moment when Jules Vuillemin published his *Philosophy of Algebra* (1962). I myself wrote my masters dissertation on Cavaillès, with Canguilhem. There was also Michel Serres, who taught us, who gave excellent lectures and who knew the history of mathematics well. He also wrote, by the way, an article on Foucault's *History of Madness*, called 'The Geometry of Madness';[7] Althusser had told us that it represented the first attempt to read the book as a structuralist text, in the precise sense of a *mathematical* structuralism.

PH: Was Lacan himself aware of this tradition of thought? Why did he lean towards mathematical logic, towards Frege and so on, in his 1965 seminar?

YD: The role of logic was something peculiar to Lacan. It came from him. It didn't come from us, contrary to what some people say, people who say that we 'logicized psychoanalysis', etc. This isn't true. It was Lacan who made us work on Frege; it wasn't our proposal. Frege still hadn't been translated. For us it followed, fundamentally, from the primacy of theory. For us, structuralism was basically a new way of asserting the primacy of theory. It was a new form of theory in which the mathematical aspect necessarily came to the fore. We had no problem with the claim that there was a *logic* of the unconscious, in the strong sense of the term.

EB: But how did this join up with Lacan's work?

YD: As I said, it was Lacan who demanded it [*l'a demandé*]. I think that Lacan had always considered that there could be a logic of the unconscious, a calculus of the unconscious, a logic of the unconscious structured as a language – a logic of the unconscious. Lacan had always thought this.

PH: Already in the speculation on 'logical time' (1945), for example.[8]

YD: That's it. Lacan had been trained in mathematics by a rather peculiar fellow, Georges Théodore Guilbaud. Guilbaud gave a series of private seminars to three

---

    7   Michel Serres, 'Géométrie de la folie', *Mercure de France* 1188 (August 1962), 683–696 and 1189 (September 1962), 63–81; 'The Geometry of the Incommunicable: Madness', trans. Felicia McCarren, in Arnold I. Davidson, ed., *Foucault and his Interlocutors*, ed. Arnold I. Davidson (Chicago: University of Chicago Press, 1997), 36–56.
    8   Lacan, 'Logical Time and the Assertion of Anticipated Certainty' [1945], *Écrits* (Paris: Seuil, 1966).

great figures – Benveniste, Lévi-Strauss and Lacan. He was a professional, academic mathematician, who wrote very little but who published some extremely ingenious articles on topics that pushed the boundaries of the discipline, for instance on topology. In any case, we weren't the ones who passed the virus on to Lacan, it was more of an encounter. Lacan was already working on the idea of a *formalization* of the unconscious, and he had had the idea of the matheme for a long time.

PH: Though it seems to become more radical over time.

YD: Yes indeed; there was the encounter with us, and we were very enthusiastic about it, insofar as we took it to be a very pure form of the theoretical.

EB: Perhaps this is something very French, by the way, this preference for mathematics over logic. Set theory was, obviously, the jewel in the mathematical crown; for Bourbaki it was the pillar of the system.

YD: Once again, this goes back to Cavaillès: his secondary doctoral thesis was on set theory,[9] and his main thesis was entitled *Formalism and the Axiomatic Method*.[10] Bourbaki considered modern, structural mathematics to begin with sets: different structures are built on them, but the foundation is set theory. Bourbakism was, in a way, Russell's revenge on Poincaré.

EB: Yes, though David Hilbert and the Hilbertians were more important to the Bourbakists than Russell, both in the presentation Cavaillès gave of them and in the ideology of the 'working mathematician' (or as we would say, in the Bourbakist version of the 'spontaneous ideology of the scientists [*savants*]', to use Althusser's expression). Lautman and Cavaillès were, moreover, very strong in philosophy.

YD: Their death was a tragedy for France: the intellectual history of France wouldn't have been the same if they hadn't been killed.

EB: Yes, it changed a lot of things. The death of Cavaillès and Lautman was a catastrophe for French philosophy. Their project was kept alive by Canguilhem (and Althusser had built on it, even if he was not directly concerned by mathematics), and the obsession of our generation was to pick up where they left off, to restart what had been interrupted. Do you remember that preface Foucault

---

9   Jean Cavaillès, *Remarques sur la formation de la théorie abstraite des ensembles* (Paris: Hermann, 1938).

10   Cavaillès, *Méthode axiomatique et formalisme* (Paris: Hermann, 1938).

wrote for Canguilhem's *The Normal and the Pathological*, where he talks about the two branches of French philosophy, one oriented towards the concept and the other towards consciousness or existence?[11] The first branch had been interrupted, and several of us wanted to continue and renew it.

YD: This is very important. It's why we insisted so much on Canguilhem's text on the concept.[12]

EB: We went back to the concept, but we also turned towards something new . . .

YD: . . . and what was new, fundamentally, was the role of the human sciences: linguistics, anthropology, psychoanalysis, structuralism, and Marx, our own 'Marx'. You know, Cavaillès's last word in *On the Logic and Theory of Science* (1946) roughly says: our generation must replace the philosophy of consciousness with a philosophy of the concept.[13] So I think, in the end, we remained faithful to this legacy, in *our* conception of structuralism. We had more means, more ways of developing this 'strong' structuralism, this conceptual structuralism: we weren't limited to mathematics, as Cavaillès was, since for us the concept at work in maths was also the one at work in Marx, in Freud. It was above all this: Marx, Freud and mathematics.

PH: You put Marx before Freud, Althusser before Lacan? In the *Cahiers* themselves it would seem that Lacan's influence is more in evidence.

YD: The *Cahiers* were something that happened *between* Althusser and Lacan, and certainly with an explicit predominance of Lacan. That's clear. Why? Because the *Cahiers* took shape around the theory of discourse and epistemology. To see the relation with politics that this represented, one has to understand the relation between the *Cahiers pour l'Analyse* and the *Cahiers Marxistes-Léninistes*, in which we also participated, Miller, Regnault and me, etc.

The *Cahiers Marxistes-Léninistes* were launched towards the end of 1964 (and the *Cahiers pour l'Analyse* one year later, towards the end of 1965). The first issue begins with a text written by Miller, 'The Function of Theoretical Training',

---

11   Foucault sees a general 'dividing line' running through the various other oppositions that shape the field of modern French philosophy, 'one that separates a philosophy of experience, of meaning, of the subject, and a philosophy of knowledge, of rationality, and of the concept' (Foucault, 'Life: Experience and Science', trans. Robert Hurley, in *The Essential Works*, vol. 1: *Aesthetics, Method, and Epistemology*, ed. James D. Faubion [London: Penguin, 1998], 466). Cf. Peden, 'The Fate of the Concept', CF2, 3.

12   Cf. Hallward, 'Theoretical Training', CF1.

13   Cavaillès, *Sur la logique et la théorie de la science* [1946] (Paris: Vrin, 1997), 90.

a text conceived along the same lines as the later *Cahiers pour l'Analyse*.[14] How does this text conceive of politics? Politics involves an education in theory, against ideology. Rancière explains all this very well, in his *Althusser's Lesson* (1974).[15] Unlike Étienne, Rancière was intrigued by Lacanianism, and he was furthermore very close to Milner, they came from the same *khâgne*. All this was bound up, of course, with personal relations: I was friends with Étienne, and with Miller, and through Miller also with Milner; Rancière was friends with Milner, but not with Miller; Étienne wasn't close with either Rancière or Miller, etc. You need to understand that this whole business, the story of the *Cahiers Marxistes-Léninistes* and of the *Cahiers pour l'Analyse*, only concerned a small group of around twenty people, all inside the École Normale – with the sole exception of Badiou, who left the ENS too early and who left, precisely, as a Sartrean, to spend a few years as a teacher in Reims, a rather quiet town . . .

PH: Meanwhile there was an argument between Miller and Rancière, after the *Reading Capital* seminar.

YD: Yes there was an argument, it's a minor story but it was uncomfortable for Althusser, and the role of peace-keeper fell to me. Miller had mentioned the concept of a metonymic causality in our 'Action de la structure' (CpA 9.6:102), but this text hadn't been published yet, and it circulated at the ENS in manuscript: we had written it in September-October 1964, at the same time we were preparing for the seminar on *Capital* (which took place the following spring). Like the text itself, we had developed the concept together, as a group. Rancière then used the idea of metonymic causality to make sense of something in Marx, which was perfectly in keeping with what we were all saying at the time. Well, he added a footnote in the text for *Reading Capital* to reference this unpublished text; and in any case, no one has written about this period, about the project of the *Cahiers Marxistes-Léninistes*, etc., better than Rancière himself in his *Althusser's Lesson* (1974).

What you have to understand is that, in the year 1965, the student group at the heart of the UEC thought that, in a way, there was nothing more that could be done [within the Party]. They had been used, as Étienne explained, against the 'Italians'; they had been manipulated by the party leaders, and so began moving towards a split. From then on it was about creating their own group, the group that eventually became the UJC(ml) (Union des jeunesses communistes marxistes-léninistes). The UJC began to exist in the autumn of 66. This group

---

14   Jacques-Alain Miller, 'Fonction de la formation théorique', présentation des *Cahiers marxistes-léninistes*, reprinted in Miller, *Un Début dans la vie* (Paris: Gallimard, 2002), 86.

15   Jacques Rancière, *La Leçon d'Althusser* (Paris: Gallimard, 1974); *Althusser's Lesson*, trans. Emiliano Battista (London: Continuum, 2011).

affirmed both an Althusserian theoretical rigour *and* the Chinese Cultural Revolution. When Althusser drew on Mao Zedong's texts on contradiction,[16] he said that he used them precisely on account of their theoretical rigour, and not in order to take political sides with the Chinese against the Soviets. This argument was very important at the time, all the more so since, although the war in Algeria was over, it continued in Vietnam. You can't understand the student mobilization in 68, if you forget that it started in the Comités de Vietnam de Base,[17] in an open battle against the French Communist Party: the party said 'peace in Vietnam' and we said the 'FLN will win!' We thought that the PCF position was opportunist, as usual, and would refuse the struggle and the victory in order to have peace. They started up in 1965, these Comités de Vietnam de base. There was thus a political conjunction between this mobilisation regarding Vietnam on the one hand, and the theoretical orientation of the *Cahiers Marxistes-Léninistes* on the other.

PH: But these first *Cahiers* were solidly established over the course of 1965, and so preceded the creation of the UJC by more than a year?

YD: That's it. The *Cahiers Marxistes-Léninistes* are the fruit of the Cercle d'Ulm, which is to say the circle of *normaliens* in the UEC. Miller and I wrote that introductory text for the first issue in October 64. The political head of the *Cahiers Marxistes-Léninistes* was Robert Linhart, a very close friend of mine and of Miller's. Then there was Benny Lévy, who entered the ENS in 66. These *Cahiers* were conceived as a sort of intermediary institution, halfway between a political group and a theoretical journal, to support what we called the 'schools of theoretical training'. These schools were set up in various universities in Paris, so as to disseminate more or less the positions you find in *Reading Capital*: they taught Althusser's Marx, the theory of revolution. Rancière was one of the teachers in these schools, which began to operate in the autumn of 1965, and which thus coincided with the Cultural Revolution.

The same people were behind the *Cahiers Marxistes-Léninistes* and then the *Cahiers pour l'Analyse*. But over time the *Cahiers Marxistes-Léninistes* became more and more intensely political, while the *Cahiers pour l'Analyse* were more purely theoretical. When you say that, in the end, one can't find much politics in the *Cahiers pour l'Analyse*, in a way that's true; it moves more and more towards an emphasis on epistemology. Its last issue, on formalization, is the one that goes furthest in the direction of a 'theoreticist' version of structuralism.

---

16   Althusser, 'On the Materialist Dialectic', in FM, 194; cf. 211–212, 94n.6.
17   Cf. Kristin Ross, *May 68 and its Afterlives* (Chicago: University of Chicago Press, 2002), 90–92; Julian Bourg, 'The Red Guards of Paris: French Student Maoism of the 1960s', *History of European Ideas* 31:4 (2005), 472–490.

PH: And this last issue is also the one in which Badiou's influence seems most marked.

YD: Yes, Badiou joined the *Cahiers pour l'Analyse* after joining Althusser. He wrote a text on Althusser in early 1967, 'Le (Re)commencement du matérialisme dialectique',[18] which was a very important article for him. He sided with Althusser on account of his rigour. He had already been defending Lacan for a long time, for the same reason, and this is why, when Badiou joined the *Cahiers pour l'Analyse,* it obviously didn't pose any problems. And when he joined, he brought a knowledge of mathematics and of logic that the others didn't have.

PH: To go back for a moment: did this double fidelity to Althusser and Lacan become more problematic after the internal split within the *Cahiers Marxistes-Léninistes* (in late 1965) that gave rise to the *Cahiers pour l'Analyse?*[19]

EB: Faithful to the Chinese Cultural Revolution, the UJC began sounding the trumpet of anti-theoreticism well before 68. I saw this from Althusser's side. I remained Althusser's faithful supporter during all these years.

YD: And I was the mediator, as always.

EB: As you well remember, Yves, Althusser had been accused of theoreticism well before 68, by the PCF on one side and by the Maoists on the other. Exactly the same rhetoric came from both sides: they said, 'you are forgetting the class struggle, you are forgetting that praxis governs theory', etc. By that stage we were no longer at the ENS: from 1965 to 67 I was in Algeria, doing my military service as a teacher, and Yves was doing the same in Madagascar. But I would receive news from a friend of Linhart's, Jacques Broyelle (who later switched to the right, well before Glucksmann), who told me that our friends had agreed to join the editorial board of the *Cahiers Marxistes-Léninistes*, and that I should join too. I wanted to verify things for myself and I asked, I can't remember whom, Macherey, I think, for more information. I then discovered that they had already signed me up – the usual method. In the end I decided not to join.

But I was very close to Linhart, and upon returning to Paris I met up with him. I remember the formulation that summed up the basic issue for him. I told him, 'theory is necessary, there must be a relative autonomy of theory, which doesn't negate the importance of the class struggle, but all the same, we can't do without theory.' I stuck to our *credo*, albeit now in a somewhat defensive way.

---

18   Badiou, 'Le (Re)commencement du matérialisme dialectique', *Critique* 240 (May 1967), 438–467.

19   See Hallward, 'Theoretical Training', CF1.

And Robert told me: 'But Étienne, who gives the *orders*, as far as theory's concerned? The theoretician cannot give himself orders! The orders have to come from the people, the masses.' They were thus already vigorously anti-theoreticist, and the *Cahiers pour l'Analyse* must have seemed even more theoreticist to them than Althusser himself.

YD: Yes, but the real turning point, Étienne, as you must know, came when the people of the UJC were invited, in the summer of 1967, by the Chinese Communist Party. It's when they came back that they began to prepare for what they called *l'établissement*, the idea that intellectuals should go to the factories and learn from the workers. This is when anti-theoreticism reached its most violent pitch. Immediately afterwards the first members of the UJC established themselves in the factories.

PH: Let's go back to the *Cahiers pour l'Analyse*. Did you initially conceive of them as consistent with the *Cahiers Marxistes-Léninistes*, as part of a coherent project? Or were they the result of a split, a break?

YD: I would say that to begin with the project was coherent, in the sense that in both cases it was a matter of theoretical training [*formation*]. We were going to engage in politics through theoretical rectification. But this ended very rapidly.

EB: That's right. Miller and Linhart had been very close, but in late 1965 quarrelled over the *Cahiers Marxistes-Léninistes* issue on literature, which Linhart suppressed.[20] Linhart was intoxicated with politics and with Leninism. A little younger than us, he had marked his entrance into our group (the Cercle d'Ulm) in a spectacular way, showing that he knew almost the whole of Lenin's work by heart. Linhart more or less identified with Lenin. He had read the thirty volumes of his complete works, and memorized them. I don't mean that Miller and Milner were against Lenin on the contrary, there was indeed also a very algebraic Lenin – but for them it wasn't the fundamental reference.

YD: While they began with the same orientation, the two *Cahiers* diverged very quickly. The project of a 'theory of discourse' went more and more towards formalization, towards what the last issue of the *Cahiers pour l'Analyse* turned out to be – which is to say, towards a position rather distant from psychoanalysis. There was a real evolution. It's obvious when you look at the importance of the ninth issue, on the genealogy of the sciences. I took part in the interview with Foucault, by the way, in the Salle Cavaillès [at the École]: it began at about 4pm, we continued until roughly 8pm. We were seven or eight, I can't

---

20   Cf. Hallward, 'Theoretical Training', CF1, 28.

remember exactly who was there. It was October/November 67 and the result was that beautiful text by Foucault (CpA 9.2).

EB: Yes, it's the core of what he subsequently turned into a book, which became *The Archaeology of Knowledge* (1969).

We also need to mention someone else, who wrote in the *Cahiers* under the pseudonym Thomas Herbert: this was Michel Pêcheux, who committed suicide in 1983. He was a student in philosophy at the ENS one or two years before us. Pierre Macherey did some seminars on his work, which are available on his website.[21] Pêcheux was very brilliant, with an immense range of cultural reference, scarred by a dreadful personal and familial history. Placing himself at the centre of a theoretical configuration in which he wanted to renounce neither epistemology, nor psychoanalysis, nor linguistics, nor formalization, nor Marxism, he pursued the dream of synthesis right to the end . . . This resulted in work that was sometimes a little scholastic, and sometimes very strong.

YD: The theory of discourse suited him very well. He devoted himself to it, and it allowed him to combine together a general theory of ideologies, translation, psychoanalysis, Marxism, linguistics, etc.

PH: And concretely: how were the issues of the *Cahiers* conceived and produced?

EB: The *Cahiers pour l'Analyse* were essentially Miller and Milner.

YD: The real core was, in my opinion, Miller, Milner and Regnault. Then there were those who joined in: Pêcheux [Herbert], Mosconi, even Bouveresse. It was very much a project run by *normaliens*.

EB: Yes, it was very, very *normalien*!

YD: What allowed people like Mosconi, Bouveresse and others to relate to the project was the theory of discourse.

EB: It drew together students of logic on the one hand and students of the humanities on the other, including Derrida's big issue, which infuriated Lévi-Strauss. Derrida, by the way, had a great animosity towards Lévi-Strauss, which never left him; I'd say that as far as theory goes, Lévi-Strauss was perhaps his main enemy.

---

21   Pierre Macherey, 'Idéologie: le mot, l'idée, la chose: de Thomas Herbert à Michel Pêcheux' (2006–07), http://stl.recherche.univ-lille3.fr/seminaires/philosophie/macherey/macherey20062007/macherey17012007.html.

YD: Miller liked Derrida a lot, he had been his student at the ENS. In 66–67 Miller was in his final year at the École, and they discussed things together. Derrida was interested in the *Cahiers,* and he gave them this text (CpA 4.1), this chunk of what would become *Of Grammatology* (1967). They were very happy with it. Don't forget the practical side, too: once the journal was launched, the problem was to get hold of enough copy to fill its pages.

EB: They also wanted to make a name for themselves. There was that side to it too.

YD: Some texts were essential to the project, for instance Miller's texts, Regnault's very beautiful text on Descartes and Machiavelli (CpA 6.2), and Milner's fundamental text on the *Sophist* (CpA 3.5) (to which he always remained faithful). Other texts were more makeshift: there's Althusser's text on Rousseau (CpA 8.1), because Rousseau was on the programme for the *agrégation* that year, and there was, for instance, Bouveresse's dissertation on Fichte (CpA 6.7), Grosrichard's dissertation on Molyneux's problem, (CpA 2.3), or Mosconi's on Condillac (CpA 4.2) – those were the MA dissertations we all had to do. Except the last two issues, these were different; here they managed, somehow, in that year 1967, to recruit a few high profile figures, for instance Antoine Culioli, François Dagognet, Jacques Brunschwig (whose very technical article on Aristotle's logic played a decisive role for Lacan, in the theory of the negative existential proposition, the famous not-all [*pas-tout*]), etc.

EB: During that period structuralism became powerful, that's why.

YD: And those last issues of the *Cahiers* were published by Seuil, thanks to François Wahl, who published Lacan's *Écrits* (1966), and who wrote the only philosophical book on structuralism that existed at the time; it appeared just before May 68.[22] These last issues are clearly more professional, more coherent; sometimes, with the other issues, we had to improvise.

PH: But always in line with the theory of discourse?

EB: Yes; this idea of a theory of discourse didn't designate a fixed method, but a field, a set of priorities, which allowed for a kind of competition between several ways of conceiving things, some more formalist, others more historical, others metaphysical.

YD: Yes, there was a certain very strong theoretical core, drawn up in that programmatic text on the action of the structure (CpA 9.6). During those years,

---

22   François Wahl, *Qu'est-ce que le structuralisme?* (Paris: Seuil, 1968).

the key years of 1966 and 67 and those first months of 68, it was through the *Cahiers* that structuralism became known in France. And you have to recognize that there is, after all, a unity in the *Cahiers pour l'Analyse,* from Cavaillès to Canguilhem, to Foucault, etc., whose *Archaeology of Knowledge* had been deeply marked by the *Cahiers* – and in the end there is relatively little Lacan. The Lacan who figures there is the Lacan who deals with discourse and science.

PH: And yet psychoanalysis is very present in the journal: there are Leclaire's seminars, the texts by Green, Tort and Nassif texts, the Schreber extracts, etc.

EB: I think that Miller had a good relation with Leclaire, who of all Lacan's disciples was the most interested in all this.

YD: Of course the relation with Lacan remained important. His seminar still took place at the ENS. But necessarily, the *normaliens* had to keep a certain distance; they realized, of course, that they couldn't contribute to the theory of analysis unless they became analysts themselves (which is why Miller later underwent psychoanalysis, in the 1970s). It wasn't tenable, the idea that there could be a commensality between analysts and non-analysts, around the appropriation of analytical theory by a theory of discourse.

PH: And after 68 it appears that the *Cahiers* themselves were no longer tenable. Did you abandon the *Cahiers* in the immediate aftermath of 68?

YD: 68 made everything explode. Afterwards it's another story that begins. The main actors of the *Cahiers* all joined the Gauche Prolétarienne. They were gripped by politics, and were completely engaged. You have to remember that the *Cahiers Marxistes-Léninistes*, the UJC(ml), were *against* May 68, almost to the end. During the whole of the summer of 68 the UJC tore itself apart, it was terrible. That's how the Gauche Prolétarienne took shape, around Benny Lévy, precisely with the exclusion of Linhart, who was condemned to *l'établissement*, to establish himself in the factory;[23] Linhart's establishment at Citroën was a condemnation, it was like in China, when people were sent for re-education at a pig farm . . .

PH: And was this predictable, was it unsurprising that the *Cahiers* editors would throw themselves into Maoist politics, and become engaged in organizations like the Gauche Prolétarienne?

---

23   Robert Linhart, *L'Établi* (Paris: Minuit, 1978); cf. Virginie Linhart, *Volontaires pour l'usine: Vies d'établis 1967–1977* (Paris: Seuil, 1994).

YD: Yes, all this was predictable. In the spring of 68 Miller was teaching philosophy at Besançon. Besançon was a hotspot of revolutionary syndicalism, with *les gars de la Rhodia*, etc.

EB: I remember a phone call from Miller, telling us that the revolution had begun in Besançon, with the creation of the first Soviet, with the workers of the Rhodiaceta and the revolutionary students, etc. We found a small car and a little petrol in a jerry can (by now France had run out of petrol) and the four of us immediately drove to Besançon, to arrive the following day – at which point the Soviet had already ceased to exist, because the workers had decided they no longer wanted anything to do with the leftist students . . .

YD: It's true that this was quite striking, to see people as far removed from politics as François Regnault and Jean-Claude Milner, people with such refined tastes, etc., taken with the Gauche Prolétarienne . . .

If we go back a little, a decisive moment was marked by the philosophy courses for scientists. Althusser organized these courses in the autumn of 1967 through to April 68 – but I don't know how they began.

EB: If you read the correspondence we exchanged at the time (which is now in Althusser's archives at the IMEC), the correspondence of the Groupe Interne de Discussion Philosophique, which took shape after *Reading Capital* (1965), when Badiou had joined us, you'll see that we were trying to develop a complete philosophy, on the basis of the ideas presented in *Reading Capital*, together with Spinoza, the notes we prepared on the theory of discourse,[24] etc. And you'll see that there were scientists among the correspondents: there was for instance a young chemistry professor, a communist comrade, Jean-Marie Savéant.

Althusser had decided – and this is what he explains in the first course[25] – that scientists were spontaneous materialists, and philosophers spontaneous idealists. Consequently the class struggle in theory was to a certain degree incarnated, within the university, by the relation between philosophers and literary scholars on the one hand and scientists on the other. Pierre Macherey had always had a great pedagogical talent; he was passionate about teaching and was looking for students. And Pierre had the idea that, after *Reading Capital*, there ought to be courses for non-philosophers – this was his idea. In 1965–66 he established an introductory course, once a week, in which he talked about Descartes, Hegel, etc. Althusser thought it was a brilliant idea, and arranged for several of us to take turns intervening: Michel Fichant,

24   Althusser, 'Three Notes on the Theory of Discourse' [1966] in HC.
25   Althusser, 'Philosophy and the Spontaneous Philosophy of the Scientists [*savants*]' [1967], in PSPS.

Regnault, Badiou, etc. The first published text to come out of this was Badiou's *Concept of Model* (1969).

YD: Which was hugely influential amongst young leftist students of mathematics, after 68 – but it's a terribly sectarian book. This was the period in which Badiou was more Althusserian than Lacanian, in which he used Althusser to criticize Lacan. In his text on zero (CpA 10.8) he basically says: Lacan is ideology. Don't forget, by the way, that the last issues of the *Cahiers* were finished well before May 68, and well before their actual publication; the ninth issue (published in the second trimester of 68) had been completed by the end of 67. And the last issue, which only appeared in the first trimester of 69, had already been finished by March-April 68. These last issues take up more or less the same ideas as the courses for scientists, and it's the same people talking: Badiou, Regnault, and Thomas Herbert.

EB: With these courses, perhaps Althusser wanted to do something parallel to the *Cahiers pour l'Analyse*, but which would be less elitist.

YD: Oh, I'm not sure. In any case, 68 blew everything up.

Translated by Cécile Malaspina.

CHAPTER TEN

Strong Structuralism, Weak Subject: An Interview with Yves Duroux

Paris, France, 7 May 2007

Peter Hallward (PH): Students at the École Normale (ENS) launched two theoretical journals in the mid 1960s, the *Cahiers Marxistes-Léninistes* and the *Cahiers pour l'Analyse*.[1] The latter emerged through a split with the former towards the end of 1965. You were all students of Louis Althusser; what role did he play in the organization of the journals?

Yves Duroux (YD): Althusser always kept a certain distance from the connected projects of the *Cahiers pour l'Analyse* and the *Cahiers Marxistes-Léninistes*. His distance in relation to the *Cahiers pour l'Analyse* was real, but the theoretical core of what Althusser said in *Reading Capital* (1965) for example vis-à-vis symptomal reading, is also to be found in our text 'Action of the Structure' (CpA 9.6), a text which circulated *before* the seminar on *Reading Capital*. Miller, Milner and I wrote this text; Miller was the one who wrote up it, but it involved discussions among the three of us. We were very interested at the time in Marx's work on labour and labour power, on the 'converted form [*forme apparente*]'[2] of labour power, which is one of the central points of this text, and which justifies the idea of *analysis,* in a very particular sense. Analysis meant: to seek out the point by which the imaginary element of the structure can be made to topple over. For us, subjectivity was *included* in the structure. It was not something . . .

PH: . . . external, free . . .

YD: . . . precisely. And this is why I maintain that there were two structuralisms. We distinguished our 'strong' structuralism from the 'weak structuralism' of Lévi-Strauss. (Today, on the contrary, I am struck by the fact that there

---

1   Cf. 'Marxism', *Concept and Form* website, cashiers.kingston.ac.uk/cahiers/concepts/marxism.

2   The German *die verwandelte Form* is sometimes translated in French as *la forme apparente*, for instance to translate a phrase in *Capital* volume 1, ch. 20: 'The converted form in which the daily value, weekly value, etc., of labour-power is directly presented is that of time-wages' (Marx, *Capital volume 1*, trans. Ben Fowkes [New York: Vintage, 1977], 683). The value of labour-power appears, in its converted or commodified form, as wages; again, 'money is precisely the converted form of commodities, in which their particular use-values have been extinguished' (251).

are young people like Patrice Maniglier who totally rehabilitate Lévi-Strauss.[3] I have a hard time getting young people today to understand that Lévi-Strauss was not in fact our idol. This is why, in a rather perverse fashion, we opened up the *Cahiers pour l'Analyse* to Derrida, in order to knock down Lévi-Strauss; and he was furious [*laughter*]). And why did we take a distance in relation to this first sort of structuralism? It had to do with Lévi-Strauss' theory of the model: he says that the model remains distant from experience. In our version of structuralism, by contrast, in our strong structuralism, experience is *included* in the structure. This is why there is a redoubling of the structure: a virtual/actual structure. In a way it's quite Deleuzian: structuring/structured. It's quite Spinozist.

PH: Nature *naturans* and *naturata*.

YD: Yes. *Reading Capital* is one of Althusser's major texts, and in a certain way it is very close to this intellectual reference [*envoi*], this theoretical reference.

PH: And in certain respects, you and your friends anticipated it, and at such a young age.

YD: We had a sort of theoretical insolence. We were between 20 and 23 years old. Miller was 20–21 years old. I was 23. For us it was a question of audacity, of theoretical audacity. Rereading this text 'Action of the Structure' (CpA 9.6), you can see that we were trying to be at the forefront of rigour and knowledge. We cite, for example, Foucault's *Birth of the Clinic,* which had come out in the spring of 1963. We cite him against Merleau-Ponty; we immediately saw Foucault as being against Merleau-Ponty. Ours was a double Foucault: simultaneously the Foucault of *The Birth of the Clinic* and that of *History of Madness*. This is why we referred to our initial project as theory of discourse, or discourse theory [*théorie du discours*]. We took Foucault's side on a rather contested point, which was his interpretation of the *cogito*, where there was . . .

PH: . . . the famous debate with Derrida.[4]

---

3   Patrice Maniglier, 'Faire ce qui se défait: la question de la politique entre Sartre et le structuralisme', *Les Temps Modernes* 632–634 (July-October 2005), 425–448.

4   With Descartes, 'madness has been banished. While *man* can still go mad, *thought*, as the sovereign exercise carried out by a subject seeking the truth, can no longer be devoid of reason.' (Michel Foucault, *History of Madness*, trans. Jonathan Murphy and Jean Khalfa [London: Routledge, 2006], 47). Cf. Jacques Derrida, 'Cogito and the History of Madness' [1963], in *L'Écriture et la différence* (Paris: Seuil, 1967); *Writing and Difference*, trans. Alan Bass (Chicago: University of Chicago Press, 1978).

YD: Absolutely, and we took Foucault's side. That must have been in spring 1964. I recall very well the discussions we had at the time. We said: we will make Freud and Marx cohere together, but not at all as the Frankfurt School attempted to do, around alienation, etc., but around a theory of the structure and not around a theory of the subject. We did not want to redo what the Germans had tried to do in the 1920s-30s, at the time of the first Freud-Marx liaison. This question of the Freud-Marx relation has helped shape Western critical thinking from the 1920s through to our generation. In *Anti-Oedipus* Deleuze and Guattari take up the Freud-Marx question again, and Badiou comes back to it in *Being and Event,* when after distinguishing the three orientations of thought (constructivist or programmatic, generic, transcendent), at the end of this chapter he says a rather strange thing. He says: *but there is perhaps still something else around Marx and Freud.* It's very enigmatic.[5]

PH: This would be the path of the subject.

YD: He did not develop it again, but it is one more echo of the Marx-Freud relation. And, just a digression on Badiou: Badiou, who joined the *Cahiers pour l'Analyse* later, did so from a stance that wasn't the same as ours. He was much more Althusserian than we were, in an almost dogmatic sense. When [in 'Mark and Lack', CpA 10.8] he criticizes Miller's article 'Suture' (CpA 1.3), he is criticizing two things. He is criticizing the idea that it is possible to deduce from Frege's logic anything for a theory of the subject. He thought that this wasn't true, that it was forced. He called it ideology. He said that it is necessary to refer logic to what it is, which was to say, at the time, simply the theory of formal writing [*théorie des écritures*]. It's quite incredible, when you reread these texts. The thing that is most caricatural is his *Concept of Model* [1969], the end of *Concept of Model,* it's astonishing. And, on the other hand, he considered that there was something ideological in Lacanianism itself. Why? Because he was against the idea of lack. This is a point, you know, that has always been a problem for Badiou. He is against this theory of lack – of the structuring lack. Later in his work this took very complicated forms, around the void, etc. But in any case, for us, the main idea was the redoubling of the subject; the subject, insofar as it is *absent* at the structural level, has effects of wholeness [*effets de plein*] at the structured level. It was very important for us that there could be this topological redoubling – to pass below the bar (in Lacan's sense of the term).

---

5 'A fourth way, discernible from Marx onwards, grasped from another perspective in Freud, is transversal to the three others. It holds that the truth of the ontological impasse cannot be seized or thought in immanence to ontology itself [. . .]. Its hypothesis consists in saying that one can only render justice to injustice from the angle of the event and intervention' (Badiou, BE, 284–285).

PH: And why, in order to understand this relation between subject and struc-ture, is it necessary to take an analytic approach, specifically? Analytic and not, say, the sort of genetic or 'dialectical' method attempted by Sartre, for instance?

YD: An analytic approach is necessary because one always sets out from what is structured. One always sets out from the structured, but there is a point in the struc-tured which represents, which is the place-holder, precisely, of the point of lack in the structure itself. Analysis is, precisely, the detecting of this point. It consists in locating what could be called the utopic point [*utopique*] or the infinite point.[6] This was connected to the ideas that Lacan had been advancing, namely that inter-pretation consists in grasping certain signifiers which weigh more than others, since it is on the basis of them that one might then reconstitute an unknown discursive chain, a chain of signifiers that remains unknown for its subject.

PH: And this point was a point of liberation in relation to what is structured?

YD: Well, this here is very complicated. Rather than a point of freedom, it is a point to be transformed. Our idea was that, for example, when Marx analyzed labour and labour power, it was properly from there that he referred back to the question of exploitation, of the extortion of surplus labour. This point, of the extortion of surplus labour, is not seen – so there was an analytical grasp or clarification of this otherwise inaccessible point, a point which would then *open up* to the political point. The political point was an effect of the theoretical grasp or clarification (which is why all this was theoreticist . . .), the grasping of this theoretical point on the basis of which the structure could move, pivot, be transformed.

PH: And on the basis of which the proletariat could grasp itself as subject?

YD: No, we were totally against the idea of the proletariat as subject.

PH: But then how are we to understand the 'transformation' in question? Is it a matter still of a properly revolutionary project (following Althusser's neo-Leninist logic: 'without revolutionary theory, no revolutionary movement')? The status of the theory-practice relation, I suppose, must have been a question that Robert Linhart (of the *Cahiers Marxistes-Léninistes*) often asked you?

---

6   Cf. Jacques-Alain Miller, 'Action of the Structure'. Every structure includes a 'lure' or 'decoy' [*leurre*] which *takes the place* of the lack [*tenant lieu de manque*], but which is at the same time 'the weakest link of the given sequence', a 'vacillating point' which only partially belongs to the plane of actuality. The 'the whole virtual plane (of structuring space) is concentrated' in this vacillating point. The place of this function 'can be named the utopic point of the structure, its improper point, or its point at infinity' (CpA 9.6:97). These are the points at which the '"transcen-dental" space of structuration' intersects with 'experiential, structured space'.

YD: No, it was Rancière who asked it *après-coup*, in his *Althusser's Lesson* (1974). Rancière says: you are the philosopher-kings, and this is enlightened despotism. Rancière's text is magnificent. It's magnificent, but I'm against it, because ultimately it rewrites the prevailing idea of the time, which is: we must synthesize the ideas of the masses, rather than clarify a scientific understanding of the forces that oppress the masses and thus distort their ideas. It takes up again the elementary Maoism of the immediate post-68 period, this Maoism which shattered the entire construction of the *Cahiers pour l'Analyse*. This was the most violent point of struggle against Althusser – the idea that when push came to shove Althusser was locked away in his study and far from the masses. Hence, the importance of synthesizing the ideas of the masses, the revolt of the masses . . . In Rancière, this takes on more anarchist forms, whereby *all* theory represses revolt, etc. Our dear Alain Badiou also went along with this in the years 1971–73.

PH: So, returning to our *Cahiers*; to launch the journal you took points of reference from Marx, from Lacan: it nevertheless remains pretty abstract!

YD: That's the least one can say . . . I tell you, it is a masterpiece of theoreticism. You really have to admit that. It was the project of arrogant young people. It's for this reason that I say someone like Pierre Macherey was more pedagogical; he had more historical culture. Our a-historicism was terrifying, in a way. You need to understand: we were very young, and aspired to theoretical rigour – whence the investment in the word 'theory'. 'Analysis' was, I would say, a derivative of the word 'theory'. For Althusser, the word was theory, for us it was analysis, but it was the same thing, the same thing that we sought to render more operational. Analysis meant the grasping of this utopic point, the deployment of the structure, in order, let's say, to open a place for action on the structure. There is the action of the structure itself, which shapes ordinary reality, but action *on* the structure presumes that the action of the structure has been located and understood.

PH: And what is the relation between this action and that of the subject, the subject as it can be understood in the dialectical tradition, and even the subject in the sense of the Cartesian cogito, which Lacan reworks in certain respects?

YD: This would be a very long discussion by itself. I will simply say that the structured subject is the phenomenological subject.

PH: And therefore imaginary.

YD: That's it. It's the phenomenological subject, and we acknowledge it by saying that it can be understood as a description of what is structured. It's the same as that strange idea of Althusser's, suggesting that Husserl was very useful for explaining ideology.

PH: By phenomenology you mean, essentially, ideology and the imaginary, is that right?

YD: Exactly: Lacan's imaginary, Althusser's ideology, phenomenology as description (but not theory), a faithful description because it's blind . . .

PH: That is to say 'pre-scientific', or even 'Aristotelian' (from before the scientific revolution) . . .

YD: As Koyré said, an Aristotelian conception of things is undoubtedly the best theory of common sense; it's pre-Galilean, pre-Newtonian, the best description of lived experience. Koyré was very important for us, perhaps more important than Bachelard. If you reread our text ['Action of the Structure'] you'll see that Canguilhem's text on the concept appears right away (CpA 9.6:94), on page two. This confirmed the idea that our theoretical work was about doing work on the concept, starting with the primary concept of *structure*, that is to say the concept of structure insofar as it *included* the concept of subject. This was very important for us: never separate the subject from the structure. We therefore had to redouble the subject. The problem is that we said nothing about practice. You raise the question of the subject as practical subject: we didn't say anything about it.

PH: At the time did you feel this to be an absence, or as something that wasn't immediately necessary? In the Marxist tradition, obviously, theory and practice go hand-in-hand . . .

YD: Just after this text ['Action of the Structure'], you must read the next text that Miller wrote, on theoretical training or formation [*la formation théorique*]; it was written around the same time, two months later, for the first issue of the *Cahiers Marxistes-Léninistes*.[7] It's another text at which Rancière, later on, would aim his bazooka. The basic idea was that rigorous traversal of the imaginary is what authorizes all practice. We said nothing about practice as such. It's on this idea that, in a way, the *Cahiers Marxistes-Léninistes* were founded, with some immediate tensions that emerged right away. We said that we would authorize practice, but what, which practice? In a certain way, I would say that there was a sort of equivocation between this theory of analysis, in the sense that I just mentioned (seek out the utopic point etc.), and the Leninist theory of the weak

---

7   Miller, 'Fonction de la formation théorique' (présentation des *Cahiers Marxistes-Léninistes*), reprinted in Miller, *Un Début dans la vie* (Paris: Gallimard, 2002).

link that Althusser develops in his 'Contradiction and Overdetermination',[8] in the sense that it was necessary to identify on and cut the weakest link in the chains of domination. We were under the impression that there was a relation between this practice and the practice of analysis, the practice of analysis being itself a practice.

PH: Analysis here, you mean psychoanalysis?

YD: Yes, a practice that seeks out a certain number of signifiers . . .

PH: . . . the signifiers that identify the weak link of the imaginary . . .

YD: . . . through which one might cause the imaginary to topple over, the imaginary in which the subject will be able to re-establish itself, having traversed its illusions [*leurres*] as so many symptoms. We could say that the theory of the symptom in Lacan was very close to this theory of redoubling – the symptom as return of the repressed, etc. We had the impression that we held the world between theory and practice, via the *detour* of theory. What Lacan said against psychoanalysis understood as a blind practice of ego reinforcement echoed what Althusser had said against Marxism understood as a blind practice of humanism and of technocratism (which formed a couple for him). We had the impression that this new way of conceiving the structured and the structuring opened at last onto a new practice.

That was the philosophical kernel of the thing, which I might call, to evoke the atmosphere of the times, an *enthusiasm* for theory. We really thought that we had found some keys: the Marx of Althusser, the Freud of Lacan, and in a way, the work of Foucault, who was not yet well known (he was for us, but less for others).

PH: I suppose Foucault, too, was still quite young.

YD: He had written *History of Madness* and *The Birth of the Clinic*: in each case it's the same gesture. In our texts of the time we would always say: Foucault's major work is *The Birth of the Clinic*. This lasted through to *The Archaeology of Knowledge*, which Foucault wrote *before* 1968. And then at that point a cycle came to an end. It's true that May 68 brings all this to an end.

PH: Was the general idea, in the *Cahiers*, to open a space, to liberate the potential of a subject that might come to terms with or re-establish itself in a more genuine way in relation to the structured, in relation to everything that tended to imprison it in the imaginary, in its ego, in its illusions, etc? Did you think that Sartre, say,

---

8   Cf. Louis Althusser, 'Contradiction and Overdetermination', in FM, 95–98.

was unable to achieve this because his chosen point of departure was not theory but precisely a praxis which was *already* free, free in an ontological sense?

YD: Yes, we turned things upside-down: we set out from the subjugated subject, and conceived freedom as the end and never the beginning.

PH: You never prescribed what this freedom ought to do. And so there was no need to connect it to ideas of justice, for instance, or with the universalization of freedom.

YD: No, the fundamental point was indeed the primacy of theory. Insofar as theory allows us, to put it crudely, to pass to the structuring dimension [*le structurant*], we need to act on this dimension.

PH: And the structuring dimension cannot be grasped except through a theory such as that developed by Marx or by Freud . . .

YD: Absolutely.

PH: Common sense experience, say, doesn't allow it to be understood; the real mechanics of capitalist exploitation cannot be grasped by experience alone?

YD: No. And it's on this point that everything turns upside down after 68, when things spin around 180 degrees, and people begin to say 'we must set out from the workers' consciousness', etc. – whereas Althusser had never stopped telling us that the workers, *like* the capitalists, were living under the same illusion. We didn't realize that, in the process, we were repeating a very old philosophical gesture. We repeated the Platonic trajectory, in our own way, under a very specific form. We were unaware of it. Actually, Althusser, who was a crafty old dog, was aware of it, but we were unaware, or much less so. In the recent talk I gave on Rancière[9] I said that he had needed to commit a double parricide – of Althusser, and of Plato. It's true, and he said nothing to contradict me.

PH: As conceived in the aftermath of 68, practice won't have any further need of theoretical authorization.

YD: Practice will figure as an abrupt emergence or apparition [*surgissement*] without cause.

---

9   Yves Duroux, 'La Querelle interminable: Rancière et ses contemporains', in *La Philosophie déplacée: Autour de Jacques Rancière*, ed. Laurence Cornu and Patrice Vermeren (Paris: Éditions Horlieu, 2006), 17–26.

PH: And without authority.

YD: An eruption without cause which in a way is authorized by its result. It is not authorized by anything preceding it. In a way, we wouldn't have been completely opposed to this idea, except that we absolutely needed it . . .

PH: . . . to pass via theory.

YD: That's it. This is why our politics was never anything other, at least in the first instance, than theoretical training – consider again that small text, contemporary with the text 'Action of the Structure', which opens the *Cahiers Marxistes-Léninistes*.[10] We see clearly, in the end, why things ended up drifting apart. To begin with there was no separation between the projects of the *Cahiers pour l'Analyse* and the *Cahiers Marxistes-Léninistes*. But from the moment when people began doing their theoretical training, they said, that's all well and good, we've understood what you've said, and now what are we going to *do*? And there the *Cahiers pour l'Analyse*, precisely, had nothing more to say, we remained within the theory of discourse. And the best moments of the *Cahiers pour l'Analyse*, by the way, are not the texts in it, but are the half-page or page that open each issue.

PH: The forewords.

YD: They are all in keeping with the inaugural text, 'Action of the Structure' (CpA 9.6). That is why, in order to understand properly the trajectory of the *Cahiers pour l'Analyse*, it is necessary, at least up until and including issue eight, to set out from this text from 1964 and to understand that they all have the same theoretical filiation – and otherwise we filled out the issues as best we could. I should add that by this stage I was no longer there at the ENS; I was absent for one and a half years, then I returned.

PH: Why are the forewords signed with proper names? I imagine that the conversations around them must have been intense, a matter of collective invention. Why did you not keep them either anonymous or collective?

YD: Because Miller was too sensitive about the risk of concept theft. When the text from 1964 was passed around it was not signed. And he reacted, after *Reading Capital*, because of Rancière's text (apropos of structural causality) . . .[11] Miller is someone who imposes himself – and I have the contrary tendency, which is absolute effacement. It doesn't matter, the point was not

---

10   Miller, 'Fonction de la formation théorique'.
11   Cf. Jacques Rancière's interview in this volume, 268.

decisive. It's true that intellectually this text was born in my head. And it's true that I made that grandiloquent comparison to a famous text of German Idealism which was co-written by Hegel, Schelling and Hölderlin.

PH: The first programme, or manifesto?[12]

YD: Exactly. I said that it resembled it. No one knows who wrote this manifesto. Today people think it was Schelling – that Hegel dictated it, Schelling wrote it and Hölderlin laughed! I would place myself in Hölderlin's position, but of course this is all rather mythological.

PH: In any case, you all were part of a moment of transition. Did you see it as the moment after Sartre?

YD: On this score an event took place that was extremely important. *Critique of Dialectical Reason* came out in September/October 1960, and in April 1961 Badiou and Terray invited Sartre to the École Normale Supérieure to talk about it. It's the last time that Sartre and Merleau-Ponty saw each other, because Merleau-Ponty died two months later [3 May 1961]. It was held in the Salle des Actes. I would say that it was the apogee of something, and also the end. It wasn't Althusser's article on the young Marx[13] that had this effect, as nobody had really noticed it; it was a small article in a journal of communist intellectuals, *La Pensée*. Nobody had noticed it. The most intellectually prestigious text was instead *Critique of Dialectical Reason*.

In a way the year of 1961 was also the moment of the student mobilization for the end of the Algerian War, which would only come about the following year, in the month of April, when dreadful things occurred. There was the notorious demonstration by Algerians against the war, in which I was one of the rare French people to have participated. I was taken by a friend called Mathiot, whose father had helped the FLN. The French police threw people into the Seine. I was 40 metres away, so I saw it. It remains one of the traumas of my existence, to have seen such savagery. 200 people were killed. It was horrifying. And now it has been turned into a memorial site in France. There is a plaque on the St. Michel bridge; a film has been made. Right. I was barely 20 years old at the time, and it was a horrifying shock. In these circumstances there was an enormous political mobilization, though not one in which theory played much of a role. Sartre was as good a point of reference here as anything else.

There was an encounter; there were heterogeneous elements which came together and merged at a given moment. Althusser, who had been turning

---

12   This is the so-called earliest or 'Oldest System Programme of German Idealism' (1796).
13   Althusser, 'On the Young Marx' [1961], in FM.

things around in his head for a long time – why did he make that alliance with Lacan? He made the alliance with Lacan for a reason which is to my mind very important. It is because he realized that there was something at stake in psychoanalysis which could not be reduced to the reductive notion that the Marxists had of it – namely an engagement with the implications of Georges Politzer's work. The Lacanian critique of Politzer was very important. Politzer had written his *Critique of the Foundations of Psychology* (1928) along the following lines: Freud is brilliant, but his metapsychology is worthless. What is required is the *concrete* of psychology (and this is why the words 'concrete' and 'lived experience' became our number one enemies). Freudian metapsychology, according to Politzer, is a sort of abstract machinery which has no relation to lived experience. Lived experience, the concrete – all this was very Sartrean. Politzer was a major figure and his book was the shibboleth of the day, everyone had read it.

The critique of Politzer made by a student of Lacan, Jean Laplanche, in a 1961 text in *Les Temps Modernes,* played a decisive role.[14] Althusser always told me that this is what had turned his ideas about psychoanalysis (and thus also about Lacan) upside down, enabling him to forge that Freud-Marx junction in an entirely original way.

PH: And, by implication, did this critique also bear on Sartre, on the primacy of praxis in relation to the theoretical? And on the political as much as on the philosophical level?

YD: Yes, but wait, not on the political level, on the contrary. We found Sartre very good on the political level, for instance we really liked his text on Franz Fanon.[15] Sartre's political commitment is something we found remarkable, impressive. We simply thought that he lacked the theory of his commitment.

PH: So was your aim to supply the theory of that commitment?

YD: Yes, and by supplying it, commitment for us became a consequence. I would say that we viewed the abstract energy of commitment from afar, since it did not serve us as a foundation. The major word was 'detour'. There's no getting round it [*c'est embêtant*], the *detour* of theory. As Plato said, it is a matter of 'the second

---

14   Jean Laplanche and Serge Leclaire, 'L'Inconscient: Une étude psychanalytique', *Les Temps modernes* 183 (1961); 'The Unconscious: A Psychoanalytic Study', trans. Patrick Coleman. *Yale French Studies* 48 (1972), *The French Freud*, ed. Jeffrey Mehlman, 118–175. Laplanche and Leclaire's text emphasizes 'how far the contribution of psychoanalysis is from descriptions given in the realm of phenomenology' (129).

15   Jean-Paul Sartre, 'Preface', in Frantz Fanon, *The Wretched of the Earth* [1961], trans. Constance Farrington (New York: Grove, 1968; http://www.marxists.org/reference/archive/sartre/1961/preface.htm).

navigation'.[16] One does not confront the hard reality [*la dureté*] of the world directly. It is necessary to take the detour of theory. Ultimately that was our project.

PH: And if it is confronted directly, what happens?

YD: If you try to confront it directly then in a certain way you are broken by it. At best one makes a heroic assault. In French national memory this is symbolized by the *cuirassiers de Reichshoffen*: in the war of 1870 between France and Germany, the Germans had machine guns and the French charged, swords drawn. They all died.

PH: The English version is 'The Charge of the Light Brigade . . .'. And someone like Sartre, then, appeared as someone who wanted to confront the world directly?

YD: At bottom the problem was that we couldn't have cared less about the Communist Party [PCF]. We need to be honest. We were in the Union des Étudiants Communistes [UEC], which was something completely different to the PCF. It was a place of great freedom, which the party regarded with a great deal of mistrust. It was made up of young students, mainly the humanities groups from the Sorbonne. At the very most, it must have had seven to eight thousands student members. That's all there was at the time – whereas today there are 200,000 students in the central Paris universities.

PH: Yes, though how many communists?

YD: Alright, but at the time things were different. There was a student movement which was organized by a student union and within this student union was the UEC, which precisely had been preoccupied by this question of the war of Algeria. It was the place where everything happened. I never joined the Communist Party, but Étienne [Balibar] did. So he reflected more on the strategy of the Communist Party. I was never really interested in that. Miller and I were not interested in the Communist Party itself. For us, it stood condemned in advance. So this is ultimately why our project was politically – it must be admitted – rather imaginary. If I take a retrospective view, I would say that, and taking our foregrounding of theory into account, it was politically speaking imaginary. At the limit, as imaginary as Sartre's own conception of things, Sartre who also saw himself as a fellow traveller of the PCF, to which he wanted to add something. He wanted to add praxis, a foundation of freedom, let's say, to the worthy cause of the Communist Party – that worthy cause of the party that could nevertheless be thrown off track by bureaucratism, etc.

---

16   See for instance Plato, *Phaedo*, 99d.

As for us, in a way, we were not interested in the relation to the Communist Party. Not at all. That was where Althusser's strategy (and perhaps it wasn't deliberate, I'm not sure) of saying 'the science of Marx, the theory of Marx' allowed things to fall into place. And so, in a way, we fabricated (because after all it was a sort of fabrication [*fabrication*]) what I'm calling that strong programme of structuralism, in opposition to the structuralism of Lévi-Strauss and of Roland Barthes.

PH: You set out from the fact that in the work of Lévi-Strauss, and of Barthes also, there was precisely no place for the subject?

YD: Right, clearly there was no place for the subject. We considered that the most important problem was to reintroduce the subject into the structure; whereas they made a structure without subject. That's what they say, plain as day.

PH: And when Althusser said, for example, that 'history is a process without a subject', etc.?

YD: Yes, but the 'process without a subject' is the Althusser afterwards, the Althusser of the *Reply to John Lewis* (1973).[17] In any case, it is a process without subject in the sense that the action of the structure is not itself the action of a subject. So, for us, it was exactly the same thing. Simply, to reintroduce the subject appeared indispensable to us in order to have the duality of the structuring and the structured. The action of the structuring is precisely not the action of a subject. At the level of the structuring there is a lack. This lack is *represented* by an imaginary. And this lack is the pivoting point of the structure. The goal is to reach or touch this pivoting point. For us, for example, it was the point touched by the analysis of the extortion of surplus labour in Marx, and, let's say, the point indicated by the primary signifiers in psychoanalysis, according to the way we saw things at the time. The same goes for the seminar of Serge Leclaire (CpA 1.5; CpA 3.6; CpA 8.6). This is why Leclaire interested us; he was seeking this sort of primary signifier. Leclaire went looking for this sort of signifier at the point closest to the lack, which it was necessary to attain in order to be able to operate. And in our approach it was linked with the idea of the weakest link, in Lenin. That would not be entirely rigorous today (and was not even at the time). But that, in short, was the idea.

If the question of the subject concerns you, you should note that we cut it into two, in order to treat the phenomenological subject as an imaginary subject – imaginary, yet obviously indispensable for human existence. It is not possible to do otherwise. We never considered that it did not exist, on the contrary. It

---

17   See Althusser, 'Reply to John Lewis' [1973], in ESC, 50–51; cf. Althusser, LP, 121–124.

was an effect, granted, but an effect exists as much as its cause. We were not neo-Platonists; we were Spinozists. The effect's mode of existence follows that of the cause.

PH: But it remains an effect deprived of any power of transformation.

YD: Of course, since it is imaginary. As for transformation at the level of the structuring; there are nodal points, and these points are the sites of a practice.

PH: And it would thus be possible to shed light on the stakes of that practice in accordance with the detour of theory.

YD: Exactly. The basic idea – formulated in an unbelievably speculative way, it must be said – was that there are sites where practice ought to intervene. This is also the idea of the link, as I've said, of the weakest link, of the *kairos*, of the important moment.

PH: This remains, by the way, the guiding idea of Badiou's philosophy. In certain ways he has remained entirely faithful to this project.

YD: What's very strange is that at the time of the *Cahiers pour l'Analyse* this was not Badiou's own position, not at all. Back then he was Althusserian in an almost caricatural way. He had therefore not understood what was really happening in our project, and he rediscovered it by his own means, beginning with his *Theory of the Subject* ([1982]) onwards. In some ways his thinking continues today in the same vein. It's become more sophisticated, developed, etc., but he remains pretty close to the initial project. It's true, then, that in a sense Badiou is the most faithful to this project. That is why he maintains that there are ultimately two paths, in contemporary philosophy: on the one hand, Lacan and Althusser, and, on the other, Deleuze and Foucault. But then he never cared much for Foucault.

PH: But he does not understand Foucault, in my opinion.

YD: No, he doesn't understand him at all. I agree.

PH: He believes (or believed) that Foucault was merely a 'classifier of encyclopaedias', etc. whereas that is not at all what matters to him. What matters in *The Order of Things* are the moments of transition: the moments of Sade, of Cervantes, and then of himself and his contemporaries. These are moments in which the structured field starts to break up, in which everything is liberated from the established rules. It's just as you said: a certain moment of saturation arrives, and there are points at which the structuring operations begin to crack.

YD: Exactly, that was precisely our position. Rancière, on the other hand, was the one who took the most distance from our project. He did this through the liquidation of theory altogether. His project became the negation of theory. Rancière's major book is *The Ignorant Schoolmaster* (1987).[18]

So today the question is to know where we are to go from here. We are in a very curious situation. The thread of those years exists, in a way, you are right, with Badiou and Žižek, but for me this configuration remains obscure. I do not really know if there are any others. Okay, there is Rancière. He opened another path. But I don't know if there's anything else. I do not know enough about the international arena. I am German-speaking and don't know what's happening in the Anglo-Saxon world in relation to such things. I don't like the idea that there is now merely a sort of 'critical thinking', I don't care for these overly generic expressions. So the question is: is there anything that is in confrontation with Badiou, Žižek etc.? That is to say, in strong confrontation.

PH: It seems to me that what is missing is an insistence on political *will*, on the practice which is committed to changing the world – an insistence which follows Marx, in knowing that what *matters* is to change the world, and not only to interpret it. We need an account of such a transformative will, but one that is firmly related to the determinate, historical world, the world to be transformed. Badiou proposes a powerful theory of transformation, but in my opinion his ontology is too abstract and the additions or concessions he makes in *Logics of Worlds* also remain too abstract. The crucial mediations are still missing. Everything that has to do with society, with the economy . . .

YD: Alain despises all that, and always has. We were 21–22 years old at the time. Later on we learned a thing or two. Later I left for Madagascar where I was confronted with armed struggle. I have memories of arms shipments arriving from Zanzibar, and of the Malagasy who had to be prevented from doing things that would have got them killed immediately. My friends and students when I was there were among those who later launched an insurrection in 1972 (now they're all neo-liberals; at the time they were Maoists). Balibar was in Algeria. So, we learned some things about the world. Meanwhile, when the university at Vincennes was created, many of my students were from Latin America. My courses were typed up and given to miners in Bolivia, you see. These were ultra-theoretical courses on *Capital*. So we continued in this way, but we could see that the world was a lot more complicated than we'd thought.

What happened is that in a certain way someone like Alain Badiou persisted,

---

18   Rancière, *Le Maître ignorant: Cinq leçons sur l'émancipation intellectuelle* (Paris: Fayard, 1987); *The Ignorant Schoolmaster*, trans. Kristin Ross (Stanford: Stanford University Press, 1991).

I would say, in a sort of philosophico-theoretical distance or gap [*écart*]. In order to give this gap as much consistency as he could, he was obliged, in a way, to cut himself off from the rest of the world, and so to have, undeniably, a rather superficial view of the world. In a sense he kept something, but he lost the world.

At a certain level everything we fought for in those days was defeated. The Cultural Revolution was defeated and communism in general was defeated, since it disappeared from the face of the earth. I think that everything now has to be rebuilt. I've come to recognize that the function of philosophy is much more complicated than we originally thought. Philosophy cannot cut itself off from the world.

PH: How do you conceive of philosophy, now, in its relations with politics, for example, or with the sciences?

YD: Philosophy, in my opinion, has to pass through [*traverser*] the social and human sciences. Why? Because the social and human sciences are and have always been disciplines for apprehending the world. What did Marx do? He passed through the political economy. Had he not passed through it, what would he have done? He would have remained with the slogans of *The Communist Manifesto,* which were not especially original. He admitted that himself. For me this point is still very important. Philosophy cannot be isolated from the world and from politics. The question of its relation with this passing through, for me, is open. I know that this is the theory-practice question, but that is also an overly abstract question, in a sense. Philosophy *connects.* I don't think it's up to philosophy to exhort. Badiou is still somewhat drawn to the idea that philosophy should exhort, should fulfil a protreptic function: to give sermons or be prophetic.

I think, then, that there is a politics of knowledge [*savoir*], and a politics of knowledge can be a knowledge of politics. Philosophy's task is to draw out of this points of intersection, points of dislocation, etc. I think that the knowledges of the human sciences are knowledges of investigation, and that philosophy *articulates,* you see. What did Foucault do? Foucault, as he liked to say, introduced 'philosophical fragments into historical building sites'. I've always liked this expression – along with the political meaning it had for Foucault, who tried to problematize our contemporary situation, our actuality.

Translated by Steven Corcoran.

CHAPTER ELEVEN

All of a Sudden, Psychoanalysis:
An Interview with François Regnault

Paris, France, 1 May 2008

Peter Hallward (PH): The *Cahiers pour l'Analyse* were launched at the end of 1965. Were you still at the École Normale (ENS) at the time?

François Regnault (FR): No. I started there in 1959 – Jacques-Alain Miller arrived in 1962, Jean-Claude Milner in 61, Alain Grosrichard in 62, and Alain Badiou well before, in 56 I believe; I never saw him at the ENS. I stayed until 63 and got to know Miller, Milner, etc., in Louis Althusser's seminars on Marx. I remember very well a presentation by Miller on Descartes that was truly remarkable; everyone was fascinated. I got on well with him. Then I left to do my military service, in 1963–64 and 1964–65, as a teacher at the Prytanée military school in La Flèche. I returned to Paris each weekend, and I saw Miller and Milner regularly, and they told me of their idea to found the new *Cahiers pour l'Analyse*, the first issue of which was published in January 1966. Remember that Lacan had begun his seminar at the École in January 1964; I attended his seminar on 'Science and Truth' (CpA 1.1), given on 1 December 1965. It was around this time that Miller and Milner decided to create a *Cercle d'Épistémologie*, to discuss the history of the sciences, etc.

PH: Was it Lacan's arrival at the École that inspired the launching of this *Cercle d'Épistémologie*?

FR: No, not only, several things inspired it. First, there was certainly Althusser's interest in the sciences, and notably his decision to drop the distinction between 'bourgeois' science and 'proletarian' science. The French Marxist-Leninist tradition had always maintained this distinction, but Althusser, inspired by Canguilhem, by Bachelard, and by the history of the sciences, thought it absolutely necessary to get rid of it.

Secondly, and more profoundly, it was at this time that French academic thinkers were making the transition from phenomenology to logic and to epistemology. I remember when I was in *khâgne* [i.e. the second year of preparatory classes for applicants to the ENS] that the topics we had to prepare were always taken from phenomenology: consciousness, the intentionality of consciousness, lived experience, and so on. We were a bit fed up with it. And all of a sudden a constellation of problems converged around the rue d'Ulm [i.e. the ENS], which were quite complex, but which could be called 'structuralist'. These problems concerned Lévi-Strauss and the elementary structures of kinship, structuralist linguistics, Jakobson etc. – don't forget that Milner studied grammar and linguistics; he passed the *agrégation* in linguistics and not in philosophy. And also Lacan had introduced the idea of the unconscious being structured like a language. So from this moment on the landscape changed.

PH: And people were reading Cavaillès too, regarding mathematics and logic?

FR: Yes, thanks to Canguilhem we had read a lot of Cavaillès, notably his book *On Logic and the Theory of Science* (1946). Canguilhem was never keen on phenomenology, he was more of a logician and an epistemologist, and a historian of the sciences. But he was isolated. When I was at rue d'Ulm, and we went to Canguilhem's courses at the Sorbonne, there would be four or five of us in the classroom. It wasn't fashionable to do the history of sciences. On the other hand, the day that Canguilhem was named president of the *agrégation* [the French university-level teaching diploma], all of a sudden a whole crowd of students began attending, in the month of May/June, to prepare for the following year . . .

PH: Yes, Canguilhem was the president of the jury of the *agrégation* in philosophy for some key years, from 1964 to 1968, I think.[1]
      And did 'phenomenology' at the Sorbonne at the time essentially mean the German tradition, and more Husserl than Heidegger? Or were Sartre and Merleau-Ponty the main points of reference?

FR: Yes, phenomenology at the university per se meant Husserl, and thus also Ricoeur, as Husserl's translator and commentator. The Hegelian tradition, represented by Jean Hyppolite (who was director of the ENS) was dimly viewed in university circles. Neither was Sartre's work as such much present in the university, though the publication of *Critique of Dialectical Reason* (in 1960) was very important. A lot of people at the ENS read it. As for us Althusserians, we read it, too, but we read it as already outdated. And I recall vividly the time when Hyppolite invited Sartre to the École, in April 1961, to give a lecture in the Salle des Actes;[2] Canguilhem was there, Althusser and Merleau-Ponty were there, etc. – and, moreover, it was the last time that Sartre would see Merleau-

---

1   As suggested by the École Normale's archives listed at http://cirphles.ens.fr/IMG/file/caphes/bib/inventaire%20des%20archives%20G_%20Canguilhem.pdf.
2   See Alain Badiou's recollection of 'the day Sartre came to the Ecole Normale', in the spring of 1961 (Badiou, 'Jean Hyppolite', *Pocket Pantheon*, trans. David Macey [London: Verso, 2009], 42–44).

Ponty, a meeting that he relates in detail in his homage to Merleau-Ponty.[3] It was an important event; Sartre appeared somewhat isolated in a world which was moving away from him.

PH: In his *Critique,* Sartre presents a sort of 'structuralist' anthropology, but individual praxis remains determinant.

FR: Yes, that's right; for Sartre, the key thing to understand isn't what structures do, but what individuals do with the structures that are imposed on them.

I should also add, if we want to complete the landscape of the time, that there were also Heideggerians at the ENS, notably Jean Beaufret and Dominique Janicaud, who didn't share in the growing enthusiasm for the sciences.

PH: So, interest in logic remained pretty marginal until that point.

FR: Yes, pretty marginal. It was obligatory to study it a little for the BA in Philosophy, and for the *agrégation,* and at the École there was a logic specialist, Roger Martin. But it remained a small current of no great importance. Afterwards, all my comrades started to become interested in logic, in mathematical logic, etc., but that was new. We should leave to one side the fact that Alain Badiou had always worked on mathematics. I was the one, by the way, who introduced Badiou to the *Cahiers pour l'Analyse,* since in 1965 I took up a post as a schoolteacher in Reims, where Badiou was already working. He had just left the school for the university, a new university. We got to know each other immediately; I told him about the *Cahiers* and he immediately enlisted in the project.

PH: Wasn't he still allied to Sartre at the time?

FR: It's hard to say: yes and no. There was, in his way of thinking, too much science, too much history of philosophy and mathematics for him ever to have been completely Sartrean. And he was already interested in psychoanalysis. He had given a presentation on Lacan, at the ENS, even before Althusser invited Lacan (and before I started at the École). We were younger than he was. Indeed, he could have easily reacted contemptuously to our journal as a childish project, but instead he joined it right away. So the *Cahiers pour l'Analyse* were always represented by six people, through to its end: Miller, Milner, Duroux, Badiou, Grosrichard and me.

---

3   Jean-Paul Sartre, 'Merleau-Ponty vivant', *Les Temps modernes* 184–185 (1961), 304–376; 'Merleau-Ponty vivant', trans. Benita Eisher, in *The Debate Between Sartre and Merleau-Ponty,* ed. Jon Stewart (Evanston IL: Northwestern University Press, 1998), 565–629.

PH: Why, within the general field of this valorization of logic and the sciences, was there a particular interest in Lacan and in psychoanalysis?

FR: The particular interest in Lacan came entirely from the fact that once Althusser – who had well-known and rather complicated mental problems, and had been in analysis for some time already – learned that Lacan's seminar at Saint-Anne was no more, he invited him to rue d'Ulm. It must be appreciated that Althusser's madness, his psychosis, played an organic role in introducing psychoanalysis into the field of thought of the time. The Communist Party had always found psychoanalysis troubling, and had been reluctant to accept it.

The first session of Lacan's seminar at the ENS took place in the Dussane theatre on 15 January 1964. At the time, Lacan had a rather bizarre reputation (I leave aside Badiou, who had already taken an interest in his work). I had read him a little and I understood nothing at all; people tended to think of him as an eccentric [*fantaisiste*]. And at the same time psychoanalysis did not interest us, since for philosophers (at the time) psychoanalysis did not exist: it dealt only with sexuality, it didn't enter into the true field of thought, etc. Everything started when Jacques-Alain Miller attended Lacan's seminar, and experienced it as a bolt from the blue. And Milner too. Afterwards they said to me, come along, and so on – they were very enthusiastic. And for Miller, this *coup de foudre* was reinforced by the fact that he then met Lacan's daughter, Judith, who became his wife soon afterwards.

So, at precisely this moment, psychoanalysis all of a sudden became a field of reflection for philosophy. And as Lacan was also interested in mathematics, logic, linguistics, and so on, when psychoanalysis entered the field it entered in a rather clever or artful way. Hence the name *Cahiers pour l'Analyse*, in which 'analysis' has to be understood to mean two things: on the one hand, analysis in the broadest sense of the philosophical tradition harking back, let's say, to Pappus of Alexandria, to analysis and synthesis, etc. At the time we often cited a phrase by the great mathematician Galois, who wrote: 'here we are pursuing the analysis of analysis'. So, it meant analysis in the mathematical sense, in algebra. And on the other hand, it meant psychoanalysis.

PH: The *Cahiers* also contain several other points of reference. There is Plato, for example, and notably his *Parmenides,* in your own article 'Dialectic of Epistemologies' (CpA 9.4). There is also Frege and the elementary status of the numbers zero and one.

FR: That's right: Frege's *Grundlagen der Arithmetik* (1884) provided us, on the basis of his reflections on one and zero, with a totally new theory of the subject, one that was no longer the subject of phenomenology.[4]

---

4   Cf. Hallward, 'Theoretical Training', CF1.

PH: And here, the text that forms the point of departure is 'Action of the Structure' (CpA 9.6), right?

FR: Yes. I was no longer at the École, but Miller, Milner and Duroux saw each other on a daily basis and that text came out of their discussions, after Lacan's first seminars at rue d'Ulm. The outcome was a new theory of the subject, which was unexpected, but which later led to a confusion that became notorious. Our theory, oriented by Althusser, Lacan and Foucault, was an anti-humanist theory. Then later, in a quite peculiar development, there came along some people who detested us, people like Luc Ferry, Alain Renaut, and so on. They started at the ENS after us. They said: you, you structuralists and *soixante-huitards*, you are anti-humanist and that's why you abolish the subject.[5] Whereas we defended the subject, in fact – but it was Lacan's subject, and not the subject of psychology. Ours was a fragmented subject, a 'localized [*ponctuel*] and vanishing' subject, to use Lacan's terms.

PH: And it was a subject that retained a certain force, all the same, a certain causality, however minimal.

FR: Yes, indeed.

PH: This seems like an essential aspect of the question, if we recall the argument between Miller and Rancière about the origins of the concept of metonymic causality.

FR: Yes, Miller thought that this concept was stolen from him; I remember some dramatic scenes, when Miller was quite beside himself: he thought he'd worked hard, only to have been done a disservice, by Rancière and also somewhat by Althusser.

PH: It seems Althusser worked closely with you all, as his students, with Rancière and Macherey, with Duroux and Badiou, and the other participants of *Reading Capital*.

FR: Yes, and around this time (in 1965) this collaboration began to intensify. Althusser had phases of absolutely extraordinary exaltation, in which he was so enthusiastic he could make anyone work on anything. Then afterwards, there were phases of dejection, of insomnia. At the time when I worked with him, things were still going well. But when I saw him again in 68, he was going through

---

5   Cf. Luc Ferry and Alain Renaut, *La Pensée 68: essai sur l'anti-humanisme contemporain* (Paris: Gallimard, 1985).

a period of despondency; he was at the hospital during the events, which he followed from afar. All this to say that in those moments of effervescence we all worked together on all sorts of things, and obviously there were moments when questions about the authorship of this or that idea didn't really come up.

PH: And regarding the political side of things: what happened between the *Cahiers Marxistes-Léninistes*, which began at the ENS in late 1964, and these new *Cahiers pour l'Analyse*, launched in late 65?

FR: Ah! Well the political movement expressed in the *Cahiers Marxistes-Léninistes*, and the epistemological concerns explored in the *Cahiers pour l'Analyse*, took shape at the same time. Miller helped with the setting up of the *Cahiers Marxistes-Léninistes*, along with Robert Linhart and the others. The break dates from the contentious eighth issue of the *Cahiers Marxistes-Léninistes*, prepared in late 1965, which included Milner's article on Aragon, and my article on Gombrowicz (cf. CpA 7.Intro). Again, I was no longer at the ENS so I can't account for the political relations in detail. But the comrades – Robert Linhart, Jacques Broyelle – made it known that these articles were not desirable. So the issue in question was not published. And those of us involved with the issue considered this to be an unacceptable act of censorship.

PH: Apart from this dispute, were there divergences of philosophical or political principle?

FR: I think that the interests Miller and Milner had in psychoanalysis and linguistics were not considered fundamental by the hard-line Marxist-Leninists, and were scorned as 'idealist'.

PH: Even though Althusser himself had written articles on this, for example his 'Freud and Lacan' (1964)?[6]

FR: Yes, but Althusser was an exception, and Linhart and Broyelle didn't agree with that side of his teaching.

PH: All the same, for you it wasn't as if a choice had to be made between Althusser and Lacan, right?

FR: Oh no, not at all, in any case not during the years in question. We had to choose afterwards, after 68. Once they'd left the ENS, after May 68, Miller and Milner joined Gauche Prolétarienne, and during this time took no interest in

---

6   Louis Althusser, 'Freud and Lacan' (1964/1969), in LP.

psychoanalysis. Miller no longer went to Lacan's seminars, and worked for some time at a factory in Rouen, I believe for six months. And then when Gauche Prolétarienne started to dissolve, which Jacques-Alain and Jean-Claude were quick to anticipate, they decided that it was necessary to move on to something else. By contrast, Linhart and Badiou both continued to take the political route.

PH: Right. But in 1966–67, during the period of the *Cahiers* properly speaking, did you all have a feeling of solidarity, with Linhart and the others?

FR: Yes, certainly. It was a very rich period of thought, with Foucault, Althusser, Barthes, etc., including Michel Serres and people like that. At the time we all took a constant philosophical interest in what other people were doing; there was no hatred or friction. Milner relates all this very well in his book *Le Périple structural*.[7] I remember that we once invited Foucault, for instance, to give a course at the ENS, and he duly began his course, which was called 'Penser la finitude [Thinking Finitude]'. But he didn't like being back at the École, so, capricious as he was, he only gave one session. But we were very interested in him, and his *History of Madness* (1961) played an important role in the *Cahiers* project. I should add that shortly afterwards Derrida also began teaching at the ENS, where he gave his courses on Husserl.

PH: Yes, it could be said that Derrida offered a sort of post-phenomenological critique of phenomenology. So how did he figure with respect to the *anti*-phenomenological project of the *Cahiers*?

FR: He was doing his own thing. But Miller liked Derrida a lot and always defended him. It was Miller who solicited Derrida's contribution to issue 4 (CpA 4.Intro). Later, during the argument between Foucault and Derrida concerning Descartes and the *History of Madness*, Jacques-Alain took Derrida's side, and I was more on the side of Foucault.

PH: And when you consider the question today, what in your view are the most interesting or important aspects of structuralism?

FR: You need to remember that at the time the word 'structure', which is now absolutely self-evident, was a quasi-incomprehensible word. People were so used to phenomenology that they didn't really understand what it meant. I clearly recall a presentation that Jules Vuillemin, a great logic specialist and professor at the Collège de France, gave on the notion of structure in

---

7   Jean-Claude Milner, *Le Périple structural* [2002] (Paris: Verdier, 2008).

mathematics; it became an important reference point for us. Basically he said that if you want to talk about structures in a rigorous way, you must keep to the field of mathematics – and if you want to talk about them in a non-serious way, then that's quite dangerous (such was Vuillemin's suspicion of the human sciences). Then there was Lévi-Strauss's *Elementary Structures*, but we didn't refer to it very much; it's not a work that's easily used outside of ethnology. And then, of course, there was Lacan's idea that 'the unconscious is structured like a language'. From a phenomenological perspective, the subject is so bound up in *lived* and conscious reflections that the notion of a structure foreign to the subject was a rather bizarre idea, exactly like the idea of the unconscious for that matter. If for example you did some work on Racine's theatre, at the time questions people tended to ask about a particular aspect of the text were always of the sort: 'Was this intentional? Was Racine conscious or cognizant of this? Was he the author of this structure?' and so on.

But the line of inquiry becomes more subtle and more intelligent, as soon as one asks: How can the subject be caused? How might we speak of the cause of a localized [*ponctuel*] and vanishing subject? From his first seminars on Freud's technical writings,[8] Lacan distinguishes between the Ego, which is an object, and the (unconscious) subject, which is not an object, and this shed light on the problematic.

PH: From this perspective, can we still make sense of the old notion of a subject's intentional or deliberate will, or accommodate the notion of 'project' in Sartre's sense of the term? Can one dispense with these things, if the aim is to continue working in the revolutionary tradition, and notably in the Leninist tradition, as urged by Althusser? You end your article on Gombrowicz, for example, with the formula: 'one does not revolutionize clichés, one only revolutionizes structures' (CpA 7.3:70). But who is this 'one'? Who is the subject of the verb 'to revolution-ize'? Who is the subject of the revolution, from this perspective?

FR: I don't remember the immediate context very clearly: I had read Gombrowicz's *La Pornographie* on the train one day, wrote the article in one go and gave it to Miller, who found it very good; he said that they might like to publish it in the *Cahiers Marxistes-Léninistes*, etc. But it must be an allusion to Althusserian Marxism: one revolutionizes structures [*on révolutionne les structures*].

PH: In other words, revolution proceeds at the level of the mode of production.

---

8   Jacques Lacan, *Le Séminaire I: Les écrits techniques de Freud* (Paris: Seuil, 1975); *Seminar I: Freud's Papers on Technique* [1953–54], trans. John Forrester (New York: W.W. Norton, 1988).

FR: Yes, exactly. As for the question of the will, then, and of Sartrean freedom: I recall the response Lacan gave one day in an interview in Belgium, when he said to the journalist 'as for freedom, I *never* speak about freedom!' The will is no doubt a more complicated question, and moreover both Badiou and I greatly admire Schopenhauer's book *The World as Will and as Representation*, which already shows that we're not working within the ordinary limits of the field. But if I adopt Lacan's standpoint, the will is a concept he only uses in relation to Sade, in relation to perversion and the will to inflict suffering, etc. Will is left to one side. Your question makes me recall Badiou's and Derrida's amazement when it was announced, not so long ago, that the will [*la volonté*] would be included as a topic for the *agrégation*. This took place shortly before Derrida's death. Both of them were amazed; you need to remember that the landscape had changed so much that for many years the question 'what is the will?' was not raised at all.

PH: Indeed! And as far as I am concerned, I think that it is high time to raise the issue anew – but that's a question for another day.

FR: In any case, as regards the political line that people took at the time, before and after May 68, whether they were Marxists, Marxist-Leninists, Communists or Maoists, neither the will nor freedom played a commanding role. Nor did engagement in Sartre's sense of the term. The question was posed differently, in terms of militancy [*militantisme*], determination.

PH: And can we really talk about militancy and determination without referring in one way or another to the will and voluntary action?

FR: Yes, I think so: in reality you had the duty to campaign [*militer*] for this or that cause, without consulting your freedom. If you were not in agreement then you were considered a traitor. Those were the political categories: betrayal, petit bourgeois vacillation, and so on – but not freedom or the will, no, not at all. We had to speak about militancy in another way. As far as I was concerned, militancy and campaigning bothered me, I didn't much like it, I did it out of duty, but at the same time . . .

PH: Since 'duty' isn't necessarily much better than 'will' . . .

FR: . . . quite [*laughter*]. There was a sort of oppression at work in the political organizations of the time, as much in the hard-line Marxist-Leninist organizations, as in Badiou's Maoist organization (the Union des Communistes de France – Marxistes-Léninistes). I was never in either the Gauche Prolétarienne, or in Badiou's group, but I followed them both assiduously, and I took part in their initiatives on many occasions. Once, when many of them were facing prosecution, I served on a joint committee to raise substantial sums of money to pay for the costs of the trials (it was necessary to gather subscriptions, to contact all sorts of intellectuals and film makers, to borrow money, and afterwards the money had to be divided up, etc.). Miller and I also went to do an industrial investigation in Lorraine for the newspaper *J'Accuse*, asking questions of workers, members of the petty bourgeoisie, trade unionists, and so on, and we turned it into a somewhat Kafkaesque text. But *J'Accuse* did not want it, deeming it too literary (though it was eventually published in *Les Temps Modernes*).[9] However, all this occurred well after the *Cahiers* period.

PH: So what happened with the *Cahiers* during May 68? Was everyone turned upside down by the events?

FR: Yes, but not straightaway. During May 68 itself we were busy working on the *Cahiers pour l'Analyse*, with research on linguistics, etc., and not at all with politics. I clearly recall that Jean-Claude Milner and Jacques-Alain Miller didn't support the events of May 68 themselves.

PH: No doubt their work was interrupted . . .

FR: . . . yes, exactly. Only afterwards did this change. As for me, I was still teaching at Reims. On May 13 I recall having seen the enormous demonstration passing in front of the Sorbonne, one hundred thousand people, and I said to myself, the Gaullist regime can't go on like this any longer – that was the major watchword of the day, 'things can't go on like this'. At that time, Judith Miller was campaigning in Besançon, and took me along, together with her husband (Jacques-Alain) and Milner. We formed an action committee at the University of Besançon. We stayed for three days and in the process we exchanged one world for another, all of a sudden. It truly was a conversion for Miller and Milner, a road to Damascus experience: from then on they worked only on politics, with the action committee, etc., from which they dismissed out of hand all the professors who were starting to say 'yes workers have difficult working hours but we do too'. We went to the factories where there were strikes, etc. Then I had to return to Reims, and got stuck there: it was impossible to travel, there was no petrol left, there were no trains, nothing at all, For me militancy began a little later, when I was appointed to (the University of Paris 8 at) Vincennes, that is to say in 1969.

---

9   Jacques-Alain Miller and François Regnault, 'La Vie quotidienne dans l'empire du fer', *Les Temps Modernes* 297 (April 1971).

PH: Yes, in that extraordinary department, with Deleuze, Lyotard and company.

FR: It was Foucault who brought us, all in one go. In this new Paris university, along with philosophy, both linguistics and psychoanalysis were also introduced right away. Serge Leclaire headed the psychoanalysis department, and Foucault had brought, among others, all the people from the *Cahiers pour l'Analyse*. It was tremendous. You can ask Badiou, he will remember this clearly: I was at his place in Reims, and we couldn't decide whether to go. We said, 'we will be co-opted'. His father, a great mathematics professor, was also there, and his wife, who was also a militant; she said 'we shall all stay in the provinces' etc. We thought it over. Badiou said 'yes that's very nice, but we may also wind up as minor provincial bigwigs, which isn't a great deal better'. And after a little while, Badiou senior said 'listen, that's enough, you shall go to Paris, end of story'. (Well, I'm summarizing things . . .). So we went to Vincennes, where we met up again with Linhart, Miller, Balibar, Rancière, Lyotard, and others, with Foucault and Châtelet; Deleuze came later.

PH: And how long did you stay there?

FR: I stayed in the philosophy department through to 1974. By then I'd become fed up, because in some ways the department had gone bad, which is to say that many younger lecturers had stopped giving classes, which annoyed all the students, who were falling back into a kind of leftism. After a while Badiou and I decided to try to get rid of some of them, it was intolerable; but we couldn't manage it. So Miller invited me to move to the psychoanalysis department, and I went despite the fact that I was not at all a specialist in psychoanalysis. Nevertheless, I'd been influenced by Lacan, and I began teaching. I remained in the psychoanalysis department until my retirement, in 2004.

PH: And during this time you also worked at the theatre.

FR: Yes, but that's another topic!

Translated by Steven Corcoran.

CHAPTER TWELVE

The Chains of Reason: An Interview with Alain Grosrichard

Paris, France, 11 December 2008

Knox Peden (KP): To begin, could you say a few words about the origin of your participation in *Cahiers pour l'Analyse*?

Alain Grosrichard (AG): Let's distinguish between the origin and the beginning. I began to participate in the *Cahiers pour l'Analyse* from its first volume, published in January 1966. Its title, 'Truth', speaks volumes about the ambitions of the 'Cercle d'Épistémologie de l'École Normale Supérieure' whose instrument the journal was. As for the origin, it came about for me during my first year at the ENS, in October 1962, which was also the first year for Jacques-Alain Miller, who was with Jean-Claude Milner the true founder of these *Cahiers pour l'Analyse*. Like Miller, I had decided to take up studies in Philosophy with Louis Althusser, our *caïman*, serving as our director. This led me to get to know the other young philosophers who were already at the school: Regnault, Macherey, Balibar, Duroux, Rancière . . . Milner, who was pursuing studies in linguistics, did not let this keep him from being very active in the discussions of this little group that gathered around Althusser. This was when Althusser devoted his seminar to a rereading of Marx that was hardly orthodox in the eyes of the official intellectuals of the Communist Party. Against their global and teleological interpretation of Marx, he located an 'epistemological break', in the Bachelardian sense, between the still Hegelian young Marx and the Marx of the *German Ideology* and of *Capital*, who was more Spinozist than Hegelian. This second Marx provided him with the elements of a theory of ideology, conceived as a system of representations that owes its coherence to the subject's misrecognition of structural causality, i.e. of the economic and social order that determines it. This reference to Spinoza in the Althusserian reading of Marx oriented our first readings of Lacan, wherein the 'ego', based in the imaginary, also saw itself defined as an instance of the subject of the unconscious's misrecognition insofar as it was determined by the symbolic order itself. In short, through Spinoza, we could think Marx and Lacan together. Having said this, the fact that the first volume opened with 'Science and Truth' (CpA 1.1), which Lacan allowed us to publish first, tells us that in 1966 it was under the auspices of the latter that the *Cahiers* was born.

KP: And why Spinoza at this moment?

AG: Macherey or Balibar would have a better response for you. But Althusser had already referred to him in his 1961 article on the 'Young Marx' (FM, 49–86). And when I started attending his seminar on *Reading Capital*, it was clear that everyone was wearing lenses shaped by Spinoza. Of course the first volume of Gueroult's *Spinoza*, on the first book of *Ethics*, was not published until 1968.[1]

KP: But Spinoza had been the subject of his course at the Collège de France during the 50s and 60s.

AG: Yes, and I suppose that Althusser had followed it. Spinoza's name was also found on the lips of Lacan. He had already cited a proposition of the *Ethics* as the epigraph of his doctoral thesis in 1933, and you know that at the start of his first seminar at ENS, in January 1964, he compared the fate dealt him by the International Psychoanalytic Association to the excommunication pronounced against Spinoza in his time.[2] In any case, lacking Gueroult's *Spinoza*, we made assiduous use of his *Descartes selon l'ordre des raisons*.[3]

KP: Gueroult was no Marxist, however.

AG: No, no more than Lacan, who made a great case for his own Descartes. What counted for us, as well as for Althusser, is that Gueroult taught us to read a philosophical text 'according to the order of reasons'. You could even say that we held this formula as a kind of slogan . . . But let's get back to my first year at the ENS. In 1963, in his seminar dedicated to Politzer's *Critique des fondements de la psychologie*,[4] Althusser introduced us to Lacan's work, whose audience up until that point was limited almost exclusively to the practitioners of psychoanalysis. Among the presentations we could choose to do, one was on Lacan. Miller was charged with this assignment and he dove into *La Psychanalyse*, the journal where Lacan had published his articles. As I recall, this was St. Augustine's *Tolle, lege!* for him, a sort of illumination. His presentation was impressive especially because he presented a Lacan who was perfectly rational with no trace of the obscurantism that results from a first reading of his texts. It was then, between 63 and 64, that our interest for Marxist theory as Althusser had developed it converged with our burgeoning interest in the writings of Freud, which we read, as Lacan had, in the light of Saussurean linguistics.

KP: But there is another concept that comes into play: Science. You say that Althusser distinguished between the Spinozist Marx of *Capital* and the Hegelian

---

1   Martial Gueroult, *Spinoza I: Dieu* (Paris: Aubier, 1968).
2   See Jacques Lacan, SXI, 3–4.
3   Gueroult, *Descartes selon l'ordre des raisons*, 2 vols (Paris: Aubier, 1953).
4   Georges Politzer, *Critique des fondements de la psychologie* (Paris: Rieder, 1928).

'young Marx'. This Spinozist Marx was also someone for whom, in his view, science was at stake. Any thoughts regarding this valorization of science in his reading of Marx?

AG: Althusser tried to theorize the distinction between science and ideology. According to him, dialectical materialism alone, such as he found it formulated in Marx and Engels, but above all in Lenin, deserved to be qualified as scientific, and distinguished from ideology, which was defined as a system of imaginary representations more or less put into play through different interests. But he did not think science was reducible to the pronouncements of scientists, even those most worthy of the title. A scientist can also construct an ideological representation of his own scientific practice and it is up to philosophy, following Spinoza's example in the appendix to Book I of *Ethics*, to identify this misrecognition and what it consists of so that it might be theorized. Althusser dedicated a seminar in 1965–66 to a critical examination of the 'spontaneous philosophy of the scientists' (PSPS, 69–165). I remember hearing lectures by Bourdieu and Passeron there . . .

KP: But what was the relation between the concept of science and that of analysis, which the *Cahiers pour l'Analyse* aimed to promote? And how does this relate in turn to the relation between analysis and psychoanalysis? Was psychoanalysis but one particular example of analysis in a general sense, or did you consider it as the model of analysis as such?

AG: To answer that, we would need to return to the programmatic texts: the foreword to the first volume, for example, signed by Miller. Having defined epistemology as 'the history and theory of the discourse of science [*la science*]' and further defining this discourse as 'a process of language that truth constrains', the text continues by saying: 'We dub analytical, finally, any discourse whose function can be reduced to that of putting into place units that produce themselves and repeat themselves, whatever the principle may be that it assigns to the transformations at play in its system' (CpA 1.Intro). And we name 'analysis properly speaking [. . .] the theory that deals with concepts of element and combination as such'. There you have an expansive concept of analysis that allows us to group together most of the work published in the *Cahiers pour l'Analyse*. Regarding psychoanalysis, our interest was clearly dependent on the Saussurean rereading of Freud that Lacan had done. What we found 'analytic' in this context was this promotion of the signifying chain as the determinant of a subject without substance, reduced to this pure point of enunciation that is the Cartesian cogito, which Lacan paradoxically established as the point of emergence of the subject of the unconscious. But alongside Althusser and Lacan, we recognized yet another master: Georges Canguilhem. Many of us attended his seminar at the *l'Institut d'Histoire des*

Sciences. I wrote my undergraduate thesis under his direction, as did Miller. The subject that I treated fit into the programme of our *Cahiers* since it was a question of the problem concerning the analysis of perception. I gave a summary of it in the second volume of the *Cahiers pour l'Analyse.*

KP: We'll come back to this, but first a question on Canguilhem. Jean Cavaillès was his friend and comrade during the Resistance, and Canguilhem spoke with great admiration for his works of history, philosophy, and mathematics. Cavaillès privileged analysis and considered it more important than intuition or other models of knowledge. He situated himself in a trajectory that descended from Bolzano, or even earlier, and that called for an arithmetization of analysis.[5] This emphasis on analysis is striking. Is this why Canguilhem supported the *Cahiers pour l'Analyse*?

AG: What is certain is that Canguilhem was interested in what we were doing and that he supported us. You will have noticed that a citation of his ('To work on a concept . . .' etc.) figured in the epigraph of the *Cahiers.* Invited by Althusser, he came to the ENS for a session of his seminar especially dedicated to him. This was when Macherey delivered a remarkable presentation on 'Canguilhem and Science' in front of Canguilhem himself.[6] Lacan also appreciated his work. In 'Science and Truth', he cites this passage from 'What is Psychology?', published in the next volume (CpA 2.1), where Canguilhem wrote, not without ferocity, that there are two ways of leaving the Sorbonne: one up top, which leads you to the Pantheon, and another, that of academic psychology, which slides you down the hill along rue St. Jacques, landing you before the police station: his way of showing that psychology is nothing but a pseudo-science in the service of political power.

KP: What was his attitude toward Marxism and the connection that you made between Marxism and his own work?

AG: He expressed some reservations in a rather grumbly manner. (Our friend François Regnault does a marvellous impersonation of it). He'd continue to have more reservations against some of us, especially those who belonged to the student cell of the Communist Party, when Althusserian Marxism started to be replaced by 'Mao Zedong thought' and particular reference to the Chinese Cultural Revolution. This was obviously not yet the case in 1963. But we need to

---

5   See Jean Cavaillès, *Sur la logique et la théorie de la science* (Paris: PUF, 1946).
6   Cf. Pierre Macherey, 'Georges Canguilhem's Philosophy of Science: Epistemology and History of Science', in *In a Materialist Way*, eds. Warren Montag and Ted Stolze (London: Verso, 1998), 161–188.

remember that before the creation of the *Cahiers pour l'Analyse*, we worked on another publication, the *Cahiers Marxistes-Léninistes* which had chosen Lenin's affirmation as its epigraph: 'The theory of Marx is all powerful because it is true'. This lasted until the day when two articles by Regnault and by Milner, which were to be included in a volume on the theme of the novel, were rejected, after a lively debate among the comrades led by Robert Linhart and Benny Lévy. In their eyes, these two articles no doubt represented a petit-bourgeois revisionist perspective. Still, it was this rejection which served as the origin of the creation of the *Cahiers pour l'Analyse* in 1966.

KP: So there was a scission at the heart of the *Cahiers Marxistes-Léninistes* and the *Cahiers pour l'Analyse* came out of this split?

AG: Yes. The other comrades went on very different paths. Some decided to become workers in factories, for example. The volume of the *Cahiers Marxistes-Léninistes* was never published, however. It was thrown out. As for the articles by Milner and Regnault, they were published much later in volume 7 of the *Cahiers pour l'Analyse*, entitled 'From Myth to the Novel' (CpA 7.2; 7.3), a volume to which Georges Dumézil agreed to contribute (7.1) as well. However, he was also not a Marxist. That's the least one could say . . .

KP: In sum, you made use of all the available structuralist tools.

AG: Yes, but we didn't use them all the same way.

KP: Milner uses the word 'hyperstructuralist' to describe the project of *Cahiers pour l'Analyse*.[7] Do you agree?

AG: I think that, in effect, what he and Miller wanted to construct was a general formal model, a sort of pure logic of the signifier capable of operating in very diverse fields and discourses, stretching from mathematical logic to psycho-analysis and going through anthropology and mythology. We were obviously far away from phenomenology.

KP: A hot topic in France, in those days.

AG: That's right. From Hegel to Merleau-Ponty, it was the dominant discourse. We also talked about it at the ENS of course, enough that the young Derrida had come to support Althusser for the position of director of philosophical studies. At

---

7   Cf. Jean-Claude Milner, *L'Oeuvre claire: Lacan, la science, la philosophie* (Paris: Seuil, 1995).

the Sorbonne where we followed some courses, such as Canguilhem's, I also attended Derrida's lectures on Husserl. He came to ENS to speak to us about *Logical Investigations*, at the same time as he was preparing *Speech and Phenomena*. However what left the deepest impression on me was the seminar he gave on Rousseau, from which he would develop the book that made him known to the general public: *Of Grammatology*. We had published an excerpt of this before its publication in Volume 4 of our *Cahiers* (CpA 4.1). Derrida delivered a rather disrespectful reading of Lévi-Strauss, who wasn't pleased at all.

KP: Did Derrida support the *Cahiers pour l'Analyse*?

AG: Let's say that Derrida was not our most solid supporter. Even if he liked speaking with us, he did not really identify with the project. Also, he kept a prudent distance with respect to our political engagement, which I think he judged rather naïve and utopian. Though it is true that he was interested in Lacan's reading of Freud, he followed a path that was his own.

KP: Incidentally, one of my colleagues, who wrote his dissertation on the young Derrida, suggests that his article on 'Freud et la scène de l'écriture', published in the summer 1966 issue of *Tel Quel*, in many respects came out of the debate between André Green and Serge Leclaire on the status of affect.[8]

AG: That's very possible. Since you bring up Leclaire, I should mention that we invited him in November 1965 to come speak to us about his analytic practice. Lacan had just founded the l'École Freudienne de Paris in June 1964. One of the original aspects of his school – something that elicited protest on the part of colleagues who were attached to their exclusive domain – was that he wanted to open its doors to non-analysts. Like Freud, Lacan refused to make psychoanalysis a branch of medicine and to reduce it to psychotherapy. Insofar as the practitioners of the concept took up the vocation of theorizing, we had a proper place in the Freudian field in his eyes. We were also convinced that in cultivating our garden there, we would make the best of all possible Freudian fields. We did seek, however, to know a bit more about analytic prac-tice and its relation with theory. So Leclaire held regular seminars over a number of years and their notes were published in the *Cahiers* (CpA 1.5; 3.6; 8.6). Even Lacan himself came a few times to chat with us at night. He joined us late one night and strolled from rue d'Ulm back to his flat on rue de Lille. On the way, he was kind enough to invite us for champagne in a café. And when I say champagne, we're talking Dom Pérignon, grand cru. However

---

8   Edward Baring, *The Young Derrida and French Philosophy, 1945–1968* (Cambridge: Cambridge University Press, 2011), Chapter 6.

there was nothing patronizing about the way he treated us. He smoked his cigar and told us funny stories . . . Speaking of funny stories, I do remember this prank that I'm not going to tell you because you are a serious person and this will lead us to anecdotes.

KP: Go ahead.

AG: Only because you insist, here we go. Among the scientific students at ENS, there were a few brilliant minds who liked to make fun of the circus that squeezed themselves into the auditorium every Wednesday at half past noon to listen religiously to the weekly pronouncements of Saint Lacan. Among them, my neighbour in the dorm, a nice guy, was an electro-physicist. Now, I didn't know this until after the investigation, but he had invented a means to interfere with Lacan's microphone from his room. So one Wednesday, when Lacan was in the middle of his talk, we heard music –*piano piano* at first but then *riforzando* – taking over his voice until it overtook him completely. I remember thinking that it was Bach's Mass in B minor, if it was not the Magnificat. In any case, it was religious music, with organ fugues and choral harmonies. What was hilarious was that Lacan continued to speak as if nothing was happening, and no one in the audience dared to lift a finger to observe that somehow there was something wrong with the sound . . . And to put the icing on this rather delirious cake, the prankster and his accomplices had taken the care to put a few smoke bombs under the platform so that Lacan, still continuing to speak, would finally disappear, in the eyes of his faithful followers, in a thick cloud of smoke.

KP: Is this true?

AG: Totally, as much as the whole truth can be said. But what happened afterwards was actually quite edifying. That night, Lacan called me, 'Listen, Grosrichard. Find me the guy who played this prank, I have a few words for him.' I was quite flattered to be trusted to play the role of Dupin in this crazy story and I started to investigate. My detective sense brought me logically to knock on the door of my neighbour. He confessed to being the mastermind. I told him, 'Lacan would like to speak with you.' Anyone else would have been shaking in his boots. Not him. 'O.K. let's go.' And so we went to rue de Lille into the waiting room of Lacan's clinic. The door opened, Lacan saw us and I presented him with the individual. I slipped away and thought, 'Damn! This is going to get rough!' Big mistake: they spent an hour together discussing modern science and its applications. Lacan was enthusiastic. My friend too. I never came back for him. But Lacan was like that: surprise, in every domain . . . Also, when he asked me something, he gave me this feeling that I knew much more that I thought I did. Not always. Often he kindly let me know that I was nothing but an imbecile. But he had this Socratic side that often surprised me with the fact that I wasn't. I remember one day when he invited me to lunch to talk with him about the blind, a theme I was writing about for my thesis. Because of him, by dessert, I realized I saw things much more clearly than I feared when I had blathered some thoughts over appetizers, regarding the quandary that was Molyneux's problem.

KP: Let's discuss your thesis, which was certainly related to the agenda of the *Cahiers pour l'Analyse*.

AG: That's right. Canguilhem had suggested that I study the history of this problem that Molyneux had posed to Locke, which he reproduced and attempted to resolve in the second part of *An Essay Concerning Human Understanding*. In the beginning, the problem was posed in a purely formal way: let us suppose that someone born blind learned by the sole means of touch to distinguish the globe and the cube, and imagine that, all of a sudden, his eyes regained the sense of sight. Question: by the use of his eyes alone, would he be able to distinguish which is the cube and which is the globe? Locke, basing his answer solely on what he'd learned from his empiricist theory of perception as the combination of elementary ideas, responded in the negative. And yet later on the problem would resurface for a number of philosophers, from Leibniz to Condillac, by way of Berkeley, Voltaire, Diderot and many lesser-known philosophers. Some respond yes, others say no, and yet others say yes if and only if the blind person is also a geometer, etc. What I wanted to show was how this little formal structure, deep within the discourse of such or such a philosopher, functions like a tell-tale sign of different philosophical positions, the idealism of Berkeley for example or the materialism of Diderot. This approach was thus in line with the *Cahiers pour l'Analyse* (CpA 2.3).

But this was only the first aspect of my work. There was a second aspect. Since this problem was one for which philosophers proposed purely speculative solutions, it was also illuminating to go into the history of medicine and more precisely eye surgery. And on this point, I was in Canguilhem's field. In 1728, if I remember correctly, the surgeon William Cheselden very successfully operated on a young man born blind with cataracts such that the abstract psychological subject who was somebody born blind at the outset became a 'subject supposed to know' incarnate. It was expected that once the bandages were taken off we could have a clear and trustworthy response to Molyneux's problem since it was founded in experience. In fact, we quickly realized that the response was not obvious for all sorts of reasons tied to his post-operational reactions.

In the end, the history of this problem took me to a third field: the relations between knowledge and power, which Foucault's work would radically reshape. In terms of my own trajectory, I ended up working on a series of writings in the history of the problem that were published in the 1770s by the Chevalier de

Mérian (CpA 2.4). He was the permanent secretary at the Academy of Berlin, founded and directed by Frederick II, the very model of the 'enlightened despot'. Seeing that the problem had neither been resolved speculatively nor experimentally, he submitted to the sovereign a project that he believed would please the philosopher-king. Given that our five senses provide the primary material of all our knowledge, as he basically put it, why not increase the profitability of these tools in rationalizing the production of knowledge? Let us create a sort of seminar on practical epistemology that would also be a workshop of knowledge where the division of perceptive labour would take over for philosophical analysis. This would permit in turn the resolution of a harmful social problem. Each year, a number of mothers abandon their babies. Instead of letting them starve uselessly, we should take them from their unworthy mothers at birth and solidly cover their eyes such as to basically artificially recreate the conditions of those born blind. Let's bring them to the seminar. Over seven years, we'll then train them methodically to use their tactile senses, which are manifestly underutilized by those who can see since they double what is already seen. Some of them could specialize in the development of other senses like smell, sound, taste, just as the perfectly tuned statues of Condillac. And then, the day when our precious children of Minerva reach their age of reason, *tada!* We remove the covering from their eyes and Molyneux's problem will finally cease to be one. This is not all. How many new kinds of questions would these young children bring to us in their new light! How many prejudices of these future priests of science would finally be swept aside! As Mérian concludes, outside of its humanitarian vision, it is a highly philosophical project that would have the further advantage of being easy to put into place. The king's order is all that would be required to make it reality . . . Fortunately, Frederic II had the wisdom of abstaining from this project. One could also point to this argument for accusing the century of the Enlightenment for having prepared the grounds for fascism, Nazism and god knows what other crimes against humanity.

KP: But couldn't we say that, all the same, the *Cahiers pour l'Analyse* sought to defend Enlightenment rationalism against a certain phenomenological romanticism which was focused more on interiority or feeling.

AG: Yes, the Enlightenment that we wanted to reclaim was that of d'Alembert, of Newton of the *Principia*, who Lacan refers to, through the work of his master Koyré . . .

KP: Lacan was also a close reader of Heidegger. Were you?

AG: No, I have to admit that the forgetting of being left me rather indifferent.

KP: I asked Milner the same question because he wrote on Plato's *Sophist*, also a key text for Heidegger. He responded that he didn't spend much time with Heidegger's work back then either.

AG: On the other hand, we'd already taken up in our own way what Lacan would later call 'antiphilosophy'. In 1974, he himself implemented it, along with linguistics, logic and topology, in the educational programme of the Department of Psychoanalysis at the University at Vincennes. It was not a question, to be clear, of considering philosophy as a whole as an enemy to vanquish. To be an 'antiphilosopher' is still to be a philosopher but in a different way. Freud loved to cite Heine, for whom the conceptions of the world that the philosophers constructed only appear to be coherent because they have filled the holes of their systems with their nightcaps. To mark, through analysis, the places where the signifiers played the function of this 'stop-gap' in one or another of these discourses, this approach, if you like, was antiphilosophy, for me at least. There were many ways of doing this. Althusser delivered a 'symptomatic' reading. With Derrida, this would become deconstruction. With Foucault, archaeology and genealogy were posed against the old theme of the history of ideas. As for myself, I practised a form of antiphilosophy without knowing it. Obviously when I read Badiou, who practises it as well as he speaks of it, that seems boastful.

KP: That's doubtful. At the end of your introduction of Mérian's text, you wrote these lines: 'The techniques for knowing Nature within man, which require and allow it to be dissected and de-composed, allow in return their reassembly according to a constructed order, which is no longer that of chance and habit, but of a nature ordered by reason. Because reason is in man the product of a natural progression, the order imposed by reason will be the only genuine natural order. Man makes use of what nature gives him in order to perfect his nature' (CpA 2.3:112). I think Foucault is saying something similar in *The Order of Things*.

AG: Oh really?

KP: Was he important for your work?

AG: Certainly, and not only because he was on the entrance committee the year Miller and I entered the ENS. In the following years, he taught in Tunisia and was thus far away from us. Physically, I mean, for we followed his publications quite closely.

KP: The passage I just cited also recalls the concept of 'suture' such as Miller developed it in reference to Frege and his theory of numbers (CpA 1.3). What use did you make of this concept? It seems to me that in this passage you're describing a similar process wherein man operates a sort of closing-in on himself.

AG: That's probably true. But, in my view, your remark bears more directly on my article on Rousseau. In 'Gravité de Rousseau' (CpA 8.2), I tried to integrate Althusser's reading of *The Social Contract* with my own understanding of what he presented as a series of 'discrepancies' (CpA 8.1). According to him, in this text there was an 'unthought' or an 'unsaid' that caused a disequilibrium in Rousseau's discourse, which made it theoretically unbalanced and thus led him to bring about nothing more than provisional moments of equilibrium. In this unsaid, one could recognise an 'absent cause' producing a chain of symptomatic effects on the level of effective discourse. I picked up this idea of discrepancy in my article in order to apply it to the sum of Rousseau's work. At the time, we (with the notable exception of Jean Starobinski, in *La Transparence et l'obstacle* [1957]) still opposed Rousseau the labourer of the concept, the author of the *Social Contract*, to Rousseau the writer, author of the *New Heloise*, the *Confessions*, the *Dialogues* and the *Reveries*. In short, there were two Rousseaus, a division the critics shared: for the philosophers there was the philosophical Rousseau, for the literary critics there was the literary Rousseau. These two Rousseaus were what I tried to think together, in showing that the Rousseau of the *Confessions* was not this proud *ego* who, once his theoretical work was accomplished, decided to bare himself before the public declaring that, 'I am the best of men, despite what they say', but rather that this 'I' of the *Confessions* was theoretically necessitated by a fundamental defect [*défaut*] in his theory. To summarize very quickly, the subject of the autobiographical work is, ultimately, the foundation that lacks in the theoretical work. If he is not what he is, everything risks collapsing [*S'il n'est pas ce qu'il est, tout risque de s'écrouler*].

KP: What really struck me in your article is how you highlight the desire that labours over and animates Rousseau's oeuvre from beginning to end. You seek to procure the set's structure without, for all that, failing to inscribe it in a history.

AG: Let's say, if you like, that I read it as if it were a diachronic form given to the structure, to invoke what Lacan said about myth as it was analyzed by his friend Lévi-Strauss. I was impressed by this 'hyperstructuralism' that Miller and Milner elaborated, but what really bothered me was that it was difficult for me to use in my reading of the texts of those called the *philosophes* of the eighteenth century. When it concerned Montesquieu, Diderot, Voltaire, and Rousseau, all of them held an essential relation with language, and knew how to make admirable use of it in the fight against prejudice. Instead of outlining their ideas in systems, they had at their disposal the most diverse forms of expression: tales, novels, theatrical works, dictionary articles, letters . . . *The Persian Letters*,

Jacques the Fatalist, *Candide*, the *New Heloise* are 'antiphilosophical' novels, each in its own way and in its style. It was difficult to formalize them in Millerian terms!

KP: Evoking Rousseau's 'theology', you write that its essential character is that 'it allows for the restoration of an order wherein the subject rediscovers its unity and ceases to be infinitely alienated in representation' (CpA 8.2:60). But you show the way in which this unity of the subject is undiscoverable, unless it is situated in an ego which is nothing but an imaginary decoy. And you conclude from this that, for Rousseau, 'the subject is unnameable' (64). This impossibility for the speaking subject of making a unity of himself, to have a name that is really his own is something that we have already encountered in Plato's *Sophist* (cf. CpA 3.4; 3.5).

AG: And elsewhere too! It is the unique feature of the subject of the signifier. In this regard, Rousseau himself was Lacanian when he declared, at the start of the Confessions: 'I am other'. A little attentive reading suffices to notice that he lived and felt, in and through his discourse, as a divided subject, as a 'lack of being'.

KP: Which justified an entire volume of *Cahiers pour l'Analyse* dedicated to Rousseau (CpA 8).

AG: Yes. We even had a republication of his *Essay on the Origin of Languages* at the same time. But I think that this interest for Rousseau also came from the fact that we imagined that our theoretical practice had something to do with the Revolution. And the *Social Contract* was the Bible of the French revolutionaries – notably Robespierre. We were also able to interpret the Terror as the effect in the real of 'the unthought of Jean-Jacques Rousseau'. No doubt, we should have studied the *Discourse on the Arts and Sciences* more closely: the critique that he had developed of the society of consumption in his time would have prepared us to conceptually confront May 68, which would erupt a year later. But I jest . . .

KP: In any case, after and despite May 68, the *Cahiers* seemed to come back to their initial programme. Volume 9, 'Genealogy of Sciences' (CpA 9) came out in the summer of 1968 and the tenth, on 'Formalization' (CpA 10), the winter of 1969.

AG: I think that they were already ready by the start of 1968, a moment when no one could predict what would happen a few months later. But I am not the right person to speak to about this, since I was no longer in Paris after October of 1967. I had just passed my *agrégation* in philosophy and had to finish my military service. Since I had no wish to wear the uniform, I chose civil service and was appointed to the French *lycée* in Casablanca, Morocco.

KP: So you were missed at the May events?

AG: Let's say I missed them. I burned with impatience for the academic year to end so I could jump on the next plane to join my friends. That's what I did. In August, I was in Besançon, together with Miller and Milner writing tracts and distributing them at the gates of the factories, and I don't remember talking much about formalization. And also, returning to Morocco, I was part of an underground Maoist group that aimed at no more and no less than the overthrow of the Moroccan monarchy. In fact, this ended badly: my Moroccan friends were arrested and sentenced, for the most part, to thirty some years in prison. As for me, I was politely asked to leave the country and I found myself as a lecturer in philosophy at the University of Aix-en-Provence, where I taught Spinoza and was a militant in Gauche Prolétarienne. But my participation in this was rank-and-file, following the orders of the Parisian intellectual leaders of the group.

KP: And so the *Cahiers pour l'Analyse* was terminated after the publication of the tenth volume.

AG: We had other fish to fry. Lacan, who valiantly continued his seminar, no longer at the ENS where he had been chased out, but at the Department of Law just in front of the Pantheon, was clearly sad to see these youths taken in by the illusion of this revolution that they heaped praises on. He tried, with his theory of the 'four discourses', to make them see that this revolution did nothing but take them back to their starting place, just like the revolution of heavenly bodies.[9] 'You want a master, you will have him!' he announced to the troublemakers of Vincennes. He was not mistaken and he would soon track down his lost flock, returning them to the fold under the guiding staff, no less firm than illuminating, of Jacques-Alain Miller. The time of *Ornicar?* had come, and that would be another adventure.

KP: Final question: in your view what remains today of the *Cahiers pour l'Analyse*? Is it still a reference in the intellectual life of Paris?

AG: That presupposes that there is still an intellectual life in Paris, which Milner seriously doubts.[10] There are, in any case, still those who work today so that we don't end up brain dead. As for the question of what remains of the project, your questions are already the beginning of an answer, are they not? As for me, I would say that the project of the *Cahiers pour l'Analyse* has had its time. It was a

---

9   Cf. Lacan, SXVII.
10   Cf. Milner, *Existe-il une vie intellectuelle en France?* (Paris: Verdier, 2002)

logical time, that which precisely structures analysis.[11] Like the fable of the three prisoners in Lacan – our chains are nothing but the sequences [*enchaînements*] of reason – at the start we were looking at each other as if in the mirror. The time of understanding and explaining what united us or what separated us had lasted a few brief years. May 68 sounded off the moment of conclusion in the real, and the small team dispersed. And we really were a team, even a real sports team. Even if there was nothing like a match-up between the members of the Cercle d'Épistémologie and the football team at ENS (half-orange jersey, black shorts), it was largely composed of philosophers (Balibar, Bouveresse, Duroux, Mosconi, Rancière . . .), for the most part brought up in Althusser's school. Althusser was himself a big fan of football. He came to the training sessions, and encouraged us from the sidelines and every time that a match of the French team was on the television, he explained to us why the *Bleus* had lost and what would have been the better strategy to surely win. Good theoretical lessons where we took careful notes. This did not keep us from regularly scoring against the students of the *Polytechnique* or the *École des impôts*. But in the end, what was the importance of all this? We will demolish them the next time, persuaded as we were with Lenin that 'the theory of Marx was all powerful because it is true'. Perhaps it is this sort of certitude that lacks among youths today, even those nourished by Badiou and Žižek, and that keeps them from rediscovering the spirit that animated our project.

They are lacking something else too, that you wouldn't know just from reading the *Cahiers*. We should really reprint these great voices that gave us so much to think about and which can no longer be heard. The voice of Lacan, those of Canguilhem, Foucault, Barthes, Derrida. And the voice of Althusser. A little anecdote, to conclude on a musical note?

KP: Sure.

AG: Althusser also loved the opera. In the spring of 1964, Maria Callas had come to perform a series of special shows at Palais Garnier. La Callas performing *Norma*, we couldn't have missed that! We went with him to the show. La Callas was divine, very much so. A memorable night. What was also unforgettable was that a few days later we learned that the day before, when she was reaching for the sublime highs of the aria 'Casta diva . . .', her voice broke. This was the beginning of the end.

Translated by Tzuchien Tho.

---

11   Lacan, 'Logical Time and the Assertion of Anticipated Certainty' in E 197–213/161–175.

CHAPTER THIRTEEN

The Force of Minimalism:
An Interview with Jean-Claude Milner

Paris, France, 28 November 2008

Knox Peden (KP): In your book, *L'Œuvre claire* you describe the *Cahiers pour l'Analyse* as the culmination of the 'first Lacanian classicism'. You describe the project as 'hyperstructuralist', suggesting that it adheres to Lacan's own hyperstructural conjecture, which can be stated: 'Any given structure has distinctive properties.'[1] How did this conjecture inform the *Cahiers pour l'Analyse*? And in what sense would you say that the *Cahiers pour l'Analyse* were 'hyperstructuralist'?

Jean-Claude Milner (JCM): We need to understand that in speaking of a first classicism and hyperstructuralism, I'm proposing my own interpretation, and that I'm proposing it after the fact. These terms did not exist when the *Cahiers pour l'Analyse* was constituted. It is certainly possible that some or even most of the participants would not recognize themselves in my interpretation of the enterprise. This is a first remark.

I think that ultimately we cannot grasp this brief venture that was the *Cahiers pour l'Analyse* if we do not consider the structuralist movement unfolding at the time and, moreover, the two-fold interpretation that one can make of structuralism. There are two possibilities. Either a given structure has no properties, which means that a structure only has properties if it is particularized (a particular phonological system, a particular system of kinship, etc.) Or instead, and this seems to me especially explicit in Lacan, a given structure in which no particular term is specified is in fact already endowed with properties. I think that this is what Lacan was presenting in the appendix to 'The Purloined Letter' (E, 54–61/41–48). Drawing on mathematical frameworks, Lacan tries to show that, given a minimum of possible particularizations, we can produce distinctive properties [*des propriétés non-quelconques*]. Hyperstructuralism seeks to establish the non-arbitrary properties of an arbitrary structure. These non-arbitrary properties are born from the very functioning of an arbitrary structure. The latter is thus a creator of properties; it is, in a certain sense, active. It seems to me that this is the programme that dominates the first part of Lacan's work, what I call the first classicism. I was very responsive to this programme; it can

---

1   Jean-Claude Milner, *L'Œuvre claire: Lacan, la science, la philosophie* (Paris: Seuil, 1995), 104. The French reads: '*La structure quelconque a des propriétés non-quelconques.*'

be seen in my article 'The Point of the Signifier' (CpA 3.5), and I would suggest in Jacques-Alain Miller's text 'Action of the Structure' (CpA 9.6) as well.

Let us consider the idea that the structure can have an action; what is this action? This action consists in making singularities emerge via the play of the structure alone. Whence the active character of the structure. Whence the active character as well of the signifier, the present active participle [*le signifiant*] opposing the perfect passive participle of the signified [*le signifié*]. Now, Lacan rarely considered the signified. In privileging the active participle, the signifier, he in fact extracted it from the signifier/signified pairing. He broke this pairing. He chose to distribute [*verser*] the signifier on the side of what he calls pure action, pure in that it is posited in itself and not in inverse symmetry with passivity. In making a theory of the action of the structure, one makes a theory of the signifier as active; one demonstrates that the signifier is only a signifier insofar as it generates a structure and that the structure is only a structure to the extent that it generates the relation of a signifier to another signifier.

KP: In the Foreword to the first volume Jacques-Alain Miller says: 'We define epistemology as the history and theory of the discourse of science [la *science*] (its birth justifies the singular)' (CpA 1.Intro). Two things are striking in this passage: the precision of the singular – la *science* – but also the emphasis on the history and theory of the *discourse* of science and not the history and theory of science per se. Why this emphasis on singularity? And, moreover, how did you and your colleagues conceive this relationship between science and its own discourse?

JCM: Here again I am not sure that I can speak for all those who participated in the *Cahiers pour l'Analyse*. The reflections on the plural and the singular with regard to science came up very early on because this had been an objection against the *Cahiers* from the outset, most notably from the Althusserians. François Regnault wrote an article bearing precisely on the varying approaches to epistemology according to whether science is considered as either one or plural (CpA 9.4). In my view, science in the singular only makes sense if it is reduced to the cut or break [*coupure*] between science and non-science. And yet, from the point of view of science, there is fundamentally only one single structure of the cut; and *this* is what grounds the singularity of science. This doesn't exclude the possibility that there could effectively be many different sciences, but if we keep to structure, the cut between science and non-science is found in all the sciences. Under different forms, perhaps, but it is the same structure of cut. This is how I grasped the question of epistemology at the moment of the *Cahiers pour l'Analyse*.

But I can be more precise. Already at this time, and here again I'm still speaking as an individual, I was troubled by the fact that in Lacan's writings science in the singular was essentially mathematical physics. Now, let's consider, alongside structuralism and structural linguistics, biology, which in the 1960s was beginning to be referred to as the epistemological model for structural linguistics; this is the moment when the notion of the genetic code began to become the dominant paradigm. I was struck by the fact that I saw no direct resemblance between mathematical physics from the point of view of its paradigm and the paradigm of structural linguistics or that of biology. I accorded much importance to the fact that it was necessary to preserve this diversity, on the one hand, and on the other to maintain the notion of science in the singular. My response was as follows: science in the singular is the cut between science and non-science; and yet, the cut between science and non-science recurs under diverse forms in mathematical physics, in linguistics, in genetics. A key historical point: I remind you that all of this must be reinterpreted in the light of an intellectual world where Popper didn't exist.

KP: Related to the notion of *coupure*, this is something you discuss in *Le Périple structural* and *L'Œuvre claire*, is the signal importance of Alexandre Koyré and this notion of what you call 'extended Galileanism' ['*galiléisme étendu*'].[2] Could you say more about the reading of Koyré at this time? He was obviously important for Lacan. How did this notion of Galileanism as a definition or a way to talk about modernity and modern science figure in your thinking at the time?

JCM: We should distinguish between what I thought at the time and what I say today. The term Galileanism is one that I forged rather late; I'm not saying that it didn't exist before me, but if it did, I never encountered it. I used it in *L'Œuvre claire* and *Le Périple structural*, but this was not a term that was used in the *Cahiers pour l'Analyse*; Galilean science, yes, Galileanism, no.

Why did I speak of Galileanism in *Le Périple structural*? Essentially so that I could introduce the notion of an 'extended Galileanism'. In fact, if I did not have to introduce extended Galileism, I would not need to talk about Galileanism. And the notion of Galileanism is not Koyréan at all. But in the *Cahiers pour l'Analyse* Koyré was clearly the reference. If you like, I would say that, it is not exactly a paradox, but from the point of view of the presentation of terms, there has been a displacement in the notion of the epistemological break. The epistemological break is a term that was invented by Bachelard, and Koyré did not really use this notion. What he describes is the emergence of a new figure of science, marked by Galileo. Something was at stake, a genuine reversal with respect to what had preceded it. For the first time in history, mathematical entities did not serve as the means to think the eternal but rather the

_____

2   Milner, *L'Œuvre claire*, 95. On Koyré, see 33–76. Cf. Milner, *Le Périple structural: figures et paradigme*, 2nd edition (Paris: Verdier, 2008), 205, 275–376.

transient [*le passage*]. For an Aristotelian, there is a difference in nature between the world of celestial beings, which follow mathematical laws since these beings are eternal, and the sublunary world, the earthly world, which is subject to generation and corruption and to which mathematical entities do not apply in an explicative way. But, Koyré says, with Galileo something absolutely particular happens: firstly, the celestial beings are not perfect beings – the problem of sunspots, etc. – and, even so, this does not prevent mathematical laws from being defined for them; secondly, mathematical laws can be defined for the sublunary world.

Under the influence of Althusser, we thought that the Bachelardian notion of the epistemological break or cut [*coupure*] allowed us to describe the rupture [*rupture*] that Koyré described. I am not sure that Koyré himself would have accepted this formulation. All the same, you can see how we were led to think of this notion of cut in itself as the fundamental notion – I was, at any rate. To think the notion of cut itself is to think it as a structural notion; thus it is effectively the same notion that permits us to understand the epistemological break as Bachelard described it and the discursive displacement that Koyré described.

KP: At one point in *L'Œuvre claire* you suggest that the ideal informing the *Cahiers* was an ideal of analysis rather than an ideal of science per se,[3] which raises a question about this relationship between the two terms, *la science* and *l'analyse*. How was this relation understood? Was psychoanalysis to be understood as one variant of a more general concept of analysis? Or was it the fundamental analysis in question?

JCM: What I said in *L'Œuvre claire* and what I say later in *Le Périple structural* turns around the question of mathematization. Science here, with the definite singular article (*la science*), is mathematical physics. It makes use of mathematics in the fullest sense of the term; Descartes was at the same time a mathematician and a physicist – I'm thinking of the *Dioptrics*. Einstein was not a very good mathematician, but that's of little consequence. There is no doubt that what he used in the theory of relativity were quadratic equations, perfectly defined in mathematics. By contrast, structuralist linguistics uses very little mathematics in the strict sense. In fact, it does not use it at all.

Thus, the first question: if we consider structuralist linguistics as a variant of Galilean science, does this not mean that we understand mathematics differently or that, in the Galilean operation, strict mathematization is only a variant among others within a larger operation? With Lacan, you find attempts at strict mathematization. I take the example of the appendix of the 'Purloined Letter' – but it's not true, if you take the definition of the signifier as 'the signifier

---

3   Milner, *L'Œuvre claire*, 37.

represents the subject for another signifier', that this formula is from the outset mathematical or even could be mathematized. If we turn to Marxism, it served as one of the variants, one of the forms of the epistemological break during the time of the *Cahiers pour l'Analyse*; with respect to the political economy that had preceded it, it was thought of as a Galilean science of economy and of social formations more generally. And yet, the dimension of strict mathematization is practically absent here. The literalized [*littéralisé*] formulas of *Capital* are not mathematical formulae in the strict sense of the term. We could not carry out any mathematical operation with them, whether simple or complex. We could even say that for Marx the notion of surplus value, were it to confront mathematics, appears precisely as irreducible to a calculation. One is tempted to say that economists can calculate everything *except* for surplus value.

We encountered this paradox very early. For my part, I feel like it was not clearly resolved until much later on, even if I now think that the resolution was already latent in the notion of analysis. The resolution itself however, in my case, appeared after the fact, after many years. The notion of analysis means that what is essential in Galilean science is not the use of mathematics. Mathematics is only one of the possible variants of what is essential and what at the time of the *Cahiers pour l'Analyse* we called, precisely, *analysis*. Later, in *Le Périple structural*, I called it – and this clearly represents a displacement – literalization [*littéralisation*].[4] Galilean science exists the moment that there is literalization; mathematization is one of the possible forms of literalization, but it is not the only one. Here we have a general point of view on the notion of Galilean science; I developed it in a particular way with respect to linguistics in my *Introduction à une science du langage*.[5] We could say that with the notion of literalization the relation between science and analysis becomes clear and precise. But since this notion is not yet clear in the *Cahiers*, the relation between science and analysis remains obscure there.

To respond to your last question, psychoanalysis was understood as one of the forms of analysis. The hypothesis of the *Cahiers pour l'Analyse* was that you could find exactly the same analysis in Freud that you would find in, let's say, Spinoza and that you would find in Marx. I don't think that this position can be fully supported.

KP: I'd like to move now from epistemology to ontology and ask about a remark you make near the end of *Le Périple structural*. I quote: 'The most obvious mark of structuralist ontology resides in the inseparability of being and position.'[6] This is a striking, clear, and succinct definition of structuralist ontology. Would

---

4   Milner, *Le Périple structural*, 338.
5   Milner, *Introduction à une science du langage* (Paris: Seuil, 1989).
6   Milner, *Le Périple structural*, 360.

you describe the *Cahiers pour l'Analyse* as an ontological project in these terms?

JCM: I think that it was an ontological project, most certainly. You cite *Le Périple structural*; I remark there that in Saussure there was an overturning with respect to the western ontological tradition, since he separates being and unicity.[7] In classical ontology, being and the one went together. Whereas what we find in the *Course in General Linguistics* is the definition of a type of being that is fundamentally not one. And this is in my view what Lacan grasped in defining the signifier as representing the subject for another signifier. This means that the alterity 'for an other' is at the heart of the one of the signifier. Somewhere, I believe it is in 'L'Étourdit', but I am not sure, Lacan posits that the signifier only represents 'for' [*le signifiant ne représente que 'pour'*].[8] This means that the signifier in its being [*en tant qu'être*] cannot be one. It is impossible to think it at the same time as being and as one. There is an ontological project and I think this can be seen in the *Cahiers*. Perhaps I'm mistaken, but it seems to me that the text where this appears most clearly is 'The Point of the Signifier' (CpA 3.5). What I tried to show in this text, however tentatively, is the way in which Plato – who, Lord knows, is the figure most associated, in the philosophical tradition, with the effort to tie being and the one together – proceeds to their disjunction in the *Sophist*. Which is to say that being is under the form of a chain.

KP: It's fascinating to see in 'The Point of the Signifier' the use of a new concept in its earliest development – i.e. 'suture' – in an analysis of Plato. Why this return to Plato, and the texts of *Sophist* and *Parmenides* in particular, in the *Cahiers*?

JCM: On this point, I think that, though the article itself was personal, many shared the interest for what I would call texts of pure logic, whether it was Plato's 'logical' texts, in other words the *Sophist* and the *Parmenides*, or Hegel's *Logic*, or mathematical logic, all the texts of this kind. Our interest in Plato was not a 'return' to Plato. It is not to be separated from other interests: why Russell on Gödel? Why Frege? What interested us in these texts at the time was the possibility of reasoning about terms without any particular substance and making particular or even singular properties appear. Since they didn't depend on a particular substance, these properties must depend on the necessity of the structure itself. This supposes that the structure is itself productive of properties. Without being

---

7   Ibid., 15–57.
8   See also Lacan, 'The Subversion of the Subject and the Dialectic of Desire': 'My definition of the signifier (there is no other) is as follows: a signifier is what represents the subject to another signifier. This latter signifier is therefore the signifier to which all the other signifiers represent the subject – which means that if this signifier is missing, all the other signifiers represent nothing. For something is only represented to' (E, 819/693–694).

aware of this at the time, this comes down to admitting that analytic judgments can be productive; from that, the importance of Frege, who tried, in explicit opposition to Kant, to base arithmetic in analytic judgments. This was also the source of Plato's importance: we could show that the Socratic dialogues rely on the hypothesis that in analyzing one proposition of his interlocutor, Socrates could find entirely new propositions. In the chain of the *Sophist*, it is by analyzing one term that we make new terms appear. We thus rediscover, through another path, the word *analysis*. I see there today what Lakatos would have called a hidden lemma, and which I would summarize, in reference to Kant: 'Certain analytic judgments are productive.' We also rediscover here, through another path, what I would today call hyperstructuralism.

It is true that Russell would surely have rejected this lemma. Russell nonetheless shared a common point with Plato; with him too, you withdraw all particular substance from terms. You reason on terms and show the constraints that are not based in experience and which are, for an empiricist like Russell, just as constraining as empirical constraints. Put differently, the empiricist in the English tradition will say: 'You cannot do whatever you like with an empirical object; it resists.' Well Russell said: 'You cannot do whatever you like with a logical object; it resists.'

KP: Another question concerns the relationship between the concept of number and the concept of being, which was a particular concern for the *Cahiers* at this time. For Badiou, it seems, at best the relationship between mathematics and the ontology that Miller was attempting to develop was an analogy, whereas it seems that Miller wanted to insist that the logic that he was drawing from Frege had an ontological bearing. I wanted to ask about your thoughts on this because your own position in 'The Point of the Signifier' (CpA 3.5) is not totally clear.

JCM: I think that here there is something that few understood at the time, and it's that I'm talking about Plato in making the hypothesis that Plato did not know what number was, or did not have a complete understanding of it. And why? Because he did not have the concept of zero. This means that when Plato reasoned – and I think this is an extremely important point – when he reasoned on numbers, he reasoned always in reference to the numbers which could have a geometrical representation, and this is tied to the fact that he did not have the concept of zero. Whence the importance of Frege's text on the zero, and the importance of the questions Leibniz poses: is it that the geometrical point is of the order of the zero or the order of the one? At the time, I had an ontological hypothesis; in my view, the signifier exploded classical ontology and the logic of the signifier announced the formal laws of this upheaval. Though it provided the instruments of thought, mathematical logic remained subordinate in relation to this hypothesis. It seems to me that Miller was close to this position. Badiou, at this time, thought on the contrary that ontological discourse must not free itself from the laws proper to mathematical logic.

I am in complete agreement with your diagnostic concerning the past; I cannot speak for the present period. Badiou has developed his own doctrine, very complete but evolving. For example, between *Being and Event* and *Logics of Worlds* there is a displacement and this displacement is deeper still if we think of the period of the *Cahiers*. As for Jacques-Alain Miller, I don't know what he would say on this question today.

For my part, as I said, in 'The Point of the Signifier' (CpA 3.5) I accord much importance to the fact that Plato, having no idea of zero, was unable to have a complete idea of number. And this means that when he constructs his chain with a finite number of terms, we must understand that this is the homonym of a modern chain wherein there would be one, two, three, four, five terms; it is not the same chain since for Plato 'one' has no predecessor, since there is no zero.

KP: For Heidegger as well, the *Sophist* was a key text, and this relationship between being and non-being was a central concern. Was Heidegger in play, as it were, at the time? Were you were familiar with Heidegger's take on the *Sophist*?

JCM: I believe that, on this score, there is a major difference among the various members of the *Cahiers pour l'Analyse*. Personally, I had no familiarity with Heidegger's texts at the time. Don't forget that I did not have a philosophical education. I was a linguist by training. At the end of the 1960s, my knowledge was classical, which is to say that all I knew were the texts of Plato, Descartes, Kant . . . and by personal choice, I read a lot of Leibniz and Hegel. Heidegger was not at all familiar to me. I have since read and worked on him, but in a completely different context. By contrast, I know that Jacques-Alain Miller had a profound familiarity with Heidegger.

KP : In your work in the past decades you've held a critical position on the *Cahiers pour l'Analyse*. In *Le Périple structural*, you describe your own personal encounter with Noam Chomsky's work as 'a total reversal of perspective.'[9] You emphasize in particular his abrogation of epistemological minimalism in favour of 'a hypothesis about structure rich enough to account for linguistic acquisition.'[10]

For you, did Chomsky's project, which insists on the physiological and biological components of speech and language, supervene on the efforts of the

---

9   Milner, *Le Périple structural*, 375n.19.
10   Ibid., 350.

Cahiers pour l'Analyse? Did the reintroduction of *phusis* in Chomsky's project compromise the 'logic of the signifier' developed in the *Cahiers*?

JCM: This was not the point of the reversal. The point of the reversal was precisely to consider that a theory should advance the most complex hypotheses possible. Obviously this sends us back to a Popperian epistemology. From the point of view of the history of ideas, it would be very interesting if someone would investigate the history of Popper's reception. I think that it was in 1960 that things really got underway. In 1960, Popper begins to be known in the English-speaking world and it is at this same moment that a separation gets made between Francophone and Anglophone epistemology. Francophone epistemology had been extremely important, even internationally. Koyré's works had exerted a great influence; in particular, they were at the basis of Kuhn's works. In truth, Kuhn was a product of Francophone epistemology. This epistemology had several characteristics and one very important one: its total indifference to logic. Anglophone epistemology on the contrary accorded much importance to the logical form of scientific reasoning. Nonetheless, they shared a common conviction: theoretical minimalism. A scientific theory must rest on the smallest possible number of axioms.

The translation of Popper into English modified this approach. But, at the time, Popper remained unread in French. A separation was thus established. Anglophone epistemology, in particular in the United States, would take the Popperian path, totally separated from Francophone epistemology, which would persist in its ignorance of Popper. Without knowing it, we were – and here I speak in a general sense, not only of the *Cahiers pour l'Analyse*, but also the Althusserians – we were inscribed in this moment during which Popper was in the process of transforming the horizon of epistemology in the Anglophone world, without us having any real awareness of it at the time.

The book of Chomsky's that I alluded to is *Aspects of the Theory of Syntax*; I read it on the airplane on the way to MIT in September 1966 and I later translated it into French.[11] Chomsky developed a Popperian style epistemology in this book. It is through him and not Popper that I discovered this epistemology and this was the occasion for my total intellectual reversal. Chomsky actually did not mention Popper. No one knows exactly why. Did he not know who he was? In which case, he seems to have rediscovered Popperian theses for himself. Another enigma for the history of ideas. In any event, it was clear that Chomsky had accomplished an important epistemological operation at the heart of linguistics. He withdrew from linguistic structuralism the evidence it had enjoyed up to that point; one of the ways he did this was in referring linguistic

---

11   Noam Chomsky, *Aspects de la théorie syntaxique*, trans. Jean-Claude Milner (Paris: Seuil, 1971).

structuralism – and I think he was right on this point – to an epistemology of a minimalist variety.

Having done this, Chomksy was able to point out two facts: (a) that structuralism devoted itself to an epistemology without knowing it, (b) that this epistemology was not self-evident. Then he argued that in truth one can construct an epistemology that was exactly the inverse, maximalist and not minimalist. Here, from the point of view of the maximalist epistemologist, structuralism appears as a weak, meagre enterprise. Since it is not really falsifiable! This was the case above all if linguistic structuralism was not hyperstructuralist; for as long as one considered that a given structure [*une structure quelconque*] did not have properties, then one was incapable of defining the properties of a structure in general. And this meant that the notion of structure, in itself, became an empty notion.

This was the true reversal for me, what I talked about in *Le Périple structural*. I was educated as a minimalist epistemologist, I discovered that this did not go without saying. After this, Chomskyan linguistics witnessed a development that was more and more naturalist, but this was not the reversal for me. Let's be clear. For me, I had been very sceptical of these developments when I was working in the Chomskyan framework. Not for reasons of right or legitimacy because, after all, sure, why not? Why not say that linguistic structures are inscribed in the body? That's not what shocked me. My objection – I've put this in writing – was that to the extent that we cannot give experimental proofs, then, to say that it is physiological is simply to baptize objects. To say that the transformations – the linguistic transformations that Chomsky will ultimately abandon, but that's another story – represent, in the last instance, neurobiological processes, why not? But when we don't have observations or admissible proofs from neurobiology, this is just talk. And this is the source of the extreme scepticism that, beyond Chomsky, I have sustained against cognitivism, which seems to me to be a way of avoiding the question of empirical proof. It so happens that I've attended discussions between the representatives of neurosciences and cognitivists. The representatives of neuroscience say to the cognitivists: 'Come on, you're just telling stories! We want to see some observations that neuroscience can accept.' The cognitivists then say, 'No! Since what we are constituting is the set of rules that allows us to account for observable behaviours.'

KP: 'The conditions of possibility.'

JCM: That's it. I said to myself: this is Cartesian reasoning. It simply led Descartes to construct a physics that revealed itself inconsistent and a physiology that revealed itself inconsistent. But I come back to maximalist epistemology. Just as a neurophysiological or neurobiological approach has little effect with regard to the approach found in the *Cahiers pour l'Analyse* – it was not our concern – so too does the emergence of a maximalist epistemology constitute a valid objection. In other words, there is a question to be asked: is the '*Analysis*' such as it appeared in the title of the *Cahiers pour l'Analyse* an analysis that was going to shoot for minimalism, that is to say the smallest possible numbers of principles for obtaining the largest number of consequences, or ought it be maximalist, with the largest possible number of hypotheses so that falsification would be possible? Historically, it was the first path that was chosen. It could not have been otherwise since Popper was unknown to us.

KP: I think it's true that the dominant theme in the *Cahiers pour l'Analyse* was an effort toward a minimal number of suppositions for the maximal application. But it seems like there was some resistance, even within the journal itself and I'm thinking in particular of André Green's contribution (CpA 3.2), where he tries to reintroduce a notion of affect, which has some sort of physiological element. But it does seem that there's a firmer move toward formalization in later issues, that this effort to introduce affect goes away, and that Leclaire effectively wins over Green. Do you have any comments on Green's contribution?

JCM: I think that your description is right. That was what happened. Leclaire had certainly sought not to lose the finesse of empirical analysis of psychic phenomena, but at the same time he did not want to lose the horizon of epistemological minimalism. This is what made the thing interesting and at the same time, even if it was exterior circumstances that brought the *Cahiers pour l'Analyse* to a halt, I think that the tensions between the two sides would have become insurmountable very quickly.

Today, I would distinguish two types of figures: either there is an instance of falsification or there is not. I would say that when there is no instance of falsification, the only weapon that we have is minimalism. On the other hand, when falsification is possible, we should reason in Popperian terms. Now, there are domains where falsification is impossible, where there is no instance of falsification. I'm thinking for example of the Darwinian hypothesis of natural selection. I doubt that it is falsifiable, in the strict sense of the term. Its force lies in its minimalism; in other words, minimalism reclaims its rights.

If you look at the work of Freud, which Popper treated rather disdainfully, minimalism is the horizon, for example when in *The Interpretation of Dreams* he settles for a negative denomination for the unconscious; it's that he doesn't have access to an instance of falsification that would allow him to give a positive characterization of it. That said, we find in Freud a nice example of Popperian reasoning in the *fort/da* game. This is reasoning by falsification, and it is a maximalist epistemology since Freud departs from a system that had one single principle, the pleasure principle, to go toward a system wherein the pleasure principle no longer sufficed. This means that the criterion of the minimum is not sustainable. And why is it not sustainable? Because the child's game falsifies the theory in which the pleasure principle is the only one that exists.

KP: That's a good example. But couldn't we perhaps say that, more than an instance of Popperian reasoning, Freud's reasoning 'beyond the pleasure principle' is almost more Lakatosian. I wanted to ask you something about the relationship between Lakatos and Popper – I know that this takes us away from the *Cahiers pour l'Analyse* a bit, but you've addressed this relation in your work – and Lakatos's critique of Popper's strong falsficationist principle. Lakatos has an image I like. He says it's not that nature shouts 'no!' to the scientist's theorem, but instead 'inconsistent!'[12] The theory is forced to undergo revision and change, but it is not wholly falsified. This is an image which itself evokes Cavaillès's insistence on the notion of 'erasure' ['*rature*'] in science's development.[13] For Lakatos, no theorem will ever be complete or finished; it will always be interrupted.

In your chapter, 'The Doctrine of Science' in *L'Œuvre claire* you present an evocative image that aligns the Lacanian unconscious with the infinite as an intrinsic property of the universe: 'The infinite is that which says no to the exception of finitude; the unconscious is that which says no to the privilege of self-consciousness [*la conscience de soi comme privilège*].'[14] For Lakatos, nature, by shouting 'inconsistent,' questions and supports at the same time the self-conscious subject of science. It seems that the project of the *Cahiers pour l'Analyse* sought to show how the subject is at the same time buttressed and tenuous in its own constitution in similar terms.

JCM: Yes, I would not be against this distant echo, since at that very moment, if we could have had access to Lakatos, that would have excited us. But these are the misfires of history. I am not against this echo, but I would like to remind you that *L'Œuvre claire* is not in the *Cahiers pour l'Analyse*. Reciprocally, my object in *L'Œuvre claire* was not to re-examine the *Cahiers*. So what you say, yes, I do not disagree . . . with a simple addition. I'll present it in my own terms, but don't think I'm betraying what was presented under other pens than mine in the project. This is what I would like to add: the convocation that was at work at the time, was that the moment of what says 'no' is itself sutured. This is where you got the mode of reading, for example, which consisted in searching a text for the point where something was in some way passed over in silence, and to affirm

---

12   See Imre Lakatos, 'Falsification and the Methodology of Scientific Research Programmes' [1970] in *The Methodology of Scientific Research Programmes*, eds. John Worrall and Gregory Currie (Cambridge: Cambridge University Press, 1978), 8–101.

13   Cf. Jean Cavaillès, *Sur la logique et la théorie de la science* (Paris: PUF, 1946).

14   Milner, *L'Œuvre claire*, 66.

that this is where the essential occurred. So in effect there is a relation with Lakatosian epistemology, except that the point of inconsistency that one discovers and that was hidden is also immediately the condition of the apparent consistency of what was visible.

KP: You've said that *L'Œuvre claire* is not about the *Cahiers pour l'Analyse*, but it does have the sense of a balance sheet, a looking back. And I would say that there are lines of continuity between the two, for example, in this notion of contingency becoming necessity and the subject as being the site where that happens. It seems to me that that's also in 'The Point of the Signifier' (CpA 3.5), that that's something you're trying to work through as a very young man and that you come back to in *L'Œuvre claire*. And again, you bring in Popper, and you have this wonderful phrase where you say he presents us with a version of science wherein 'the referent must be able to be – logically or materially – other than it is. But that's contingency. [. . .] The set of contingencies as science grasps them, in theory and practice, is the universe.'[15] So from there, I want to ask you if you think that this project of the *Cahiers* has anything contemporary about it. Are these questions still in play today in French intellectual life? And is there a way to read your efforts then with your current work and develop some new questions out of this project?

JCM: I would say that this is true for the *L'Œuvre claire*, since you alluded to it, but this is true for many of the things that I have written. When I wrote *L'Œuvre claire*, I had studied a lot of Lakatos, Holton, Feyerabend, Quine, Duhem; this literature was much discussed in the milieu of Chomskyan linguistics. But in a more particular manner, I was very impressed with the book of Ernst Mach on the physics of Newton.[16] In sum, what I wanted to do with *L'Œuvre claire* was a rereading of Lacan in the manner that Ernst Mach had reread Newton, in isolating the axioms, in examining if they are inconsistent etc. Why did I do this? Simply because I asked myself the question: Does it stand up? Does something remain of Lacan if we submit it to a questioning of the Ernst Mach sort? Can we formulate a finite number of fundamental propositions? Are these propositions consistent within themselves? Is there one or a number of inconsistent points? In fact, *L'Œuvre claire* was an attempt to submit Lacan to examination, but this is an examination that Lacan, I dare to say, passed. I concluded that I was not mistaken at the time of the *Cahiers pour l'Analyse* in giving importance to Lacan.

If I make this remark, it is because not all the texts that were important to me at the time of the *Cahiers pour l'Analyse* underwent the test in a positive way. For

---

15   Ibid., 61.

16   Ernst Mach, *The Science of Mechanics* [1883] (La Salle, IL: Open Court, 1989).

example, it's clear to me, rereading the texts of Althusser, that if I passed them through the Ernst Mach test they would fall apart. This is also true, in my view, for Canguilhem. I would say the same thing for Koyré. There is a historical part that is absolutely important, but the general propositions seem to me today to be extremely weak. This is to say that not all the points of references you find in the *Cahiers pour l'Analyse* necessarily stand up to re-examination. Lacan, yes, very certainly. Marx, very certainly also, even if I interpret Marx in a manner totally different from mine at the time. So, to respond to your question, you are right in judging that much that I have done in recent years is a re-examination of questions that were already present for me at the time of the *Cahiers pour l'Analyse*, but the response is not always of the same nature. In certain cases, it stands up to examination and in certain cases the results are unfavourable.

KP: So would you say that we need to 'find new answers for old questions'?

JCM: Maybe, or that from old questions, we should build new questions. Since you pose the question of intellectual life as it is today, I think that it has turned away from the questions posed at the time of the *Cahiers pour l'Analyse*. For example, I believe that all ontological questions are totally out of play. I think that the will to pose questions on the productive character of a structure, all these kinds of questions no longer command attention. I even feel that the general mode of questioning which was that of the *Cahiers pour l'Analyse* is a mode of questioning that has become very distant. I said that we were in a world where Popper did not exist and now Popper does. I do not mean that he has the last word, but he exists. We must also not forget that at the moment we were writing – this is also true for Lacan and Foucault – French was a vibrant intellectual language and still had a certain audience. 'French Theory' existed. I think this is no longer true today. I think that what is said in French, by the fact alone of being said in French, is inaudible. To say it another way, I think that French is a dead language.

KP: Though it must give you some hope that a few Anglophones are at least discussing the *Cahiers pour l'Analyse* . . .

JCM: Yes, yes. I am very happy about this. But this is to say that there is a displacement.

KP: There's clearly a wistful sense at the end of *Le Périple structural* and you introduce this pessimism where you say it's as if this type of questioning never happened, or a pessimist would think that it never happened.[17] Would it even be

---

17   Milner, *Le Périple structural*, 368.

desirable in your view for these ontological questions to come back, to be discussed again?

JCM: I'm not fond of 'comebacks'. You know, Busby Berkeley once wrote, before he tried to kill himself in fact, 'there is no comeback for a has been'. In fact there is no 'comeback' *except* for the 'has been'. But what I mean is that what was called 'French Theory' and had enjoyed a certain celebrity in the Anglophone world only represents a portion of the things that were going on. This is the first point. The second point, and here I have deliberately not brought it up since its demonstration would be too long, I now think that among the great authors, the great discursive interventions in French in the latter part of the 20th century, that one of the greatest will have been that of Foucault. More important, in my view, than Deleuze.

Now, the world of the *Cahiers pour l'Analyse* was a world in which Foucault and Deleuze were just beginning to exist. They had just published major books, but all the same the essential was still to come. And I believe that Foucault constitutes one of the very important shifts of the 20th century. I think that, even on the question of ontology, he could have been a fundamental interlocutor, but things did not happen like that; the *Cahiers pour l'Analyse* were interrupted, and then, from a certain moment, he himself did not want to have an interlocutor in France.

KP: Deleuze is an interesting case, because it seems only now, in the Anglophone context, that people are reading *Difference and Repetition* as a work deeply engaged with structuralism. But I have the sense that Deleuze wasn't really being read by 'structuralists' at the time.

JCM: You are right. Deleuze began to be important later on, at a moment when structuralism had begun to decline.

KP: It seems to me that the *Cahiers pour l'Analyse* is a chapter in a much longer French history, the history of a certain rationalist way of thinking that resurges from time to time.

JCM: Yes, I think that there is continuity in which Descartes indeed plays a part. But I would not put it in terms of rationalism. I would say that there is in the French tradition a sort of prose of thought, but we desire or need these writings to encounter questions along the way that make prose explode. I think of Descartes' *Meditations* and Pascal's *Pensées*; I could add Cavaillès's last text. This is not German systematicity, which is architectural; this is on the order of the sequence or chain [*enchaînement*] of reasons, which is linear. This is also not the pleasing coordination of English (I think of Locke, Berkeley or Hume) which avoids, at least in appearance, concatenations and points of explosion. In the continuity that I am thinking of, the effect of the sequence remains, regardless of the length of the chain; it remains even if the chain at one point has an encounter with an element that breaks it. Yes, I think that there is something of this order that appears in the *Cahiers pour l'Analyse*, extending to their interest for the notion of a signifying chain.

Yes then to a continuity, but this must be corrected by taking into account particular historical circumstances. The *Cahiers pour l'Analyse* were produced by very young people who came directly from their university education; they testify to something that happened in certain places in the French university at the time. I described this moment in *Le Périple structural*; theory, which had had Germany and the German language as its privileged place, was in certain respects displaced or errant, with no longer any place nor language. I think that with Althusser, there was the will to make the French language, and in the French language Paris, and in Paris the university, and in the university the École Normale of the rue d'Ulm, and in the École Normale of the rue d'Ulm his own seminar, his own teaching, become the place of reception for this errant theory. We were seized by this moment; even if the *Cahiers pour l'Analyse* depended on Lacan and not Althusser, I believe they were animated by a conviction that came to them from Althusser: the tranquil conviction that France had by then already become the natural language of the concept. This was at once a moment for the French language and a moment for what I am calling the wandering [*errance*] of theory, a wandering both geographic and linguistic, born from the observation that the German language could no longer be the language of the concept, because of 1933, and the conviction that the English language had long since ceded to market forms. Need I add that I now think, as I speak to you today, that these games around languages arise from, or amount to, a mirage?[18]

Translated by Tzuchien Tho.

---

18   The French reads: '*Dois-je préciser que ces jeux autour des langues relèvent, selon moi, au moment où je vous parle, du mirage?*'

CHAPTER FOURTEEN

To Get Rid of the Signified:
An Interview with Jacques Bouveresse

Paris, France, 15 January 2009

Knox Peden (KP): To start, could you say something about the origin of your participation in the *Cahiers pour l'Analyse*?

Jacques Bouveresse (JB): That's a little difficult. First of all, these things are really distant from me now and my memories are a little imprecise. At the time, we were a team, a gang – I'm not sure how I should put it – who found ourselves together at rue d'Ulm [i.e. the ENS]. But I held a position that was, I think, already very marginal in many ways, because I had started to study Wittgenstein. I was very interested in analytic philosophy. I had begun to learn mathematical logic very seriously and had begun teaching in 1966. So I was an assistant at the Sorbonne then – it was still called Sorbonne at the time – teaching mathematical logic. I was surrounded by people whose interests were for the most part, let's say, very different. There were extremely committed Heideggerians, in the style of French Heideggerianism, that is to say, Heideggerians whom we could say without any exaggeration were not merely sectarian, but generally more sectarian than German Heideggerians. It is a French phenomenon, a type of Heideggerian idolatry. So there were Heideggerians, and then there was also what we could call structuralism; of course here I'm using the term extremely generally.

But inside this structuralist constellation, the dominating force was really 'Lacano-Althusserianism', which was a phenomenon that was born around this time. I had myself just arrived at the ENS in 1961 and I already kept a distance from all this. 'Lacano-Althusserianism' was a rather surprising phenomenon. It was born from Althusser's encounter with psychoanalysis, first, and then more precisely with Lacan. And I think we can date this meeting with some precision: I think the beginning of all this was Jules Vuillemin's inaugural lecture at the Collège de France, which must have been in 1962, if I remember correctly. There – I see it as if it were yesterday – at the exit, Althusser says, 'Lacan is here, I should go talk to him'. Lacan had attended this inaugural lecture of Vuillemin, who was already an exception. He was already very interested in logic at that point and he was in the middle of working on his monumental work, *The Philosophy of Algebra*; he may have already published the first volume.[1] He was among those who had truly started to introduce logic and a philosophy inspired by logic into France – at the same time that Granger did so; they were the two big exceptions of the time. Althusser had been at the ENS at the same time as Vuillemin. Vuillemin, Althusser, and Granger were more or less the same age. They knew each other well, and Vuillemin and Granger had been students of Jean Cavaillès. Vuillemin explained to me once that, 'to do what I have done', i.e. to work on the philosophy of logic, the philosophy of mathematics, 'that's the least you can do when you had Cavaillès as a teacher'. So there was a legacy that was transmitted to them.

That's to describe a bit of the context. I took up a role that was complicated and a bit unstable since I was already in some regards very far from all this. I remember having attended Derrida's course, which was called 'The Idea of Ontology in Husserl and Heidegger,' and most of us left with a headache. Most of the people who found themselves in the Cercle d'Épistémologie could not stand this sort of philosophy and we couldn't really understand it. We found it completely irrational. In the Heideggerian context, science, which is very significant for me, was treated, to put it as mildly as possible, in a very contemptuous way. So these were the kinds of things that were ignored, and especially the human sciences, at the moment that they had in fact become very important. The Heideggerians were livid about the human sciences at the very moment that they had, on the contrary, become extremely important. This was the moment when linguistics had become very fashionable, anthropology too. So linguistics meant Saussure, Hjelmslev and Jakobson, who were not in fact the most representative figures of linguistics. I don't think they are. Chomsky's *Syntactic Structures* was published in 1959. We should have been interested in this, but of course we did not discover it until much later.

KP: So it was the Cercle d'Épistémologie who asked you to participate?

JB: Yes, yes, they asked. I no longer remember whether it was Miller or Milner or both of them. You will have noted the '*liminaires*' [introductions], as they were called; we called them the '*limilners*' in the *Cahiers pour l'Analyse*, which were written by Miller and Milner most of the time. I found them almost incomprehensible. They were written in a language that was so hermetic, so precious. I think that there was a respect for what I did or what they thought that I did. I remember clearly that what interested me at the time was Wittgenstein and Frege, and other similar authors. Not so much French epistemology but, well, we will speak about this later, because it is an important aspect of the problem.

---

1   Jules Vuillemin, *La Philosophie d'algèbre, t. 1: recherches sur quelque concepts et méthodes d'Algèbre Moderne* (Paris: PUF, 1962, second edition, 1993).

So again they probably asked me to participate in the Cercle because I was interested in logic and epistemology and because perhaps they were really convinced that there were things to be done in this domain and maybe I was capable of doing them. But my participation remained completely formal, because I don't remember having participated in the meetings of the Cercle. Did they even have meetings? I don't really know.

KP: I noticed that in the volumes of the *Cahiers pour l'Analyse* themselves, your name is always listed with the Cercle d'Épistémologie, but never with the editorial board.

JB: Yes, I think – obviously we must distrust our memoires – I believe I never participated either in a meeting of the Cercle d'Épistémologie or of the editorial board.

KP: You spoke a little bit about the role of Heidegger, of Heideggerian idolatry and it's clear that in the *Cahiers pour l'Analyse* there's a critique of phenomenology from beginning to end. But at the same time we know that Cavaillès's engagement with phenomenology cannot be reduced to a complete rejection. There were also others like Suzanne Bachelard, Jean-Toussaint Desanti, Granger, Vuillemin, who continued to engage in the project of Husserl, if not Heidegger, in the fifties and sixties. So there was a difference at the heart of French phenomenology itself.

JB: I would say that it was Suzanne Bachelard above all; she was the one who understood Husserl very well.[2] Our paths crossed in 1965, passing the *agrégation*; she had given a course on Husserl's *Logical Investigations*, a text that she knew very well. Ten years later it became difficult to find someone who could give a good course on *Logical Investigations*, in part because Heidegger had supplanted Husserl, especially the early Husserl. The later Husserl was relatively well known, thanks to Ricoeur and Derrida. But the early Husserl is still classical, and shares many common points with analytic philosophy; this did not escape people like Gilbert Ryle for example. This Husserl had already started to become less known. So Suzanne Bachelard had a very good knowledge of Husserl. Vuillemin and Granger also, but they had a much more critical position.

KP: Similar to Cavaillès's position, I imagine.

---

2   In addition to Suzanne Bachelard, *A Study of Husserl's Formal and Transcendental Logic* [1957], trans. Lester E. Embree (Evanston: Northwestern University Press, 1968); see Bachelard, *La Conscience de la rationalité: étude phénoménologique de la physique mathématique* (Paris: PUF, 1958).

JB: They were even more critical than Cavaillès. As for Desanti, it's obvious; his thesis was called *Les Idéalités mathématiques*,[3] a truly phenomenological title. So clearly there's a whole lineage here that's interesting, because Vuillemin had succeeded Merleau-Ponty at the Collège de France, when Merleau-Ponty died in 1961. Actually, there's not really anything like a succession at the Collège de France. The fact is that we passed from a philosopher like Merleau-Ponty, who was probably the best representative of French phenomenology, to something fundamentally different, which meant a more emphatic opening toward the Anglo-Saxon world, to logic. So I think Suzanne Bachelard was the one who remained closest to phenomenology. I had many discussions with her, which was not always very easy because she had difficulties with analytic philosophy. They all had problems with it, but she had the most. For example, she had an enormously difficult time accepting the idea that Bertrand Russell might be a great philosopher. She found him dull.

There was this idea that philosophy was a literary discipline, that it ought only to concern writers, those who knew how to write. This was an extremely important difference. The style, the mode of writing counted infinitely more for French philosophers than for Anglo-Saxon philosophers. I am not saying that it doesn't count at all because there were analytic philosophers, Anglo-Saxons as we say, who were great writers. Quine for example had a remarkable style. But Carnap didn't, neither in English nor in his own language. So Suzanne Bachelard had real difficulty reading this sort of philosophy and she found it a little puerile, a bit simplistic. As for me, this surprises me still. I find the kind of philosophy done by people like Bertrand Russell to be anything but puerile. Actually, it's extremely difficult most of the time. It was a bit like Poincaré. We have the impression that he is very easy when we read him. He wrote in superb French, very clear, but when we see what is going on in the background . . .

So, we remained at a stage where a truly French tradition dominated. What this meant was that we were interested in a number of foreign authors, but most of the time these foreign authors were German and very rarely English or American. This ties in to a phenomenon that I have described often, because it really struck me. After the end of the Second World War, it was obvious, or it should have been, that the centre of gravity of philosophy had changed in a spectacular way as a result of the emigration. Practically all the best minds of that generation had left Germany or Central Europe, Austria, Poland, etc. Gödel and many more, Carnap, Popper. And they found themselves either in England or the United States, a few started again in Australia and New Zealand. Or actually, I believe New Zealand was a little different.

It was a bit paradoxical because I was a Germanist by training and I was

---

3   Jean-Toussaint Desanti, *Les Idéalités mathématiques: recherches épistémologies sur le développement de la théorie des fonctions des variables réelles* (Paris: Seuil, 1968).

enormously interested in German literature. I even thought about passing my *agrégation* in German. And all of a sudden, just as I started to do so – I didn't know English at the time – I learned English to read Anglophone philosophers. I was immediately struck. I felt like I'd found just what I needed, namely philosophers that I understood. In fact I understood them rather well except for what concerned the technicalities of logic. This was obviously something that people like us didn't know anything about. We had to learn everything. So I started to become interested in this and it turned out that, for reasons we'll have to consider more closely, formal logic was something that also interested many Lacanians and Lacan himself. In 1970–71, I had done a French translation of Carnap's *The Logical Syntax of Language*, which had never been published and will no doubt be published soon. Well, I hope that this will happen in the next year. Gallimard has agreed to publish it.[4] But you see the point. We practically had to wait forty years for this translation to be published. This means that there really has been an important transformation, and it took a long time, this realization that there are some things really worth knowing in philosophy written in English. You should know too that I still hear it said, fairly recently, by people who are not idiots, that English is not really a philosophical language. I also heard people like Jean-Luc Nancy and Philippe Lacoue-Labarthe, who were Derridians, say that philosophy is not to be done in English, or something like that. At a given moment, it was done in Greek, then in Latin; in the seventeenth century, it was done in French and then, well, it was German that took over. This was how things were.

KP: In an interview with Jean-Jacques Rosat, you said that there is an almost nationalist element in philosophy of science in France and in particular with the Althusserians.[5] There's the need to 'buy French'. It's obvious that they were very interested in Canguilhem and Bachelard.

JB: Absolutely. There was a French tradition in epistemology that supposedly represented the only epistemology worthy of the name. In certain respects, Bachelard was thought to have created epistemology, thanks to what we call the 'epistemological break'. But before him there were many extraordinarily important authors, Poincaré, Duhem, Meyerson. For example, we are rediscovering Meyerson; people have started rereading Émile Meyerson, who is remarkable. But here in this situation, there is the application of a familiar Althusserian schema, which is to say that a science begins to exist due to an epistemological

---

4   Rudolf Carnap, *The Logical Syntax of Language* [1934], trans. Amethe Smeaton (London: Kegan Paul, 1937). As of November 2011, Carnap's volume remains unpublished in French.

5   Jacques Bouveresse, *Le Philosophe et le réel: entretiens avec Jean-Jacques Rosat* (Paris: Hachette, 1998).

break. Galileo had created dynamics due to a break of this sort. Darwin had created . . . you get the idea. There was this succession of epistemological breaks, which marked the start of a new science each time, and epistemology was the product of a creation of this sort. But this is a French phenomenon, which is to say that there really should have been a few Germans deserving of reference. In any case, all those who were referenced by the Anglo-Saxon tradition were excluded. So in a general way, all the scientists, what was called the spontaneous epistemology of the scientists, were considered as totally not worthy of interest. This meant that the contributions made by authors such as Helmholtz, Mach, Boltzmann, or Poincaré himself, were considered to be of very little interest. Well this was what interested me. I had already begun, for example, to read Boltzmann, whose philosophical and epistemological work is still quite unknown. I had already begun to read Hertz, Hertz's *The Principles of Mechanics*, which was published in 1894. The introduction to this book is a true classic in epistemology. And at the time it was almost impossible to convince anyone that this sort of thing could count as epistemology.

Now this was strange because this was a recent phenomenon. Bachelard would not have reacted like this. Bachelard knew Mach for example, whom he held in high regard. He would not have spoken like Althusser's students. It's the same with Popper. This is also a fascinating phenomenon. When Popper's *The Logic of Scientific Discovery* was translated, it had a preface by Jacques Monod, who opened with something like, 'here, finally, is this powerful book translated into French'. Monod was surprised that people were not interested in this book sooner, paying attention instead to what he called 'the most obscure extravagances of German metaphysics'. In other words, the references of French philosophy remained turned toward what we called the 'the blue line of the Vosges', i.e. Germany.[6] We may think that Monod was wrong, but the fact is that we had our eyes fixed on Germany. As for Germany, that meant Heidegger. He was at any rate the only philosopher of calibre who remained. Practically all the others were gone. Cassirer had died. I don't remember when Husserl died, but he was no longer really part of the discussion as people considered him to have been supplanted by Heidegger. In short, the reactions to publishing Popper were surprising. Canguilhem for example, whom I knew quite well, was indignant. He asked me, 'But why translate this book? What reason is there for translating this book? What we have in France is much better'. He meant Bachelard. I told him, 'Listen, if this book contains things that you and others don't agree with, you can express your disagreement. But these sorts of books need to be translated. It needs to be known, needs to be read, it needs to be discussed.'

---

6   The expression '*la ligne bleue des Vosges*' was used by the French premier Jules Ferry in the aftermath of the Franco-Prussian War in 1870 as a reminder that Alsace, on the other side of the line, was in Germany.

This is to describe the climate, which was a climate that was extremely difficult and that was hard for me to support, because I was caught in a desperate battle of trying to persuade people. I don't mean that I was persuading people that Popper was right; no, I was simply persuading them to open his books, to go look at what Popper had really said. I believe I was the first to publish an article on Popper in a French newspaper. I think that that was in 1974, in *Le Monde*. They requested an article on Popper and I managed to get it done. It was even accepted without being truncated, because they wanted to cut it. I said, 'No, come on, we never talk about Popper. We need to make more of an effort.' They tried but the general mindset was basically as follows: Popper was thought to be a more subtle positivist, and thus more dangerous than the members of the Vienna Circle. Marxists saw him in this way, for example. He was more dangerous in their eyes, because the theory of falsifiability had the appearance of being more plausible, more acceptable. So we must take stock of the fact that Popper's situation was not that much better than Carnap's. It was even worse in certain ways. Then all of a sudden everything changed. I don't remember exactly when, at the beginning of the 80s or around then, all of a sudden Popper became practically fashionable. Carnap never became fashionable. In my view, Carnap is one of the greatest philosophers of the twentieth century. But he was not at all thought of in this way in France. In general, he was thought of as a narrow-minded positivist, *grosso modo*.

So that was the state of mind. But it's more complicated than you'd think at first with the Cercle d'Épistémologie, because they had a certain respect for logic and formalism that they separated, or rather that they found convenient to separate in every possible way, from the philosophy it could have been in dialogue with. The philosophy of the Vienna Circle was something that was categorically rejected and then there was modern logic, or rather, mathematics and the use to which they put it. The use they made of it was one thing, but there was also logic, its possibilities and the possibility of employing it in a completely different way, for example what Lacan had tried to do. Now that's a whole chapter that we'd have to talk about, because Lacan had shown the greatest respect for logic and mathematics, but it must be said that he didn't know much about them.

KP: For Lacan, as for the editors of the *Cahiers pour l'Analyse*, the interest in logic was inseparable from formalism and the search for precise forms. In the *Cahiers pour l'Analyse*, there was an accent put on the 'singular', the singular of *the* logic of the signifier, for example. But the question of formalism was much larger than linguistics. In any case, it's clear in your contributions on Fichte and Wittgenstein that you were criticizing the accent on singularity and the primacy of a certain form of discourse.

JB: Yes, you're right. I had developed the habit of looking instinctively at original texts, which is to say that each time I formulated a judgment on a philosopher my initial reaction was suspicion and I always had to go read the texts. I did this with Hilbert, for example, because I wanted to understand what exactly formalism in mathematics was. And as soon as you did this, you noticed that the discourse that you were hearing most of the time came from people who didn't have a real idea of what real mathematical formalism was. Take, for example, the controversy between formalism and intuitionism in philosophy and mathematics, the great controversy between Hilbert and Brouwer; people did not really know about this.

But then there was an idea that was strictly associated with structuralism, the idea that one should be interested in the signifier and in the play of signifiers and forget the signified. Well, I schematize a bit, I simplify things, but let's say that people were very opposed at the time to any apparently Platonist theory of signification. The dream was even to get rid of the signified. This explains why someone like Lacan was interested in Carnap's *Logical Syntax of Language*. Because Carnap's *Logical Syntax of Language* defended a point of view that was rigorously syntactic and claimed that we can pass over semantics, or more precisely that syntax is capable of providing a theory of signification which would be all that we'd need as a theory of signification. Now this may seem surprising and paradoxical, but I think that the mentality of these structuralists was often not too far from this. Basically, they would have loved to get rid of the notion of signification and this was what Derrida had started to do, in another way, with the idea of deconstruction. The signified had to be deconstructed. And if you deconstructed the signified, what effectively remained was the signifier and then the more or less serious or frivolous games that we can try to play with the signifier. So, if you like, this might partially explain this interest in formalism.

You mentioned the two articles that I published. To explain a bit about what's happening in the Fichte article (CpA 6.7), it was taken from what was at the time called a *diplôme d'études supérieures*[7] on the legal and political philosophy of Fichte, under the direction of Raymond Aron. And to give you a sense of how strange this situation was, I did it at Althusser's recommendation. But the specific idea of working on Fichte came from Vuillemin. Vuillemin had given a course at the ENS in 1961–1962, if I remember correctly, and he explained to us that much remained to be done on legal philosophy, on Fichte's political philosophy. Many texts were not translated at the time, by the way. I worked principally on German texts. And at this time, I was still very close to German philosophy. I had begun discovering Wittgenstein a little bit. I think the *Tractatus* was translated in 1961. So some of us read it; we understood *nothing*. And when I say nothing, I mean nothing. We did not understand the least bit of logic. It was not complex logic, not difficult logic, but we

---

7   The *diplôme d'études supérieures* is roughly equivalent to a master's thesis.

didn't have the minimal logic that was required. We totally lacked the background in the tradition that was necessary to understand what was going on. Frege was an author with whom we were not, so to speak, familiar. Claude Imbert had begun to translate him, but I can still say that we weren't familiar with him, and if we had read him, I doubt we would have had the means to understand him. It was a universe that was completely foreign. But I had already effectively begun; I was already drawn to Wittgenstein. I more or less had a premonition that he was a truly important philosopher. At any rate, it was the style of those in charge of the *Cahiers pour l'Analyse* to contact people who had completed theses on an interesting subject, and to invite them to write an article and publish it. Knowing that I had completed a thesis on a subject that was, basically, little studied, and was relatively unknown, as not much had been published on legal philosophy and the political philosophy of Fichte, this is what they did with me in the case of Fichte.

In the case of Wittgenstein, I don't remember if it was they or I who proposed it, but what happened was that *Die Bemerkungen über die Grundlagen der Mathematik,* [*Remarks on the Foundations of Mathematics*] was published in 1967. So I took this book out from the library of the ENS – in principle, they purchased books as soon as they appeared – and I was basically dumbfounded, literally. The fact was that this book did not resemble anything that I was used to in the philosophy of mathematics. This was someone who said that 'the quarrel of realism and formalism in mathematics such as it had occurred is of no interest. This will disappear very soon and there are other things to be done in the philosophy of mathematics, e.g. the clarification of the grammar of mathematical statements' etc. In any case, you know all this, but to me this was a novelty, a considerable novelty. So, at the time the book was fairly poorly received. There were two aspects of the philosophy of Wittgenstein – the philosophy of mathematics and anthropology – and they did not really interest many people. And yet, these were the two things that, to the contrary, interested me the most. So, taking up the philosophy of mathematics, I wrote this article, with the means of interpretation that were at my disposal, which weren't really too well developed (CpA 10.9). Today, I'd like to think I'd be capable of doing better than that, but I had a certain credit for what I did at the time. And this totally interested the people in the Cercle d'Épistémologie, because obviously this was philosophy of mathematics. It was Wittgenstein, so it must be said that he enjoyed a great prestige, and I must say that this was largely due to his enigmatic character. So it totally worked. An important philosopher ought to be surrounded by an aura of mystery. An immediately accessible philosopher like Carnap doesn't interest people. Yes, Suzanne Bachelard's reaction was a bit like this. Philosophy should be a little impenetrable.

KP: We might say that Heidegger and Wittgenstein are alike in this way.

JB: Sure, why not. They share something in this point of view, absolutely, in this same category of history – but still, extremely different. But you are right, on this point, there is an analogy. And I think that Wittgenstein has been recognized more easily and has been perceived more easily as a continental philosopher than Carnap for example; there is no comparison. People may not know him very well, but in the *Tractatus* there are these final propositions, all the same: 'Whereof one cannot speak, thereof one must be silent'. This really excited people. There was the question of metalanguage.

For example, there's an article by Blanchot that I have cited somewhere, I think in *La Rime et la raison*,[8] on metalanguage as it concerned Wittgenstein where he says, 'Ah yes, Wittgenstein is very good because he demonstrates that there is no metalanguage.' Well this enormously excited Lacan. But this obviously all rested on an approximate understanding of what Wittgenstein had really said. With Blanchot this was clear. With Lacan, this was less clear but no less true. In short, you see that there were all these ambiguities. So I think that a large part of what intrigues you was constructed from ambiguities, almost misunderstandings. The Cercle d'Épistémologie was interested in Wittgenstein, and I was too, but it is clear that we were not at all investigating the same thing.

KP: Your critical position in this regard is evident in your contributions. I'm thinking in particular of your epigraph taken from Alain that you chose for your article on Fichte.

JB: It's good that you mentioned this because I was just thinking of it. I wondered: would they accept it? 'It is certain, in the light of [Kant's] Critique, that socialism as a party depends on this initial error of wanting to go from the concept to existence.' I figured, given the mindset of the *Cahiers pour l'Analyse*, that they were not going to tolerate this, especially because Alain was an extremely religious philosopher. Be he also incarnated French radicalism. And so, they accepted it, they left the thing as it was.

KP: And then in your article on Fichte when you speak of 'the misadventure of analytic reason', we have a kind of 'immanent critique' of the project.

JB: Yes, so I remained absolutely marginal. I took no account of what we might call the underlying ideology of the Cercle. It's true. I was interested in two authors, Wittgenstein and Fichte, and I wrote exactly what I wanted, what I thought about them, without the least bit of pressure to revise.

---

8   Bouveresse, *Wittgenstein: La Rime et la raison – science, éthique, et esthétique* (Paris: Minuit, 1973).

KP: Another question on formalization. It's clear that there was a transformation over the course of the existence of the *Cahiers*. It seems to me that at the beginning there were two tendencies, one toward formalization, toward abstraction, and another effort toward reconciling formalization with the vital and affective concepts found in psychoanalysis. I think of André Green, for example. But it's clear that in the end, formalism was dominant. But even there your articles can be read as exposés of the *aporia* of formalism. And this is striking because your article on Wittgenstein appeared in the same volume as Alain Badiou's 'Marque et Manque' (CpA 10.8) which is also a critique of Miller in his use of mathematical formalism. It's clear, even at the time, that you and Badiou had taken different positions on mathematics. But in any case, it's striking to see you and Badiou so close like this, for the first and last time, I imagine.

JB: Yes, probably. But here we should emphasize that Badiou had and still has a real understanding of mathematics, which Miller obviously didn't have; this is absolutely clear. Badiou has written books that have really shocked me, for example his book on the concept of model, which made a lot of noise (CM). Here there was a failure to understand Carnap. There was a sort of hatred against Carnap, which was really representative of the time. Not only did he incarnate positivism, but technocratic capitalism too – something close to this. There were even those who went so far as to place bourgeois logic to one side, and then, on the other, true logic, or the good one. So there was at once this interest in formal logic alongside a considerable suspicion with respect to its representatives for political reasons. First of all, most of the time these representatives belonged to the Anglo-Saxon world, the American world. And basically the American world was capitalism, technocracy, and all that. One should not forget that we were judged according to this sort of criteria, not really on what we wrote or more precisely on the content of what we wrote.

For example, each time things started to change, when it became possible from time to time to publish these authors, these representatives of analytic philosophy, or to write articles on them, the reaction provoked in certain French philosophical contexts, in the context of the most politicized context of French philosophy, was pretty much invariably: 'What is the political point of view behind this? What is the political background?' I'm not exaggerating; this was really what happened. They didn't say, 'What did they write?', 'What do they mean?', no, 'What is the political intention?'

KP: That's a Marxist tendency. And there was Althusser's course on the spontaneous philosophy of the scientists where we find a variant of this analogical thought (PSPS, 69–165). Althusser had greatly criticized phenomenology for borrowing theological concepts. That's the critique: this is nothing but theology. But at the same time his philosophy had borrowed concepts from the Marxist canon. The name 'materialism' is equivocal in this regard, the idea that, since proletarians are materialist in their practice, and I am with them, therefore my philosophy – what was previously my 'theoretical practice' – is 'materialist' also.

JB: Well, I knew Althusser very well and I had excellent relations with him because he was, speaking personally, extremely warm and not at all dogmatic. In fact, he invited Granger, Vuillemin, and me to the ENS. In 1966, I taught a course. So this didn't bother him at all. The dogmatism that is so characteristic of his disciples did not apply to him at all. He did not proselytize his philosophy, so to speak. But his disciples were another story. I found myself in the middle of these people, soldiers, if you like. They had a military conception of philosophy. We leave from the countryside and we launch waves of assault. This was the language used by Pierre Raymond, who worked on philosophy of mathematics. If we launch the first wave, and this isn't enough, we will launch a second wave. Whatever, but this scared me a little. Intellectually, they really were Stalinists. Well, they were hyper-intelligent Stalinists, how's that! I mean I rubbed shoulders with the most brilliant of this generation, intellectually speaking. Not necessarily serious, that's another thing. But brilliant, that they were.

There were disparities, as we just noted. Badiou, once again, was very competent on questions of formalism, of logic. This is clear. The others were not. So obviously these things are in the *Cahiers pour l'Analyse* – the title itself was already really surprising. I mean, 'The zero is the lack'. Now that's a play on words, a 'pun'. That's it, nothing more, because there's nothing serious in this article that compares the problem of zero in Frege with lack in the Lacanian sense.

KP: But Miller's argument is that yes indeed, there is a relationship between the two. It's precisely that zero is the mark of lack.

JB: Given that at the time I was in the process of reading Frege and doing so seriously, I had the feeling that Miller had really understood nothing. He didn't even really try. In the end, we could discuss this at length for it's always a problem knowing at what point we can judge an analogy absurd and unproductive. It's not easy. Most of time we do not know. We have a certain idea, we say that we can pull something out of one analogy, but out of another we can't.

KP: It's clear that you were troubled by these more or less precarious relationships between science and politics or ontology and politics. I know that you were marginal to the project but do you think the *Cahiers pour l'Analyse* is a living document today? What are its effects in your view?

JB: It's a little hard for me to respond. It's surely a living document, an extremely interesting document, from the point of view of cultural sociology at least. I think that it's an irreplaceable document. It was the sixties. Future generations will probably make use of it as one of the most characteristic phenomena of the time. As to what remains in terms of the content or substance, this is difficult to say. I said once, with regard to the behaviour of the Althusserians, that this had created above all bad philosophy, pseudoscience, and imaginary politics. Well, I think it was 'an imaginary politics'. I remember a discussion with Vuillemin. Vuillemin was justifiably surprised that one could call what they did political action, this procedure that consisted of tracing a line of demarcation between materialism and idealism.

But this was unbelievable, for they did this in a totally arbitrary way! For example they had decided that Husserl was not good because he was an idealist. Frege was good because he was a realist, *thus* a materialist, because Frege thought that, first there is being and then thought, something which arrives after and depends on being, and does not create it in any case. Obviously they forgot that Frege was a very reactionary thinker and even an anti-Semite – for as much as they knew it, because I don't know if they did know this. None of this had any importance. The members of the Vienna Circle like Carnap, Neurath, were all people on the left, in certain cases very much on the left. Carnap was called '*der rote Professor*', 'the red professor'. Well, I tried to tell them, 'Since what counts above all for you is politics, you might consider that these people here are not the ones to beat up on, these are not the enemies!' 'But yes, yes, yes!' Because, here again, they don't have science, they don't have good theory, etc. They might be right politically speaking, but by accident.

So my spontaneous reaction would be to say, there you go, what remains is relatively little. But in saying this, I feel like I'm committing an injustice. Because when we compare it with the current situation, it was a period that was extremely lively. An enormous number of things happened. We should take into account the fact that one of the reasons why I felt closer to them, a feeling that I would not have had spontaneously, was the distance with respect to the traditional university. We had a certain common point in that we were fed up with 'Sorbonne' philosophy – we were not the first because many other people have had this experience – and in my case the history of philosophy. This practice of philosophy that still largely exists in France consists, basically, of confounding philosophy with the history of philosophy. French philosophers are in general good historians of philosophy; they are often among the best in this domain. Gueroult, for example, was absolutely remarkable. I attended the final courses of Martial Gueroult at the Collège de France, in the 1970s, I think. I attended the last two years; I saw the book on Spinoza being written. And the election of Vuillemin to the Collège de France was made possible by Gueroult. It's Gueroult who invited Vuillemin to the Collège de France.

But my point was that I was personally very irritated and extremely disappointed by the philosophical education that one received at the Sorbonne. It was a surprising period. There were people like Vladimir Jankélévitch who taught moral philosophy, which I found simply to be rhetoric. There were also a great number of historians of philosophy, people like Maurice de Gandillac, who taught medieval philosophy. And then there were people on the other hand that I appreciated, like Raymond Aron. Politically speaking I was always diametrically opposed to Raymond Aron, but I knew him quite well. I still lunched with him a bit before the time of his death. Aron had a chair in sociology but not in philosophy proper. What dominated was still metaphysics, the history of philosophy and I would say theology, because there was, there *is* in French philosophy an extremely tight relationship that is maintained between theology and philosophy and that subsists through people like Jean-Luc Marion, for example, who is really typical of the great Catholic philosophy and who has become an academician.[9] Well that, I was horrified by that. So there, in an instant, seen from this angle, I'd say '*Vive les Cahiers pour l'Analyse!*', without hesitation!

Translated by Tzuchien Tho.

---

9   Jean-Luc Marion was elected to the Académie Française, one of the highest honours for a French scholar, in 2008.

CHAPTER FIFTEEN

Only in the Form of Rupture:
An Interview with Jacques Rancière

Paris, France, 2 May 2008

Peter Hallward (PH): I know you weren't part of the *Cahiers pour l'Analyse*, far from it, and that you can't talk about the journal directly. But I'm grateful for your answers to some questions regarding the general context of the project, the political discussions and theories that surrounded it and what was going on at the École Normale Supérieure in those years. When did you arrive at the ENS?

Jacques Rancière (JR): In the autumn of 1960. Jean-Claude Milner in 61 and Jacques-Alain Miller in 62.

PH: And the *Cahiers Marxistes-Léninistes*[1] were launched at the end of 1964, is that right?

JR: Yes, that's right. Robert Linhart arrived at the École in 63, and his friend Jacques Broyelle arrived in 1964. They represented the 'political' hard core of the project, if you like, against the theoreticist tendency that dominated in the Althusserian milieu.

PH: What was your own role in the *Cahiers Marxistes-Léninistes*?

JR: It was my idea, actually. For me it was, in the beginning, simply about reviving the propagandist activity of the Cercle des Étudiants Communistes de L'École Normale Supérieure (the Cercle d'Ulm). But the Communist *normaliens* [i.e. students at the ENS], who participated in this revival alongside me had become Communists under Althusser's influence. And what was supposed to have been a simple informational bulletin of the *cercle communiste d'Ulm* [the circle of Communist students at the ENS] became in fact an instrument for propagating Althusserianism amongst the Communist students.

At the time there were two tendencies in the Union des Étudiants Communistes (UEC): those we called 'the Italians', people influenced by the Italian Marxists (or by dissident French Marxists like Henri Lefebvre), who

---

1   See Frédéric Chateigner, 'D'Althusser à Mao: Les *Cahiers Marxistes-Léninistes*', *Dissidences* 8 (2010), 66–80.

emphasized recent changes in capitalism, the idea that one had to adapt to neo-capitalism. They gathered around the journal *Clarté*, which was basically in favour of opening up politically, for a wider, more open, more culturally-oriented politics aimed at young people; they approved of the policy of peaceful coexistence [with capitalism] proclaimed by Khrushchev – ideas to which the French Communist Party (PCF) did not really adhere. The Italians had just taken over the leadership of the UEC from those loyal to the PCF. Then there were, to the left, the Trotskyists, and those we called the 'pro-Chinese'.

Linhart was already the main organizer of the *Cahiers Marxistes-Léninistes*, and his basic position was not to enter ideological quarrels and to affirm, first and foremost, the necessity of theory and of a new foundation of practice on this basis. But this led to an ambiguity: when the *Cahiers* were presented at the UEC congress in 1965, they were held up by the Party leaders, by the orthodox, by those loyal to the PCF, as an example for the young – who should study and work on theory rather than discuss the political orientation of the Party. In this same congress Linhart made a declaration: 'we are not "pro-Chinese" in disguise'. But in fact, in a way, we were! All those who participated in the *Cahiers Marxistes-Léninistes* were more sympathetic to Mao's theses than to the official thesis of the Party, but we played a sort of double game. The line was: the Communist students should busy themselves studying Marxism, rather than discussing Party politics.[2] This implied, for us, that theory should arm us against the politics of the Party, while it appeared to be a declaration of loyalty towards the Party. This was, in fact, also Althusser's position. Except that Althusser was willing to wait-and-see, forever, whereas Linhart was a strategist ready to pick the right moment to split the organization.

PH : The *normaliens* of the *Cahiers* were thus dealing with the theoretical forma-tion. Were they thus reinforcing the distinction between the ENS and the University, in parallel to the theory-practice distinction: theory for us, and mili-tant practice for the others?

JR: Not really. In the UEC circle at the ENS there were very active people and at the Sorbonne there were students who were very committed to theory, in particular the philosophy group.[3] In *La Leçon d'Althusser* I talk a little about these students, who were very active, who criticized Bourdieu when he came to the École, etc., and wanted to promote collective forms of work.[4] They were

---

2   Cf. Jacques Rancière, *Althusser's Lesson* [1974], trans. Emiliano Battista (London: Continuum, 2011), 18–19.

3   See Julian Bourg, 'The Red Guards of Paris: French Student Maoism of the 1960s', *History of European Ideas* 31:4 (2005), 482–483.

4   Althusser's intervention against the syndicalist left in late 1963 was partly triggered, Rancière notes, by 'the student strike led by the FGEL [la Fédération des Groupes d'Études de

critical of the organization of knowledge, they anticipated many of the questions that emerged in 68. And Althusser intervened to denounce this 'ideological' drift amongst the young in the most violent terms. He insisted on the fact that the students were there to learn, to acquire the science that would deliver them from their petit-bourgeois ideology. It is science that must direct politics, etc.; the legacy of this insistence is the article Althusser wrote against the students at the end of 1963.[5] And this coincided with a change in the Cercle d'Ulm; the 'elders', who had been very active during the Algerian war were leaving the Ecole, and the rest of us had just arrived: Miller, Milner, Linhart, etc. We were thus in the position to take over the cercle, if you like.

This was our point of departure: in the first place comes theory, rather than critique of the PCF, or a fight for or against the Italians, or the pro-Chinese. It wasn't simply 'we do the theory and the others do the action', but rather: 'we do politics that pass through a theoretical training or formation [*formation*] first'. Linhart's big project in the UEC circle was this: first we need to take care of theoretical training. Even my text, published in *Lire le Capital*,[6] wasn't initially written for the book at all, but to help with the sort of school of theoretical training that Linhart wanted to set up. The theoretical training was to allow the gathering of people on a Marxist, scientific basis – that was the idea.

There was, then, a twofold theoretical and political aspect to the project. Even the name of the *Cahiers Marxistes-Léninistes*, in the end it was I who proposed it but not at all in the sense of an adherence to Beijing; we chose it because there was Miller who wanted to call them 'Marxist' (this was the theoretical aspect), and Linhart 'Leninist' (to accentuate the directly political side).

Lettres, at the Sorbonne] in November 1963, whose main – and notable – slogan was "Sorbonne to the students", and the intervention by the FGEL's secretary, Bruno Queysanne, during the inaugural lecture of Bourdieu and Passeron's seminar at the École Normale Supérieure. In Queysanne's intervention, in his questioning Bourdieu and Passeron about the political status of a sociological research project about academic learning that protracted the authoritarian division of academic labour, Althusser recognized his enemy: here was leftism [*le gauchisme*], the subordination of science to politics, the aggression of illiterate politicians against researchers' (Rancière, *Althusser's Lesson*, 39–40).

5   Louis Althusser, 'Problèmes étudiants', *La Nouvelle Critique* 152 (January 1964), 80–111; 'Student Problems', partial trans. Dick Bateman, *Sublation* (University of Leicester, 1967), 14–22, revised and republished in *Radical Philosophy* 170 (November 2011). Althusser takes for granted the idea that 'the pedagogic function has as its object the transmission of a determinate knowledge to subjects who do not possess it', and is therefore 'based on the absolute condition of *an inequality between a knowledge and a lack of knowledge*' (Althusser, 'Student Problems', *Sublation*, 18). Cf. Rancière, 'On the Theory of Ideology: The Politics of Althusser' [1969], trans. Martin Jordin, *Radical Philosophy* 7 (1974), retranslated by Emiliano Battista as an appendix of *Althusser's Lesson*, 125–154.

6   Rancière, 'Le Concept de critique et la critique de l'économie politique des *Manuscrits de 1844* au *Capital*', in Althusser et al., *Lire le capital*, 2 vols. (Paris: Maspero, 1965), vol. 1, 93–210; 'The Concept of "Critique" and the "Critique of Political Economy" (From the *Manuscripts* of 1844 to *Capital*)', in *Ideology, Method and Marx: Essays from Economy and Society*, ed. Ali Rattansi (London: Routledge, 1989), 74–180.

Marxist-Leninist soon became a name indicating sympathy with Chinese communism, but here it wasn't at all a Maoist affirmation. It was a simple compromise. It was a compromise between those who wanted first to write, think, and work in theory and those, like Linhart, who wanted to act first of all. It was a link between activists and theoreticians.

PH: And the new theoretical training in question, was that first of all a matter of learning the science needed to understand capitalism? Or was it about interrogating the status of theory and of science as such, of pursuing an epistemological project in the large sense?

JR: Not at all, it wasn't linked to a general epistemological project. It was essentially about teaching Marxism, considered as an existing science, to militants. But at the same time, the science we were supposed to learn was not the one taught in the Communist Party's schools but that of authentic Marxism, which we sought to exhume with Althusser. The job of the *Cahiers Marxistes-Léninistes* was really to extend the work of the UEC, for which 'scientific training' quite simply meant 'Marxist training'. We insisted on the difference between science and ideology, between theory and lived experience, but there was no reference to the tradition of French epistemology, etc.

PH: And Sartre, was he no longer a point of reference?

JR: Sartre was soon overtaken by the rise of structuralism and Althusserian Marxism. For my part, I arrived at the Ecole in 1960; phenomenology was still dominant, and Sartre's influence was still strong. But this situation changed very quickly. 1960–61 was the year of Jean Beaufret's last seminar at the École, it symbolized the end of the period of Heidegger's importance. When I arrived at the École I was still very marked by Sartre. His big book on dialectical reason had come out and I had read it passionately.[7] Then, there was Sartre's famous lecture at the ENS in April 1961, in the Salle des Actes; Sartre gave a very poor presentation.

PH: This was an important moment, many of your contemporaries mention it too; do you remember the topic?

JR: I think that it was a lecture on possibility. The subject was, basically, how 'the possible' is wrested from the impossibility of being human. It was extraordinarily weak. He was then attacked by several people in the audience, by Althusser in a rather polite way, and more sharply by Roger Establet, who was at the heart

---

7   Jean-Paul Sartre, *Critique de la raison dialectique* (Paris: Gallimard, 1960).

of the UEC circle and who pressed him along Althusserian lines, saying more or less 'your philosophy is a philosophy of consciousness, and your praxis is only that of consciousness, which supposes a transparent cogito', and so forth. For me this marked a disillusionment with Sartre; that evening marked the beginning of Sartre's movement out of our horizon. I believe that those of my generation who were there felt the same way, even though Sartre's influence can still be felt, for instance in Badiou, who remains a great Sartrean.

PH: This is quite a clear line of transition. Was there a lot of discussion when the *Critique de la raison dialectique* (1960) came out?

JR: Absolutely not. Sartre's visit to the ENS was precisely to celebrate its publication, but it was more like a burial. I never saw anyone again (at the École) discussing Sartre. The *Critique* is a book that came too late; he wanted to talk about history, to refer to anthropology, to engage a little with Lévi-Strauss, etc., but it didn't work. It really was the swan song of existentialism. And when I entered the UEC in 1963 Sartre wasn't a point of reference anymore at all.

PH: The Algerian war (in which Sartre had played an important role) was coming to an end and I suppose that for young people at the time the question of colonialism didn't have the same urgency anymore?

JR: Yes, the war was over and the young people of the UEC turned to other things, to student life and the organization of knowledge. No one talked about the colonial question in France anymore – it was a period in which the spirit of *cartiérisme* dominated, the doctrine of the journalist Raymond Cartier, who said we had to concentrate on mainland France, that the time of the colonies was over. The problem of the colonies disappeared completely from theoretical and political discussion, and the reflection on the international situation began to find a new orientation, towards the idea of a third-world revolution. It was the time of the Cuban revolution, of mobilization in the Arab world, and it was soon going to be the time of the Chinese Cultural Revolution, etc. Political reflection at the time was about local participation in a global movement. But it was essentially a question of a more or less distant sympathy, as it would be regarding the American war in Vietnam a little later. In France people didn't feel implicated in the same way, and we acted without the immediate problem of solidarity, the war on the home front, etc. which had been issues during the Algerian war. After 1962 the French government was no longer engaged in any colonial war, and therefore there was no reason for this aspect to be pre-eminent. Instead it was a moment of hope in a new era of global revolution, the moment of the third-world.

PH: And those in your group who emphasized political action, on militants, but who also refused any reference to consciousness, to will, to engagement; did they manage to conceive of political action without falling more or less into a kind of economic determinism? The Sartre of the 1950s liked to say that 'Marxism gives us a grip on the historical situation', and thus helps us to act in order to transform this situation. With Sartre it's still fairly clear who he means by this 'us'. Whereas this isn't so obvious, a little later! Can we conceive of militant action without reference to consciousness, to the notion of a project, the deliberations of a subject, etc.? How did you resolve those questions within the orientation of the *Cahiers Marxistes-Léninistes*?

JR: Everything is mediated by theory. The idea is to go through theory, through science, in order to have a grip on the situation. And science tells us, precisely, that the subject is only a 'support' or medium ['*support*'] of the relations of production, etc. What Marxist science says is that one has to liquidate all theories of will, all theories of engagement, in order to think the place of what is done in a historical and actual situation, understood in a way that only science can accomplish. Politics is conceived in ways mediated by theory, I would say, in theory as much as in practice, if you see what I mean.

But one has to understand equally that, at that time, to choose the camp of theory and of science was *also* to choose the camp of rupture, of revolution, the camp of Marxism's autonomy, of its exteriority to the Communist Party's political apparatus, but also to the whole of the existing order. Don't forget that what is at stake at the heart of Althusserianism (even if its conception of history becomes so sophisticated that the aim is lost from view) is still a refutation of evolutionist theories, of a certain conception of historical evolution that leads to socialism, and thus of the idea of a peaceful passage, etc. Theory says that the revolution can only proceed in the form of rupture, and not in the form of a peaceful evolution. And this indeed encouraged most structuralists, in 1968, to become radical political militants.

PH: Those who then became militants without reserve, those who (like Linhart) 'established' themselves in the factories, etc., did they conceive of this militantism as the prolongation of this same project, authorized by theory? Or as a rupture and a passage to a different conception of politics, and thus also to a different conception of the subject? Is there not, in the new reference to the Chinese Cultural Revolution after 67 precisely a kind of hyper-voluntarism?

JR: Those were the politics of the UJC(ml), and then of Gauche Prolétarienne after 68, precisely a politics of rupture with the Althusserian logic. When the UJC constituted itself as an autonomous political organisation, it did so inevitably in a logic of rupture with Althusser and the Communist Party.

Here there was a sequence in two stages. The first moment of rupture amongst the Althusserians was in 1965–66, when I was no longer at the École: there was a split between those who enlisted in the project of a theoretical re-foundation, of the kind undertaken by the *Cahiers pour l'Analyse* (starting with Miller and Milner), and those who chose the path of practical action, like Linhart and Broyelle. And then, in a second moment, the 'theoreticists' and the activists were reunited in 1968, against the Althusserians who stayed in the PCF. What is interesting is how people came back together: what took place in 68 would turn upside down the relation both to theory and to organization. The UJC and then the GP gave the 'establishment' of militants in the factory an important role. But establishment involved two things at the same time: gaining a way in to the factories, organization of militant cells, getting a foothold in the workers' domain; but it also involved a transformation of the intellectual, a re-education of intellectuals – and thus an end to the idea of intellectuals bringing theory to the masses. Both aspects were at play. There was what we could almost call an ethical aspect, a new kind of intellectual militant, and in the second place there was the instrumental aspect, a recognition that in order to do things in the factories you have to be there.

PH: And before this renewal of 68, was the break of 1965–66 perceived as irreversible, fundamental?

JR: Yes, Linhart and the UJC completely cut themselves off from those who left to found the *Cahiers pour l'Analyse*. It was a genuine rupture, which began, as far as I remember, with this issue of the *Cahiers Marxistes-Léninistes* that Linhart and the Cercle d'Ulm refused to distribute, an issue on literature, with texts by Milner and Regnault (cf. CpA 7.Intro). That was the moment of a real break. The *Cahiers Marxistes-Léninistes*, from then on printed with red covers, would afterwards concentrate on the political stakes, even though one still finds the same double game at play, for instance with the long (unsigned) text by Althusser on the Cultural Revolution,[8] which indicated a kind of rallying to Maoism, but still in very theoretical, veiled and convoluted terms.

And then in 68 the UJC found itself moving somewhat against the current of events, since Linhart, in early May, defended a version of the theory according to which this movement of May 68 was just a social-democratic manipulation designed to undercut the workers movement, and he denounced it violently. After which the UJC militants chose various paths: some gravitated towards the *Humanité Rouge*, the Parti communiste marxiste-léniniste de France and other

---

8   [Louis Althusser], 'Sur la révolution culturelle', *Cahiers Marxistes-Léninistes* 14 (November 1966); 'On the Cultural Revolution', trans. Jason Smith, *Decalages* 1:1 (16 February 2010), http://scholar.oxy.edu/cgi/viewcontent.cgi?article=1003&context=decalages.

'hard-core' Marxist-Leninist groups, others joined Gauche Prolétarienne, and yet others would fade away, etc. And the committed structuralists, people like Miller and Milner, who had taken their distance from Linhart's project since 66, also joined Gauche Prolétarienne. Let's say that 68 redistributed the relations between theory and practice.

PH: I'd like to go back to the *Cahiers* themselves a little. The new *Cahiers pour l'Analyse*, launched in January 1966 by Miller and Milner – as far as you could tell, were they initially conceived as a kind of theoretical-epistemological supplement to the *Cahiers Marxistes-Léninistes*, or rather as a new, independent project, or even in competition with the older *Cahiers*?

JR: I didn't take part in the *Cahiers pour l'Analyse* at all and so I can't say much about it. But it would be wrong to say that the *Cahiers pour l'Analyse* were a theoretical supplement to the *Cahiers Marxistes-Léninistes*, even if there was no contradiction on a theoretical level between the two: the *Cahiers pour l'Analyse* sought to develop the structuralist theory within which a renewed Marxism was taking its place. It was about exploring this paradigm at all levels, and this implied working with people who were not directly involved in militant action. They wanted to intervene in what appeared to be the great debate of the day, that is to say – in the terms proposed by Cavaillès – the struggle of the philosophy of the concept against the philosophy of consciousness.[9] They took sides, of course, in favour of the concept. They wanted to renew an anti-phenomenological French epistemological tradition, whose reference points were names like Cavaillès, Canguilhem, Foucault (who had been influenced by Canguilhem, his thesis supervisor), etc.

Apart from this, the *Cahiers pour l'Analyse* also corresponded, of course, to the period in which Lacan arrived at the École, in 1964. I believe that Lacan quickly realized that he could rely on the *normaliens* to help shake the structures of the psychoanalytic profession a little, in order to constitute his own school. In 64–65 there was a first meeting to constitute what would later become the Freudian School of Paris; there was a small group of *normaliens* – Miller, Milner, Grosrichard and me. Lacan had positioned us so as to counterbalance psychoanalysts like Serge Leclaire. Lacan saw that he could use Miller and the others to help him create exactly the kind of theoretical paradigm that could help him take power in his milieu. There was a strategic dimension to all this.

So the *Cahiers pour l'Analyse* were created to extract the theoretical,

---

9   'The term consciousness does not have a univocal application – no more than the thing has a unity that can be isolated. [. . .] It is not a philosophy of conscience, but a philosophy of the concept that can yield a doctrine of science' (Cavaillès, *Sur la logique et la théorie de la science* [1946] [Paris: Vrin, 1997], 90).

conceptual aspect of the structural-Marxist paradigm, in brief, whereas the UEC was there to deal with the practical side. At the same time the practical side underwent its own evolution, while the theoretical aspect remained a little ambiguous: in 1967 there was the 'philosophy course for scientists' (organized by Althusser), which was part of the great project of an epistemological re-founding. There was still the project of laying a theoretical foundation for politics, but this first had to pass through a general theory of diverse practices, and political practice wasn't the priority of either the Cercle d'Épistémologie or the *Cahiers pour l'Analyse*.

PH: Did it seem coherent at the time, for those who were trying to devise a theoretical foundation for political action and for Marxism, to pass through Canguilhem and Lacan, through epistemology and the 'logic of the signifier', etc.? Or did this seem to be not only a 'detour through theory', a kind of Althusserian detour, but even perhaps a kind of distraction or deviation?

JR: Remember that it was Althusser who had defined a kind of equivalence between Marxist materialism and structuralism. There was thus a clear link between Marxism as a general theory and structuralism as a materialist paradigm, in opposition to an 'idealist' philosophy of consciousness. The Lacanian 'procession of the signifier' thus functioned, like Marxist relations of production, as a form of constraint misunderstood or ignored by the ideologues of consciousness, praxis and lived experience. And Canguilhem (who had overseen Foucault's thesis and who had exerted a strong influence on several of us, not least on Balibar), Canguilhem appeared to be the representative of a tradition of scientific thought in opposition to phenomenological idealism. You might have thought, then, that there was a common theoretical ground to all this. But in practice this wasn't the case. There was for instance the famous argument around the issue of the *Cahiers Marxistes-Léninistes* on literature, conceived by the *Cahiers pour l'Analyse* people and rejected by Linhart (CpA 7.Intro).

   At the time I was teaching at a lycée [high school] with huge classes of 40–50 students, so I was thus completely cut off from all this and heard only echoes of what was going on. Linhart summoned me, because he wanted to lean on the 'good' Althusserians, as opposed to the 'bad' ones, so to speak. It was the moment the UJC was launched, but I had no time at all to get involved. The following year I moved to the Fondation Thiers, so between 65 and 68, apart from ties of friendship, I had hardly any links at all with the projects at the ENS. And with Miller there had already been this dismal business with *Lire le Capital* in 65.

PH: Concerning the authorship of the concept of metonymical causality?

JR: Yes, that's it. When he read my text about the seminar on *Capital* – initially written only for our lectures in theoretical training – he was furious, he said that I had stolen his concepts. It was very violent. At the time I knew that Althusser was planning to publish the seminar in a volume – the future *Lire le Capital*. I said that I would withdraw my text, but there was pressure from Althusser and others for it to appear anyway, with a footnote referencing Miller, etc. After 65, I no longer saw Miller, and so I was thus never involved in all the things surrounding the *Cahiers pour l'Analyse* and the Cercle d'Épistémologie. I was never invited. Well, I was still a friend of Milner's, but otherwise I remained entirely to one side of all this.

PH: Considered from a distance it seems a little exaggerated, Miller's reaction regarding metonymical causality. Weren't there variants of this idea in several others who sought to think 'structural causality' at the time, in Althusser and around Althusser – Miller no doubt, but also Duroux, Macherey, you . . . ?

JR: Well, you need to understand that Miller was initially very invested in the seminar on the *Capital,* but he subsequently withdrew, because he wanted it to be a closed seminar, a seminar for researchers, whereas Althusser preferred a public seminar (which it eventually became). As a result Miller did not attend any of the sessions. The seminar took place between the end of 1964 and the spring of 65 (and the first issue of the *Cahiers Marxistes-Léninistes* appeared in the autumn of 64). At the end of the seminar he presented himself as having been excluded from what was going on; he said that his concepts had been stolen, he accused Milner (who had participated in the seminar) of not having kept him informed, etc. All this was complicated by the complex structure of the Althusserian group: I had not been associated with the organization of the seminar and at the same time, as I had been asked to talk about the relation between *Capital* and the young Marx, I had the strategic role of declaring the break that established scientific Marxism. Althusser created concentric circles around him, in this way.[10] For instance, I heard only later about the existence of a 'Spinoza circle' grouped around him, an almost clandestine theoretical cell; I never participated in it, but there were people like Duroux, like Badiou, like Balibar. There was this sort of elaborate machinery of circles, more or less informal, that mediated between Althusser and the others, between politics and theory.

PH: And after this Miller cut himself off from you and from Althusser?

---

10   Cf. Althusser, *The Future Lasts Forever*, trans. Richard Veasey (New York: New Press, 1993), 208.

JR: I don't know about Althusser, but with the *Cahiers pour l'Analyse* Miller constituted, in effect, his own theoretical space, where the organizing point of reference for thinking the structuralist paradigm was Lacan more than Marx.

PH: I suppose that for Linhart and his friends these new *Cahiers* were little more than an esoteric, ultra-theoreticist deviation?

JR: Yes, of course. One side denounced pure activism, the other pure theoreticism. A familiar structure!

PH: And this idea of structural causality, central to analysis of the '*action* of the structure' (to use the *Cahiers*' phrase [CpA 9.6]), and which was implicated in the rupture between the two tendencies: could it have, in principle, served as mediation between theory and practice, once all reference to consciousness, to the subject, to militant will, etc. was removed? And this way, through the analysis of causality, it would be possible not only to study history, but to understand how to make history?

JR: Yes certainly, it allowed for a kind of double attitude. First one could say, here we are presenting theory, as far as can be from any thought of engagement, of lived experience; this theory refutes false ideas, idealist ideas about the relation between theory and practice. But one could also hope that theoretical practice itself might open up other fields for new ways of thinking about political practice ... In fact it didn't open any such fields. But this delay [*différement*] also corresponded to Althusser's strategy, to the slightly naïve idea that we would gradually gain influence in the intellectual milieu, that we would expand, and that while appearing to remain faithful to the PCF we might win over this or that person.

PH: Understood. And in the meantime, during these years 66–68, did you already have an idea of what your own subsequent itinerary would be, your projects in the archives, the works that would result in *La Nuit des prolétaires* (1981), etc.? I mean, well before *La Leçon d'Althusser* (1974), did you already foresee a break with the theoretical/scientific orientation?

JR: Not at all! I didn't even have a project, in any sense. That's not how things work. You find yourself in a conjuncture, you're caught up in what is going on – and what is going on could be the Algerian War, it could be Althusser, structuralism, etc. Whether it's a matter of militant political action or of debates around a theoretical point of view, you find yourself in a conjuncture and your orientation depends on what is happening around you. At the time there was a whole context, a whole set of possibilities that allowed you to take part in something new, to follow the new wave. You are gripped by the new, you try to think of the new, you try to measure up to the new, and you don't think it in strategic terms. At the time I didn't have any long term theoretical project, nor any strategic or career project, etc. On top of everything else I was teaching at the lycée, I had little time for thinking about the future. You had to run around like a madman preparing classes for the next day, etc. – all this had nothing to do with great projects of theoretical renewal. But at the same time I became aware of the gap between the kind of magisterial position we were aspiring to, as the bearers of scientific knowledge, and the realities involved in teaching young people.

Having said that, it's true that Althusserianism represented a huge restriction, a restriction of things that were recognized as theoretically valid, even with respect to our students, who had diverse interests – ranging from surrealism to Simone Weil, all sorts of things. Even with respect to Marxism and the revolutionary tradition, Althusserianism greatly narrowed the field of Marxist thought and history. All this to say that, at the time, I was living in a sort of bubble. I taught my classes. After a year at the lycée I found a way out, and moved to the Fondation Thiers, a completely different situation: a completely sterile environment, with fifteen people working in an old building, working on their dissertations. I myself was working on my dissertation, and spending a lot of time in the countryside. So all through these years I was living at quite a distance from the world, and heard only echoes: I was sure that the Cultural Revolution was a great thing, but only knew about it through the *Cahiers Marxistes-Léninistes*, you see.

Well, in this context May 68 was a bit like the return of the real, in all sorts of ways. But at the time I didn't at all know what I was going on to do, I didn't have a long term plan.

PH: In early 1969 you joined the new philosophy department at Paris VIII-Vincennes, along with many of your former colleagues from the ENS?

JR: Yes, right away; I was solicited by Foucault, who created the department. Foucault later implied that he'd tried to balance various political tendencies, but this is a complete joke: he just asked Althusser and Derrida to help him find young people who were supposed to be good, that's all. I didn't hesitate: after 68 we wanted to be somewhere where things might happen, while also being able to work on our dissertations.

PH: What was your dissertation about, by the way?

JR: It was on Feuerbach, on the concept of man in Feuerbach – but I didn't finish it, and I didn't publish any of it. All the same, this is where I realized that

Althusser's and Foucault's interpretations of Feuerbach didn't work, that the theoretical forms underlying his theory of man, of humanity and of humanism had nothing to do with their constructions.

PH: Ok. A last question: when you think about it now, what sort of philosophical legacy has structuralism left behind? The *Cahiers pour l'Analyse* were abandoned almost immediately after 68, and forgotten for a while, or almost. Today there is a renewal of interest, here and there, and questions concerning the relation between structure and subject, between action and logic, between the real and mathematics, are being taken up again, in various ways, for instance through the work of Badiou, Žižek's reading of Lacan, etc.

JR: Maybe. Theoreticians like Badiou and Žižek are pursuing the Althusser-Lacan alliance, albeit through new mediations. Even their Lacan is different from the one of the earlier era. At the time, Lacan was the symbolic; their Lacan is the real. At the time no one would have thought of founding a theory of the renewal of communism or Leninism on the Thing, horror, the act, not at all! For the *Cahiers*, the link was made through the symbolic. The 0 and the 1, the elements of a logic of the signifier, etc., this is precisely not horror, it is not the Thing, abjection, etc. There is indeed a whole Lacanian thematic of the real (which Badiou initially confronted with the *mise en scène* of the struggle of courage against anguish, in his *Theory of the Subject* [1982]), but this wasn't really the perspective of the 60s. Badiou subsequently reframed Lacan as a dialectician. Every system is cobbled together, of course, and in Badiou one finds a complicated arrangement between the Althusserian vision of philosophy grasping the rationality of science, the Lacanian conception of the real and a strong Sartrean inheritance, all assembled within a Platonic logic. But yes, it has to be said, that in the end there is, effectively, an Althusserian-Lacanian tradition that has, in a sense, maintained itself and that was able to produce, through bizarre transformations, work as different as that of Milner, Žižek or Badiou.

PH: And do you feel entirely distant from all this?

JR: Yes, completely – first of all I have had absolutely nothing to do with Lacan, and as soon as I arrived at Vincennes I distanced myself from Althusserianism, that is to say, not only from a particular person or way of thinking, but from the whole scientistic tradition that had nourished Marxism, structuralism and all the attempts to connect them. It was a break with the vanguardism of those who believed they had the science that the masses needed to liberate themselves, but it was also a break with any attempt to make the intelligence at work in emancipatory practices depend on a global explanation of the world or of being.

PH: Right. And these days, are you continuing to work on your long series of studies on the politics of writing in the nineteenth century, on aesthetics, on democracy, etc.?

JR: Yes, when I can, I am working on a book about the aesthetic regime of art, a book that attempts to grasp its logic through a certain number of specific or punctual events: a theoretical text, a staging in the theatre, a review of a performance, an exhibition of decorative art, etc. What I am interested in is always how, in the most concrete and subtle ways, a regime of perception and of thought is transformed.

Translated by Cécile Malaspina.

CHAPTER SIXTEEN

Theory from Structure to Subject: An Interview with Alain Badiou

Paris, France, 6 May 2007

Peter Hallward (PH): I'd like to begin with some anecdotal details. The *Cahiers pour l'Analyse* were launched in 1966. What was happening at the École Normale Supérieure at that time, that is, around 1964–65? What is the Cercle d'Épistémologie, and how did the journal come to be launched?

Alain Badiou (AB): First I should admit that I don't know all that much about it. I was no longer at the École Normale. I arrived there in 1956 and left in 1961. I'm older than this project. I first left for the provinces and then did my military service. So, in the years 1962–63, the preliminary years of all this, I was actually pretty far from the intellectual scene of the ENS. All the farther, in fact, since I was mainly caught up in writing fiction at the time; I was busy with my novels *Almagestes* and *Portulans*.[1] I thus only joined up again with this process after a distinct gap; I will tell you about that later. I only made a connection with the *Cahiers* project in 1966–67.

PH: In other words, once the *Cahiers pour l'Analyse* were launched.

AB: Yes, I wasn't really incorporated into the editing of the *Cahiers pour l'Analyse* until 1967. So in addition it was to be a very brief experience, since, as you know, it was interrupted in 1968. That is the first point I want to make. I am a belated element, belonging to another generation. For even if there are only a few years of difference, ideologically and philosophically these few years are very important. In particular, I had a Sartrean background and training, for example.

PH: And was Sartre a reference for the other members of the Cercle? His name doesn't appear much in the *Cahiers*, if at all.

AB: No, no, the others had no Sartrean background. They were far removed from and very critical of Sartre. The situation began to change as of 1963–64: the two decisive events of those years were the moving of Lacan's seminar to the

---

1 Alain Badiou, *Almagestes* (Paris: Seuil, 1964); *Portulans* (Paris: Seuil, 1967).

École Normale Supérieure, and Althusser's cycle of seminars leading up to *Reading Capital*. None of that existed when I was at the ENS (1956–1961). Instead, there was a dispersed, hesitant progression – investigations that were tentatively oriented in the direction of what was starting to happen, structuralism, whose foundations were in fact laid down in the readings we were doing at the time, in the discussions we were having, in particular the rather delayed, retrospective discovery of Lévi-Strauss. The reading of his *The Elementary Structures of Kinship* was very important for me.

PH: From 1948–49.

AB: That's right, though for at least ten years the book actually remained unread by anyone other than specialists. Then, it became a public reference. Linguistics, an engagement with structural linguistics, phonology, the discovery of both Trubetzkoy and Jakobson, the epistemological significance of mathematics, of formal logic (itself very seldom taught at the time) – these were all things we discovered on our own, as best we could. At the time there was only a single teacher who dealt with any of these things, Roger Martin. So, this involved a certain effort, a certain engagement with mathematics and logic.

PH: Were you already engaged on that path at the time?

AB: Yes, I had a training in mathematics, but even those who didn't nevertheless became interested in it – or at least, those of us who belonged to the small group who were bound up in this philosophical movement. We began to read the analytic tradition, Carnap and then Wittgenstein. And so through all of that we began to cobble together a few things, into which the discovery of Lacan would soon be inserted. In fact I was quite involved with the (philosophical) discovery of Lacan, since already in 1959 I started to become familiar with the *Revue sur la psychanalyse*, that is, with Lacan's first public texts. Althusser also started to take note of them, around the same time, and I once went with Althusser to Lacan's seminar at Sainte-Anne – it must have been in 1960. Hyppolite also participated in Lacan's seminars, as is well known: in other words, the guarantor of the Hegelian and phenomenological tradition, Hyppolite himself, also moved – if I may say so – toward these innovative elements. And then, encouraged by Hyppolite and Althusser, I gave the first systematic account of Lacan at the ENS in 1960, or perhaps in 61.

So, that was the general atmosphere of the period: an interest for structuralism, an interest in formalization, an interest in linguistics, and an interest in Marxism. There was also the idea that the teaching inherited from traditional philosophy, in its most recent phenomenological modality, should be replaced by a new set of theoretical tools. The human sciences became a very important reference point, and this helped instil a scientistic aspect to our work: a reference to scientificity, to science, which Althusser would subsequently systematize.

So what you have to understand is that we were really constituted in a mixed environment. On the one hand, we had a Sartrean training and background, and we continued to maintain considerable interest in Sartre. The year 1960 was also the year of publication of the *Critique of Dialectical Reason*. Along with Emmanuel Terray and a few others, we read it passionately, we debated it. Moreover, at the same time as us, Sartre was also discussing the structural current and the human sciences, and the *Critique of Dialectical Reason* bears the mark of these discussions. So we recognized each other in these discussions, even if some of us were in tension with this latest effort of Sartre. For, on the other hand, we were perhaps already more committed to the alternative theoretical approach. In this, there was an element of conviction which went far beyond pure philosophy, because it also involved discussions about the *Nouveau Roman* of Robbe-Grillet and the cinematic *New Wave*. There was a general feeling that there had been a kind of fundamental transformation in the intellectual climate.

And this was also the moment when we started to contest and criticize the legacy of the Communist Party. For, it must not be forgotten that this period is situated right in the middle of the Algerian war – that is fundamental. A difference with those who came later is that the Algerian war was finished. For us the Algerian war was still a key point, after all – the struggles around the war, the demonstrations against it, relations with the FLN support network set up by Francis Jeanson, and the permanent threat, which weighed on everybody, of being sent to fight in the colonial war! Everyone had to do his military service. In this context we experienced the political conflict as very violent, since the old apparatuses no longer functioned, were unable to deal with the situation. The stance of the French Communist Party was indecisive. There was an element of transformation after de Gaulle's arrival in power, but the war in Algeria continued.

So overall, the Sartrean heritage formed a fundamental reference point for a whole group of us, but there was also this sort of transformation, still somewhat obscure, which brought about a new way of comprehending things, a new relation to the question of the scientific paradigm. And there were also very important mutations in the artistic order, and so on.

PH: How should we situate the *Cahiers Marxistes-Léninistes* of the ENS in this milieu?

AB: The *Cahiers Marxistes-Léninistes* began around 1964–65, since they were tied to the Sino-Soviet split and even to the development, to the first stirrings, of the Cultural Revolution. The creation of the *Cahiers Marxistes-Léninistes* was linked to a split with the Union of Communist Students (UEC). There always was a considerable number of communists at the École. The group of communist students was significant and, moreover, it was linked to the Communist Party cell of the École, which contained a considerable number of communist teachers, including Althusser. This communist apparatus at the École entered into crisis – rather fundamentally, it seems to me – concerning, on one hand, some new ideas, the reformulation of Marxism, but above all the Vietnam war and, more generally, the Communist Party's position on the colonial question and the question of the national liberation struggles. The young people, strongly marked by the anti-imperialist struggles, considered the Party's official position to be timorous and uncertain. Other criticisms were to follow later. But the vector was the conflict between Third-Worldism and the French Communist Party (PCF) as such, that is, between the idea that the fundamental stage of contemporary history was the wars of national liberation, and the trade-unionist and nationalist orientation conserved by the PCF apparatus.

There would be two successive splits in the Union of Communist Students, splits which defined a configuration that would persist for a long while to come. *Grosso modo*, there would be a Trotskyist split and a Maoist split.

The Trotskyist split gave rise to the creation of the apparatus which has best withstood the test of time, that is, the Ligue Communiste Révolutionnaire, led by Alain Krivine, Daniel Bensaïd, etc. And then there was the 'Chinese' split, that is to say, the one that gave rise to the UJC(ml), the Union des Jeunesses Communistes – Marxistes-Léninistes.[2] These two splits each had their representatives at the École Normale Supérieure. It can be said that with the UJC(ml) there was actually a merging of something of the Chinese experience, of the Sino-Soviet split after the Cultural Revolution and of a significant, active fraction of the French intelligentsia. They are the ones who created the *Cahiers Marxistes-Léninistes*.

PH: And during this time you were appointed to a teaching post in Reims and busy writing novels . . .

AB: Yes, when French Maoism was created (I call French Maoism not all the pro-Chinese organizations, but basically that novelty comprising the crystallization around Maoism of a concentrated, intense and creative part of the French intelligentsia), I was living in the province, general secretary of the PSU of La Marne, a novelist . . . And so really somewhat out of the loop.

Two things would bring me back within the centre of gravity emanating from the École Normale in Paris. The first was the arrival of my friend, François

---

    2   See Hervé Hamon and Patrick Rotman, *Génération 1. Les années de rêve* (Paris: Seuil, 'Points', 2008), 128–135.

Regnault, in Reims in 1965–66. Regnault was part of the *inner circle* of the *Cahiers pour l'Analyse*, a friend of Miller and of Milner, and a Lacanian. Meanwhile I had continued to read Lacan; I did not go to his seminars but I continued to read his books, the journals, etc. Regnault arrived in Reims at the start of the academic year of 1965. We became great and deep friends. It was he who told me of the *Cahiers pour l'Analyse*, Althusser's seminar and the tensions between the two. Because watch out! The Lacanians and the Althusserians were not entirely the same people. There were overlaps and exchanges, but these were nevertheless two distinct groups.

PH: How were the *Cahiers pour l'Analyse* themselves launched? Were there divisions among the editorship of the *Cahiers Marxistes-Léninistes*? And there was that dispute between Miller and Rancière, in 1965.

AB: Yes, there was Miller's famous trial of intellectual plagiarism against Rancière over the concept of 'metonymic causality'. Miller thought that Rancière had stolen this concept from him. It was a painful story, since all the participants were in the same Althusserian circle . . . But despite everything, even prior to this episode, the Lacanians were already somewhat in their own separate world. They assigned more importance to Lacan than to Marxism, Althusser, etc. This difference became more heated with the plagiarism affair. Ultimately, [in 1965] the whole group (Miller, Milner, Regnault . . .) withdrew from Althusser's *Reading Capital* project. They decided to create their own organization, the Cercle d'Épistémologie, and their own journal, the *Cahiers pour l'Analyse* (while still maintaining links with Althusser: after all Althusser published his text on Rousseau in their journal [CpA 8.1]). Furthermore, there was already a germ of the tension that would soon turn into the tension between the Maoists (including Miller and Milner) and Althusser and the Althusserians. Althusser and the Althusserians (Macherey, Balibar, etc.) did not join the Maoist organizations. They remained in the Communist Party. Only Rancière would play an intermediary game, as always.

PH: Okay. So when Miller and his friends created the Cercle d'Épistémologie, was the main issue at stake political, or more '*epistemological*' in a broad, large sense, that is, a mix of a certain scientific-philosophical inheritance and a new psychoanalytic orientation?

AB: I think that what they understood as structuralism was what I'd call a certain Lacanian interpretation of scientism. They sought to find in scientism itself, in the extreme forms of formal thought, something to support the Lacanian theory of the subject. In my view that is why Miller's text 'Suture' (CpA 1.3) is programmatic. It is a fundamental text in this regard, because this is the text that manifests the synthetic genius for which Miller must undeniably be recognized: he shows that for Frege the logicist reconstruction of the theory of numbers conceals an operation which can only be interpreted as the operation of a subject. I would say that this was the general orientation.

Their alliances, in addition, were very broad. In the journal, one finds Bouveresse, for example, who would become the mainstay of analytic philosophy in France. So as always with the young, there was much confusion.

But in the end, the primitive operation – which also seduced me, as I've often admitted – is this idea that it's not because one engages in the most extreme formal rigour and takes up the intellectual power of mathematics, of logic, etc., that one must necessarily erase or abolish the category of the subject. I think that was Lacan's major philosophical influence. That is, the ability to bring together, in a thoroughly unusual way, a theory of formal structures, which he developed as the logical theory of the signifier, and a theory of the subjective adventure.

I think that from this viewpoint Lacan succeeded where Sartre, in his furthest effort, didn't really succeed. For if you think about it, the *Critique of Dialectical Reason* is also an attempt of this kind. Note that the subtitle of the *Critique* is *Theory of Practical Ensembles*. It's an emblematic title: 'theory of ensembles', or *sets*, is the formal structures side of things; 'practices' is the aspect of constituting praxis, the aspect of the subject. The great difference is that for Lacan and for us, including myself today, formal dispositions are in a position of condition *for* the possible development of the subjective figure. Sartre, however, unfortunately remained within a genetic theory. He wanted to engender structures on the basis of praxis. He took praxis as elementary. What interested him [in the *Critique*] was the genesis of monumental history, understood as having ultimately only a single operator, the interaction of different individual freedoms or liberties. Sartre's goal was somewhat the same as ours: to maintain at all costs a theory of the subject, while also doing justice to the human sciences, doing justice to Braudel, to history, etc. Simply he conserved a Hegelian element, which was a genetic element. For Sartre, everything was to be engendered; he wanted to show how all these figures were engendered on the basis of an absolutely simple and initial determination, which is practice. And with a sole contingent element, scarcity, and the operator of nihilation [*néantisation*] that is praxis, we are supposed to be able to generate formally all the practical ensembles, seriality, the group in fusion, the organized, statutory group, the party, the state . . .

I think the reason why this project of Sartre didn't seem to work in the eyes of young people at the time – even for that fraction of the young who in a sense shared his objective – was because he tried to maintain this genetic operation. We were no longer in a position to believe in it. That is to say, we were no longer able to believe in the engendering of the general system of formal structures on the basis of the simple intentionalities of consciousness.

And so we worked the other way around. We began by assuming the formal construction as such, the general system of structures, but we then tried to see in what breach, in what crack, in what disruption of this system, the subject and freedom might possibly spring up. This is what I have done until this very day, it must be said.

In addition, Sartre continued to cling to a process of legitimizing the Soviet Union. In 1960 he still sought to legitimize the Communist Party of the Soviet Union, that is, to legitimize an alienated form of the process of emancipation. What was the reason for Stalin's terror? If you read the second volume of the *Critique of Dialectical Reason,* the one which is unfinished, you start to realize that it's always a question of Stalin. I think that Sartre's problem was Stalin. Moreover, I think that this was also Althusser's problem. Now, the stance of young people at the time was instead: 'Stalin is finished'. With Mao and with the Cultural Revolution, something else had begun right on the inside of the socialist countries, so Stalin was no longer our problem. We were learning from the Chinese who said 'Stalin, well, he had some merits, there were pros and cons; in any case we'll figure all this out in a thousand years'. This was very characteristic of the Chinese: they said that Stalin must not be constituted as a problem. If Stalin is constituted as a problem, we are doomed. For the true problem is instead to constitute *our* political scene, which lays claim to the socialist heritage, which takes on this heritage absolutely (Stalin included, for that matter), but which also goes beyond it.

Though it might seem strange, this is what I see as the source of what has always stupefied foreign and hostile observers, namely that strange fusion of Lacanianism and Maoism which characterized the most intense and creative fraction of the young French intelligentsia between 1965 and 1980, and indeed well beyond (since I belong to this genealogy). Now the fusion of Lacanianism and Maoism is entirely pertinent here because, as regards the relation of structures and subjective freedom, Lacan is the one who developed the alternative apparatus to Sartre's. That is why, from the viewpoint of politics, it was the Lacanians who were ready to receive Maoism, precisely as a hypothesis which did not claim to legitimate alienation and terror via the inertia of the economic and the socialist state. It was a hypothesis that stated: it is necessary to make use of internal contradictions, of the subjective novelties, the revolts, in order to develop a radical critique of the socialist state itself. It's clear that this is how things were heading. Indeed, I have always found it absolutely rational and by no means contingent and absurd, the fact that it was the Lacanians who became Maoists.

PH: A moment ago you said that the essential operation of the *Cahiers* was that of thinking together the primacy of mathematical, scientific formalism *with* the category of the subject. I recognize in this the priorities of Miller, of Milner, of

Regnault, of Duroux also, and others . . . But not so much of the Badiou of 1967! Your article 'Mark and Lack' (CpA 10.8) is presented as a critique of Miller's 'Suture' and his logic of the signifier. You refuse the idea of a 'logic' that could think the subject (the non-identical). You insist on the 'psychotic' aspect of science, the expulsion from its domain of any trace of a subject. Through and after 68, of course, the subject becomes the central category of your thought. (You reaffirm, perhaps, an aspect of your earlier Sartrean inspiration?) But how did you understand this question, at the time of your participation in the *Cahiers* (1967–68)?

AB: In 1967, I was indeed at the extreme point of a strict formalism. I pushed much further than my friends the detailed study of the recent developments of mathematical logic, notably the sectors in full effervescence comprising set theory (Cohen's theorem) or the new non-standard theory of numbers (and wrote a paper on this in the *Cahiers*, of course [CpA 9.8]). The fact that my thought is rooted in Platonism, which I've never denied, even when I was a convinced Sartrean, sometimes leads me to oscillate between a radical priority of the question of the Subject, on the one hand, and on the other a pre-eminence of the Idea, or of the truth, whose intelligible substructure, whose purest model, is to be found in the historical development or life [*vie*] of mathematics. Subjectively, for me this means that politics and mathematics constitute the two major 'appeals' ['*appels*'] on the side of what I call the 'conditions of philosophy', and that these two appeals are always in tension.

I only came to find the conceptual form of that tension once I understood that the most significant mathematical events might also provide the key to the subjective process of truths. That was the entire aim of *Being and Event*, in the crossing, through the concept of genericity, of the mathematics of the pure multiple and the post-evental subjective trajectory that constructs a truth. In 1967, just before the political storm, my meditations were on the side of formal structures. For the ten years following it, I was rather on the side of political subjectivity. Philosophy really began for me after these oscillations, at the start of the 1980s.

PH: I'd like to return for a moment to the status of science, of structuralism, etc. From the very first volume of the *Cahiers*, the insistence on science is very emphatic. And science, roughly speaking, is Galileo, Descartes and mathematical formalization, that 'literalization' of mathematics which was to become, as you know much better than me, more and more intense in Lacan. I wonder if there was not in that formalizing ambition, that singular search for the clear and distinct, something like the equivalent of that primordial clarity of consciousness to be found in Sartre, precisely. In Sartre, consciousness illuminates itself from the start; here, there is scientific work, 'Science' with a capital 'S', which clarifies itself in primordial and literal formalization. There is precisely no plurality of sciences, no historical and technical plurality, as we find in Bachelard or Canguilhem (who are nevertheless among the figures who inspired the *Cahiers'* authors). The link between Canguilhem and the *Cahiers* is not entirely obvious.

AB: No, it is not obvious at all, I absolutely agree with you. I think that what was retained from Canguilhem and Bachelard is limited to two things. For me it was first the idea of a fundamental constitutive relation between philosophy and science. In itself that is ultimately anti-Sartrean. I remember that Sartre liked to say, in terms that lose their poetry in literal translation: 'morality's an asshole, but science is nothing at all.'[3] For us, inheritors of the French epistemological tradition, there was no way that philosophy could escape its confrontation with scientific discipline. So there is this first point, which is simultaneously prospective and reactive. It is prospective because it creates a new situation, roughly termed 'structuralism'. But it is also reactive since people such as Sartre, and in a certain sense Bergson too, had already tried to escape from that tyranny of science. We are dealing with a cyclical phenomenon here, which can be observed very clearly in the history of French philosophy, between the vitalist and existential tendencies on one side and the formalist and conceptual ones on the other.[4] At the start of the twentieth century, this is very clearly seen in the couple Bergson-Brunschvicg. It is obvious that people such as Bachelard, and Canguilhem, but also Cavaillès and Lautman, and then Desanti, and also me, are in a certain way all among the descendents of the Brunschvicgian current of French philosophy. Yet Sartre, who detested Bergson, is actually much more part of the Bergsonian filiation. So this is the first point: to restore an inextricable link between philosophy and science.

The second point that was retained was that science, far from consolidating empiricism, is *anti*-empiricist. That is the absolute break made by French epistemology from Anglo-Saxon epistemology. We see very clearly with Bachelard, but also with Canguilhem, that not only is science not empiricist, but that it is the principle school of non-empiricism, that it forms the principle critique of empiricism itself. Whether it's a matter of Galileo, Descartes, etc., or even the Canguilhemian conception of the life sciences, it is axiomatic decisions and conceptual constructions that prescribe empirical experimentation and not the reverse. That is Bachelard's theory in a nutshell: scientific apparatuses are theory embodied, experimentation is always an artifice, the theoretical and formal hypotheses come first. The historians and philosophers of the sciences, such as

---

3   TN: The French reads, '*la science, c'est peau de balle, la morale, c'est trou de balle*'.
4   Cf. Michel Foucault, 'Life: Experience and Science', trans. Robert Hurley, in *The Essential Works*, vol. 1: *Aesthetics, Method, and Epistemology*, ed. James D. Faubion (London: Penguin, 1998), 466–469.

Koyré, come to the aid of this view. They prove that in reality Galileo never made a single experiment and, moreover, that if he had carried any out, they would have contradicted his conceptual decisions, etc. That is the second point: philosophy is all the closer to science for science's being theoretical and not empirical. French epistemology, in which Meyerson must be included, is conceptualist and anti-empiricist. This is why it is entirely ignored and contested in the Anglo-Saxon milieu, of course, which has always considered it dogmatic, typically French, that is to say *a priorist*, or even idealist.

We structuralists certainly shared this conceptualist view. But the differences that you point out are evident. For Bachelard and Canguilhem the centre of gravity of what is called science remains physics. Even in Canguilhem, who was above all concerned with the life sciences, we sense clearly that his scientific paradigm is physics, since he was squarely a companion of Bachelard. The most important discussions concern issues like general relativity, the origins of physics, the relations between conceptualization and experimentation, etc. Yet for Lacan and for the Lacanians that we were and are, in reality the centre of gravity of science is mathematics. As Lacan said: 'our aim, our ideal, is formalization'.

PH: What you describe fits Lacan more generally, and his refusal of imaginary forms of identification, of the adaptation of the subject to his 'natural' and social environment, etc.

AB: We mustn't forget the motif, so important at the time, of the 'human sciences'. We thought that formalization could be extended to the human sciences. Didn't Lévi-Strauss call upon group theory to come to the aid of the theory of kinship relations? Well, the paradigmatic human science became linguistics. And as the paradigmatic science was linguistics, there turned out to be a much greater and more immediate proximity with mathematical logic. It's exactly here that the Lacanian figure of the logic of the signifier will establish itself. This logic will operate in a sense between natural language and formalization.

PH: Indeed, because as Miller explains, 'We define epistemology as the history and theory of the discourse of science' (CpA 1.Intro) – which is also to say, it's a matter of science on one hand, and discourse on the other.

AB: Yes, absolutely. Discursivity will be the fundamental category.

PH: This remains the case even in your ontology, in *Being and Event*.

AB: Indeed. In it I maintain that mathematics is the only admissible discourse on being qua being.

PH: What I find most striking about the *Cahiers* project is the attempt to extend such a notion of science, i.e. one dominated by mathematics (such that in the end there is only one science, or Science as such) to the domain of the subject, and in particular of unconscious subjectivity, which is to say, classically, to all that seems to escape measure and quantification.

AB: That is the core of the question. If we assume that there is one science and that this science is ultimately what touches the real; if as Lacan said, the real is the 'deadlock of formalization', meaning that it is only attained in the element of formalization, then how can we have any access whatsoever to that which subtracts itself from the evidence of this scientificity? To that which is an exception to formalization? To the point which is 'out of structure' (i.e. that which I call, in *Theory of the Subject*, the 'outplace' ['*horlieu*'])? This exception is the unconscious, the pure subject, the rupture, the revolution . . .

PH: . . . lack . . .

AB: Yes, lack, grace, the event . . . French philosophy, or at least what's been creative in it over the last forty or more years, is virtually structured by the system of names it gives to the figure that is placed in exception, that is produced *as an exception* to an apparatus [*dispositif*], moreover to an apparatus that is conceived as pertaining to science. Even if this is a metaphor, then when all is said and done the real is conceived in the regime of science and no longer in the region of spontaneous perception, as the phenomenologists proposed to think it, as a correlate of consciousness. The world, for us, pertains to scientific objectivity; it is indifferent to humanity, etc. Nevertheless, it is in the regime of the exception to this objectivity, precisely, that something can be grasped which maintains the figure of the subject, the figure of universality.

Here there is a general movement of thought (common to our generation of creative French philosophers), wherein we all agree on the fact that the world (or that which is) is arranged as a matter of formal objectivity, one that is foreign to consciousness and valid on its own terms. One might then think it's only a question of pure scientism. This is perhaps how Ray Brassier, for example, interprets the movement of French philosophy. But for me and many others, it is precisely because this formal objectivity exists that one can search for and define the point that exceeds it. And in this point the subject, or its possibility, takes place.

PH: Okay. But you're familiar with the 'Anglo-Saxon' (and moreover Hegelian) objection. This applies perfectly well to the domain of mathematics, we might say, and up to a point it's easy to see what Duroux and Miller have in mind when (following Frege) they talk about 0 and 1. But how can we go from this mathematical domain to the conditioned freedom of a *subject*, that is to say, of a being endowed with a will, a living and sexed being, a being that has a body, that exists in the natural and historical world, that is socialized in specific conditions, etc.? Don't we need operators of mediation that might enable the passage between mathematical and natural, 'human' or historical situations? What are those operators? As conceived by the Lacanians of the *Cahiers*, is psychoanalysis able, on the sole basis of a formalizing theory of the signifier, to do justice to this whole empirical aspect of things?

AB: I don't at all think that psychoanalysis is capable of this, and besides it is not interested in this problem, since that is not its objective. It is a discipline of the clinic, and not a protocol of knowledge of the empirical subject. I think that it simply needs the conditions which enable it to construct the particular and limited stage or scene in which the cure is deployed. Psychoanalysis is not a theory of the world. It is quite the opposite of a theory of the world. Even Lacan's complicated operators, which have an air of generality, ultimately have as their filter the construction of a particular experimental apparatus for a particular procedure.

PH: The subject faced with his discourse, etc.

AB: Yes. If, by contrast, we are to ask about philosophy, I would say that, yes, mediation is needed. We need to assume that between the pure multiplicity thought by mathematical formalism and everything that has a body (including the Subject, which also has a body), there operates a singular localization. Such a localization authorizes us to speak not only of being but of a world. You know that I call this mediation a transcendental [*un transcendental*].[5] From this viewpoint, and this is what I said in the very interesting discussion on *Logics of Worlds* with Andrew Gibson (at the British Library, in 2007), it's true that *Logics of Worlds*, in which the concept of a transcendental appears, and then that of a body, is partially a response to long-standing Anglo-Saxon objections.

PH: Let's come back a little to the question of scientism, of structuralism, that peculiar mixture between mathematical formalization and Lacanian inspiration. For Regnault, Miller and Milner, was psychoanalysis their primary point of reference?

AB: At the time they were not psychoanalysts, and only one has become one: Miller. But they were all deeply stamped by Lacan's teaching. The attempt of the

---

5   See Peter Hallward, 'Order and Event: On Badiou's *Logics of Worlds*', *New Left Review* 53 (October 2008), 97–122.

Cahiers pour l'Analyse was essentially to constitute an independent Lacanianism which would not be immediately linked to psychoanalysis as such.

PH: Miller insisted on this from the very beginning; he begins his discourse on 'Suture' (CpA 1.3:37) by presenting himself as a non-analyst.

AB: Exactly (and he engaged in self-criticism about this later on). He often told me that 'we tried to declare that we were stronger than Lacan, for being able to create a Lacanianism without having to pass through all the trouble of psycho-analysis. But in reality we were presumptuous, and destined to return every-thing to psychoanalysis, after all.' Miller dedicated himself to organizing this return after the Maoist parenthesis, from 1972. It's true that Lacan saw us as a sort of dissidence at the time, around 1966. Miller told me several times that Lacan was a bit vexed by the *Cahiers pour l'Analyse*. He saw them as a presump-tuous attempt to escape from the rigours of psychoanalytic training.

PH: Ok. Let's go back now to your own trajectory for a moment. In the mid 1960s, then, you were together with Regnault for a time, and Regnault was already active in the *Cahiers*. When did you decide to become part of the Cercle?

AB: The decisive years were 1966–67. Moreover, they can be considered the peak years of what was called structuralism, in all aspects.

PH: There was Foucault's *The Order of Things* . . .

AB: . . . and Derrida's three fundamental books; there was Althusser's seminar, and *Reading Capital* [by Althusser and his students]; there was Lacan's teaching at the École Normale Supérieure, there was the creation of Maoist dissident groups in politics, there was the creation of the Comités Vietnam de Base, very important, because these were the first cells to practise a new type of activism. All that was in 1966–67. They were major formative years! Extraordinary years! There was a fabulous intensity to those two years. As Patrice Maniglier says, the miraculous year of what is called structuralism is 1967.

PH: And May 68, it did not spring up like that, from the void.

AB: Not at all. The highest pitch of the action was articulated around the highest effort of thought. [Going back to 1966–67:] from in my retreat in Reims, Althusser first asked me to run a course at the ENS, which I did on the question of literature (which yielded the article in the *Cahiers Marxistes-Léninistes* on the relations between literature and ideology).[6] A little later, Althusser asked me to participate in his course of philosophy for scientists, organized in 1967.

PH: That became *The Concept of the Model*?

AB: The story of that lecture course on the concept of the model is a veritable allegory of the moment. There were supposed to be two sessions: the first took place and the second didn't, because it was supposed to take place right at the beginning of May 68! That was the Althusser side of things. And then symmetrically, as it were, Regnault introduced me to Jacques-Alain Miller, and eventually I joined the editorial group of the *Cahiers pour l'Analyse*. At the time the group comprised Grosrichard, Milner, Miller, Regnault and me. There were five of us. So this was the time that I began to write articles for the *Cahiers pour l'Analyse*, namely 'Mark and Lack' (CpA 10.8) and the one on non-standard analysis (CpA 9.8).

PH: It seems to me, all the same, that these last two issues (9 and 10) of the *Cahiers* are different to the others. It's as if you put these two issues together yourself.

AB: I think I had some influence at the time, due to the fact that during these two years I was closely tied, in friendship, not only with François Regnault, but also with Jacques-Alain Miller. I certainly had some influence over the composition of these issues on account of the technical knowledge I had of the most recent formalisms. But they were also influenced by Jacques-Alain Miller's own evolution, and by the general context. In addition, these two issues were published in a more official way, because they were produced by Éditions du Seuil, whereas before this the production was rather artisanal; and lastly they were distributed too late, in any case one of them was distributed after 68.

PH: In 1969. But all the work had been done before May 68?

AB: All the work had already been done. The final adventure of the *Cahiers pour l'Analyse* consisted, sometime after [May] 68, I think at the end of 1968 or the start of 1969, in a last meeting of the editorial committee. Grosrichard was absent, but Miller, Milner, Regnault and I were all there. We met at a time when Miller and Milner were heavily involved in Gauche Prolétarienne. I was not in Gauche Prolétarienne myself, but we had not yet created the UCF-ML (Union des Communistes de France Marxiste-Léniniste), so I appeared as an

---

6   Badiou, 'L'Autonomie du processus esthétique', *Cahiers Marxistes-Léninistes* 12/13 (1966), 77–89.

independent Maoist (I was still in the PSU, where I led a Maoist tendency which later caused a split and then rallied to form the UCF-ML). The question at issue in this meeting was whether we would continue the *Cahiers pour l'Analyse* in the new political context, regardless, or if we would give up. Jacques-Alain adopted a hesitant position, as he often does; Regnault and I were rather for continuing. I put forward suggestions for continuing, arguing that, overall, there were aspects of some of the theoretical questions we were working on that could be considered separately from the immediate political questions. And Milner was violently against continuing. He thought that none of it made sense any longer, etc. The meeting was very difficult. The situation was tense and did not lead to anything. This meeting marked the end of the *Cahiers pour l'Analyse* project.

PH: At the time, did you have any ideas in mind for further issues?

AB: there was a project for an issue, I think, on the idea of hierarchy, to which Miller was very attached, because he had a solid grasp of the theory of types, the hierarchy of languages in Russell. There were one or two projects like that, which we had already discussed. But after May 68 we scarcely met. This is because when 68 erupted Jacques-Alain was in Besançon, I was in Reims, and the political demands were so intense that we no longer saw each other. So we called a meeting, an *ad hoc* meeting, to deal with this issue. It was held at Regnault's place; it was at once violent and confused, and we inevitably proceeded toward a negative conclusion.

PH: Before that, in 1966–67 there were regular editorial meetings?

AB: Yes, yes, there were regular meetings, on the whole every month, a little less, a little more, that depended on the moments, and besides, meetings that were terribly tiring, because Jacques-Alain was an extraordinary stickler for details, meetings involving infinitely long discussions (which Regnault narrates brilliantly) bearing simply on the form and colour of the cover, which dragged on for hours; he was obsessive about these sorts of questions!

PH: And ordinarily, how were the topics for each of the issues decided?

AB: The issues were decided on the basis of a sort of central theme, but it also depended a little on what we had available, on things that we'd asked for or which occurred at the time, things that 'would be interesting to talk about' . . .

PH: . . . for example, Derrida's text was longer than expected . . .

AB: Exactly, that's right.

PH: Was there much of a difference between the editorial committee and the Cercle d'Épistémologie as such?

AB: In my opinion, during the period of my participation the Cercle d'Épistémologie was dead, an empty shell. In the period I was there, I actually had no contact with Bouveresse, and I only met with Duroux once or twice; Grosrichard was no longer there, and I never saw any of the others. The group made up of Jacques-Alain Miller, François Regnault, Milner and me decided everything. In my view, the Cercle d'Épistémologie only existed when all these people were together at the ENS. But in 1967–68, none of them were still there.

PH: Do you regret the fact that the journal came to an end as it did, in this rather sudden way? In many respects, it could be said you subsequently returned to it; you came back to the questions of formalization, of logic, of structure, and so on, already in *Theory of the Subject* [1982] and even more so thereafter. How do you conceive the *Cahiers* project today? Do you still maintain a certain fidelity to the journal's original ambition?

AB: I think that, on the philosophical level, there can be no shadow of a doubt about that. It was politics that liquidated the *Cahiers pour l'Analyse*. Now, it was by no means a political journal. The *Cahiers* were not in a position to endure the open political tension that began after 68 – that's obvious. Don't forget that what followed was a period of ten years in which we all did nothing but politics.

PH: And were you, too, more or less completely involved in political practice during those years? Did you leave to one side the questions of formalization, etc., for a while?

AB: To a certain extent, yes; I only returned to them around 1974–75, with the seminars that would lead to *Theory of the Subject*. In the period from 1968 to 1972, in those four years, whether it was Jacques-Alain Miller or myself, we were caught up in political decisions in the most activist sense of the term. I think it was very difficult to continue a common project. But from another perspective, the problem from which we set out and which ultimately gave the *Cahiers pour l'Analyse* their general legitimacy, namely a more Lacanian than Sartrean version of the correlation between the theory of the subject and the formal theory of structures (to give it a very simple name), this project has continued to drive my philosophical research, absolutely.

I think that little by little I was left as the only one from the old team who remained faithful to the initial project. Because those who have remained in the Lacanian orbit properly speaking brought things back down to psychoanalysis.

They became or returned to being disciples of Lacan, and abandoned philosophy. They even became antiphilosophers. Jacques-Alain Miller was the first to do so, of course, but Regnault also in a certain sense. As for Milner, he was a linguist by training. He hasn't succeeded in imposing, on a grand scale, his theoretical vision in this domain, but it nevertheless seems to me that this vision was original and profound. In addition, in relation to Regnault or Miller, Milner was without doubt the most 'political'. He had a potential ambition in that direction. Little by little he has helped to organize (in a manner that's remained faithful to Benny Lévy) a distinctive ideological current, whose recent avatars, linked to a singular interpretation of the name 'Jew' and its historical pertinence, are nevertheless thoroughly reactionary. When all is said and done, this reactionary normativity now dominates his work [*emporte tout*].

Clearly the Althusserians (Balibar, Macherey, my friend Emmanuel Terray, in certain respects Rancière, who is an anti-Althusserian Althusserian), that is to say the non-Lacanians, have followed an entirely different trajectory. They are working in a far more historicist problematic, more in debate with Foucault than with Lacan. They are closer to a debate with classical Marxism, less tied to hypotheses of formalization. Overall, it is a different trajectory, even if on isolated political questions I have often been very close to them. And we should give credit where it is due: unlike Benny Lévy, Miller, Milner, and even Regnault, they are not renegades.

In the intellectual world, May 68 ultimately produced three distinct orientations. A first orientation is dominated by fidelity to the initial kernel of the event, which tries to develop a theory of the compatibility between subjective exception and the formal theory of structures, such that, furthermore, this compatibility not only doesn't block but demands political radicalism.

PH: . . . and which continues on the anti-humanist path.

AB: Absolutely. Let's call this orientation, Lacano-Maoism. Clearly we are no longer Lacanians nor Maoists. But Lacano-Maoism endures, as a possible figure of thought, one deployed in philosophical-conceptual space but also in practice and in politics. Today, I embody this tendency.

Then, second, there are those who have returned the project back within the psychoanalytic institutional space, who have cut it off from philosophy or from more general ambitions, and who have also cut it off from radical politics. That is to say, they have become either members of the Socialist Party, nothing at all, or even Sarkozy supporters, it doesn't much matter. I would say that this is the re-institutionalization of this project within the restricted disciplinary space that first gave rise to it. Here we find Miller and his followers.

And then, third, there are those who got caught up in an explicitly reactionary drift, and who think it is necessary to return back to before the 1960s, who say that we must have done with the 1960s. These are the renegades, generally sectarian supporters of 'democracy' against 'totalitarianism', who ultimately drape themselves in the American flag.

The post-68 sequence gave rise to this little galaxy of positions, one that stretches from a reconstituted extreme right to a continued extreme left, crossing an institutional centre. This is the trajectory of the small world of this period, and at bottom it has its own logic. You have to see that it was in the ordeal of May 68 and its consequences that these things were structured and deployed. In this sense, it is also legitimate to say that May 68 marked the end of the *Cahiers pour l'Analyse,* in the twofold sense of its cessation and its realization.

Translated by Steven Corcoran.